The Good Vegetarian Travel Guide

HEADWAY BOOKS

First published in 1995 by Catherine Mooney and Headway Books
Birch Hagg House, Low Mill, York, YO6 6XJ

© Catherine Mooney, 1995

ISBN 1 899583 01 7

Printed at Redwood Books, Trowbridge, Wiltshire.

For Francis

a rather special omnivore
(thankyou for waiting)

Introduction

When I first approached publishers with my idea to produce a vegetarian travel guide in 1987, I was in many ways a fortunate new writer. A literary agent had agreed to act on my behalf and, although I was an unknown, we were optimistic about our chances. Our optimism, however, was to be short-lived. The reaction in the publishing world was universal: too faddy, not appealing to a wide enough readership, and (one remark I remember particularly well from an established publishing house), 'there's no future in vegetarianism'.

With hindsight I'm glad I was turned down. While I lacked experience in writing and publishing I felt I already had a keener sense of the scope of the potential readership of a vegetarian travel guide than the large publishing houses we were approaching with our idea. My lack of confidence in the publishing world (a lack of confidence which has remained unshaken ever since), prompted me to set up my own company and take a sideways step with the subject matter of my book which was launched as *The Healthy Holiday Guide* - a directory of places to stay which could accommodate vegetarians but which also catered for other special diets and served fresh, wholesome food.

Of course six editions and eight years later the picture is greatly changed and the provision for vegetarians has come full circle and presents a different set of problems. In 1987 there were very few vegetarian-friendly establishments, and amongst those which were extant I was plagued by the cheese omelette brigade who claimed to cater for vegetarians but simply omitted to put bacon on the ubiquitous full English Breakfast Platter served each morning. These days on tourist board lists, it is hard to spot a place which does NOT claim to cater for vegetarians and those on special diets, though with what degree of competence they are able to provide tasty, imaginative and conscientiously produced meat-free fare is hard to discern. Looking for a needle in a haystack was an easier job, I was to discover, than looking for the right needle in a haystack full of wrong needles.

So how have I collected my information and what criteria have I used for my selection? Before revealing this may I make an admission.

I Am Human.

Although for the last two years I felt like a walking database full of information about vegetarian hotels and restaurants, regrettably I am not: each entry in the book has been culled from thousands of leaflets, letters, lists of information and previously collected data. While it may be obvious to you that there is a wonderful vegetarian and wholefood café at the end of your street which has been established since 1966 and has won several major awards, if I have not been given the information from my sources, and your café is not at the end of my street, I'm afraid it will not be obvious to me. There is a simple solution to this problem. Write and let me know so that I can include it in the next edition of the guide.

Neither have I been able to visit every establishment and check it out. This is called lack of funding. I can think of no nicer way to spend three years than visiting thousands of vegetarian hotels and restaurants and dining on sumptuous meat-free meals. It would also have been nice if someone could have paid me to conduct this enterprise (incidentally it is amazing how often I receive letters from people volunteering, for a small fee, to undertake this part of my research for me!). I am afraid I have had to rely on information provided by the establishments themselves

- and trust to its veracity. Added to this problem is the fact that hoteliers and restaurateurs are exceptionally busy people - the latter group particularly so - and they are, to a man, application-form-phobic, in many instances I have had to rely on information I have been given from other sources. I have done my best to provide as comprehensive a directory of places which competently cater for vegetarians as is humanly possible. I hope I have succeeded.

These problems notwithstanding, the further problem of selection remained. I did not want to produce a guide to *exclusively* vegetarian places for several reasons. First of all, there are many, many establishments which I know to be extremely competent at catering for vegetarians (some have vegetarian owners), but feel, for reasons of having to earn a living and appeal to a wider number of guests, that they must also provide carnivorous fare. Secondly many vegetarians - though not all - are happy to stay in a place which serves vegetarian food as well as meaty meals, and I would rather give you the information to enable you to make a choice than withhold names of places which may be useful (exclusively vegetarian establishments are marked in the margin with a prominent V - they're easy to spot).

However the decision to include places which are not exclusively vegetarian presented a further problem with selection in that so many places these days claim to offer a vegetarian choice on the menu, but do so perfunctorily offering a tired salad and a microwaved reincarnation of drummed-into-service soya beans. In making these decision I was particularly hampered by not being able to visit each place and check it out. So I have tried to select the very best of establishments - choosing those places which seem to display an awareness of other important nutritional matters which, while not exclusively the prerogative of vegetarians, reflect conscientious attitudes towards food, the way it is grown, the way it is eaten and the way it is prepared. Places that use their own organically home-grown vegetables, for instance, or have free-range eggs, bake their own bread or always use fresh produce in cooking. Of course it has not always been possible to find such places in some of our urban deserts, for instance, and in these cases I have tried to find the nicest places possible - sometimes a little way of town - where your meat-free needs will be met.

By the same token, I am sure that we have all visited pizza chains and been confident that we are able to order a salami free meal. I do not think you need my help in tracking down a chain restaurant - they seem to abound on every high street. So I have tried to direct you to places where there is a greater abundance of vegetarian choices on the menu - and of course the exclusively vegetarian establishments are also clearly marked.

So . . . gentle reader, I hope my endeavours enable you to find good vegetarian food on your travels. If I have failed in any respect - please let me know. If anywhere has been omittted (or, more importantly, wrongly included), again, please let me know. I rely very much on the help and recommendations of those who use my books - and I thank you in advance for your positive criticism and suggestions.

Happy travelling.

Catherine Mooney

Birch Hagg House, January, 1995

C O N T E N T S

ENGLAND

SCOTLAND

WALES

HOW WE COLLECTED OUR INFORMATION

This first edition of *The Good Vegetarian Travel Guide* was compiled from information received on detailed questionnaires which were completed by participating establishments in 1993/4. It has not been possible to verify the information that has been given by visiting each place and accordingly the information provided in this book is presented in the good faith that it is correct but with the recommendation that customers check with a particular establishment before booking to ensure that the provision meets their requirements and has not altered since the information was compiled.

HOW TO USE THIS BOOK

This guide is divided into four sections: *England, The Channel Islands, Scotland* and *Wales*. The *England* section of the book is divided into 11 principal areas in which the English counties within these areas are listed alphabetically; hotels and guest houses are listed within each county section under an alphabetical list of cities, towns and, if they are especially significant, villages. Establishments themselves are listed alphabetically by name under their city, town or village heading.

Scotland, Wales and *The Channel Islands* are smaller sections so it was not thought necessary to divide them into area by area sections. Instead the regions within *Scotland* and *Wales* (and the islands for *The Channel Islands*) are listed alphabetically and within that format the listing is the same as for the English entries.

The information given about each establishment is largely self-explanatory but the following should be noted:

The prices for B. & B. are per person per night and represent the cheapest high season price offered by each establishment - this is usually based on the price of a couple sharing a room; single rooms may cost significantly more than the B. & B. price given. Although prices were correct at the time of collecting our information, it is advisable to check the price before booking.

The reference to access for the disabled is based on the information we have been supplied with by the establishments. It has not been possible to verify the extent of the provision for those with varying degrees of physical disability. It is advisable to check before booking.

We have tried to keep abbreviations to a minimum, however the following have been used throughout the book:

V	= Totally vegetarian establishment	ORG	= Organic
N/S	= No smoking	WH	= Wholefood
V	= Vegetarian	STD	= Standard
VE	= Vegan		
S.D.	= Special diets		
B/A	= By arrangement		
G.H.	= Guest House		

The South West

Avon

ACCOMMODATION

BADMINTON

Petty France Hotel
DUNKIRK, BADMINTON. AVON, GL9 1AF. TEL: (01454) 238361 FAX: (01454) 238768

Georgian & Regency house in private gardens at edge of Cotswolds. French/English food.
OPEN ALL YEAR.   V, VE, SD, ORG., STD.   N/S DINING R. LICENSED.   CHILDREN & PETS.   EN SUITE, TV &
BEVERAGES IN ROOMS.   WHEELCHAIR ACCESS TO PUBLIC AREAS, 4 GROUND FLOOR BEDROOMS.   CREDIT
CARDS.   EB. & B. FROM £42.50

BATH

Bath Breaks
102 OLDFIELD PARK, BATH, AVON, BA2 3HS TEL: (01225) 425951

Victorian house with panoramic city view. Excellent vegetarian breakfasts.
OPEN ALL YEAR. V STD. NO SMOKING. CHILDREN WELCOME. BEVERAGES & TV. B. & B. £17.50 - 20.

Cedar Lodge
13 LAMBRIDGE, LONDON RD, BATH, AVON, BA1 6EJ.   TEL: (01225) 423468

Cedar Lodge is a unique detached Georgian house which was built during the reign of George III. and is listed as being of both architectural historical importance. It stands in its own grounds with aprivate car park at the rearand the front of the house overlooks the Avon valley and the hills which surround the city. Your hosts, Mr and Mrs Beckett, offer excellent bed and breakfast accommodation in beautifully furnished and individually designed bedrooms, such as The Pine Room, with its half testerbed, the twin-bedded Mahogany Room and the double-bedded Walnut Room. Tea, coffee or soft drinks are there to greet you on arrival and evening meals can be prepared by arrangement. You are within easy reach of the city centre - there are frequent bus services which pass the door - and the Kennet an Avon Canal and countryside walks are also nearby.
OPEN ALL YEAR. NO SMOKING V B/A. CHILDREN. TV, EN SUITE & PRIVATE BATH AVAIL. B. & B. FROM £19

Haydon House
9 BLOOMFIELD PARK, BATH, AVON, BA2 2BY   TEL & FAX: (01225) 427351 / 444919

From the outside Haydon House looks like many another unassuming Edwardian detached house so typical of the residential streets of Bath. Inside, however, 'an oasis of tranquillity and elegance' prevails; certainly the proprietor, Magdalene Ashman, has done everything possible to make your stay - so near and yet so far from the tourist throng of Bath - a truly happy and welcome one: rooms are tastefully decorated (lots of Laura Ashley and soft furnishings) and, although breakfast is the only available meal, this too has a little special something added (porridge is served with whisky or rum and muscavado sugar, for instance, and a fresh fruit platter is available for less staunch appetites).
OPEN ALL YEAR. NO SMOKING. V BFAST.   CHILDREN B/A. EN SUITE,
TV & TEA/COFFEE-MAKING IN BEDROOMS.   CREDIT CARDS.   B. & B.
FROM £26 (3 FOR THE PRICE OF 2 MID-NOV. TO MID-MAR.).

Holly Lodge
8 UPPER OLDFIELD PARK, BATH, AVON, BA2 3JZ TEL: (01225) 424042 FAX: (01225) 481138

Large Victorian house set in its own grounds with magnificent views over the city.
Extensively renovated retaining original features (marble fireplaces, ceiling cornices, etc).

OPEN ALL YEAR. NO SMOKING. V, S.D. B/A. CHILDREN B/A. EN SUITE, BEVERAGES, T.V. & PHONE IN ROOMS. CREDIT CARDS. B. & B. FROM £34.

Leighton House

139 WELLS RD, BATH, AVON, BA2 3AL TEL: (01225) 314769

leighton House is a fine Victorian residence which stands in its own grounds enjoying magnificent views over the city and surrounding hills; it is family owned and run, and each of the spacious en suite bedrooms has been tastefully decorated and furnished (the house also enjoys the benefit of its own car park and is just 10 mins walk from the city centre). A hearty breakfast is served in the charming dining room, and the beautifully prepared 4-course dinner (*from Tues. - Sat. Nov. - April inc.*) is complemented by an excellent wine list; vegetarians and those on other special diets are sympathetically catered for. Bath is one of only three United Nations World Heritage Cities and its history dates back to the Bronze Age; modern Bath owes much of its character to the Georgians, and present day visitors are lured by its many museums, art galleries and parks, as well as its splendidly elegant shops and antique markets.

OPEN ALL YEAR. N/S DINING R. V, S.D. B/A. LICENSED. CHILDREN WELCOME. PETS B/A. EN SUITE. BEVERAGES & T.V. IN ROOMS. ACCESS, VISA. B. & B. AROUND £57.

Milton House

75 WELLSWAY, BEAR FLAT, BATH, AVON, BA2 4RU TEL: (01225) 335632

Lovely Georgian home. Vegetarian breakfast on request.

OPEN ALL YEAR ex Xmas & New Year. V STD. CHILDREN WELCOME. BEVERAGES & TV. B. & B. AROUND £18.

21 Newbridge Road

BATH, AVON, AVON, BA1 3HE TEL: (01225) 314694

Attractive Victorian family house with spacious rooms and views. 1m from Bath centre on the A4 road to Bristol. Jan & John Shepherd, for health reasons, follow special diets. Though not vegetarian, they have a good knowledge of various dietary requirements.

OPEN Feb. - Nov. NO SMOKING. V, VE, D & G-FREE, WH, BA. CHILDREN WELCOME. T.V. IN LOUNGE. BEVERAGES AVAIL. B. & B. FROM £15.

Oldfields

102 WELLS RD, BATH, AVON, BA2 3AL   TEL: (01225) 317984 FAX: (01225) 444471

This beautiful Victorian building, constructed of the warm, honey-coloured stone for which Bath is famous, has been lovingly restored by its owners, the O'Flahertys, who have complemented the spacious architecture, moulded ceilings, high windows and marble fireplaces with such 20th C. refinements as Laura Ashley wall coverings and delicate pastel paintwork. Although breakfast is the only meal available at Oldfields the O' Flahertys are a health-conscious couple and offer, in addition to the traditional breakfast fare, a healthy alternative with wheatmeal bread, muesli (the heavy-duty variety) and herbal teas. Incidentally you are invited to *linger* over breakfast, with unlimited coffee, tea, toast & newspapers for those who like to dawdle at this hour.

OPEN ALL YEAR ex. Xmas. V, DIAB, S.D. B/A. DISABLED ACCESS: 2 ground floor rooms but showers and wc do not allow wheelchair access. CHILDREN WELCOME. 8 EN SUITE ROOMS. BEVERAGES & T.V. IN ROOMS. CREDIT CARDS.

The Old Red House

37 NEWBRIDGE RD, BATH. TEL: (01225) 330464

Romantic Victorian guest house with stained glass windows and canopied beds. B'fast is served in a sunny conservatory - hearty or healthy, the choice is yours. Private parking.

OPEN ALL YEAR. NO SMOKING. V STD. S.D. B/A. 1 GROUND FLOOR R. CHILDREN WELCOME. PETS B/A. EN SUITE, TV & BEVERAGES IN ROOMS. ACCESS, VISA. B. & B. £17.

Parkside Guest House

11 MARLBOROUGH LANE, BATH, AVON, BA1 2NQ   TEL: (01225) 429444

Parkside is an Edwardian family house, with a serene atmosphere, situated on the fringe of Bath's famous Royal Victoria Park and the famous Royal Crescent; it has a delightful town garden, and it is just a short, beautiful walk from thence to the city centre. Parkside has a total of five bedrooms - three of which have en suite facilities, with colour TV and welcome tray - and the breakfast menu includes a choice of traditional and health food; evening meals, with vegetarian specailities, are also available.

V, VE, S.D. B/A. ORG. WHEN AVAIL. WH. STD.   OPEN ALL YEAR.   NO SMOKING.   OVER 5S ONLY.   PETS B/A.   B. & B. AROUND £20.

Smiths

47 CRESCENT GARDENS, UPPER BRISTOL RD, BATH, AVON, BA1 2NB   TEL: (01225) 318175

Recently renovated Victorian house 5 mins city centre; friendly welcome. B'fast only.
OPEN ALL YEAR.   NO SMOKING.   S.D. B/A.   CHILDREN WELCOME.   BEVERAGES & T.V. IN ROOMS.   1 ROOM EN SUITE.   B. & B. AROUND £16.

Somerset House

35 BATHWICK HILL, BATH, BA2 6LD   TEL: (01225) 466451

Somerset House is a listed Regency building perched atop of Bathwick Hill with splendid views across to the city. Jean and Malcolm Seymour spent some years as restaurateurs in the Lake Distict specialising in imaginative, home-cooked food using fresh, local ingredients. Now joined by their son Jonathan, they have brought their high culinary standards to Bath and guests in the south west can now dine on excellent meals prepared from organically home-grown, wholefood and/or local ingredients; all bread, cakes, pâtés and soups are home-made and, as the Seymours like to add a bit of intellectual spice to their already savoury fare, you are likely to find food for the mind, as well as the palate, on the menu and wine list (their Shrove Tuesday menu featured, for instance, a Pease Soup for Lent which the Seymours found in the 18th C. recipe book of the otherwise anonymous Mr Farley).

OPEN ALL YEAR.   NO SMOKING.   VE, VEG,STD. SD, WH, ORG.   LICENSED.   OVER 10s WELCOME.   CREDIT CARDS.   EN SUITE & BEVERAGES IN BEDROOMS, T.V. LOUNGE.   B. & B. £25-34.

Wellsgate

131 WELLS ROAD, BATH, AVON, BA2 3AN   TEL: (01225) 310688

Victorian residence. Veg. options at b'fast & generous jugs of orange juice on the table.
V, VE, S.D. B/A. NO SMOKING.   OPEN ALL YEAR.   CHILDREN.   EN SUITE, TV & BEVERAGES IN ROOMS.

BATHFORD

Bridge Cottage

NORTHFIELD END, ASHLEY RD, BATHFORD, AVON, BA1 7TT TEL: (01225) 852399

Natural stone-built cottages/coach house. 2 luxury S/C suites. Pretty garden. Quiet village.
OPEN ALL YEAR.   N/S DINING RM.   V, VE, SD, BA.   CHILDREN WELCOME.   WHEELCHAIR ACCESS.   EN SUITE, BEVERAGES & TV IN ROOMS.   B. & B. FROM £18.

The Old School House

CHURCH ST, BATHFORD, BATH, AVON, BA1 7RR   TEL: (01225) 859593

Converted village school; rooms with views & 2 ground floor rooms. Home-made food.
OPEN ALL YEAR.   NO SMOKING.   S.D. B/A.   LICENSED.   DISABLED ACCESS: 2 GROUND FLOOR, LEVEL-ENTRY BEDRS AVAIL.   EN SUITE, BEVERAGES & T.V. IN ROOMS.   CREDIT CARDS.   B. & B. FROM £29.50.

BRISTOL

Arches Hotel

132 COTHAM BROW, COTHAM, BRISTOL, AVON, BS6 6AE   TEL; (0117) 924 7398

ETB 1 Crown Commended. A small, friendly private hotel 100 yards from the main A38 and ½ to 1¼ miles from central stations. All rooms are comfortably furnished (some have en suite facilities). The hotel is renowned for its cleanliness and firm beds. The very reasonable tariff includes a continental breakfast, in addition to which there are six choices

of vegetarian, vegan and traditional cooked breakfasts. Although evening meals are not served, there are several good vegetarian restaurants within a 2 to 10 minutes walk.
OPEN ALL YEAR, (ex. Xmas).   N/S in public areas.   V, VE & S.D. STD.   CHILDREN WELCOME.   PETS WELCOME.
BEVERAGES & T.V. IN ROOMS.   CREDIT CARDS. B. & B. FROM £21.50.

Basca House

19 BROADWAY RD, BRISTOL, BS7 8ES   TEL: (0117) 942 2182
Elegant Victorian house in a quiet residential area close to A38. Beautifully restored. Home-cooking. Vegetarians can be accommodated by arrangement.
OPEN ALL YEAR ex. Xmas. NO SMOKING.   V, VE, S.D. B/A. CHILDREN WELCOME. TV & BEVERAGES IN ROOMS.
B. & B. £18, Sgle. £19, D. £9.

Vicarage Lawns

BRISTOL RD, WEST HARPTREE, BRISTOL, BS18 6HF   TEL: (01761) 221668
Comfortable country home amidst an acre of lovely walled gardens in the pretty village of West Harptree. Well-appointed bedrooms have garden views. Wholesome b'fasts.
OPEN ALL YEAR. NO SMOKING.   V, S.D. B/A.   CHILDREN WELCOME. SOME EN SUITE ROOMS. BEVER-
AGES & T.V. IN ROOMS.   T.V. IN LOUNGE. B. & B. FROM £15.

RESTAURANTS

BATH

CANARY, 3 QUEEN ST, BATH, AVON
TEL: (01225) 424846 V STD.   50% NO SMOKING.

CIRCLES RESTAURANT, JOLLYS, MILSOM ST, BATH, BA1 1DD
TEL: (01225) 462811 V STD. SOME NO-SMOKING SEATS.

CLARETS, 7A KINGSMEAD SQUARE, BATH, AVON, BA1 2AB
TEL: (01225) 466688 V STD. 1 N/S ROOM.

THE CROWN INN, 2 BATHFORD HILL, BATHFORD, AVON, BA1 7SL
Excellent food prepared to order. Serving food 12 - 2, 7 - 9.30
TEL: (01272) 852297 N/S GARDEN R. V STD. CHILDREN.   PETS B/A. CREDIT CARDS.   WHEELCHAIR ACCESS.

DEMUTH'S RESTAURANT & COFFEE SHOP, 2 NORTH PARADE PASSAGE,
ABBEY GREEN, BATH.
TEL: (01225) 446059 OPEN Mon. - Sat. 9.30 - 6, SUN. 10 - 5.   V. STD.   NO SMOKING. LICENSED.

HANDS DINING & TEAROOM, 9 YORK ST, BATH, AVON, BA1 1NG
Charming small restaurant situated in a Georgian House; freshly prepared meals.
TEL: (01225) 463928 V STD. NO SMOKING. L. FROM AROUND £4. LICENSED. DISABLED ACCESS.

Sally Lunn's House

4 NORTH PARADE PASSAGE, BATH, AVON, BA1 1NX   TEL: (01225) 461634
Sally Lunn's is the oldest house in Bath. Excellent vegetarian options.
V, VE STD. NO SMOKING. LICENSED.   CHILDREN WELCOME. Booking Essential Sat. & Sun. Evenings.

BRISTOL

THE BAY TREE, 176 HENLEAZE RD, HENLEAZE, BRISTOL.
TEL: (0117) 962 1115 V STD. CHILDREN WELCOME. TAKEAWAY SERVICE.

BOUBOULINA'S GREEK RESTAURANT, 9 PORTLAND ST, BRITOL.
TEL: (01170 973 1192 V STD. CHILDREN WELCOME. LICENSED.

CHERRIES, 122 ST MICHAELS HILL, BRISTOL, AVON, BS2 8BU
TEL: (0117) 929 3675 V, VE EXC. 50% N/S.

MILLWARD'S VEGETARIAN REST, 40 ALFRED PL, KINGSDOWN, BRISTOL.
TEL: (0117) 924 5026 V STD. NO SMOKING.

McCREADIE'S WHOLEFOOD RESTAURANT, 3 CHRISTMAS STEPS, BRISTOL
TEL: (0117) 929 8387 V, VE EXC. OPEN MOST WEEKDAYS. THURS. - SAT. EVES. CHILDREN WELCOME.

MILAGROS, 88A QUEENS RD, BRISTOL, AVON.
TEL: (0117) 923 8697 V STD. CHILDREN WELCOME.

THE ROWAN TREE, THE TRIANGLE, CLIFTON, BRISTOL.
TEL: (0117) 927 7030   V EXC. WHEELCHAIR ACCESS. CHILDREN WELCOME.

Cornwall & Isles of Scilly

ACCOMMODATION

BODMIN

Hendra Country House

ST KEW, HIGHWAY, NR WADEBRIDGE, BODMIN, CORNWALL, PL30 3EQ TEL: (01208) 841343
FAX; (0208) 841343

ETB 3 Crown Commended. A Grade II listed building, Hendra is a large 19th C. centrally heated house situated in peaceful countryside close to the sea and numerous sandy beaches. Accommodation is in very comfortable guest rooms with have been equipped with a range of helpful amenities including electric blankets, TV and beverages. The food is excellent: all meals are prepared from fresh produce, home-grown whenever possible, and the delicious breakfast features home-made preserves. There is an imaginative, extensive vegetarian menu.

OPEN Feb. - Dec. inc. V STD. N/S DINING R. CHILDREN & PETS WELCOME. LICENSED. EN SUITE., TV & BEVERAGES IN ROOMS. B. & B. FROM £23.50.

BUDE

ATLANTIC HOUSE HOTEL, SUMMERLEAZE CRES, BUDE, EX23 8HJ
TEL: (01288) 352451 EN SUITE, TV & BEVERAGES IN ROOMS. CHIDREN WELCOME. CREDIT CARDS.

CALSTOCK

DANESCOMBE VALLEY HOTEL, CALSTOCK, PL18 9RY
Villa in tranquil wooded valley; highly acclaimed cuisine using fresh, local produce.
TEL: (01822) 832414 OPEN Easter - Oct. V, S.D. B/A. N/S DINING R. LICENSED. OVER 12S WELCOME.
ALL ROOMS EN SUITE. BEVERAGES. D. B. & B. AROUND £85.

COVERACK

V

THE CROFT, COVERACK, NR FALMOUTH, CORNWALL.
Vegetarian non-smoking B. & B. Sea views from every room.
TEL: (01326) 280387 OPEN ALL YEAR. V, VE EXC. CHILDREN WELCOME.

CRACKINGTON HAVEN

CRACKINGTON MANOR, CRACKINGTON HAVEN, EX23 0JG (08403) 397/536
Meals prepared from local produce where possible. Gym, sauna, solarium & pool.
OPEN ALL YEAR. V STD, S.D. B/A. NO SMOKING. LICENSED. DISABLED ACCESS. CHILDREN WEL-
COME. T.V. IN LOUNGE.

FALMOUTH

LERRYN HOTEL, DE PASS RD, FALMOUTH, CORNWALL, TR11 4BJ
Detached hotel 80 yds sea front. Excellent food including vegetarian & vegan options.
TEL; (01326) 312489 OPEN ALL YEAR. V, VE S.D. STD. CHILDREN & PETS. EN SUITE, TV & BEVERAGES. B. & B.
AROUND £25.

Melvill House Hotel

52 MELVILL ROAD, FALMOUTH, CORNWALL, TR11 4DQ TEL: (01326) 316645

Lovely centrally heated hotel, refurbished, yet retaining its Victorian atmosphere, close to town & beaches. Large car park.
OPEN ALL YEAR ex. Xmas. V, S.D. B/A. N/S BEDROOMS, DINING R. OVER 7S WELCOME. LICENSED. EN SUITE,
BEVERAGES & T.V. IN ROOMS. D., B. & B. FROM £21.

Tresillian House Hotel

3 STRACEY ROAD, FALMOUTH, TR11 4DW TEL: (01326) 312425/311139

ETB 3 Crowns Commended. Small, friendly, family run hotel in a quiet road near the main sea front and close to the beach and coastal walks at Falmouth. The 12 comfortable, en suite bedrooms have each been tastefully decorated and furnished with a good range of amenities including colour TV, hair dryer, radio intercom and baby listening service. The cooking is excellent: traditional food is served in generous portions, in an attractive dining room with lovely garden views, and after-dinner coffee is served in the comfortable lounge.

OPEN Mar. to Oct.   V, DIAB, GLUTEN-FREE & LOW-FAT B/A.   N/S DINING R & 1 LOUNGE.   LICENSED. CHILDREN WELCOME.   EN SUITE, BEVERAGES & TV IN ROOMS.   D., B. & B. AROUND £26.

HELSTON

Caerthilliam Farmhouse

THE LIZARD, HELSTON, CORNWALL, TR12 7NX   TEL: (01326) 290596

330 yr old farmhouse with sea views & beautiful walks. Excellent food inc. free-range eggs. OPEN Mar. - Nov. inc. V STD, VG & SD BA WH, FRESH VEG. NO SMOKING. CHILDREN WELCOME. BEVER-AGES IN BEDROOMS.   B. & B. FROM £13.50.

Tregildry Hotel

GILLAN, MANACLAN, HELSTON, TR12 6HG TEL: (01326) 231378 FAX: (01326) 231561

Tregildry Hotel is beautifully situated on the Cornish coastal path and enjoys panoramic sea views over Falmouth Bay. You are very close to Helford River (Frenchman's Creek) and a private path leads down to the secluded beach where there is safe bathing. The area is excellent for birdwatching and fishing, and boat hire is available nearby. Enthusiastic walkers will enjoy the opportunities afforded by the coastal path and inland walks. OPEN Mar. - Oct.   V, S.D. B/A.   N/S DINING R. & BEDROOMS.   LICENSED.   CHILDREN & DOGS WELCOME.   EN SUITE, BEVERAGES & TV IN ROOMS.   B. & B. £25-31.

ISLES OF SCILLY

Covean Cottage Guest House

ST AGNES, ISLES OF SCILLY.   TEL: (01720) 22620

Charming little house overlooking the sea on the peaceful island of St Agnes. Meals are home-cooked from fresh, local produce. OPEN Jan. - Nov.   V & SD BA.   N/S DINING & COTTAGE.   OVER 12s.   GROUND FLOOR BEDROOM.   EN SUITE & TV.   BEVERAGES IN BEDROOMS.   L., B. & B. FROM £25.50.

Glandore Guest House

PORTHLOO, ST MARYS, ISLES OF SCILLY, TR21 0NE   TEL: (01720) 422535

Glandore is a large, peaceful, family-run, guest house which stands near the shore in over ½ an acre of grounds, enjoying magnificent views over the sea from Tresco in the West over to Lower Moors in the East. Most of the five comfortable, centrally heated guest rooms have en suite facilities, and a real fire blazes in the lounge grate in cooler weather. The food is excellent: vegetarians and those on special diets can be accommodated with notice, and much of the cooking is prepared from local or home-grown produce (including delicious pesto with plenty of fresh basil). Packed lunches and flasks can be provided on request. OPEN 8 Apr. - 16 Oct.   V, VE, S.D. B/A. ORG, WH STD. N/S DINING R. & PUBLIC ROOMS.   OVER 7s WELCOME. BYO WINE.   V, VE, S.D. B/A.   SOME EN SUITE, BEVERAGES IN ROOMS.   B. & B. £22.50, D. £9.50.

Star Castle Hotel

THE GARRISON, ST MARY'S, ISLES OF SCILLY. TEL: (01720) 22317 FAX: (01720) 22343

Star-shaped garrison built in 1503. Now a comfortable hotel overlooking the sea. OPEN Mar. - Oct.   N/S DINING R.   V STD, VE & SD B/A.   CHILDREN & PETS WELCOME.   LICENSED.   EN SUITE, TV & BEVERAGES IN BEDROOMS.   CREDIT CARDS.   D. B. & B. FROM £40.

Four Seasons

LITTLE PORTH, HUGH TOWN, ST MARY'S, ISLES OF SCILLY, TR21 0JG   TEL: (01720) 22793

2 mins from Porthcressa Beach. Food prepared from fresh produce where possible. OPEN Easter - Oct. inc.   N/S DINING R & 1 BEDR.   V B/A.   LICENSED.   OVER 7S ONLY.   SOME EN SUITE ROOMS.   BEVERAGES IN ROOMS.   T.V. LOUNGE.   D., B. & B. FROM £27.

Hell Bay Hotel

BRYHER, ISLES OF SCILLY, TR23 0PR   TEL: (01720) 22947

An old Scillonian farmhouse forms on Bryher. Most food prepared from fresh produce. OPEN Mar. 22nd - Oct. 6th V B/A.   N/S DINING R. LICENSED. CHILDREN WELCOME. PRIVATE BATHR. BEVERAGES & T.V. IN ROOMS.   B. & B. FROM £37.50.

LAUNCESTON

The Old Vicarage

TRENEGLOS, LAUNCESTON, CORNWALL, PL15 8UQ   TEL: (01566) 781351

ETB Highly Commended 2 Crowns. Elegant Grade II listed Georgian vicarage in its own grounds in peaceful seclusion near the coast. Beautifully furnished and decorated:fresh

flowers in the bedrooms. Food prepared from organically home-grown herbs, fruit and flowers, and locally supplied free-range eggs. All jams, marmalades, biscuits and cakes are home-made.
OPEN Easter - Oct.   NO SMOKING.   V, S.D. B/A.   CHILDREN WELCOME.   EN SUITE, TV & BEVERAGES IN BEDROOMS.   B. & B. £16 - 19, d. £10.

THE LIZARD

Landewednack House

CHURCH COVE, THE LIZARD, CORNWALL, TR12 7PQ   TEL & FAX: (01326) 290909
17th C. rectory in walled garden overlooking sea between Black Head & Lizard Point. Magnificent cliff path walks. Proprietress qualified chef offering exceptional comfort and attention to detail.
OPEN from April 1st   V, ORG, WH, STD. VE, S.D., B/A.   NO SMOKING.   LICENSED.   OVER 10s   CREDIT CARDS.
EN SUITE, TV & BEVERAGES IN BEDROOMS.   B. & B. £18 - 30.

LOOE

MARWINTHY G.H., EAST CLIFF, EAST LOOE, CORNWALL, PL13 1DE
Small friendly guest house on coastal path. Vegetarians welcome.
TEL: (01503) 264382 OPEN ALL YEAR. V STD. CHILDREN WELCOME. B. & B. AROUND £15.

LAUNCESTON

Highfield Country House

ST. GILES ON THE HEATH, LAUNCESTON, DL15 9SD   TEL: (01566) 772937
Elegant Edwardian house set in its own grounds surrounded by beautiful countryside. Food prepared from natural produce.
OPEN ALL YEAR.   N/S DINING R & DRAWING R.   DIAB STD.   V, VE, S.D. B/A.   OLDER CHILDREN WELCOME.   PETS B/A.   BEVERAGES IN ROOMS.   T.V.   B. & B. FROM £13.50.

MAWGAN PORTH

Bedruthan Steps Hotel

MAWGAN PORTH, CORNWALL, TR8 4BU   TEL: (01637) 860555

Splendid modern hotel amidst 5 acres of grounds overlooking the spectacular Cornish coast at Mawgan Porth. There are spacious hotel bedroom suites which have been very comfortably furnished and overlook the sea, and a number of villa suites which open out onto spacious lawns and are ideal for families (there is a children's play area in the grounds, a wonderful indoor play complex and a childrens' dining room). The food at Bedruthan Steps is outstanding: everything is home-made (including the bread, croissants and desserts), and fresh, local produce plus vegetables, fruit and herbs from the hotel's market garden, are always used in cooking. The leisure facilities are excellent: there is an indoor pool complex, tennis and squash courts, snooker and pool - and there is even an on site beauty therapist and masseuse.
OPEN Mar. - Nov.   N/S DINING R, LOUNGES & PART OF BAR.   V, S.D. B/A.   LICENSED.   CHILDREN WELCOME.   EN SUITE, BEVERAGES & T.V. IN ROOMS.   ACCESS, VISA.   D., B. & B. AROUND £35.

MEVAGISSEY

Steep House

PORTMELLON COVE, MEVAGISSEY, CORNWALL, PL26 2PH   TEL: (01726) 843732
Comfortable house in 1 acre of grounds within a natural cove with safe sandy beach; covered pool; car park.
OPEN ALL YEAR.   N/S IN BEDROOMS.   V, S.D., B/A.   LICENSED.   CHILDREN: OVER 10S ONLY.
TREMARNE HOTEL, POLKIRT, MEVAGISSEY, PL26 6UY
TEL: (01726) 842213 OPEN ALL YEAR. V STD. CHILDREN. EN SUITE, TV & BEVERAGES. B. & B. AROUND £29.

MOUSEHOLE

Carn Du Hotel

RAGINNIS HILL, MOUSEHOLE, TR19 6SS   TEL: (01736) 731233

Detached hotel in terraced gardens overlooking St Michael's Mount; excellent cuisine.
OPEN Mar. - Feb.　N/D DINING R.　V B/A.　LICENSED.　DISABLED ACCESS.　EN SUITE, BEVERAGES &
T.V. IN ROOMS.

Marconi Private Hotel

COVE RD, MULLION, NR HELSTON, CORNWALL.

Victorian house overlooking cricket field. Food prepared from fresh, local produce.
TEL: (01326) 240483　OPEN ALL YEAR.　N/S BEDRS & SUN LOUNGE.　V STD, S.D. B/A.　LICENSED.　1
ROOM DISABLED ACCESS.　CHILDREN WELCOME.　SOME EN SUITE ROOMS.　BEVERAGES & T.V. IN
ROOMS.　B. & B. FROM £13.50.

NEWQUAY

SHELDON, The Haven For Non-smokers, 198 HENVER RD, NEWQUAY.

Fresh ingredients; bread, rolls & pastries baked fresh daily; home-made marmalade.
TEL: (01637) 874552　OPEN June - Aug. inc.　NO SMOKING.　CHILDREN: OVER 10S ONLY.　BEVERAGES
ON REQUEST.　T.V. IN LOUNGE.　B. & B. AROUND £18 (based on weekly rate).

Treisaac Farm Vegetarian Guest House

ST COLUMB MINOR, NEWQUAY, CORNWALL, TR8 4DX   TEL: (01637) 880326

Treisaac Farm Vegetarian Guest House is over 250 years old; it is built of cob and granite stone, and stands amidst a large garden overlooking open fields. The surrounding countryside is typical of much of rural Cornwall, with stone-walled fields and woodland, but the spectacular cliffs of the North Cornish coast with its fine, sandy beaches are just 2 miles away. Guests are accommodated in comfortable bedrooms and the spacious south-facing lounge and dining room opens out onto the garden through French windows; in cooler weather a log fire blazes in the grate. The delicious home-cooked vegetarian food features a choice of a full vegetarian /vegan or continental breakfast and the evening meal would typically feature a choice of dishes such as Butterbean Pâté and toast followed by Millet Pilav with a rich tomato sauce and fresh vegetables followed by a home-made dessert or cheese; organic and home-grown produce is used wherever possible.
OPEN ALL YEAR.　V, VE STD, S.D. B/A.　LICENSED.　CHILDREN & PETS WELCOME.　EN SUITE & BEVERAGES
IN ROOMS.　TV LOUNGE.　CREDIT CARDS.　B. & B. FROM £15.

PADSTOW

THE DOWER HOUSE HOTEL, FENTONLUNA LANE, PADSTOW, CORNWALL, PL28 8BA

Fabulous food prepared from fresh ingredients.
TEL: (01841) 532317　OPEN ALL YEAR ex. Xmas.　V, DIAB, LOW-FAT/LOW-CAL. STD.　VE B/A.　LICENSED.
CHILDREN.　PETS B/A.　MOST ROOMS EN SUITE.　BEVERAGES & TV IN ROOMS.　B. & B. AROUND £20.

PENRYN

Prospect House

1 CHURCH RD, PENRYN, CORNWALL, TR10 8DA   TEL: (01326) 373198

Listed 19th C. 'gentleman's residence' within pretty walled rose garden. Log fires. First-rate: food prepared from fresh ingredients.
OPEN Jan. - Dec.　N/S DINING R.　V, S.D. B/A.　OVER 12s.　PETS B/A.　EN SUITE.　BEVERAGES & T.V.

PENZANCE

Ednovean House

PERRANUTHNOE, PENZANCE, CORNWALL, TR20 9LZ   TEL: (01736) 711071

Ednovean is a charming Victorian house which stands in an acre of quiet, secluded grounds in an elevated position above the picturesque village of Perranuthnoe; it has, arguably, one of the finest views in Cornwall overlooking St Michaels' Mount, and at night the lights

across the bay stretch from Mousehole to Marazion. It is a nine-bedroom hotel: each of the guest rooms is comfortably furnished and centrally heated, and most enjoy wonderful sea views. Dinner is served in a candle-lit dining room, and the delicious food has been prepared from local farm produce; there is a varied choice at breakfast, and vegetarians are also catered for. In addition to a most comfortable lounge and bar, guests may enjoy relaxing on the patio in sunny weather.
OPEN ALL YEAR.   V STD, VE, S.D. B/A.   N/S DINING R.   OVER 7s & PETS WELCOME.   LICENSED.   CREDIT CARDS.   EN SUITE & BEVERAGES IN BEDROOMS.   B. & B. FROM £18, D. £12.50.

The Higher Faugan Country House Hotel

NEWLYN, PENZANCE, TR18 5NS   TEL: (01736) 62076
Gracious country house built surrounded by 10 acres of lawns and woodlands overlooking Penzance and St Mounts Bay. Excellent food prepared from fresh local produce.
OPEN ALL YEAR.   V, S.D. B/A.   N/S DINING R.   LICENSED.   CHILDREN WELCOME.   PETS B/A.   EN SUITE, BEVERAGES, T.V., & PHONE IN ROOMS.   B. & B. AROUND £40.

PENALVA GUEST HOUSE, ALEXANDRA ROAD, PENZANCE, CORNWALL.
Small, private hotel in tree-lined avenue.
TEL: (01736) 69060   OPEN ALL YEAR; no evening meals Jul. & Aug.   V, S.D. B/A.   NO SMOKING.   CHILDREN WELCOME.   2 EN SUITE ROOMS.   BEVERAGES IN ROOMS.   T.V. IN LOUNGE.   B. & B. AROUND £16.

PORTSCATHO

ROSELAND HOUSE HOTEL, ROSEVINE, NR PORTSCATHO, CORNWALL, TR2 5EW
18 bedroom hotel set in 6 acres of National Trust and Heritage coastline; wonderful views.
TEL: (01872) 580644 FAX: (01872) 580801   OPEN ALL YEAR.   V, S.D. B/A.   N/S DINING R.   LICENSED. SOME ROOMS DISABLED ACCESS.   CHILDREN WELCOME.   EN SUITE, TV & BEVERAGES IN ROOMS.

REDRUTH

LANSDOWNE, REDRUTH, CORNWALL.
Vegetarians & vegans catered for. Comfortable accommdation.
TEL: (01209) 216002 OPEN ALL YEAR. V, VE STD. CHILDREN WELCOME. EN SUITE, TV & BEVERAGES.

ROCK

PENTIRE ROCKS HOTEL, NEW POLZEATH, NR ROCK, PL27 6US
TEL: (01208) 862213   OPEN ALL YEAR.   V MENU STD.   CHILDREN & PETS.   LICENSED.   EN SUITE, TV & BEVERAGES.   B. & B. AROUND £38.

SALTASH

Barncroft

BARN PARK, SALTASH, CORNWALL, PL12 6HG   TEL: (01752) 843643

Barncroft is a spacious, comfortable home which which stands amidst large, attractive, landscaped gardens overlooking the Tamar Estuary and beyond to Dartmoor, on the fringe of the riverside town of Saltash. Accommodation is in tastefully decorated en suite rooms, one of which overlooks the river, and one the garden; fresh flowers and a limitless tea and coffee tray add to the comfort; there is also a cosy sitting room for guests' use. A varied and imaginative breakfast is served each morning, and vegetarians are particularly welcome. A dramatically rugged coastline, sandy beaches and beautiful wooded valleys are the natural surroundings that this area enjoys, and consequently there are plenty of excellent walks; however there are several nearby National Trust properties which are well worth a visit, and there is a very good theatre at Plymouth.
OPEN ALL YEAR ex. Xmas.   V, ORG, WH, STD.   NO SMOKING.   OVER 13s WELCOME.   EN SUITE, TV & BEVERAGES IN ROOMS.   B. & B. £16.50 - 18.50.

ST BLAZEY

NANSCAWEN HOUSE, PRIDEAUX ROAD, ST BLAZEY, CORNWALL, NR PAR
16th C. house in 5 acres of grounds. Meals prepared from fresh, often home-grown produce.
TEL: (01726) 814488 OPEN ALL YEAR ex. Xmas.   NO SMOKING.   V B/A.   OVER 12S ONLY.   EN SUITE, TV & BEVERAGES IN ROOMS.   B. & B. AROUND £30.

ST COLUMB

BRENTONS FARM, GOSS MOOR, ST COLUMB, CORNWALL, TR9 6WR
Small farm close to the A30; free-range eggs, home-baked rolls.
TEL: (01726) 860632   V, S.D. B/A.   NO SMOKING.   CHILDREN.   BEVERAGES & TV.   T.V.   B. & B. AROUND
£15.

ST IVES

Boswednack Manor
ZENNOR, ST IVES, CORNWALL, TR26 3DD   TEL: (01736) 794183
Peaceful granite-built farmhouse in wildest part of Cornwall with magnificent views of
moor & sea. Meditation room, conservatory. Natural history courses. Self-catering cottage
available.
OPEN ALL YEAR.   NO SMOKING.   V. STD; VE & SD BA; WH.   CHILDREN WELCOME.   NO PETS OR TV.   2 EN
SUITE ROOMS.   BEVERAGES IN ROOMS.   B. & B. FROM £14.50, D. £7.

✇ Woodcote Vegetarian Hotel
THE SALTINGS, LELANT, ST IVES, CORNWALL, TR26 3DL   TEL: (01736) 753147
Long-established vegetarian hotel overlooking the estuary and bird sanctuary of Hayle.
OPEN Mar. - Oct.   N/S DINING, BEDRS & LOUNGE.   V EXC. DIAB, GLUTEN-FREE & SD BA.   NO BABIES/
TODDLERS.   BYO WINE.   EN SUITE & TV SOME ROOMS.   BEVERAGES ALL ROOMS.   D., B. & B. FROM £24.

TINTAGEL

**BOSSINEY HOUSE HOTEL, TINTAGEL, CORNWALL, PL34 0AX   TEL:
(01840) 770240**
Hotel in 2½ acres of grounds overlooking the coast. Heated pool, sauna and solarium.
OPEN Mar. - Oct.   V, VE, S.D. B/A.   LICENSED.   DISABLED ACCESS.   CHILDREN WELCOME.   PETS
B/A.   EN SUITE & BEVERAGES IN ROOMS.   B. & B. AROUND £30.

Trevervan Hotel
TREWARMETT, TINTAGEL, CORNWALL, PL34 0ES   TEL:(01840) 770486
White-washed building overlooking Trebarwith Strand; healthy meat-free fare.
OPEN ALL YEAR.   V, VE, DIAB. STD. LOW-CAL, LOW-FAT, ALLERG-FREE, MACROB B/A   WH, ORG STD.   N/S
DINING R. & SOME BEDRS.   LICENSED.   CHILDREN & PETS. BEVERAGES & T.V. IN LOUNGE.   B. & B. from
£13.50, D. £6.50.

TORPOINT

CLIFF HOUSE, KINGSAND, NR TORPOINT, CORNWALL, PL10 1NJ
Grade II listed house overlooking the bay. Wholefood cookery. Home-baked bread.
TEL: (01752) 823110   V, WH STD.   CHILDREN WELCOME.   EN SUITE, TV & BEVERAGES.   B. & B. AROUND £20.

THE COPSE, ST WINNOLLS, POLBATHIC, TORPOINT, PL11 3DX
The Copse is part of a mixed farm in the hamlet of St Winnolls in a lovely rural setting yet
A374 just 1m away; home-produced milk and vegetables.
TEL: (01503) 30205   OPEN Mar. - Sept.   V STD. NO SMOKING.   CHILDREN: OVER 10S ONLY.   SOME EN
SUITE ROOMS.   BEVERAGES & T.V. IN ROOMS.   B. & B. AROUND £15.

TRURO

Carvean Farm
PROBUS, TRURO, CORNWALL, TR2 4HY   TEL: (01872) 520243

Carvean is an ancient, secluded farmhouse set in 20
acres of pasture and woodland about 5 miles east of
Truro and close to the Roseland peninsula. A settlement
at Carvean was mentioned in the Domesday Book,
although facilities have improved considerably since
then! The house is about 500 yards off the road, and you
are more likely to be woken by the birds than the traffic.
The delicious home-cooking is prepared from fresh,
local produce and Carvean's Table Licence enables you
to enjoy an aperitif or glass of wine with your meal.
Friendly and informal in ambience, Carvean is an ideal base for touring Cornwall.
OPEN ALL YEAR.   NO SMOKING.   V, VE,S.D. B/A.   CHILDREN WELCOME.   PETS B/A.   EN SUITE & BEVERAGES
IN ROOMS.   B. & B. £16, D. £12.

Marcorrie Hotel

20 FALMOUTH RD, TRURO, CORNWALL, TR1 2AX.   TEL: (01872) 77374
Privately owned, family-run Victorian hotel pleasantly situated in conservation areaa few
mins'walk from town centre. Ideal base for touring Cornwall. Car parking. *RAC 3 Crowns.*
N/S DINING R. & SOME BEDROOMS.   VE, SD B/A.   CHILDREN & PETS.   OPEN ALL YEAR.   LICENSED.   EN
SUITE, BEVERAGES & TV IN ALL BEDROOMS.   CREDIT CARDS.   B. & B. FROM £19.

POLSUE COTTAGE, RUAN HIGH LANES, TRURO, CORNWALL, TR2 5LU
Six acre organic smallholding 1 mile from the sea; own vegetables, herbs and soft fruit.
TEL: (01872) 501596   OPEN ALL YEAR.   NO SMOKING.   V STD (fish may be served on request). LOW-FAT,
VE, DIAB B/A.   CHILDREN WELCOME.   BEVERAGES.   B. & B. FROM £11. E.M. £7.

RESTAURANTS

BODMIN

PANCHOS VILLA, CASTLE CANYKE RD, BODMIN, CORNWALL.
French/English/Mexican cuisine.
TEL; 901208) 74601 V, VE STD. CHILDREN WELCOME. DISABLED ACCESS.

POT COFFEE SHOP, 55 FORE ST, BODMIN, CORNWALL.
OPEN MOST DAY TIMES. V, VE, STD. CHILDREN WELCOME.

CONSTANTINE

TRENGILLY WARTHA INN, NR CONSTANTINE, CORNWALL.
TEL: (01326) 40332 V STD. LICENSED. CHILDREN WELCOME (FAMILY ROOM AVAILABLE0.

FALMOUTH

ANNABILLS TEA SHOP, 17 - 18 KILLIGREW ST, FALMOUTH, CORNWALL.
TEL(01326) 211272   V STD. CHILDREN WELCOME.   TAKEAWAYS AVAILABLE.

LAUNCESTON

**THE GREENHOUSE VEGETARIAN WHOLEFOOD RESTAURANT, MADFORD
LN, LAUNCESTON.**
TEL: (01566) 773670 NO SMOKING. V EXC. LICENSED. DISABLED ACCESS 'GOOD'. CHILDREN.

PENZANCE

ENZO RESTAURANT, NEWBRIDGE, PENZANCE, CORNWALL, TR20 8QU
V STD.   SEPARATE ROOM FOR SMOKERS. LICENSED. CHILDREN WELCOME.

THE PARROT OF PENZANCE, PENZANCE, CORNWALL.
Elegant, warm, friendly and environmentlaly aware. Owned by a vegetarian (although also
serving free-range organic meat based meals) the vegetarian options are first-rate.
TEL: (01736) 50515   V STD. LICENSED. CHILDREN WELCOME.

PIZZA WORLD, 96 MARKET JEW STREET, PENZANCE, CORNWALL
TEL: (01736) 60678   V STD. SEPARATE SMOKE-FREE SECTION. LICENSED. CHILDREN WELCOME.

POLPERRO

THE OLD BARKHOUSE COFFEE SHOP AND EATING HOUSE, THE QUAY,

PORTH LEVEN

CRITCHARD'S SEAFOOD RESTAURANT, HARBOUR HEAD, PORTH LEVEN
TEL: (01326) 562407   V STD. EVENINGS ONLY.

THE LUGGER LICENSED FAMILY RESTAURANT, PORTH LEVE, CORNWALL.
TEL: (01326) 562761 OPEN DAILY IN SEASON. V STD. CHILDREN WELCOME.

Devon

ACCOMMODATION

ASHBURTON

Cuddyford

REW RD, ASHBURTON, DEVON, TQ13 7EN   TEL: (01364) 653325

Family home in rural setting within Dartmoor National Park, whole foods including home-baked bread, free-range eggs, organic fruit , vegetables & honey from our own hives. OPEN ALL YEAR Ex. Xmas. V, VE, GLUTEN-FREE & MACRO. STD. NO SMOKING. CHILDREN WELCOME. PETS B/A. BEVERAGES IN OWN KITCHEN. T.V. B/A. D B/A (3-COURSE, £10). B. & B. FROM £12.50.

Holne Chase Hotel

NR ASHBURTON, DEVON, TG13 7NS   TEL: (01364) 631471   FAX: (01364) 631453

*ETB 4 Crown Highly Commended.*Described by a 19th C directory as "being in a particularly secluded and romantic situation", Holne Chase Hotel has been offering hospitality since 1934 and, for the last 22 of those years, the Bromage family has been providing a sanctuary from "the pressures of modern life" with an efficacy that won them commendation by the BTA since 1974. Although, as the hotel brochure points out, there are telephones and televisions in bedrooms "for those who need to keep up with the news", there is every incentive not to do so, and to spend your time instead fly fishing on the hotel's mile length of the River Dart or whiling away an hour or two on the croquet lawn or putting green. Those seeking a day's energetic walking on Dartmoor may do so safe in the knowledge that they return to the good food and a sound night's sleep that the Holne Chase Hotel has to offer.

OPEN ALL YEAR.   V STD.   N/S DINING R. WHEELCHAIR ACCESS TO ALL PUBLIC ROOMS & GROUND FLOOR BEDROOM.   EN SUITE, BVERAGES & T.V. IN ROOMS. B. & B. FROM £45.

THE OLD COFFEE HOUSE, 27-29 WEST STREET, ASHBURTON, TQ13 7DT

Charming 16th century Grade II listed. Food prepared from fresh local produce. TEL: (01364) 52539 OPEN ALL YEAR. V STD. NO SMOKING. BEVERAGES & T.V. B. & B. AROUND £15.

AXMINSTER

GOODMANS HOUSE, FURLEY, MEMBURY, NR AXMINSTER, EX13 7TU

16th C. cum Georgian residence converted to 4 superbly furnished self-catering cottages. Succulent home-produced fare used in cooking including free-range eggs. TEL: (0140488) 690 OPEN Feb. 1st - Jan. 3rd. V, S.D. B/A. NO SMOKING. CHILDREN & PETS AT OWNERS' DISCRETION. EN SUITE, BEVERAGES & COLOUR TV IN BEDROOMS. 7 DAYS AROUND £150.

BARNSTAPLE

Huxtable Farm

WEST BUCKLAND, BARNSTAPLE, DEVON, EX32 0SR   TEL: (01598) 760254

Beautiful secluded 16th C. listed building lovingly restored to reveal oak beams, screen panelling & open fireplaces (with bread ovens). On Tarka Trail. OPEN ALL YEAR ex. Xmas & New Year. V B/A.   N/S DINING ROOM.   CHILDREN WELCOME.   5 EN SUITE ROOMS.   BEVERAGES IN BEDROOMS. T.V. IN 3 BEDROOMS. B. & B. FROM £19.

BIDEFORD

Mount Hotel

NORTHDOWN ROAD, BIDEFORD, DEVON, EX39 3LP TEL: (01237) 473748

Charming Georgian building in semi-walled garden a short walk from town. Home-cooked fare cooked from fresh produce where possible. OPEN ALL YEAR. V, VE, S.D. B/A.   N/S BEDRS & DINING R. LICENSED.   CHILDREN B/A.   MOST ROOMS EN SUITE. BEVERAGES IN ROOMS. T.V. CREDIT CARDS. B. & B. AROUND £16.

YEOLDON HOTEL, DURRANT LN, NORTHAM, BIDEFORD, EX39 2RL
TEL: (01237) 474400 V, VE, DIAB STD.   LICENSED.   WHEELCHAIR ACCESS.   CHILDREN WELCOME.
PETS B/A.   EN SUITE, BEVERAGES & T.V. IN ROOMS.   CREDIT CARDS.

BOVEY TRACEY

Blenheim Country House Hotel

BRIMLEY ROAD, BOVEY TRACEY, DEVON, TQ13 9DH   TEL: (01626) 832422
Country house hotel amidst delightful grounds on the edge of Dartmoor National Park.
OPEN ALL YEAR.   V, S.D. B/A.   N/S DINING R & T.V. LOUNGE.   LICENSED.   CHILDREN WELCOME. PETS B/A.
SOME EN SUITE, PRIVATE SHOWERS & COLOUR T.V. IN ROOMS.   BEVERAGES.   B. & B. AROUND £25.

CROYDE

The Whiteleaf at Croyde

CROYDE, BRAUNTON, DEVON, EX33 1PN   TEL: (01271) 890266
"Small and intimate", this highly acclaimed guest house offers first-class cuisine.
OPEN ALL YEAR.   V, VE, S.D. B/A.   LICENSED.   CHILDREN WELCOME.   PETS B/A. EN SUITE, BEVER-
AGES & T.V. IN BEDROOMS.   ACCESS, VISA.   B. & B. FROM £27. D. £18.50.

CULLOMPTON

TREDOWN FARM, CLAYHIDON, CULLOMPTON, DEVON, EX15 3TW
Modern bungalow on a working dairy farm in an area of Outstanding Natural Beauty. Most
ingredients locally produced including home-grown produce. J26 off M5 to Wellington,
then following signs to Ford St; at top of hill turn left, then after 300 yds, turn right.
TEL: (01823) 662421   OPEN ALL YEAR Ex. Xmas.   N/S DINING ROOM & LOUNGE.   V, S.D.   B/A.   DISABLED
ACCESS.   CHILDREN WELCOME.   BEVERAGES & TV IN ROOMS.

DARTMOOR

Slate Cottage

THE GREEN, NORTH BOVEY, NR MORETONH'STEAD, DEVON, TQ13 8RB TEL: (01647) 40060
18th C. cottage offering peace and comfort, overlooking thatched houses, 13th C. church,
oak-tree'd green and undulating moorland, all in a picturesque Dartmoor village.
OPEN ALL YEAR.   NO SMOKING.   V, S.D. B/A.   OVER 12s.   TV & BEVERAGES IN ROOMS.   B. & B. FROM £20.

Two Bridges Hotel

TWO BRIDGES, DARTMOOR, DEVON, PL20 6SW   TEL: (01822) 890581

This 18th century posting inn, set in the heart of
Dartmoor some 1,000 feet above sea-level, is situated
near to the junction of the two main roads over the
moor and has boundless views on each side of the
unspoilt beauty of this lovely National Park. In the
heart of a beautiful wilderness it is therefore reassuring
to discover that the atmosphere at Two Bridges is *cosy*:
log fires warm footsore travellers in the beautifully
furnished lounge and bar, and good home-cooked food
accompanied by sensibly priced wines is the order of
the day in the dining room (cream teas are also served
daily). With some 60 acres of hotel grounds alone,
holiday-makers could walk for days within the vicinity of Two Bridges and not retrace a
single path - but the proprietors organise guided National Park walks and there is riding
and fishing to be enjoyed nearby (the West Dart River flows through the grounds).
OPEN ALL YEAR.   V STD. S.D. B/A.   N/S DINING R, LOUNGE, MOST BEDR.   LICENSED.   DISABLED ACCESS.
CHILDREN WELCOME, PETS B/A.   EN SUITE MOST ROOMS.   BEVERAGES & T.V. (+ SATELLITE) IN ROOMS.   B.
& B. FROM £24.50 (2-DAY BREAKS FROM £75 FOR D.B. & B.).

DARTMOUTH

Ford House

44 VICTORIA RD, DARTMOUTH, DEVON, TQ6 9DX   TEL: (01803) 834047
Comfortable rooms & good food, wholefood & organic where possible, much home-grown.
OPEN MAR. TO DEC.   V, S.D. B/A.   N/S PART DINING R.   WELL-BEHAVED CHILDREN & PETS B/A.   EN SUITE
SOME ROOMS.   BEVERAGES & T.V. ALL ROOMS.   B. & B. FROM £22.50. D £20.

EXETER

COPPLESTONE FARM, DUNSFORD, EXETER, EDEVON, X6 7HQ
Comfortable farmhouse in the beautiful Teign Valley just within Dartmoor National Park;
home-baked bread, free-range eggs and poultry; small adjoining cottage to let.
TEL: (01647) 52784 OPEN Easter - Oct. inc. NO SMOKING. V, VE, S.D. B/A. BEVERAGES . T.V.

The Royal Oak Inn
DUNSFORD, EXETER, DEVON, EX6 7DA TEL: (01647) 52256
ETB Listed Approved. Traditional village inn in Dartmoor National Park with all fa-
cilities. 6 real ales & home-made food.
OPEN ALL YEAR. V, ORG STD, S.D., VE B/A. N/S DINING R. CHILDREN & PETS WELCOME. WHEELCHAIR
ACCESS. EN SUITE & BEVERAGES IN ROOMS. TV AVAIL. B. & B. 17.50-25.

KINGSBRIDGE

BURTON FARM, GALMPTON, KINGSBRIDGE, DEVON, TQ7 3EY
Working farm in the South Huish Valley. Home-produce used wherever possible.
TEL: (01548) 561210 OPEN ALL YEAR ex. Xmas & New Year. NO SMOKING. V, S.D. B/A. LICENSED.
CHILDREN WELCOME. SOME ROOMS EN SUITE BEVERAGES. T.V. LOUNGE. B. & B. AROUND £20.

Start House
START, SLAPTON, NR KINGSBRIDGE, DEVON, TQ7 2QD TEL: (01548) 580254
South-facing home with log fire. B'fast features locally made bread, & free-range eggs.
Home-cooked prepared from home-grown vegetables
OPEN ALL YEAR ex. Xmas. V, DIAB & LOW-FAT DIETS B/A. NO SMOKING. BYO WINE. CHILDREN
WELCOME. SOME EN SUITE ROOMS. BEVERAGES. T.V. IN LOUNGE. B. & B. AROUND £18.

The White House
CHILLINGTON, KINGSBRIDGE, DEVON, TQ7 2JX TEL: (01548) 580580
Lovely Georgian house in an acre ofgardens midway between Salcombe and Dartmouth
and just 2 m from the sea. All food home-made from fresh local produce wherever possible.
OPEN Easter - Xmas. N/S DINING R & DRAWING R. V, S.D. B/A. LICENSED. OVER 5S ONLY. PETS
WELCOME. EN SUITE, TV & BEVERAGES IN ROOMS. CREDIT CARDS. B. & B. AROUND £35.

LEWDOWN

HAYNE MILL, LEWDOWN, NR OAKHAMPTON, DEVON, EX20 4DD
Friendly holiday accommodation for dogs and their owners in lovely old mill house; good
food prepared from organically produced fruit and vegetables; nearby walks.
TEL: (01566) 783342 OPEN ALL YEAR. V, S.D. B/A. CHILDREN. 1 EN SUITE ROOM. BEVERAGES & T.V.

LYNTON

LONGMEAD HOUSE HOTEL, 9 LONG MEAD, LYNTON, DEVON, EX35 6DQ
Lovely hotel quietly situated in beautiful gardens. Imaginative, home-cooked food pre-
pared from fresh produce when possible, served in an oak-panelled dining room.
TEL: (01598) 52523 OPEN ALL YEAR. V, S.D. B/A. NO SMOKING. LICENSED. CHILDREN WELCOME. 4
EN SUITE ROOMS. BEVERAGES IN ROOMS. T.V. B. & B. AROUND £18.

Neubia House Hotel
LYDIATE LANE, LYNTON, DEVON, EX35 6AH TEL: (01598) 52309
Beautiful Victorian farmhouse in old Lynton. Excellent healthy food. & veg. options.
OPEN Mar. - Nov. V, VE STD. S.D. B/A. N/S IN DINING R. LICENSED. CHILDREN WELCOME. EN SUITE,
TV & BEVERAGES IN ROOMS. B. & B. FROM £27.

Sylvia House Hotel
LYDIATE LANE, LYNTON, DEVON, EX35 6HE TEL: (01598) 752391
Set in England's little Switzerland, Sylvia House offers elegance at moderate terms.
Delightful en suite bedrooms. Exquisitely scrumptious fare and old-fashioned hospitality.
OPEN ALL YEAR. N/S PUBLIC RS & SOME BEDRS. V, S.D. B/A. LICENSED. CHILDREN WELCOME. EN SUITE.
TV & BEVERAGES IN ROOMS. B. & B. FROM £14.

Waterloo House
LYDIATE LANE, LYNTON, DEVON TEL: (01598) 753391
ETB 3 Crown Commended. Delightful Georgian building. Imaginative 4-course meals are
served by candlelight in an elegant dining room prepared from fresh produce. Vegetarians

are most welcome and can be accommodated by arrangement.
OPEN ALL YEAR. N/S DINING R, SOME BEDRS & 1 LOUNGE. V B/A. CHILDREN WELCOME. EN SUITE MOST BEDRS. TV & BEVERAGES IN ROOMS. B. & B. AROUND £19.

MORETONHAMPSTEAD

WHITE HART HOTEL, THE SQUARE, MORETONHAMPSTEAD, TQ13 8NF

Beautiful listed building. Fresh local produce used in cooking where possible; everything home-prepared, including pastries & sweets.
TEL: (01647) 40406 OPEN ALL YEAR ex. Xmas. V, VE B/A. N/S DINING R. LICENSED. OVER 10S ONLY. EN SUITE, BEVERAGES, T.V. & PHONE IN ROOMS. CREDIT CARDS. B. & B. AROUND £30

NEWTON ABBOT

CLEAVE HOTEL, LUSTLEIGH, NEWTON ABBOTT, DEVON, TQ13 9TJ

15th C. thatched inn, inglenook fireplace. home-cooked food prepared from fresh produce.
TEL: (016477) 223 OPEN Feb. - Nov. V STD. S.D. B/A. N/S DINING R. LICENSED. WHEELCHAIR ACCESS. BEVERAGES & T.V. IN ROOMS. VISA, MASTERCHARGE. B. & B. AROUND £22.

Lustleigh Mill

LUSTLEIGH, NEWTON ABBOTT, DEVON, TQ13 9SS   TEL: (016477) 357

Historic 15th C. riverside millhouse on edge of beautiful Dartmoor village. Exposed beams, antique furniture, home-grown produce, (eggs, milk, vegetables). Walking, riding, fishing.
OPEN ALL YEAR. NO SMOKING. S.D., WH., B/A. OVER 7s. WELCOME. PETS WELCOME. BEVERAGES IN ROOMS. TV LOUNGE. B. & B. FROM £15.

Rutherford House

WIDECOMBE IN THE MOOR, NR NEWTON ABBOT, DEVON, TQ13 7TB   TEL: (013642) 264

Large detached house in pretty gardens. Vegetarian b'fast & a choice of fresh fruit salad.
OPEN from Easter. NO SMOKING. V, VE, DIAB B/A. OVER 9S. T.V. LOUNGE. B. & B. AROUND £16.

NEWTON POPPLEFORD

JOLLY'S, THE BANK, NEWTON POPPLEFORD, DEVON, EX10 0XD

Friendly smoke-free establishment offering accommodation and food to both residential and non-residential guests. Predominantly vegetarian. Imaginative & delicious food.
TEL: (01395) 68100 OPEN ALL YEAR. V STD. S.D. B/A. NO SMOKING LICENSED. CHILDREN.

OKEHAMPTON

HOWARD'S GORHUISH, NORTHLEW, OKEHAMPTON, DEVON, EX20 3BT

Charming 16th C. Devon longhouse in 7 acres of beautiful gardens. Meals are prepared from organically home-grown fruit & vegetables.
TEL: (01837) 53301 OPEN ALL YEAR. V, VE B/A. NO SMOKING. CHILDREN: OVER 10S ONLY. SOME EN SUITE ROOMS. TV LOUNGE. BEVERAGES IN ROOMS. B. & B. AROUND £20.

Pumpy Cottage

EAST WEEK, OKEHAMPTON, DEVON, EX20 2QB   TEL: (01647) 23580

Mediaeval Dartmoor cottage in beautiful countryside, with its own herb garden & paddock. Comfortable & charming. Healthy b'fast using home-grown & local produce.
OPEN May - Oct. V B/A. NO SMOKING. CHILDREN: OVER 5S ONLY. B.& B. AROUND £14.

Stowford House

STOWFORD, LEWDOWN, OKEHAMPTON, DEVON, EX20 4BZ   TEL: (0156 683) 415

Charming former rectory in peaceful gardens. Outstanding home-cooking prepared from fresh ingredients (vegetarian meals are available with notice)
OPEN Mar. - Nov. V, S.D. B/A. N/S DINING R. LICENSED. CHILDREN B/A. EN SUITE, TV & BEVERAGES IN ROOMS. CREDIT CARDS. B. & B. AROUND £20.

OTTERY ST MARY

Fluxton Farm Hotel

OTTERY ST MARY, DEVON, EX11 1RJ   TEL: (01404) 812818

Once a 16th C. long house, a charming white-washed hotel in open country & pretty sheltered gardens. Fresh, locally purchased or home-produced ingredients used including: free-range eggs come from the house hens.
OPEN ALL YEAR. V, S.D. B/A. N/S DINING R & 1 LOUNGE. LICENSED. CHILDREN & PETS WELCOME. EN SUITE, TV & BEVERAGES IN ROOMS. B. & B. FROM £22.50 D., B. & B. FROM £28.50.

PLYMOUTH

Rosaland Hotel

32 HOUNDISCOMBE RD, MUTLEY, PLYMOUTH. TEL: (01752) 664749 FAX: (01752) 256984

Charming Victorian town house. Quality accommodation at affordable prices.
OPEN ALL YEAR. V, S.D. B/A. CHILDREN WELCOME. LICENSED. EN SUITE, TV (inc. Satellite) & BEVERAGES IN ROOMS. CREDIT CARDS. B. & B. FROM £17.

The Trillium Guest House

4 ALFRED ST, THE HOE, PLYMOUTH, DEVON, PL1 2RP   TEL & FAX: (01752) 670452

Comfortable family guest house with a homely & friendly atmosphere close to city centre & seafront. Home-cooking. Quiet area. English language courses. Reservation for car park needed.
OPEN ALL YEAR. N/S DINING R. ON REQUEST. V, S.D. B/A. CHILDREN WELCOME. EN SUITE, TV & BEVERAGES IN ROOMS. B. & B. £15 - 23, D. £11.

SEATON

THE BULSTONE, HIGH BULSTONE, BRANSCOMBE, NR SEATON, EX12 3BL

Lovely 16th C. hotel offering very high standard of cuisine & accommodation; especially welcoming to families with young children.
TEL: (01297) 80446 OPEN Feb. - Nov. V STD, S.D. B/A. N/S ex 1 LOUNGE. LICENSED. CHILDREN. PETS B/A. MOST ROOMS EN SUITE. BEVERAGES IN ROOMS. T.V. LOUNGE. B. & B. AROUND £23.

SOUTH MOLTON

Whitechapel Manor

SOUTH MOLTON, DEVON, EX36 3EG   TEL: (01769) 573797

Beautifully restored Elizabethan manor house with wonderful views; excellent cuisine.
OPEN ALL YEAR. N/S DINING R. V, S.D. B/A. LICENSED. CHILDREN. EN SUITE & T.V. IN ROOMS. B. & B. FROM £49.

TAVISTOCK

V The Stannary

MARY TAVY, TAVISTOCK, DEVON, PL19 9QB   TEL: (01822) 810897 FAX: (01822) 810898

The Stannary Vegetarian Restaurant with Rooms has, since its opening in early 1989, achieved greater acclaim than any other vegetarian restaurant, with high ratings in the leading restaurant guides and some excellent reviews in the national press. The proprietors, host Michael Cook and chef Alison Fife, provide unique gourmet creations and use many wild, unusual and exotic ingredients such as seaweeds, truffles and flowers, and many rare and uncommon vegetable and fruit varieties. In addition to the frequently changing multi-choice menu, The Stannary makes its own specialist breads, ice-creams and sorbets, preserves and exquisite chocolates, plus a range of highly successful Stannary Country Wines plus home-made cordials and many other drinks. The 16th C. Victorian house on the edge of Dartmoor offers a wealth of character: the restaurant is beautifully decorated in Victorian style and incorporates a fascinating collection of over 200 antique pottery fruit and vegetable dishes. The Orangery, a plant-filled haven, is used as a lounge by restaurant visitors as well as guests staying in one the three elegant and comfortable rooms.
N/S ex in ORANGERY. V EXC., VE, ORG, WH, STD. LICENSED. OVER 12S ONLY. 1 EN SUITE ROOM. BEVERAGES & TV IN ROOMS.   CREDIT CARDS. D., B. & B. FROM £60.

TEIGNMOUTH

FONTHILL, TORQUAY RD, SHALDON, TEIGNMOUTH, DEVON, TQ14 0AX

Beautiful Georgian house in 25 acres of private grounds. Very tranquil and peaceful.
TEL: (01626) 872344 OPEN Mar. - Dec.   NO SMOKING. V, S.D. B/A. CHILDREN WELCOME. 1 PRIVATE BATHROOM. BEVERAGES IN ROOMS. B. & B. AROUND £20.

TIVERTON

Harton Farm

OAKFORD, TIVERTON, DEVON, EX16 9HH   TEL: (013985) 209

Beautiful south-facing 17th C. farm; all produce has been organically home-grown; all bread home-baked. Herbs & flowers are grown & Harton Farm Jam is made!

OPEN ALL YEAR ex. Xmas   V, S.D. B/A. ORG. STD. MOSTLY WH.   N/S DINING R.   BYO WINE. OVER 4S ONLY. BEVERAGES IN ROOMS.   T.V.   B. & B. AROUND £16.

TORQUAY

Brookesby Hall Vegetarian Hotel

HESKETH ROAD, MEADFOOT BEACH, TORQUAY, DEVON, TQ1 2LN   TEL: (01803) 292194

Exclusively vegetarian hotel; imaginative cuisine cooked from natural ingredients including free-range eggs & organic vegetables.

OPEN Easter - Oct. inc.   V EXC.   NO SMOKING.   CHILDREN WELCOME.   SOME EN SUITE ROOMS. BEVERAGES.   T.V. IN 1 OF 2 LOUNGES.   D., B. & B. AROUND £29.

Orestone Manor

ROCKHOUSE LN, MAIDENCOMBE, TORQUAY, DEVON, TQ1 4SX TEL: (01803) 328098 FAX: (01803) 320336

Orestone Manor as built early in the 19th C. and was originally a Georgian Country Lodge. It has been substantially extended over the years and is now an exceptionally comfortable hotel: warm, inviting and full of character and charm. Its restaurant (which is totally smoke-free) has been awarded two prestigious AA Rosettes for its excellent Anglo-French cuisine (the only hotel in Torbay to be thus honoured), and all food is prepared from fresh ingredients; a tasty vegetarian option is always available. Accommodation is in beautifully furnished en suite bedrooms; each has an individual character and all have views of either the countryside or the sea. There is a comfortable cocktail lounge and bar for guests' use, and the outdoor heated swimming pool is available from mid-June to mid-September. Orestone stands in an area of outstanding natural beauty: the sheltered gardens offer a haven of peace and tranquillity, yet you are just over 3 miles from Torbay harbourside.

OPEN ALL YEAR.   N/S DINING R.   V STD, VE, S.D., WH B/A.   LICENSED.   PETS B/A.   WHEELCHAIR ACCESS TO RESTAURANT.   EN SUITE, TV & BEVERAGES IN ROOMS.   CREDIT CARDS.

Hotel Sydore

MEADFOOT ROAD, TORQUAY, DEVON, TQ1 2JP   TEL: (01803) 294489

Comfortable villa-style hotel near Meadfoot Beach; tasty & imaginative vegetarian options.

V STD, S.D. B/A.   OPEN ALL YEAR.   LICENSED.   DISABLED ACCESS.   CHILDREN WELCOME.   PETS B/A. EN SUITE, BEVERAGES, T.V. & HAIRDRYER IN ROOMS.   CREDIT CARDS.   B. & B. AROUND £25.

TOTNES

The Old Forge at Totnes

SEYMOUR PLACE, TOTNES, DEVON, TQ9 5AY   TEL: (01803) 862174

No church bells

This charming stone-built hotel was converted recently from a 600 year-old smithy; it has a lovely walled garden which makes it a rural retreat in the heart of Totnes; the property has had an interesting history and has partly reverted back to its primary use - Peter Allnutt now runs a busy wrought iron business while his wife, Jeannie, runs the hotel. The highest standard of accommodation is offered to guests: the cottage-style bedrooms are prettily and tastefully furnished, and the food (served in very plentiful quantities) is prepared from the best of healthy ingredients. A typical breakfast menu features a variety of fish and vegetarian options and, in addition to four different

types of bread, *two* different sorts of decaffeinated coffee are also offered. Healthily conscientious indeed. Traditional breakfasts are also available as well as fruit, yoghurts, waffles and pancakes. **Holder of AA Merit Award and ETB Highly Commended.**
OPEN ALL YEAR.   NO SMOKING.   V, S.D. B/A.   LICENSED.   CHILDREN WELCOME.   PETS IN CARS ONLY. DISABLED ACCESS TO SOME GROUND FLOOR ROOMS.   EN SUITE IN MOST ROOMS.   BEVERAGES & T.V. IN ALL BEDROOMS.   CREDIT CARDS.   B. & B. FROM £20.

BARNSTABLE

HEAVENS ABOVE, 4 BEAR ST, BARNSTABLE, DEVON.
TEL: (01271) 77960   NO SMOKING.   V, VE, EXC.   WH. STD.   LICENSED.   CHILDREN WELCOME.

BIDEFORD

SLOOPS, BRIDGE STREET, BIDEFORD, DEVON
TEL: (01237) 471796   V STD.   NO SMOKING AFTER 12 NOON.   ACCESS, VISA. .

THYMES RESTAURANT, THE BAKEHOUSE, QUEEN ST, BIDEFORD.
TEL: (01237) 473399   V STD.   ONLY 3 SMOKING TABLES.   LICENSED.   CHILDREN WELCOME.

BOVEY TRACEY

Devon Guild of Craftsmen

RIVERSIDE MILL, BOVEY TRACEY, DEVON   TEL: (01626) 832223
Granary cafe serving teas, coffees, light lunches annexed to specialist exhibition centre & retail shop selling work of 200 craftsmen & women; outside seating in walled courtyard.
OPEN 10 - 5. L. FROM £3.25.   V STD.   NO SMOKING.   LICENSED.   DISABLED ACCESS.   CHILDREN WELCOME (TOYS AVAILABLE).   CREDIT CARDS.

CREDITON

WILD THYMES, 100 HIGH ST, CREDITON, DEVON.
Friendly little restaurant serving a variety of wholesome meat-free dishes.
TEL: (01363) 77 2274   V, WH EXC.   NO SMOKING.   BYO WINE.   CHILDREN WELCOME.

DARTINGTON

CRANKS, CIDER PRESS CENTRE., SHINNERS BRIDGE, DARTINGTON.
TEL: (01803) 862388   V EXC.   NO SMOKING.   LICENSED.   DISABLED ACCESS.

EAST BUDLEIGH

GRASSHOPPERS, 16 HIGH ST, EAST BUDLEIGH, BUDLEIGH SALTERTON.
TEL: (013954) 2774   V STD.   NO SMOKING. DISABLED ACCESS.

EXETER

THE CAFÉ, 38 SOUTH STREET, EXETER, DEVON.   TEL: (01392) 410855
Light, airy 'conservatory' restaurant, with pleasant *al fresco* dining area, in converted chapel; excellent food. 'Thai nights'are a special feature Wednesdays & Thursdays eves.
OPEN 10.30 - 6 MON. TO SAT.   V STD.   N/S 80% OF RESTAURANT & IN LARGE GARDEN.   LICENSED.   DISABLED ACCESS.   CHILDREN WELCOME.   CREDIT CARDS.

HERBIES, 15 NORTH STREET, EXETER, DEVON.   TEL: (01392) 58473
V EXC, VE STD.   60% N/S.   LICENSED.   CHILDREN WELCOME

KILLERTON HOUSE (NAT. TRUST), BROADCLYST, NR EXETER.
TEL: (01392) 881691   V STD, S.D. B/A   NO SMOKING.   LICENSED.   CHILDREN WELCOME.

MILL ON THE EXE, BONHAY ROAD, EXETER, DEVON.   TEL: (01392) 214464
V STD.   SEPARATE N/S SECTION.   DISABLED ACCESS.

EXMOUTH

WILLOWS, 53 THE STRAND, EXMOUTH, DEVON   TEL: (01395) 264398
NO SMOKING.   VEGETARIAN.   LICENSED.   CHILDREN WELCOME.

HONITON

HONEY BEES, 160 HIGH ST, HONITON, DEVON   TEL: (01404) 43392
V STD.   50% N/S.   DISABLED ACCESS.   CHILDREN WELCOME.

NEWTON ABBOT

DEVON GUILD OF CRAFTSMEN, RIVERSIDE MILL, NEWTON ABBOT.
TEL: (01626) 832223   V STD. NO SMOKING.   LICENSED.   DISABLED ACCESS.

NEWTON POPPPLEFORD

Ⅴ **JOLLY'S VEGETARIAN RESTAURANT, THE BANK, NEWTON POPPLEFORD.**
For further details please see under the entry in the accommodation section.

TIVERTON

Ⅴ *Angel Gallery*

1 ANGEL TERRACE, TIVERTON, DEVON, EX16 6PD   TEL: (01884) 254778
Art gallery with café & takeaway serving vegetarian food with Mediterranean and world
cuisine influences. Historic castle and award-winning museum nearby.
OPEN 10 - 5, Mon-Sat.   V STD. NO SMOKING. L. FROM £1.50, TAKEAWAY.   CHILDREN WELCOME

TOTNES

Ⅴ *Willow Vegetarian Restaurant*

87 HIGH ST, TOTNES, DEVON.   TEL: (01803) 862605
Wholefood vegetarian restaurant in The Narrows at the top of Totnes. A café by day and
a restaurant by night, the Willows has a lovely garden and the food is first-rate: everything
is prepared from fresh, wholefood ingredients (most vegetables are organic) and the
desserts include soya icecream or Rocombe Farm Icecream made with organic milk.
V EXC.   NO SMOKING. CHILDREN WELCOME. LICENSED. DISABLED ACCESS.

Dorset

ACCOMMODATION

BLANDFORD FORUM

La Belle Alliance

WHITE CLIFF MILL STREET, BLANDFORD FORUM, DORSET, DS11 7BP   TEL: (01258) 452842
Elegant country house style restaurant and hotel offering first-rate accommodation; all
dishes have been prepared from fresh ingredients (local wherever possible).
OPEN Feb. To Dec. V, S.D. B/A.   N/S DINING R. LICENSED. CHILDREN WELCOME, BABIES B/A. PETS B/A.
EN SUITE, BEVERAGES & TV IN ROOMS. ACCESS, VISA, AMEX. B. & B. AROUND £33.

BOURNEMOUTH

Langtry Manor

DERBY RD, EAST CLIFF, BOURNEMOUTH, BH1 3QB TEL: (01202) 553887
OPEN ALL YEAR. V STD.   N/S DINING R & SOME BEDRS.   LICENSED. DISABLED ACCESS.   CHILD-
REN & PETS B/A.   EN SUITE, BEVERAGES & T.V. IN ROOMS.   CREDIT CARDS.   B. & B. FROM £39.50.

BRIDPORT

Britmead House

WEST BAY ROAD, BRIDPORT, DORSET, DT6 4EG   TEL: (01308) 422941
ETB 3 Crown Commended. At Britmead the proprietors, Ann and Dan Walker, put your
comfort first. The house is just a short, level walk from both the historic town of Bridport,
Chesil Beach, the Dorset Coastal Path and the harbour of West Bay, with its beaches, golf
course and walks. The seven well-appointed and individually decorated bedrooms (one of
which is on the ground floor) have many thoughtful little extras. There is an airy,
comfortable south-facing lounge and dining room overlooking the garden and beyond to
the open countryside. The food is excellent; whenever possible, meals are prepared from
fresh produce & locally caught fish. The dinner menu changes daily. Car parking.
OPEN ALL YEAR. V, S.D. B/A. N/S DINING R.   LICENSED. CHILDREN WELCOME. PETS B/A. EN SUITE,
TV & BEVERAGES IN ROOMS.   CREDIT CARDS. B. & B. FROM £19 - 26, D. £12. Bargain breaks avail.

DORCHESTER

Badgers Sett

CROSS LANES, MELCOMBE BINGHAM, NR DORCHESTER, DT2 7NY   TEL/FAX: (01258) 880697
Mellow 17th C. flint and brick cottage carefully modernised to retain such original features
as oak beams and inglenook fireplaces; all bedrooms are en suite with TV, radio and kettle.
OPEN ALL YEAR.   V, S.D. B/A.   N/S DINING & SITTING R.   CHILDREN WELCOME.   PETS B/A).   EN SUITE,
TV & BEVERAGES IN ROOMS.   B. & B. FROM £16.50.

CASTLEVIEW, 8 EDWARD RD, DORCHESTER, DORSET, ST1 2HJ
TEL: (01305) 263507   V, VE STD.   CHILDREN WELCOME.   TV & BEVERAGES.   B. & B. AROUND £14.

The Creek

RINGSTEAD, DORCHESTER, DORSET, DT2 8NG   TEL: (01305) 852251
Lovely white-washed house on Dorset coast with the sea at the bottom of the garden.
Fabulous views across Weymouth Bay. All food 'as fresh as possible'.
OPEN ALL YEAR.   V, VE, S.D. B/A.   NO SMOKING.   CHILDREN WELCOME.   BEVERAGES IN ROOMS.   T.V.
IN LOUNGE.   B. & B. FROM £17.50, D. FROM £9.50.

The Manor Hotel

WEST BEXINGTON, DORCHESTER, DT2 9DF

TEL: (01308) 897616   FAX: (01308) 897035
The Manor Hotel, the ancient Manor House
of West Bexington, snuggles in a pocket of
tree and garden on a gentle slope just a saunter
from the sea at Chesil Bank; an old stone
building, mellowed by nine centuries of sea
and sun, the Manor Hotel has, nonetheless,
every modern comfort you could wish for
together with a few welcome traditional
values of hospitality and service (crisp bed
linen, warming log fires, real ales served in
the stone-lined cellar bar); most bedrooms
have uninterrupted sea views. The food is
prepared with integrity and flair from fresh,
local and seasonal ingredients (lobster, game,
seafood, etc.), and there is a good childrens'
menu (younger guests will also enjoy playing on the swings and slides in the garden). Its
a wonderful place to come for those in search of safe sandy beaches (Weymouth, Charmouth
& Lyme Regis are within easy reach), & historic towns, houses & gardens abound.
OPEN ALL YEAR.   N/S CONSERVATORY.   V, S.D. B/A.   LICENSED.   WHEELCHAIR ACCESS RESTAURANT.
CHILDREN WELCOME.   EN SUITE, TV & BEVERAGES IN ROOMS.   B. & B. FROM £38, D. B. & B. FROM £56.

POOLE

GULL COTTAGE, 50 TWEMLOW AVE, LOWER PARKSTONE, POOLE.
Large family house overlooking Poole Park and close to harbour.
TEL: (01202) 721277   V B/A.   NO SMOKING.   CHILDREN WELCOME.   EN SUITE.   B. & B. AROUND £18.

SHERBORNE

Middle Piccadilly Natural Healing Centre

HOLWELL, SHERBORNE, DORSET   TEL: (01963) 323468   FAX: (01963) 323038

In spite of its urbane title, Middle Piccadilly
is a 17th C. thatched cottage set in the heart
of the Dorset countryside. Its proprietors de-
scribe themselves as "natural healers" and a
wide range of treatments is offered at Middle
Piccadilly including Acupressure, Bach
Flower Remedies, Reflexology and Remedial
Yoga. Guests have an initial consultation during which treatments are prescribed and during the course of their stay these are carried
out while the additional recuperative benefits
of living in a beautifully furnished cottage
and being fed exceptionally good vegetarian
cuisine also work their therapeutic magic. The food is 100% wholefood, the produce is

organic (mostly home-grown), and the menu imaginative (a typical meal might feature Vegetable Wellington followed by pears in red grape juice).
OPEN ALL YEAR EX. XMAS. V STD. WH, ORG WHEN AVAILABLE. NO SMOKING. BEVERAGES. FULL BOARD FROM £46. 2, 3 & 4 DAY PACKAGES AVAILABLE INCLUDING TREATMENTS.

SHAFTESBURY

THE MITRE INN, 23 HIGH ST, SHAFTESBURY, DORSET.
Country inn with good vegetarian specialities.
TEL: (01747) 52488 OPEN ALL YEAR. V STD. CHILDREN WELCOME. BEVERAGES & TV. B. & B. FROM £19.

SWANAGE

CROWTHORNE HOTEL, CLUNY CRES, SWANAGE, DORSET, BH19 2BT
Totally non-smoking. Real home-cooking with choice of dishes including vegetarian.
TEL: (01929) 422108 OPEN ALL YEAR. V STD. LICENSED. CHIDREN WELCOME. B. & B. FROM £18.

Seashells Vegetarian Hotel

7 BURLINGTON RD, SWANAGE, DORSET, BH19 1LR   TEL: (01929) 422794
Seashells Vegetarian Guest House is a comfortable family owned hotel which, as its name suggests, is situated immediately opposite the safe, sandy beach at Burlington Chine; beach huts, deck shairs and ice cream are all available from the hotel making in an ideal choice for a family holiday. All bedrooms are centrally heated and have been comfortably furnished and appointed - many have sea views. Meals are served in an attractive dining room: all food is home-cooked and a typical evening menu would feature Hummus with pitta bread and vegetable batons followed by Aubergine Bake and a choice of desserts such as Turkish Rice Pudding or fresh fruit salad; coffee, cheese, biscuits and mints complete the meal.
OPEN ALL YEAR. NO SMOKNG. V STD. CHILDREN WELCOME. LICENSED. EN SUITE, TV & BEVERAGES IN ROOMS. B. & B. £18 - 22.50.

Skelmorie House

50 QUEENS RD, SWANAGE, DORSET, BH19 2EU   TEL: (01929) 424643
Beautiful sea views and delicious home-cooking prepared from fresh ingredients, at this small guest house in a quiet part of Swanage. Relaxed and friendly atmosphere.
OPEN Apr. - Sept. V, S.D. B/A. N/S DINING R. OVER 5s WELCOME. SOME EN SUITE. BEVERAGES & TV IN ROOMS. B. & B. £14.50-22, D. ££7.50.

WEYMOUTH

The Beehive

OSMINGTON, NR WEYMOUTH, DORSET, DT3 6EL   TEL: (01305) 834095
Lovely thatched Georgian cottage in the picturesque village of Osmington. Healthy food is of prime importance at The Beehive, including fre-range eggs.
OPEN Feb. - Dec. V, S.D. B/A. NO SMOKING. CHILDREN: OVER 5S ONLY. PETS B/A. 1 EN SUITE ROOM. BEVERAGES IN ROOMS. T.V. IN SITTING ROOM. B. & B. AROUND £18.

FAIRLIGHT, 50 LITTLEMOOR RD, PRESTON, WEYMOUTH, DORSET, DT3 6AA
Family-run establishment with good home-cooking. All food fresh.
OPEN ALL YEAR. V B/A. NO SMOKING. CHILDREN: OVER 4S. D, B. & B. FROM £18.

RESTAURANTS & TAKEAWAYS

BOURNEMOUTH

THE SALAD CENTRE, 22 POST OFFICE RD, BOURNEMOUTH.
Vegetarian restaurant serving a wide range of dishes which varies daily.
V, VE, WH EXC. NO SMOKING. CHILDREN WELCOME.

CERNE ABBAS

OLD MARKET HOUSE, 25 LONG ST, CERNE ABBAS, DORSET.
TEL: (01300) 3680 OPEN Mar. - OCt. V STD. NO SMOKING.

LYME REGIS

PILOT BOAT INN, BRIDGE ST, LYME REGIS, DORSET, DT7 3QA
TEL: (012974) 43157 V A SPECIALITY. NO SMOKING. LICENSED. DISABLED ACCESS. CHILDREN.

THE FOOD SHOP, 67 KINGS RD, SWANAGE, DORSET.
Home-cooked savoury dishes including good vegetarian selection. Takeaway only.
TEL; (01929) 427293   V, VE STD.

TAWNY'S WINE BAR, 52 HIGH ST, SWANAGE, DORSET.
Interesting home-made dishes from around the world, including good vegetarian options.
TEL: (01929) 422781 OPEN ALL YEAR. PHONE FOR RESERVATIONS. V TSD.

FIVE AND DINE, 14 WEST ST, WAREHAM, DORSET.
Candle-lit suppers (by reservation). Good food including vegetarian options.
TEL: (01929) 552778 V STD. LICENSED.

RIVERSIDE RESTAURANT, WEST BAY, BRIDPORT, DORSET, DT6 4EZ
Seafood restaurant overlooking West Bay. Vegetarian dishes available.
TEL: (01308) 22011 V STD. LICENSED.

Somerset

ACCOMODATION

BRENDON

BRIDGE COTTAGE, BRENDON, NR LYNMOUTH. TEL: (015987) 247
Old stone house in woodland by river. Home-cooked food with garden produce.
V B/A. B. & B. FROM AROUND £15.

BRIDGWATER

THE GRANGE, STAWELL, BRIDGWATER, SOMERSET.
Lovely old house with large garden. Vegetarian b'fasts.
TEL: (01278) 722452 OPEN ALL YEAR. V STD. B. & B. AROUND £15.

LITTLE WHITLEY FARM, STAGMAN LN, ASHCOTT, BRIDGWATER.
Working dairy farm with chickens, ducks and goats. Vegetarian meals a speciality.
TEL: (01458) 210050 OPEN ALL YEAR. V STD. CHILDREN WELCOME. BEVERAGES & TV. B. & B. AROUND £13.

Parsonage Farm
OVER STOWEY, BRIDGWATER, SOMERSET, TA5 1HA TEL: (01278) 733237
Parsonage Farm is a traditional 17th C. farmhouse which is located in a quiet Quantock

Hill village directly adjacent to the parish church. It has spacious rooms, quarry tile floors and log fires, and is surrounded by an organic smallholding with large, walled kitchen garden from which are gathered the delicious vegetables, fruit and free range eggs used in cooking. Dining at Parsonage Farm is a real treat: breakfast features porridge cooked overnight in the Aga, home-made breads and jams, and house specialities of waffles or blackcurrant pancakes with maple syrup. Evening meals are predominantly vegetarian and always include seasonal fruits and vegetables. Your hosts are keen ramblers and enjoy helping guests choose walks which begin at the doorstep; additionally it is peaceful to relax in the garden.
OPEN ALL YEAR. ORG, WH, V, VE STD, S.D. B/A. NO SMOKING. CHILDREN WELCOME. PETS B/A. TV IN SITTING ROOM. B. & B. £16 - 18.

POPLAR HERB FARM, MARK RD, BURTLE, NR BRIDGWATER, TA7 8NB
Organic smallholding, herb & nursery gardens.
TEL: (01278) 723170 OPEN ALL YEAR.   V, VE EXC NO SMOKING. CHILDREN. BEVERAGES & T.V. B. & B. £13 - 17.

WEST BOWER MANOR, BRIDGWATER, SOMERSET.   TEL: (01278) 422895
Peaceful Medieaval lakeside B. & B. Home-made bread, free-range breakfasts.
OPEN Jan. - Dec. V STD. CHILDREN WELCOME. BEVERAGES & TV. B. & B. AROUND £18.

CREWKERNE

ADAMS FIELD HOUSE, WEST CHINNOCK, CREWKERNE, TA18 7QA
300-year-old former shop and bakery.
TEL: (01935) 881249 OPEN April - Oct.   V, DIAB B/A. N/S DINING R.   CHILDREN. BEVERAGES & T.V. IN ROOMS.

Merefield House

EAST ST, CREWKERNE, SOMERSET, TA18 7AB   TEL: (01460) 73112

 Merefield House is a listed 16th C. building on the edge of the historic town of Crewkerne. It is an ideal base for walking, touring or just relaxing. Imaginative vegetarian cuisine is cooked fresh daily with much produce home-grown in summer months. A typical menu might feature such delights as Crispy Mushrooms with Garlic and Chilli Dip, followed by Stuffed Vine Leaves or Hazelnut Roast Wellington with Pepper and Tomato Sauce and Chick Pea Dal. There are lots of delicious traditional desserts such as Steamed Date Pudding with date syrup and custard (a regular favourite), and to complement the meal a jug of local cider is provided on the house.
OPEN Mar. - Dec.   V, VE EXC. N/S DINING R. & ALL PUBLIC AREAS.   WELL-BEHAVED CHILDREN WELCOME. EN SUITE & TV IN 1 BEDROOM.   BEVERAGES IN ROOMS.

Yew Trees Cottage

SILVER STREET, MISTERTON, CREWKERNE, SOMERSET.   TEL: (01460) 77192
Beautiful 17th century timber-beamed cottage with attractive gardens. Excellent food
OPEN ALL YEAR. V, S.D. B/A.   NO SMOKING. CHILDREN: OVER 8S ONLY. BEVERAGES IN ROOMS. T.V. IN LOUNGE. B. & B. AROUND £18.

DUNSTER

THE OLD PRIORY, DUNSTER, somerset.
12th C. house with old fashioned walled garden. Wholefood / farmhouse cooking.
TEL: (01643) 821540 OPEN Jan. - Dec. V STD. BEVERAGES. DISABLED ACCESS. B. & B. AROUND £19.

EXFORD

Exmoor Lodge

CHAPEL ST, EXFORD, SOMERSET, TA24 7PY TEL; (01643) 831694
Located in the heart of Exmoor National Park, in the village of Exford overlooking the village green. Exclusively vegetarian and vegan. A set 3-course evening meal is offered which is prepared fresh each day. A vegan option is always available. Exmoor Lodge is not licensed but guests are welcome to bring their own wine. 94/95 Somerset Heartbeat Award for encouraging healthy eating, discouraging smoking and hygienic premises.
OPEN ALL YEAR. V, VE EXC. NO SMOKING. EN SUITE. BEVERAGES IN ROOMS. 1 GROUND FLOOR ROOM. PETS B/A. B. & B. £15-20.

GLASTONBURY

BROCK COTTAGE, 77 BERE LANE, GLASTONBURY, SOMERSET.
Small peaceful cottage overlooking Abbey grounds. Vegetarian household.
TEL: (01458) 834985. OPEN ALL YEAR. NO SMOKING. V EXC. CHILDREN. BEVERAGES. B. & B. AROUND £14.

HOPE HOUSE, 51 BENEDICT ST, GLASTONBURY, SOMERSET.
Peaceful nurturing alternative centre. Any diets catered for. Massage available.
TEL: (01458) 834451 V, S.D. STD. CHILDREN. PETS B/A. BEVERAGES & TV. B. & B. AROUND £12.

THE LONG HOUSE AT PILTON, MOUNT PLEASANT, PILTON, SOMERSET.
18th C. house in picturesque village. Emphasis on care, comfort and conversation. Vegetarian and wholefoods. Non-smokers welcome.
TEL: (01749) 8990701 V STD. CHILDREN WELCOME. BEVERAGES & TV. LICENSED. B. & B. AROUND £16.

NO 9 VEGETARIAN B. & B., 9 LAMBROOK ST, GLASTONBURY.
Comfortable top floor suite of Victorian house. Vegetarian food provided.
TEL: (01458) 831009 OPEN ALL YEAR. NO SMOKING. CHILDREN. BEVERAGES & TV. B. & B. AROUND £13.

UNICORN LIGHT CENTRE, 57 HILL HEAD, GLASTONBURY, SOMERSET.
10-choice vegetarian menu. Nwe Age library. Groups welcome.
TEL: (01458) 833238 V STD. CHILDREN WELCOME. PETS B/A. BEVERAGES & TV. B. & B. AROUND £16.

WATERFALL COTTAGE, 20 OLD WELLS RD, GLASTONBURY, BA6 8ED
Beautiful 18th C.cottage 8 mins from town. Views to Tor. Vegetarians & vegans welcome.
TEL: (01458) 831707 OPEN ALL YEAR. V, VE EXC. CHILDREN B/A. BEVERAGES. B. & B. AROUND £15.

1 MANOR HOUSE RD, GLASTONBURY, SOMERSET, SOMERSET.
Quiet location 5 mins town centre. Vegetarian or vegan b'fast.
TEL: (01458) 832185 OPEN ALL YEAR. V STD. BEVERAGES & TV. B. & B. AROUND £14.

MINEHEAD

Kildare Lodge
TOWNSEND RD, MINEHEAD, TA24 5RQ.   TEL: (01643) 702009   FAX: (01643) 706516
Beautiful historic inn with 9 de luxe en suite guest rooms. Kildare Lodge has a friendly pub with outstanding pub food and real ales. There is an extensive choice of vegetarian meals on both the pub food and dining room menus. There is a dry, smoke-free TV lounge and a 50 seat restaurant. Wedddings, birthdays, anniversary and private parties are a speciality.
OPEN ALL YEAR. V STD. N/S 95% DINING ROOM. LICENSED. CHILDREN & PETS. EN SUITE, TV & BEVERAGES IN BEDROOMS. CREDIT CARDS.   B. & B. FROM £24.50, D.B & B. FROM £29.

PERITON PARK HOTEL, MIDDLECOMBE, MINEHEAD, TA24 8SW
19th C. residence in 4 acres of woodland. Excellent food with good vegetarian options.
TEL: (01643) 706885 OPEN ALL YEAR. N/S DINING R. V STD. S.D. B/A. LICENSED. DISABLED ACCESS.
OVER 12S ONLY. EN SUITE, BEVERAGES & TV IN ROOMS. CREDIT CARDS.   B. & B. AROUND £20.

MONTACUTE

Mad Hatters Tea Shop
1 SOUTH ST, MONTACUTE, SOMERSET. TEL: (01935) 823024
OPEN Easter. V., LOW-FAT, LOW-CAL STD. NO SMOKING. CHILDREN. WHEELCHAIR ACCESS: to tea garden only.
EN SUITE, TV & BEVERAGES IN ROOMS. B. & B. FROM £15.

MILK HOUSE RESTAURANT & ACCOMM., THE BOROUGH, MONTACUTE.
TEL: (01935) 823823   N/S DINING R. V, VE STD. LICENSED. OVER 12S ONLY. EN SUITE.

NORTON FITZWARREN

OLD MANOR FARMHOUSE, NORTON FITZWARREN, SOMERSET.
Former Edwardian farmhouse. Log-fires in the dining room. Vegetarians welcome.
TEL: (01823) 289801 OPEN Jan. - Dec. V STD. CHILDREN WELCOME. BEVERAGES. B. & B. AROUND £25.

PORLOCK

Bales Mead
WEST PORLOCK, SOMERSET, TA24 8NX TEL: (01643) 862565
Small, elegant country house offering superb luxurious bed and breakfast in an outstanding & peaceful setting. Magnificent panoramic views towards both sea & rolling countryside. Ideally situated for walking/touring Exmoor and the North Devon Coast.
OPEN ALL YEAR (ex. Dec/Jan).   V, S.D. B/A. NO SMOKING. BEVERAGES & TV IN ROOMS. B. & B. £22.

Lorna Doone Hotel
HIGH ST, PORLOCK, SOMERSET, TA24 8PS   TEL: (01643) 862404
ETB 3 Crown & RAC Acclaimed. AA QQQ. 11-room, family-run hotel in Porlock village. Menu has a Somerset flavour & dishes are prepared from local, seasonal ingredients.
OPEN ALL YEAR.   N/S DINING R. V STD, S.D. B/A. DOGS WELCOME. ALL ROOMS EN SUITE. SOME CREDIT CARDS. BEVERAGES & TV IN ROOMS. B. & B. FROM £18.

Seapoint

UPWAY, PORLOCK, SOMERSET, TA24 8QE TEL: (01643) 862289

Seapoint is an Edwardian country guest house which stands on the fringe of Porlock enjoying spectacular views across the bay to the distant coast of Wales. The atmosphere is warm, friendly and relaxed: the sitting room (which overlooks the bay) is comfortably furnished and has a log fire in chilly weather, and each of the tastefully furnished en suite bedrooms have beverage-making facilities (including herbal teas). The Fitzgeralds have earned an excellent reputation for the quality of their food: wonderful vegetarian, vegan or traditional meals are served, including a first-rate vegetarian breakfast, with home-made marmalade. Evening meals are home-made from wholefood ingredients and there is a varied selection of good wines.

OPEN ALL YEAR ex. Xmas.   NO SMOKING.   V, VE, S.D., WH, STD.   CHILDREN & PETS. WINE LICENCE. EN SUITE, TV & BEVERAGES IN ROOMS. B. & B. £20.50, D. £10.50.

SHAFTESBURY

QUIET CORNER FARM, HENSTRIDGE, TEMPLECOMBE, BA8 0RA

Farm with stunning views across the Blackmore Vale. B'fast features yoghurt & fresh fruit from the garden, or eggs, & fresh filter coffee.

TEL: (01963) 63045 OPEN ALL YEAR.   N/S DINING R, BEDRS & SITTING R.   V STD, S.D. B/A.   CHILDREN WELCOME.   EN SUITE. BEVERAGES IN ROOMS. T.V. B. & B. AROUND £18.

TAUNTON

WATERCOMBE HOUSE, HUISH CHAMPFLOWER, WIVELISCOMBE, TAUN-TON, TA4 2EE

Modernised old school house in a beautiful unspoilt valley in a secluded riverside setting. Imaginative dinners are freshly prepared.

 TEL: (01984) 23725 OPEN Mar. - Oct.   V, S.D. B/A.   NO SMOKING. BYO WINE. 1 EN SUITE ROOM. BEVERAGES IN ROOMS. T.V. IN LOUNGE.   B. & B. AROUND £18.

WELLINGTON

GREENHAM HALL, GREENHAM, WELLINGTON, SOMERSET, TA21 0JJ

Large, friendly home set in a beautiful garden. B. & B. only.

TEL: (01823) 672603   V, S.D. B/A.   CHILDREN WELCOME. 2 EN SUITE ROOMS. BEVERAGES & T.V.

WELLS

THE BULL TERRIER, CROSCOMBE, NR WELLS, SOMERSET.

One of Somerset's oldest pubs. Home-cooked food. Vegetarian options.

TEL; (01749) 343658 OPEN ALL YEAR. V STD. CHILDREN WELCOME (family room).   EN SUITE AVAIL.

WESTON-SUPER-MARE

Beachlands Hotel

17 UPHILL RD NORTH, WESTON-SUPER-MARE, SOMERSET, BS23 4NG TEL: 901934) 621401

Comfortable hotel overlooking Weston's sand dunes. Menus for vegetarians and diabetics.

OPEN ALL YEAR. V, DIAB STD. CHILDREN.   EN SUITE, TV & BEVERAGES. LICENSED.   D, B. & B. AROUND £35.

Moorlands Country Guest House

HUTTON, NR. WESTON-SUPER-MARE, AVON, BS24 9QH   TEL: (01934) 812283

ETB 3 Crown Approved. Moorlands is an attractive Georgian house which has been the family home of Margaret and David Holt for over 25 years; it stands in 2 acres of mature landscaped gardens and enjoys peaceful with views of nearby wooded hills. The food is delicious and wholesome; everything has been prepared on the premises from fresh produce - some of it home-grown - and vegetarian diets can be accommodated by arrangement. Hutton is a pretty little village which stands just 3 or 4 miles from the sea at Weston super Mare; it is within easy reach of a wide range of attractions in both Somerset and North Devon, and as such is a good centre for day trips. Children are very welcome at Moorlands and pony rides from the paddock can be arranged on request.

OPEN Feb. - Oct. N/S DINING R.   V S.D. B/A.   LICENSED.   WHEELCHAIR ACCESS (& 1 ground floor room suitable for physically less able).   CHILDREN WELCOME.   PETS B/A.   SOME EN SUITE ROOMS.   BEVER-AGES.   T.V. IN LOUNGE & SOME BEDROOMS.   B. & B. FROM £16, D. FROM £8.

8 VICTORIA PARK, WESTON-SUPER-MARE, SOMERSET, BS23 2HZ
Delightful Edwardian hotel with 'secret' garden close to sea front. Good veg. menu.
TEL: (01934) 631178   V STD.   CHILDREN WELCOME.   EN SUITE, TV & BEVERAGES.   B. & B. AROUND £18.

YEOVIL

SELF-REALIZATION HEALING CENTRE, LAUREL LN, QUEEN CAMEL, NR YEOVIL, SOMERSET, BA22 7NU
Spiritual centre. Vegetarian meals made with organic produce where possible.
V STD, S.D. B/A.   NO SMOKING.   BEVERAGES.   1 EN SUITE ROOM.   B. & B. AROUND £16.

RESTAURANTS

CASTLE CARY

THE OLD BAKEHOUSE, HIGH ST, CASTLE CARY, BA9 7AW
TEL: (01963) 50067   NO SMOKING.   V EXC.   LICENSED.   DISABLED ACCESS.   CHILDREN WELCOME.

GLASTONBURY

RAINBOWS END CAFÉ 17 HIGH ST, GLASTONBURY, SOMERSET.
TEL: (01458) 33896   NO SMOKING.   V STD. VE, GLUTEN-FREE SOMETIMES ON MENU.   LICENSED.   CHILDREN

MONTACUTE

MILK HOUSE, THE BOROUGH, MONTACUTE, TA15 6XB

WELLS

THE GALLOPER RESTAURANT, WOOKEY HOLE, WELLS, SOMERSET.
TEL: (01749) 672243   OPEN ALL YEAR. ex Xmas.   V STD.   CHILDREN WELCOME.   LICENSED.

THE GOOD EARTH RESTAURANT, 4 PRIORY RD, WELLS, BA5 1SY
TEL: (01749) 678600   V STD.   NO SMOKING.   LICENSED.   DISABLED ACCESS.   CHILDREN WELCOME.

Wiltshire

ACCOMMODATION

AVEBURY

Windmill House

WINTERBOURNE MONKTON, NR AVEBURY, WILTS., SN4 9NN   TEL: (01672)539 446
Beautifully renovated miller's house set amidst stunning scenery; 1m from Avebury stone circle; comfortably furnished; excellent cuisine with home-baked bread & home-grown vegetables and natural spring water from own well.
OPEN ALL YEAR.   NO SMOKING.   V, S.D., DIAB, B/A, ORG, WH.   OVER 5s ONLY.   B. & B. FROM £16.

BRADFORD ON AVON

Barton Farm

POUND LANE, BRADFORD-ON-AVON, WILTS, BA15 1LF   TEL: (01225) 865383

Barton Farm is a beautiful Grade I Listed 14th C. farmhouse which stands in a country park adjacent to the historic Tithe Barn (the second biggest in Britain) where Robin Hood was filmed for TV in 1984. There are two rooms, both very spacious, and families are very welcome (there is a play area opposite the house). Breakfast is eaten in the huge kitchen around an 8 foot pine table: it is a generous meal consisting of orange juice, cereals, eggs, mushrooms, tomatoes, toast and the beverage of

your choice. Your host Mrs Chowles, aims to achieve a friendly, relaxed and homely atmosphere and guests are made very welcome. Behind the house is the Kennet and Avon Canal and to the side is the River Avon; you are just 5 minutes walk from the station, with its frequent services to Bath, and 10 minutes walk from the centre of the lovely old town of Bradford-on-Avon.
OPEN ALL YEAR.   NO SMOKING.   V EXC. S.D. B/A.   CHILDREN WELCOME.   BEVERAGES & TV IN ROOMS. B. & B. FROM £17.50.

Bradford Old Windmill

4 MASONS LANE, BRADFORD ON AVON, WILTS, BA15 1QN   TEL: (01225) 866842
Beautifully restored mill with timber sail gallery with lots of stripped pine and 'the flotsam and jetsam of beachcombing trips around the world'. The food is imaginative and eclectic.
OPEN ALL YEAR.   V STD. VE, S.D. B/A.   NO SMOKING. OVER 6S ONLY.   MOST ROOMS EN SUITE.   TV & BEVERAGES IN ROOMS.   B. & B. FROM £24.50.

WOOLLEY GRANGE, WOOLLEY GREEN, BRADFORD ON AVON, BA15 1TX
Jacobean Manor House built from Bath stone in the 17th C. All dishes have been home-prepared from the finest of fresh, local, and often home-grown, ingredients.
TEL: (012216) 4705 OPEN ALL YEAR. V, VE, S.D. B/A. ORG, WH WHEN AVAIL. LICENSED. CHILDREN WELCOME. PETS B/A. MOST ROOMS EN SUITE. ROOM SERVICE. T.V. B. & B. AROUND £50.

CORSHAM

RUDLOE PARK HOTEL, LEAFY LANE, CORSHAM, WILTS, SN13 0PA
Splendid country house hotel; exceptional cuisine prepared from fresh, local produce.
TEL: (01225) 810555 OPEN ALL YEAR.   V STD. VE, DIAB, CANDIDA, COEL S.D. B/A.   N/S DINING R.   LICENSED. OVER 10S (HOTEL), OVER 5S (RESTAURANT). PETS B/A. EN SUITE, BEVERAGES & T.V. IN ALL ROOMS.

DEVIZES

PINECROFT GUEST HOUSE, POTTERNE RD (A360), DEVIZES, SN10 5DA
Comfortable Georgian family house; 5 mins' walk from the centre of the ancient market town of Devizes; free-range eggs and bacon; vegetarians catered for by arrangement.
TEL: (01380) 721433 OPEN ALL YEAR.   V STD. N/S DINING R & BEDRS. CHILDREN WELCOME. MOST ROOMS EN SUITE. BEVERAGES & TV IN ROOMS. CREDIT CARDS. B. & B. AROUND £20.

Longwater

ERLESTOKE, NR DEVIZES, WILTS, SN10 5UE   TEL & FAX: (01380) 830095
ETB 3 Crown Commended. ¼ mile from the 160 acre organic farm buildings, Longwater overlooks its own parkland and lakes. Conservatory and spacious lounge with log fire. Soil Association approved, much of the organic produce used in cooking is home-grown or locally produced. Self-catering also available.
OPEN Jan 1 - Dec. 22.   V, VE, DIAB, S.D. B/A. ORG, WH WHEN AVAIL.   N/S DINING R, CONSERVATORY & BEDRS. LICENSED.   DISABLED ACCESS: ground floor rooms available (Grade 3 access).   CHILDREN & PETS WELCOME.   EN SUITE, BEVERAGES & T.V. IN ROOMS.   B. & B. FROM £20.

EAST KNOYLE

MILTON HOUSE, EAST KNOYLE, SALISBURY, WILTS, SP3 6BG
Charming old house. B'fast features farm-fresh eggs, fresh fruit juice, wholemeal bread.
TEL: (01747) 830397 OPEN ALL YEAR.   NO SMOKING.   V, S.D. B/A.   CHILDREN.   B. & B. AROUND £24.

MARLBOROUGH

Laurel Cottage

SOUTHEND, OGBOURNE ST GEORGE, MARLBORO', WILTS, SN8 1SG   TEL: (01672) 841288
Exquisite 16th C. thatched cottage with gardens; oak-beams, inglenook fireplace, etc.
OPEN Mar. - Oct.   V STD., S.D. B/A.   NO SMOKING.   CHILDREN WELCOME.   SOME ROOMS EN SUITE.   BEVER-AGES & T.V. IN ALL ROOMS.   B. & B. FROM £16.

Silbury Hill Cottage

WEST KENNETT, MARLBOROUGH, WILTS, SN8 1QH TEL: (01672) 539416
Charming thatched cottage located next to Silbury Hill and the West Kennett Long Barrow, offering relaxed and friendly hospitality.
OPEN ALL YEAR.   V, S.D. STD.   NO SMOKING.   CHILDREN WELCOME.   B. & B. £18 Sgle., £30 Dble.

SALISBURY

ELM TREE COTTAGE, STAPLEFORD, WILTS, SP3 4LJ   TEL: (01722) 790507
Character cottage with friendly atmosphere. Home-produce and personal service.
OPEN Mar. - Oct. V STD. CHILDREN WELCOME. TV & BEVERAGES IN ROOMS. B. & B. AROUND £18.

THE HOMESTEAD, STOCKBOTTOM, PITTON, NR SALISBURY, SP5 1SU
Comfortable, friendly Christian household offering wholefood home-cooked food.
TEL: (01980) 611160 V STD. NO SMOKING. CHILDREN WELCOME. BEVERAGES & TV. B. & B. AROUND £16.

Stratford Lodge
4 PARK LANE CASTLE RD, SALISBURY, SP1 3NP   TEL: (01722) 325177 FAX: (01722) 412699

Stratford Lodge is an elegant Victorian house which stands in a quiet lane overlooking Victoria Park. Your host, Jill Bayly, offers a special brand of gracious hospitality: the complementary sherry before dinner speaks volumes - and is a welcome herald to a first-rate meal prepared by Jill from fresh ingredients, some organically home-grown. It is always advisable to book for dinner lest you miss such delights as Baked Roquefort Pears followed by Salmon Steak with Herb Butter and a selection of home-made desserts, all served by candlelight on beautiful china. Each of the bedrooms has en suite facilities and has been decorated and furnished with flair - one room has a brass Victorian bed; the house has been furnished throughout with antiques and there is a lovely garden with flowering shrubs. Salisbury is a beautiful city - not the less appealing because of its proximity to so much unspoilt countryside and historically interesting towns and villages.
OPEN 2 Jan - 23 Dec. NO SMOKING. V STD, VE, S.D. B/A. LICENSED.   OVER 8S WELCOME. EN SUITE, TV & BEVERAGES IN BEDROOMS. CREDIT CARDS.

Yew Tree Cottage
GROVE LANE, REDLYNCH, SALISBURY, WILTS, SP5 2NR   TEL: (01725) 511730
ETB Listed & Approved. Spacious country cottage and smallholding (sheep & poultry). 1m New Forest & nr. to Salisbury. Ideal Southern touring centre. Walking, riding, fishing, golf, cycling. B'fast features traditional, vegetarian & vegan options.
OPEN ALL YEAR ex. Xmas/New Year. NO SMOKING. V, VE STD, S.D. B/A. CHILDREN WELCOME. BEVERAGES ON ARRIVAL & REQUEST.   T.V. IN LOUNGE. B. & B. FROM £16.

ZEALS

CORNERWAYS COTTAGE, LONGCROSS, ZEALS, WILTS, BA12 6LL
18th C. house of great character; breakfast includes fresh croissants & muffins (mint, herb or decaffeinated tea or coffee also avail.; alternative b'fast menus for special diets).
TEL: (01747) 840477 OPEN ALL YEAR. NO SMOKING. V, S.D. B/A. CHILDREN WELCOME. PETS (SMALL DOGS) B/A. 2 EN SUITE ROOMS. BEVERAGES. T.V. IN LOUNGE. B. & B. AROUND £18.

RESTAURANTS

AVEBURY

STONES RESTAURANT, AVEBURY, MARLBOROUGH, SN8 1RE
Excellent vegetarian restaurant serving fine meals prepared from fresh local produce.
TEL: (016723) 514   70% N/S. V EXC. LICENSED. DISABLED ACCESS: GOOD. CHILDREN WELCOME.

MARLBOROUGH

THE POLLY TEA ROOM, 27 HIGH STREET, MARLBOROUGH, WILTS.
TEL: (01672) 512146   60% N/S. V STD. LICENSED. DISABLED ACCESS. CHILDREN WELCOME.

SALISBURY

BISHOPS MILL, SALISBURY, WILTS.
TEL: (01722) 412127 V STD.

CLOISTERS, IVY ST, SALISBURY, WILTS.
TEL; (01722) 338102 V STD.

MO'S RESTAURANT, MILFORD ST, SALISBURY, WILTS.
TEL: (01722) 331377   V STD.

PLAYHOUSE, MALTHOUSE LN, SALISBURY, WILTS.
TEL: (01722) 320333   V STD.

SALISBURY ARTS CENTRE, BEDWIN ST, SALISBURY, WILTS.
TEL: (01722) 331728   V STD.

MICHAEL SNELL, ST THOMAS SQUARE, SALISBURY, WILTS.
TEL: (01722) 336037   V STD.

The South of England

Hampshire

ACCOMMODATION

ALDERHOLT

ALDERHOLT MILL, L. ANN PYE, ALDERHOLT MILL, SANDLEHEATH RD, ALDERHOLT, FORDINGBRIDGE, HANTS, SP6 1PU
Picturesque position beside working 14th C. watermill. Stone-ground flour/ home-made bread and fresh, local produce used.
TEL: (01425) 653130   V STD.   EN SUITE AVAILABLE.   B. & B. FROM £13.

ANDOVER

ABBOTTS LAW, ABBOTTS ANN, ANDOVER, HANTS, SP11 7DW
Country house in 3 acres of attractive gardens overlooking water meadows. Cordon Bleu cook & the garden provides much of the fresh fruit and vegetables used in cooking.
TEL: (01264) 710350   OPEN Apr. - Oct.   V STD.

BASINGSTOKE

MR & MRS DAWES, 58 ST NICHOLAS COURT, SOUTH HAM, BASINGSTOKE.
TEL: (01256) 24485 OPEN ALL YEAR.   V STD.   NO SMOKING.   B. & B. AROUND £14.

FERNBANK HOTEL, 4 FAIRFIELDS ROAD, BASINGSTOKE, RG21 3DR
Victorian building forming 18-bedroom hotel. Healthy b'fast options.
TEL: (01256) 21191   OPEN ALL YEAR.   N/S DINING R.   V, S.D. B/A.   CHILDREN WELCOME.   EN SUITE, BEVERAGES & T.V.   B. & B. AROUND £20.

BISHOP'S WALTHAM

ANCHOR COTTAGE, BANK ST, BISHOP'S WALTHAM, NR WINCHESTER.
Modern house in attractive location.
TEL: (01489) 894935 OPEN ALL YEAR.   V, S.D. STD.   CHILDREN WELCOME.   B. & B. AROUND £18.

CHANDLERS FORD

ST LUCIA, 68 SHAFTESBURY AVE, CHANDLERS FORD, EASTLEIGH, SO5 3BP
1920's detached home. A traditional or Continental breakfast option is served to guests (in your room, if you wish!). Evening meal prepared from fresh produce.
TEL: (01703) 262995   OPEN ALL YEAR.   V, S.D. B/A.   NO SMOKING.   CHILDREN: OVER 10S ONLY.   BEVERAGES & T.V. IN ROOMS.   B. & B. AROUND £18.

FAREHAM

AVENUE HOUSE HOTEL, 22 THE AVENUE, FAREHAM, HANTS
Highly acclaimed guest house offering very comfortable accommodation and healthy breakasts prepared by qualified dietican.
TEL: (01329) 232175   V, DIAB STD. VE, LOW-FAT, LOW-CAL. S.D. B/A.   CHILDREN & PETS WELCOME. EN SUITE, BEVERAGES & TV IN ROOMS.   ACCESS, VISA.   B. & B. AROUND £23.

FORDINGBRIDGE

ASHBURN HOTEL, STATION RD, FORDINGBRIDGE, HANTS.
Comfortable, warm family-run country house hotel amidst miles of scenic beauty. Renowned for food and friendly atmosphere. Outdoor heated swimming pool.
TEL: (01425) 652060 OPEN ALL YEAR. V, S.D. B/A. N/S DINING R & GARDEN R (adjacent to bar). LICENSED. CHILDREN & PETS WELCOME. EN SUITE, BEVERAGES & T.V. B. & B. AROUND £35.

HOOK

OAKLEY BARN, SEARLES LANE, HOOK, HANTS.
Restored 17th C. thatched barn with panoramic views of the Whitewater Valley.
TEL: (01256) 766104 OPEN ALL YEAR. V B/A. NO SMOKING. CHILDREN BEVERAGES & T.V.

KILMESTON

Dean Farm

KILMESTON, NR ALRESFORD, HANTS, SO24 0NL   TEL: (01962) 771 286
ETB Listed Welcoming 18th C. farmhouse in the picturesque village of Kilmeston. Log fires and a relaxing atmosphere.
OPEN Jan. - Dec. NO SMOKING. V STD. DIAB, LOW-FAT B/A. OVER 5S WELCOME. BEVERAGES ON REQUEST. T.V. IN SITTING ROOM. B. & B.AROUND £17. .

LYMINGTON

ALBANY HOUSE, 3 HIGHFIELD, LYMINGTON, HANTS, SO41 9GB
Elegant Regency house with views of the Solent and Isle of Wight from most bedrooms. Log fires. Afternoon tea. Excellent food prepared from fresh, local ingredients.
TEL: (01590) 671900 OPEN SEASONALLY. V B/A. N/S DINING R. CHILDREN 'ACCEPTED'. PETS B/A. 3 EN SUITE ROOMS. BEVERAGES IN ROOMS. T.V. AVAILABLE. B. & B. AROUND £20.

REDWING FARM, PITMORE LN, SWAY, LYMINGTON, HANTS, SO41 6BW
Farmhouse forming part of a working farm; bedrooms are cosy and beamed.
TEL: (01590) 683319 V, S.D.B/A. NO SMOKING. 2 BEDROOMS GROUND FLOOR. T.V. B. & B. AROUND £20.

STANWELL HOUSE HOTEL, HIGH ST, LYMINGTON, HANTS, SO41 9AA
Charming small hotel, beautifully equipped; ground floor rooms available.
TEL: (01590) 677756 OPEN ALL YEAR. V STD, VE, S.D. B/A. LICENSED. GROUND FLOOR ROOMS AVAILABLE, ONE WITH WHEELCHAIR ACCESS. CHILDREN WELCOME. EN SUITE, TV & BEVERAGES IN ROOMS.

LYNDHURST

FOREST COTTAGE, HIGH STREET, LYNDHURST, HANTS, SO43 7BH
Charming 300-year-old cottage with an extensive library of natural history books.
TEL: (01703) 283461 OPEN ALL YEAR ex. Xmas. N/S DINING R & BEDRS. V, VE DIAB STD. CHILDREN: OVER 12S ONLY. BEVERAGES. B. & B.AROUND £16.

PETERSFIELD

Mizzards Farm

ROGATE, PETERSFIELD, HANTS, GU31 5HS   TEL: (01730) 821656
Lovely 17th C. farmhouse in peaceful setting; 13 acres of gardens, fields. Swimming pool.
OPEN ALL YEAR Ex. Xmas. V B/A. NO SMOKING. LICENSED. OVER 6S ONLY. EN SUITE, TV & BEVERAGES IN ROOMS. B. & B. FROM £22.

TROTTON FARM, ROGATE, PETERSFIELD, HANTS, GU31 5EN
Lovely farmhouse in an area of outstanding natural beauty with many attractions within 1 hour's drive; many walks & fishing may be enjoyed within the environs of the farm.
TEL: (01730) 813618 OPEN ALL YEAR. V, B'FAST STD. NO SMOKING. V STD. CHILDREN. EN SUITE & BEVERAGES IN ROOMS. T.V. IN SITTING/GAMES R. B. & B. AROUND £19.

RINGWOOD

MOORTOWN LODGE, 244 CHRISTCHURCH ROAD, RINGWOOD, HANTS.
Charming country house hotel; excellent food prepared from fresh local produce.
TEL: (01425) 471404 OPEN ALL YEAR. N/S DINING R. V, S.D. B/A. LICENSED. CHILDREN WELCOME. MOST ROOMS EN SUITE. BEVERAGES & TV IN ROOMS. CREDIT CARDS. B. & B. AROUND £30.

ROTHERWICK

Tylney Hall

ROTHERWICK, NR HOOK, HANTS, RG27 9AJ   TEL: (01256) 764881
Magnificent, Grade II listed mansion. Sauna, gym and an indoor and outdoor heated pool.
OPEN ALL YEAR. V STD. VE, DIAB B/A. ORG, WH WHEN AVAIL. LICENSED. CHILDREN WELCOME. EN SUITE
& T.V. IN ROOMS. CREDIT CARDS.

SOUTHSEA

BEAUFORT HOTEL, FESTING RD, SOUTHSEA, HANTS.
TEL: (01705) 823707 OPEN ALL YEAR. V STD. CHILDREN. EN SUITE, TV & BEVERAGES. B. & B. AROUND £32.

THE MALLOW, 82 WHITWELL RD, SOUTHSEA, HANTS.
TEL: (01705) 293829. V, WH STD. CHILDREN. EN SUITE TV & BEVERAGES IN ROOMS. B. & B. FROM £15.

MANDALAY, 31 ST ANDREWS RD, SOUTHSEA, HANTS, PO5 1EP
TEL: (01705) 829600 OPEN ALL YEAR. V B'FAST STD. EN SUITE, tV & BEVERAGES. B. & B. AROUND £17.

WINCHESTER

'DEVER VIEW', 17 UPPER BULLINGTON, SUTTON SCOTNEY, WINCHESTER, SO21 3RB
ETB 2 Crown Commended. Attractive guest house in the peaceful rural village. First-rate
b'fast with a variety of delicious options including some healthy alternatives (low-fat, etc.).
TEL: (01962) 760566 OPEN ALL YEAR. NO SMOKING. V, DIAB B/A. CHILDREN WELCOME. PETS B/A. TV 7
BEVERAGES IN ROOMS. T.V. IN GUESTS' LOUNGE. B. & B. AROUND £19.

SANDY LODGE, 47 CHRISTCHURCH RD, ST CROSS, WINCHESTER.
Charming detached house built of flint and red brick set in beautiful gardens just 10 mins
walk from the city centre; good food, including lunch on request.
OPEN ALL YEAR. V B/A. N/S ONE OF THE TWO DINING RS & IN BEDRS. DISABLED ACCESS. CHILDREN
WELCOME. BEVERAGES IN ROOMS. T.V. AVAILABLE.

THE WYKEHAM ARMS, 75 KINGSGATE STREET, WINCHESTER, SO23 9PE
17th C. public house - one of the oldest in Winchester - offering very comfortable
accommodation and excellent food prepared exclusively from fresh, local produce.
TEL: (01962) 853834 OPEN ALL YEAR. V STD. N/S 2 OF 4 EATING AREAS & IN BREAKFAST ROOM.
LICENSED. DISABLED ACCESS. OVER 14S. PETS WELCOME. EN SUITE, TV & BEVERAGES IN ROOMS.

SHAWLANDS, 46 KILHAM LANE, WINCHESTER, HANTS, SO22 5QD
TEL: (01962) 861166 OPEN ALL YEAR. V, S.D. B/A. CHILDREN & PETS. B. & B. AROUND £18.

RESTAURANTS

ALRESFORD

THE OLD SCHOOL HOUSE, 60 WEST ST, ALRESFORD, SO24 9AU
TEL: (01962) 732134 NO SMOKING. V, S.D. LICENSED.

CHAWTON

Cassandra's Cup

THE HOLLIES, CHAWTON, NR ALTON, HANTS, GU34 1SB   TEL: (01420) 83144
Charming restaurant opposite Jane Austen's house at Chawton; cosy atmosphere. Morning
coffee, light lunches. Home-made scones, cakes & gateaux. Afternoon cream teas.
L. AROUND £3. NO SMOKING. V STD. LICENSED. CHILDREN WELCOME.

HAVANT

V **NUTMEG RESTAURANT, OLD TOWN HALL, EAST ST, HAVANT**
TEL: (01705) 472700 NO SMOKING. V EXC. LICENSED. DISABLED ACCESS. CHILDREN.

ALDERSHOT

V **THE WEST END CENTRE, ALDERSHOT, HANTS.**
Vegetarian restaurant within centre.
OPEN ALL YEAR. V STD. CHILDREN WELCOME.

FAREHAM

CHIVES, 15 HIGH ST, FAREHAM, HANTS.
15th C. building. Winner of 1990 *Les Routiers*. Vegetarian meals available.
TEL: (01329) 234170 OPEN ALL YEAR. V STD. CHILDREN WELCOME.

HOBBITS, 147 GOSPORT RD, FAREHAM.
Home-made specialities. Fresh vegetables. Vegetarians welcome.
TEL: (01329) 280244 OPEN ALL YEAR. V STD. CHILDREN WELCOME.

PORTSMOUTH

V **THE ORCHARD CAFÉ, 243A FRANCIS AVE, PORTSMOUTH.**
Portsmouth's newest vegan/vegetarian café. Meals made from fresh organic produce.
TEL: (01705) 614666 V, VE EXC. CHILDREN WELCOME.

SOUTHAMPTON

V **THE FLYING TEAPOT, ONSLOW RD, SOUTHAMPTON.**
Exclusively vegetarian restaurant. Sensibly priced and interesting menu.
TEL: (01703) 335931 V, VE EXC. CHILDREN WELCOME.

OSCAR'S, 8 COMMERCIAL RD, SOUTHAMPTON.
Eat in the company of Hollywood greats. Also vegetarian.
TEL: (01703) 636383 V STD. CHILDREN WELCOME. LICENSED.

V **THE TOWN HOUSE, 59 OXFORD ST, SOUTHAMPTON.**
Award-winning vegetarian restaurant. Gourmet candlelit dinners.
TEL: (01703) 220498 V EXC. CHILDREN WELCOME. LICENSED.

WINCHESTER

CAFÉ 13, 13 KING'S WALK, SILVERHILL, WINCHESTER, HANTS.
Continental style coffee shop. Vegetarian dishes available.
TEL: (01962) 866814 V STD. CHILDREN WELCOME.

THE ELIZABETHAN RESTAURANT, 18 JEWRY ST, WINCHESTER, HANTS.
16th C. building with galleried restaurant. Anglo-French cuisine. Vegetarian dishes.
TEL: (01962) 853566 V STD. CHILDREN WELCOME. LICENSED.

GIORGIO'S, 72 ST GEORGE ST, WINCHESTER.
Italian restaurant. Vegetarian dishes.
TEL: (01962) 863515 V STD. CHILDREN WELCOME. LICENSED.

HUNTER'S RESTAURANT, 5 JEWRY ST, WINCHESTER, HANTS.
Open for light lunches and superb dinners. Vegetarian options.
TEL: (01960) 860006 V STD. CHILDREN WELCOME. LICENSED.

LAURA'S RESTAURANT, 17 CITY RD, WINCHESTER, HANTS.
Home-made food and freshly filled baps. Vegetarian dishes.
TEL: (01962) 840358 V STD. CHILDREN WELCOME. LICENSED.

RICHOUX RESTAURANT, GOD BEGOT HOUSE, 101 HIGH ST, WINCHESTER.
Traditional restaurant with food emporia. Vegetarian dishes.
TEL: (01962) 841790 V STD. CHILDREN WELCOME. LICENSED.

WINCHESTER CATHEDRAL VISITOR'S CENTRE, WINCHESTER.
Superb refectory selling home-made snacks, including vegetarian options
TEL: (01962) 853224 V STD. CHILDREN WELCOME.

Isle of Wight

ACCOMMODATION

CHALE

Clarendon Hotel and Wight Mouse Inn

CHALE, ISLE OF WIGHT, PO38 2HA   TEL: (01983) 730431

17th C. stone-built coaching inn; excellent food, home-made from fresh, local ingredients.
OPEN ALL YEAR.   V STD, VE, DIAB., S.D. B/A.   LICENSED. CHILDREN WELCOME. PETS B/A. EN SUITE.
BEVERAGES & T.V. IN ALL ROOMS.

FRESHWATER

BROOKSIDE FORGE, BROOKSIDE RD, FRESHWATER, I.O.W., PO40 9ER

Substantial detached property with attractive terraced gardensclose to the centre of Fresh-
water. All food is home-made from fresh ingredients, including the soups and sweets.
TEL: (01983) 754644 OPEN ALL YEAR.   V, VE, DIAB STD.   N/S DINING R & BEDRS.   LICENSED.   CHILDREN.   PETS
B/A.   MOST ROOMS EN SUITE.   BEVERAGES.   T.V. IN LOUNGE.   ACCESS, VISA.   B. & B. AROUND £20.

RYDE

Hotel Ryde Castle

THE ESPLANADE, RYDE, I.O.W., PO33 1JA   TEL: (01983) 63755 FAX: (01983) 68925

Magnificent, creeper-clad castle with unparalleled views of the Solent and Straight. All
dishes have been home-cooked from fresh island ingredients.
OPEN ALL YEAR.   V STD on à la carte menu. VE, DIAB, LOW-FAT ON REQUEST. N/S part DINING R. LICENSED.
CHILDREN WELCOME. PETS B/A. EN SUITE, TV & BEVERAGES IN ROOMS. B. & B. AROUND £45

SEAVIEW

Seaview Hotel and Restaurant

HIGH ST, SEAVIEW, ISLE OF WIGHT, PO34 5EX   TEL: (01983) 612711

Exquisite hotel in the small Victorian seaside resort of Seaview; beautifully furnished with
antiques and designer fabrics; excellent cuisine prepared from fresh local produce.
OPEN ALL YEAR. V, S.D. B/A. LSMOKING IN DINING R. only at other guest's discretion. LICENSED.   CHILDREN
WELCOME. EN SUITE & T.V.   CREDIT CARDS.   B. & B. FROM £30, Sgle £40, Mid-week breaks from £46 pppn.

SHANKLIN

CHINE LODGE, EASTCLIFF RD, OLD VILLAGE, SHANKLIN, PO37 6AA
TEL: (01983) 862358 OPEN Jan. - Nov. V B/A. LICENSED. EN SUITE, TV & BEVERAGES. B. & B. AROUND £29.

Culham Lodge Hotel

LANDGUARD MANOR RD, SHANKLIN, ISLE OF WIGHT, PO37 7HZ   TEL: (01983) 862880

Attractive hotel in beautiful tree-lined road; excellent food prepared from fresh produce.
Heated swimming pool in secluded garden.
OPEN Fe. - Nov. N/S DINING R.   V B/A.   OVER 12s WELCOME.   MOST ROOMS EN SUITE.   BEVERAGES & TV IN
ROOMS.   B. & B. £16 - 20.50.

Edgecliffe Hotel

CLARENCE GARDENS, SHANKLIN, ISLE OF WIGHT, PO37 6HA   TEL: (01983) 866199

The Edgecliffe Hotel is a charming, family-run hotel,
pleasantly situated down a beautifully peaceful and
tree-lined residential road close to Shanklin's famous
cliff top walk. It has been comfortably and tastefully
furnished throughout (all bedrooms have hair-dryers
and radio alarms as well as the more usual facilities),
and the combined bar and dining room is a pleasant
place in which to enjoy both a pre-dinner drink and
the excellent food. Fresh, local produce is used wherever possible in the preparation of both traditional and
speciality dishes (both served in very generous portions), and imaginative vegetarian meals may be or-
dered by arrangement. The countryside around

Shanklin is excellent for walking - your hosts can lend you maps and advise you of good routes - and the local beach is very safe for bathing as well as offering a variety of water sport facilities.
OPEN Feb. - Nov.   NO SMOKING.   V STD, S.D. B/A.   LICENSED.   OVER 3s WELCOME.   EN SUITE MOST ROOMS.
BEVERAGES & T.V. IN ALL ROOMS.   ACCESS, VISA, AMEX.   B. & B. FROM £15.

TOTLAND BAY

THE NODES HOTEL, ALUM BAY OLD RD, TOTLAND BAY, PO39 0HZ
Charming small hotel; excellent home-cooking using fresh produce.
TEL: (01983) 752859 OPEN ALL YEAR. N/S 50% OF DINING R & SOME BEDRS.   V, S.D. B/A.   LICENSED.   DISABLED
ACCESS. CHILDREN WELCOME.   PETS B/A.   MOST ROOMS EN SUITE.   BEVERAGES IN ROOMS. T.V.

VENTNOR

HOTEL PICARDIE, ESPLANADE, VENTNOR, PO38 1JX   TEL: (01983) 852647
Attractive villa-type hotel on the Esplanade; imaginative vegetarian options.
OPEN Mar. - Oct. N/S, ex. bar area.   V, S.D. B/A.   LICENSED. CHILDREN WELCOME. PETS B/A   PRIVATE
FACILITIES, BEVERAGES & T.V. IN ROOMS.   CREDIT CARDS.   B. & B. FROM £16.50.

WOOTTON BRIDGE

BRIDGE HOUSE, KITE HILL, WOOTTON BRIDGE, PO33 4LA
Listed Georgian residence at water's edge. B'fast includes preserves from garden fruit.
TEL: (01983) 884163 OPEN ALL YEAR. V, DIAB, S.D. B/A. ORG. WHEN AVAIL. WH ON REQUEST.   NO SMOKING.
CHILDREN & PETS B/A.   SOME ROOMS EN SUITE.   BEVERAGES.   T.V. ON REQUEST. B. & B. AROUND £20.

West Sussex

ACCOMMODATION

ARUNDEL

Burpham Country Hotel and Restauran
BURPHAM, ARUNDEL, W. SUSSEX, BN18 9RJ   TEL: (01903) 882160
ETB 3 Crowns, AA 2 Star. Charming country house with garden & views over owns.
OPEN ALL YEAR.   V, S.D. B/A.   N/S DINING R.   LICENSED.   EN SUITE, TV & BEVERAGES IN ROOMS. CREDIT
CARDS.   B. & B. FROM £29.

CHICHESTER

Chichester Lodge,
OAKWOOD, CHICHESTER, W. SUSSEX, PO18 9AL   TEL: (01243) 786560

Built in 1840, Chichester Lodge is a delightful Gothic style gate cottage to a large manor house; it stands in and acre and a half of rambling old world gardens, the whole surrounded by beautiful Sussex countryside. Accommodation is in comfortable double en suite rooms, and there is a garden room with a cosy wood burning stove for chilly days. Leading on from the garden room is a spaciou conservatory full of interesting plants and shrubs. Although Chichester Lodge is in the heart of the countryside, Chichester city - with its theatre, cathedral and museum - is just five minutes drive away.
OPEN ALL YEAR.   NO SMOKING.   S.D., V. STD.   EN SUITE, TV & BEVERAGES.   B. & B. £17.50 - 22.50.

CROUCHERS BOTTOM, BIRDHAM RD, APULDRAM, CHICHESTER, PO20 7EH
Rurally set with fine view of the Cathedral. Good food made from fresh produce.
TEL: (01243) 784995OPEN ALL YEAR.   N/S DINING R, BEDRS   V, S.D. B/A.   LICENSED.   4 GROUND FLOOR
BEDRS, 1 specifically designed for the disabled.   CHILDREN. EN SUITE, BEVERAGES & T.V. IN ROOMS.

EAST GRINSTEAD

GRAVETYE MANOR, NR EAST GRINSTEAD, W. SUSSEX, RH19 4LJ
TEL: (01342) 810567   V, S.D. B/A.   LICENSED.   OVER 7S ONLY.   EN SUITE & T.V.   B. & B. AROUND £50

EAST ASHLING

ENGLEWOOD, EAST ASHLING, W. SUSSSEX, PO18 9AS   TEL: (01243) 575407
Modern bungalow in conservation village; Cordon Bleu trained hostess offers superb home cooked food using organic home grown vegetables, fruit & herbs when possible.
OPEN ALL YEAR full menu Mar. - Oct.   V, STD. S.D. B/A. BEVERAGES & TV IN ROOMS.

HENFIELD

Little Oreham Farm

NR WOODSMILL, HENFIELD, W. SUSSEX, BS5 9SB   TEL: (01273) 492931

Lttle Oreham Farm is *gorgeous*. Tucked away down a quiet country lane and next door to footpaths that will lead you (if energetic!) to the South Downs, this 300-year old listed building is a picture-book cottage; prettily pantiled and set in a beautiful garden complete with (inhabited) dovecot. Inside the house are the oak beams and inglenook fireplace that one would expect from such a cottage, and outside the barn has been comfortably converted to accommodate further guests. Evening meals are available by arrangement; your hostess, Josie Forbes prepares delicious meals from organic and wholefood ingredients, some home-grown (from the herbary).
OPEN ALL YEAR. NO SMOKING. V STD., S.D. B/A. EN SUITE, T.V. & BEVERAGES. B. & B. FROM £17.50.

PETWORTH

River Park Farm

LODSWORTH, PETWORTH, W. SUSSEX, GU28 9DS   TEL: (01798) 861362
17th C. farmhouse. All food home-prepared from fresh ingredients.
OPEN Easter - end Oct.   N/S DINING R & BEDRS.   V STD, S.D. B/A. CHILDREN WELCOME.   TV LOUNGE.
BEVERAGES IN BEDROOMS.   B. & B. FROM £16.

PULBOROUGH

CHEQUERS HOTEL, CHURCH PL., PULBOROUGH, W. SUSSEX, RH20 1AD
17th C. hotel on sandstone ridge overlooking the beautiful Arun Valley & South Downs.
TEL: (01798) 872486 OPEN ALL YEAR. V, S.D. B/A.   LICENSED. CHILDREN WELCOME. PETS B/A.   EN SUITE, BEVERAGES & TV IN ROOMS. B. & B. AROUND £40.

STEYNING

NASH HOTEL, HORSHAM RD, STEYNING, W. SUSSEX.
A beautiful 16th C. country house with lawns, paddocks and pond near to the coast and South Downs; a productive vineyard adjoins the property.
TEL: (01903) 814988 OPEN ALL YEAR.   V, VE, S.D. B/A.   NO SMOKING. LICENSED.   CHILDREN WELCOME. PETS B/A. 2 EN SUITE ROOMS. BEVERAGES & TV IN ROOMS. B. & B. AROUND £25.

RESTAURANTS & CAFÉS

ARUNDEL

HEMINGWAY'S, 33 HIGH ST, ARUNDEL, W. SUSSEX. TEL: (01903) 883378

PLAISTOW

CLEMENT'S VEGETARIAN RESTAURANT, RICKMAN'S LN, PLAISTOW
Excellent restaurant serving vegetarian & vegan food.
OPEN WED. - SAT. LUNCH & EVES. V, VE EXC. LICENSED. CHILDREN WELCOME.

POYNINGS

THE ROYAL OAK, POYNINGS, W. SUSSEX. TEL: (01273) 857389
Wholesome meals in a friendly atmosphere. Vegetarian choices.

South East England

East Sussex

ACCOMMODATION

BEXHILL-ON-SEA

'HELENSHOLME', HEATHERDUNE RD, BEXHILL-ON-SEA, E. SUSSEX.
Lovingly furnished chalet home; vegetarian cuisine made from fresh produce a speciality.
TEL: (01424) 223545 OPEN ALL YEAR. V EXC. S.D. with good advanced notice. NO SMOKING. OVER 10S WELCOME. VANITY UNITS IN 2 ROOMS. BEVERAGES. T.V. LOUNGE. B. & B. FROM £15.

BRIGHTON

'Brighton' Marina House Hotel & Langham's Guest House.

8 & 16 CHARLOTTE ST, MARINE PARADE, BRIGHTON, BN2 1AG Marina: TEL/FAX: (01273) 605349 TEL: (01273) 679484   Langham's TEL/FAX: (01273) 682843

Your Comfort is our first Concern

ETB 3 Crown, AA QQ, RAC Accalimed, TCB, ANWB. Cosy, well-maintained and family-run, the Brighton Marina House Hotel and Langham's Guest House are pleasantly furnished and well-equipped hotels, highly recommended for cleanliness, comfort and hospitality; they stand in the heart of Kemp town, the Regency side of Brighton. The bedrooms are all comfortable and elegantly furnished: single, double, twin, triple and family rooms are available, and some have en suite facilities. The rooms at Langham's Guest House are very comfortable but are more geared towards the budget price range; those at Brighton Marina House Hotel have a wider range of facilities including radio alarm, hairdryer, phone, shaver point, luggage stand and clothes brush.Traditional English fare is served but, perhaps uniquely amongst privately owned Brighton hotels, you may also dine on Indian, Chinese, vegetarian, Halal or Kosher dishes on request; if you have other special dietary requirements your host, Mr Jung, will do his very best to accommodate them; the hotel enjoys a residential licence. The Brighton Marina House Hotel is in a quiet street leading to the beach which is a minute's walk away, and the other tourist attractions of Brighton are all within easy reach. For guests on a budget, your hosts offer standard accommodation, without en suite facilities, across the road at the Langham Guest House.
OPEN ALL YEAR. V, KOSHER & S.D. B/A. LICENSED. CHILDREN WELCOME. EN SUITE, TV & BEVERAGES IN BEDROOMS. CREDIT CARDS at Marina House Hotel only. B. & B. £13.50 - 31.

Diana House

25 ST GEORGES TERRACE, BRIGHTON, E. SUSSEX, BN2 1JJ TEL: (01273) 605797
Large friendly Victorian B. & B. 50 yds sea front and close to town centre/all amenities. Evening meal by arrangement.
OPEN ALL YEAR.   N/S DINING R.   V, ORG, WH STD, VE, S.D. B/A.   CHILDREN & PETS WELCOME.   EN SUITE, TV & BEVERAGES IN R OOMS.   CREDIT CARDS.   B. & B. £16 - 18.

Rozanne Mendick

14 CHATSWORTH RD., BRIGHTON, E. SUSSEX, BN1 5DB TEL: (01273) 556584
Large, comfortable family home.
OPEN ALL YEAR. NO SMOKING. V, VE STD., S.D. B/A. CHILDREN WELCOME. BEVERAGES. T.V. B. & B. FROM £14.

LEWES

Berkeley House Hotel

2 ALBION ST, LEWES, E. SUSSEX, BN7 2ND   TEL: (01273) 476057
Elegant Georgian town house in quiet conservation area in historic county town. South-facing roof terrace. Candle-lit restaurant.
OPEN ALL YEAR. V, S.D. B/A. N/S RESTAURANT. EN SUITE, TV & BEVERAGES IN ROOMS. CHILDREN WELCOME. LICENSED. CREDIT CARDS. B. & B. AROUND £35.

RYE

Green Hedges

HILLYFIELDS, RYE HILL, RYE, E. SUSSEX, TN31 7NH   TEL: (01797) 222185

ETB 2 Crowns Highly Commended. AA QQQQQ Premier Selected. Green Hedges is a large Edwardian country house superbly situated on rising ground, with wonderful views of the ancient town of Rye and the sea beyond. It is a comfortable family home and stands in a beautiful landscaped garden, just a short walk from the town; during the summer months the heated outdoor swimming pool is available for guests' use. Breakfast is prepared from seasonal garden produce, home-made preserves and free range eggs. You can explore the cobbled streets of mediaeval Rye and are within easy reach of Royal Tunbridge Wells, the beautiful Cathedral city of Canterbury and many National Trust properties. There is ample parking in the private road beside the house.

OPEN ALL YEAR EX. XMAS.   NO SMOKING.   V, STD, S.D. B/A.   CHILDREN: OVER 12S ONLY. EN SUITE, TV & BEVERAGES IN ROOMS.   ACCESS, VISA.   B. & B. FROM £23.

Jeake's House

MERMAID ST, RYE, E. SUSSEX, TN31 7ET   TEL: (01797) 222828   FAX (01797) 222623

*RAC Highly Acclaimed & AA Selected. Winner Of Good Hotel Guide César Award 1992*This beautiful listed building derives its name from the remarkable Jeake family of Rye who built the oldest part of the house (oak-beamed and wood-panelled) in 1689. It stands on a picturesque cobbled street in the heart of mediaeval Rye and has, in its time, seen service as a wool store, a Baptist School and, for 23 years home to the American Poet and author Conrad Aitken. The house is comfortably and interestingly furnished: antiques abound and there are 'brass and mahogany bedsteads, linen sheets and lace'; there is also a honeymoon suite. Wide choice of delicious breakfast fare.

OPEN ALL YEAR.   N/S DINING R.   V, VE STD, S.D. B/A.   LICENSED. CHILDREN WELCOME. PETS B/A. EN SUITE MOST ROOMS. BEVERAGES & T.V. ALL ROOMS. B. & B. FROM £19.50

The Old Vicarage Guest House

66 CHURCH SQUARE, RYE, E. SUSSEX, TN31 7HF   TEL & FAX: (01797) 225131

Listed 16th C. building in the quiet and picturesque Church Square. Restaurant has extensive views over Romney Marsh, and the food is prepared from fresh, local produce.

OPEN ALL YEAR ex. Xmas.   V STD, S.D. B/A.   OVER 12S ONLY.   EN/S DINING R & BEDRS.   N SUITE. BEVERAGES & T.V. IN ROOMS.   B. & B. FROM £17.50.

ST LEONARDS-ON-SEA

MERRYFIELD HOUSE, 3 ST MATTHEWS GDNS, ST LEONARDS ON SEA

Large Victorian house. Exclusively vegetarian.

TEL: (01424) 424953   OPEN ALL YEAR ex Xmas.   V EXC.   NO SMOKING.   CHILDREN AND WELL BEHAVED DOGS WELCOME. BEVERAGES & TV IN ROOMS.   B. & B. AROUND £16.

WADHURST

NEW BARN, WARDS LANE, WADHURST, E. SUSSEX, TN5 6HP

Beautiful 18th C. farmhouse overlooking Bewl Water. Beams, log fires and inglenooks. Breakfast is a hearty feast of home-made jams, marmalades & preserves with local home-baked bread & free range eggs; local pubs & restaurants serve an evening meal.

TEL: (01892) 782042   OPEN ALL YEAR.   V, S.D. B/A.   N/S ex in 1 lounge.   CHILDREN WELCOME.   PETS B/A.   EN SUITE & TV IN ROOMS.   BEVERAGES.   B. & B. £19-24, SINGLE £21.

RESTAURANTS

BRIGHTON

V *Food for Friends*

17A-18 PRINCE ALBERT ST., THE LANES, BRIGHTON TEL: (01273) 202310 FAX: (01273) 202001
Licensed vegetarian wholefood restaurant in the heart of the Lanes area of Brighton.
Everything on the menu (which changes daily) has been prepared from additive-free
ingredients (some organic), and there is an excellent takeaway and home-delivery menu.
55 SEATS. OPEN 9 - 10. 50% V EXC. NO SMOKING. LICENSED. DISABLED ACCESS. CHILDREN.

V SLIMS HEALTHFOOD RESTAURANT, 92 CHURCHILL SQUARE, BRIGHTON.

Friendly health food restaurant established 16 years ago, offering a range of savoury dishes,
cakes, pastries & fresh salads. Vegetarian outside catering service.
TEL: (01273) 24582 OPEN 9.30 - 5.30. V EXC. VE, DIAB, GLUTEN FREE DIETS B/A.   50% NO SMOKING.
LICENSED. DISABLED ACCESS. CHILDREN WELCOME.

TROGS, THE GRANVILLE HOTEL, 124 KINGS RD, BRIGHTON, BN1 2FA

Fish & vegetarian dishes of a very high standard. Organic produce where possible.
TEL: (01273) 326302   V STD.

HAILSHAM

The Homely Maid Restaurant and Pie Shop

2 HIGH ST, HAILSHAM, E. SUSSEX, BN27 1BJ   TEL: (01323) 841650
Cosy 13th century cottage. Home-baked fare including vegetarian, low-fat, etc.
OPEN Mon-Fri. 9-5, Sat. 9-1.30. V. & LOW-FAT. NO SMOKING. CHILDREN WELCOME.

JEVINGTON

THE HUNGRY MONK, JEVINGTON, NR POLEGATE, E. SUSSEX.

TEL: (01323) 482178 D. 7-10, L (Sun only) 12-2. V STD. N/S RESTAURANT (allowed in sitting room)   LICENSED.

NEWHAVEN

V HEALTHIBODY WHOLEFOOD, 52 HIGH ST, NEWHAVEN.

Cosy restaurant with varied menu of light and main meals.
TEL: (01273) 512957   OPEN MON - SAT., 9 - 5. N/S 60% RESTAURANT. V, VE STD. CHILDREN WELCOME.

Kent

ACCOMMODATION

ASHFORD

WOODMAN'S ARMS AUBERGE, HASSELL ST, HASTINGLEIGH, ASHFORD.

17th C. inn. Exceptionally good food prepared from finest local ingredients, fresh herbs.
TEL: (01233) 75250 OPEN ALL YEAR Ex. Sept. NO SMOKING. V, S.D. B/A. LICENSED.

BECKENHAM

CROCKSHARD FARMHOUSE, WINGHAM, CANTERBURY, CT3 1NY

Regency farmhouse. Families welcome. Home-produced bread, jam, eggs & vegetables.
TEL: (01227) 720464 OPEN ALL YEAR. NO SMOKING V, S.D. B/A. CHILDREN WELCOME. PETS B/A. SOME EN
SUITE ROOMS. BEVERAGES.   T.V. IN LOUNGE. AMEX. B. & B. AROUND £20.

CANTERBURY

ACACIA LODGE, 39 LONDON RD, CANTERBURY, KENT, CT2 8LF.

TEL: (01227) 769955   OPEN ALL YEAR. V B'FAST STD. EN SUITE, TV & BEVERAGES. B. & B. AROUND ££17.

ALEXANDRA HOUSE, 1 ROPER RD, CANTERBURY, KENT. CT2 7EH.

TEL: (01227) 767011 OPEN ALL YEAR. V B'FAST. CHILDREN. EN SUITE, TV, BEVERAGES. B. & B. AROUND £17.

CLARE ELLEN GUEST HOUSE, 9 VICTORIA RD, CANTERBURY, CT1 3SG
TEL: (01227) 760205 OPEN 1-12. V, S.D. STD. CHILDREN. EN SUITE, TV & BEVERAGES. B. & B. AROUND £23.

DAR-ANNE, 65 LONDON RD, CANTERBURY, KENT, CT2 8JZ
TEL: (01227) 760907 OPEN ALL YEAR. V, VE STD. CHILDREN. EN SUITE, TV, BEVERAGES. B. & B. AROUND £15.

Magnolia House

36 ST DUNSTAN'S TERR., CANTERBURY, KENT, CT2 8AX   TEL & FAX: (01227) 765121 MOBILE (0585) 595970

ETB 2 Crown Highly Commended. AA QQQQ Selected. Magnolia House is a charming detached late Georgian house situated in a quiet residential street near to the city centre and just 2 minutes' drive, or twenty minutes' walk, from the university. The house itself has much of architectural interest to commend it and has been decorated sympathetically with each bedroom being individually designed and coordinated in a light, bright decor (lots of Laura Ashley fabrics and wallcoverings, and one has a four-poster); there is a walled garden with fishpond, terraces and shrubberies (the perfect place to relax in after a day's sightseeing). Ann Davies, the proprietor, tells me, "because we only take 10 guests, each one is special", and guests are aware of this special treatment from the moment they arrive, when a welcome tray is offered. Breakfast is a generous meal with a wide range of options and special diets are treated sympathetically. Evening meals are available from November to February inclusive.
OPEN ALL YEAR. NO SMOKING ex. lounge. V, S.D. B/A. CHILDREN WELCOME. EN SUITE, TV, CLOCK RADIOS, HAIRDRIERS & BEVERAGES IN ROOMS. CREDIT CARDS. B. & B. FROM £24 - 40.

ORIEL LODGE, 3 QUEENS AVE, CANTERBURY, KENT, CT2 8AY.
Period character nr. city centre. Lounge with log fire. Vegetarian b'fast.
TEL: 901227) 462845 OPEN ALL YEAR. V STD. CHILDREN. EN SUITE, TV & BEVERAGES. B. & B. AROUND £20.

THE TANNER OF WINGHAM, 44 HIGH ST, WINGHAM, CANTERBURY.
17th C. building. Separate vegetarian menu with wide range of healthy, meat-free options.
TEL: (01227) 720532 V, VE STD. S.D. B/A. OPEN ALL YEAR. LICENSED. CHILDREN. BEVERAGES & TV.

Walnut Tree Farm

LYNSORE BOTTOM, UPPER HARDRES, CANTERBURY. TEL: (01227) 87 375.
14th C. thatched farmhouse situated in 6 acres. Perfect location for walking & birdwatching in peaceful valley yet close to Canterbury. Close to channel ports.
V, VE, DIAB B/A. WH STD. NO SMOKING. CHILDREN. EN SUITE & BEVERAGES. B. & B. AROUND £19.

YORKE LODGE, 50 LONDON RD, CANTERBURY, CT2 8LF
Lovely Victorian town house.; all food prepared to suit. Lots of home-made items, including the marmalade, stewed apple and fruit salad.
TEL: (01227) 451243 N/S ex. in library. V, S.D. B/A. CHILDREN. EN SUITE, TV. B. & B. AROUND £20.

CRANBROOK

HANCOCKS FARMHOUSE, TILSDEN LANE, CRANBROOK, TN17 3PH
Fine well-preserved timber-framed family home; inglenook with log fires. First-rate food; organic and wholefood ingredients are used in cooking whenever availability permits.
TEL: (01580) 714645 NO SMOKING. V, S.D. B/A. OVER 9S. EN SUITE, TV, BEVERAGES. B. & B. FROM £21.

HARTLEY MOUNT HOTEL, HARTLEY RD, CRANBROOK, TN17 3QX
Edwardian country manor; 2 acres. Good vegetarian menu prepared from fresh produce.
TEL: (01580) 712230 V STD, S.D. B/A. ORG, WH WHEN AVAIL. N/S. LICENSED. CHILDREN. EN SUITE & TV.

DARTFORD

Rosedene Guest House

284-286 LOWFIELD ST, DARTFORD, DA1 1LH   TEL: (01322) 277042
Comfortable B. & B. Vegetarian & other diets catered for. Wholefoods on request. Payphone.full central heating, h & c in all rooms, off-road parking. Close to M25/m20/A2. 40 mins London.

V, LOW-FAT STD, S.D. B/A. OPEN ALL YEAR.   N/S DINING R & BEDROOMS.   CHILDREN.   BEVERAGES & T.V IN ROOMS.   VISA. B. & B. FROM £15 - 20.

DOVER

THE CLIFFE TAVERN, HIGH ST, ST MARGARET'S-AT-CLIFFE, NR DOVER.
Historic series of Kentish clapboard buildings. Imaginative vegetarian dishes.
TEL: (01304) 852749 OPEN ALL YEAR. V STD. CHILDREN. EN SUITE, TV & BEVERAGES. B. & B. £18 - 42.

SUNSHINE COTTAGE, THE GREEN, SHEPHERDS WELL, NR DOVER.
17th C. cottage on village green; oak beams, inglenook fireplace; evening meal available using fresh produce; all home-cooking & baking.
TEL: (01304) 831359 V, S.D. B/A. ORG, WH WHEN AVAIL. CHILDREN. BEVERAGES. TV. B. & B. AROUND £18.

SEVENOAKS

POND COTTAGE, EGGPIE LANE, WEALD, SEVENOAKS, TN14 6NP
16th C. listed house with inglenook, oak beams & quarry floors, in 3 acres of land, including fish pond. Home-made bread and cakes.
TEL: (01732) 463773 OPEN ALL YEAR Ex. Xmas. NO SMOKING. CHILDREN WELCOME. PETS B/A. SOME EN SUITE ROOMS. BEVERAGES & TV IN ROOMS. B. & B. AROUND £25.

SITTINGBOURNE

Hempstead House

LONDON RD, BAPCHILD, SITTINGBOURNE, KENT, ME9 9PP   TEL:(01795) 428020
Exclusive private country house offering luxury accommodation, excellent cuisine and friendly hospitality; Home grown produce, home-baked bread, fresh herbs.
OPEN ALL YEAR.   V, DIAB. S.D. B/A. WH STD, LOW-FAT, HIGH FIBRE.   CHILDREN WELCOME. NO SMOKING ex. smoker's lounge. PETS B/A. EN SUITE, BEVERAGES & T.V. IN ROOMS. B. & B. FROM £31.

TENTERDEN

BRATTLE HOUSE, CRANBROOK RD, TENTERDEN, TN30 6UL
Handsome Grade II listed Georgian farmhouse in an acre of gardens. Beautiful bedrooms with views. Imaginative cooking using fresh, organic, wholefood produce where possible.
TEL: (015806) 3565   OPEN ALL YEAR.   V S.D. DIAB B/A. NO SMOKING.   CHILDREN: OVER 12S ONLY. EN SUITE & BEVERAGES IN ROOMS.   T.V. IN SOME BEDROOMS.   B. & B. AROUND £30.

TONBRIDGE

POPLAR FARM OAST, THREE ELM LN, GOLDEN GREEN, NR TONBRIDGE.
Traditional Kentish Oast house; b'fast prepared from fresh ingredients where possible; special diets plus a range of diabetic foods
TEL: (01732) 850723   V, DIAB B/A. NO SMOKING. CHILDREN. BEVERAGES. B. & B., AROUND £19.

TUNBRIDGE WELLS

Danehurst House Hotel

41 LOWER GREEN RD, RUSTHALL, KENT, TN4 8TW   TEL: (01892) 527739 FAX: (01892) 514804
Danehurst is a charming gabled guest house standing in a lovely rural setting in the heart of Kent; accommodation is in tastefully decorated rooms - all of which have private bathrooms and beverage-making facilities. The food is excellent: everything has been home-prepared from fresh, seasonal ingredients, and a typical evening menu would feature Carrot and Orange Soup followed by Chicken in Cream and Tarragon (with a selection of five seasonal vegetables and baby new potatoes), and a tempting dessert, such as Strawberry and Kiwi Fruit Shortcake with Cream; an English Cheeseboard, coffee and mints would complete the meal. You are just a short distance from Royal Tunbridge Wells and the gracious country houses of Kent are easily reached.
OPEN ALL YEAR.   N/S ex. in lounge. V, S.D. B/A. LICENSED. CHILDREN WELCOME.   SOME EN SUITE ROOMS. BEVERAGES & T.V. IN ROOMS.   CREDIT CARDS. B. & B. FROM £21.50.

Scott House

HIGH ST, WEST MALLING, KENT, ME19 6QH   TEL: (01732) 841380 /870025
Grade II listed Georgian town house. Excellent breakfast including healthy options such as muesli, yoghurt and porridge as well as the usual 'Full English' fare.
OPEN ALL YEAR ex. XmaS. NO SMOKING. V, S.D. B/A. EN SUITE, TV & BEVERAGES IN ROOMS. ACCESS, VISA, JCB, MASTERCARD.

RESTAURANTS

BROADSTAIRS

MAD CHEF ON THE HARBOUR, BROADSTAIRS, KENT.
12 Vegetarian & wholefood dishes on the menu.
TEL: (01843) 869304   OPEN ALL YEAR.   V, WH STD.   CHILDREN WELCOME. LICENSED.

PIPS WINE & EATING HOUSE, 35 ALBION ST, BROADSTAIRS, KENT.
Clean Food Award Winner. Excellent vegetarian menu.
TEL: (01843) 869439   OPEN ALL YEAR.   V STD.   CHILDREN WELCOME. LICENSED.

CANTERBURY

BEN JONSON RESTAURANT, 10 GUILDHALL ST, CANTERBURY.
TEL; (01227) 769189   V STD (English & Greek).

CORNERSTONE WHOLEFOOD RESTAURANT, 25A HIGH ST, ASHFORD.
TEL: (01233) 642874   NO SMOKING.   V.   . DISABLED ACCESS: 'good for wheelchairs'.   CHILDREN WELCOME.

CROTCHETS, 59 NORTHGATE, CANTERBURY, KENT.
Excellent menu. Vegetarian food a speciality. Live jazz some nights.
TEL: (01227) 458857   OPEN ALL YEAR.   V STD.   LICENSED.

FUNGUS MUNGUS, 34 ST PETERS ST, CANTERBURY, KENT.
TEL: (01227) 781922   V STD.

CANTERBURY

FOOD FOR LIVING EATS, 116 HIGH ST, CHATHAM, ME4 4BY
TEL: (01634) 409291 V EXC. NO SMOKING.   DISABLED ACCESS.   CHILDREN WELCOME.   ACCESS, VISA.

FOLKESTONE

HOLLAND & BARRETT REST., 80 SANDGATE RD, CT20 2AA
TEL: (01303) 243646   NO SMOKING.   V EXC. CHILDREN WELCOME.

Surrey

ACCOMMODATION

CAMBERLEY

TEKELS PARK GUEST HOUSE, CAMBERLEY, SURREY, GU15 2LF
Comfortable accommodation in a large house owned by the Theosophical Society in a
beautiful and secluded estate of 50 acres, forming a wildlife sanctuary; 35 miles London.
TEL: (01276) 23159   NO SMOKING.   V, VE EXC. OTHER MEAT-FREE S.D. B/A.   BOOKING ESSENTIAL.

KINGSTON-UPON-THAMES

CHASE LODGE, 10 PARK RD, HAMPTON WICK, KINGSTON-ON-THAMES.
ETB 4 Crowns Highly Acclaimed victorian villa. Excellent food made from fresh produce.
TEL: (0181) 943 1862   OPEN ALL YEAR.   V, S.D. B/A. N/S DINING R, SITTING R & 1 BEDR.   CHILDREN.
PETS B/A.   MOST ROOMS EN SUITE, BEVERAGES, T.V. & PHONES IN ROOMS.   B. & B. AROUND £20.

RESTAURANTS

GUILDFORD

THE FORUM RESTAURANT, 'Y' CENTRE, BRIDGE ST, GUILDFORD, SURREY.
Light and airy. Vegetarian choice changes daily.

GUILDFORD INSTITUTE, WARD ST, GUILDFORD, SURREY.
Part of the University of Surrey. Coffee and freshly cooked lunches (mainly vegetarian).

MUSWELLS, 16 NORTH ST, GUILDFORD, SURREY.
Bright and lively restaurant. Vegetarian menu.

PASTA CONNECTION, 8 - 9 CHAPEL ST, GUILDFORD, SURREY.
Lively atmosphere. Hand-made pasta. Vegetarians catered for.

London and Middlesex

London

Most of the larger London hotels offer vegetarian options on their restaurant menus. However they are also, for the most part, 'business' class (i.e. expensive) and I have not thought it useful to mention them all here (although I have listed a few). However there are a number of homely B. & B.s in central London (and within tube travelling distance) that you might well not otherwise have come across, which serve vegetarian options at breakfast together with a number of other breakfasty items which vegetarians tend to enjoy (wholemeal bread, yoghurt, fresh fruit, etc). These places are also reasonably priced and I have listed them where possible.

ACCOMMODATION

N4

Mount View

31 MOUNT VIEW RD, LONDON, N4 4SS   TEL: (0181) 340 9222   FAX: (0181) 342 8494
Mount View is a smart 3-storey Victorian house which stands on a tree-lined street in a residential area. It has three tastefully decorated double bedrooms (each of which can be let as a single), one of which has en suite facilities. There is a choice of an English, Continental or health food breakfast served in a downstairs dining room opening on to the patio and garden. The nearest tube station is Finsbury Park, on the Piccadilly and Victoria lines with fast, direct access to central London.
OPEN ALL YEAR.   N/S DINING R.   V, VE STD. S.D. B/A.   CHILDREN WELCOME.   EN SUITE, BEVERAGES AND TV IN BEDROOMS.   B. & B. FROM £15.

N19

PARKLAND WALK G. H., 12 HORNSEY RISE GARDENS, LONDON, N19 3PR
Small, friendly B. & B. in Victorian family house. B'fast menu features a wide range of home-cooked dishes plus home-made jams, fresh fruit, yoghurt and wholemeal bread.
TEL: (0171) 263 3228 OPEN ALL YEAR. V, S.D. B/A.   NO SMOKING. BEVERAGES & T.V.   B. & B. FROM £23.

NW1

Liz Heavenstone's

192 REGENT PARK'S RD, LONDON, NW1 8XP TEL: (0171) 722 7139 FAX: (0171) 586 3004
Light, bright friendly apartment on top two floors of Regency terrace, in leafy 'village' of Primrose Hill. 10 mins city centre. Close to parks, cafés and restaurants. Great breakfasts including freshly squeezed orange juice, rye bread, Patisserie Pastries, yoghurt, fruit, etc.
OPEN ALL YEAR (booking advisable). V STD. VE, S.D. B/A. ORG, WH STD. N/S DINING R. CHILDREN & PETS. EN SUITE, TV & BEVERAGES IN ROOMS. B. & B. AROUND £22 - 30.

NW3

HAMPSTEAD VILLAGE G.H., 2 KEMPLAY RD, HAMPSTEAD, NW3 1SY
Typical Victorian house with many original features.
TEL: (0171) 435 8679 FAX (0171) 7940254 OPEN ALL YEAR.   V B/A. NO SMOKING. CHILDREN WELCOME. BEVERAGES & T.V. B. & B. AROUND £21.

WC1

BONNINGTON HOTEL, SOUTHAMPTON ROW, WC1B 4BH
Well-established family-run hotel conveniently situated near to most of the attractions.
TEL: (0171) 242 2828 V, VE STD.   DIAB. S.D. B/A.   OPEN ALL YEAR.   LICENSED.   DISABLED ACCESS.
CHILDREN WELCOME. EN SUITE, TV & BEVERAGES.   ACCESS, VISA, AMEX.   B. & B. FROM £47.

W9

COLONNADE HOTEL, 2 WARRINGTON CRESCENT, W9 1ER
Charming Grade II listed Victorian building in a quiet residential area of Little Venice.
Family-owned and run. 50 well-equipped bedrooms.
 TEL: (0171) 286 1052   V STD. OPEN ALL YEAR.   N/S part of DINING R & SOME BEDRS.   LICENSED.
DISABLED ACCESS. CHILDREN WELCOME.   PETS B/A.   EN SUITE, TV & BEVERAGES IN ROOMS.

SW7

ASTER HOUSE HOTEL, 3 SUMNER PLACE, SW7 TEL: (0171) 581 5888
Aster House is at the end of an early Victorian terrace in the heart of London. Country
house atmosphere is enhanced by its pretty walled garden; the elegant facade of the building
has not been marred by any hotel signs, so just ring the bell at No 3. Meals are served in
the charming L'Orangerie in an atmosphere of relaxed elegance.
OPEN ALL YEAR.   N/S RESTAURANT & BEDRS.   EN SUITE & T.V. IN ROOMS.   B. & B. AROUND £35.

THE REGENCY HOTEL, ONE HUNDRED QUEEN'S GATE, SW7 5AG
TEL: (0171) 370 4595 OPEN ALL YEAR.   V STD. VE, DIAB, S.D. B/A.   WH, ORG WHEN POSSIBLE.   LICENSED.
CHILDREN WELCOME. EN SUITE & T.V. IN ROOMS.   CREDIT CARDS.   B. &. B. FROM £99.

SE10

TRADITIONAL B. & B., 34 DEVONSHIRE DRIVE, GREENWICH, SE10 8JZ
Pleasant Victorian house near Cutty Sark & antique markets; 25 mins central London.
TEL: (0181) 691 1918   OPEN ALL YEAR.   V STD. VE, DIAB, S.D. B/A. ORG WHEN AVAIL. WH ON REQUEST.   N/S
DINING R.   CHILDREN WELCOME.   T.V. & BEVERAGES IN ROOMS.   B. & B. AROUND £20.

RESTAURANTS

NW11

All' Italiana

8 PRINCES PARADE, GOLDERS GREEN RD, LONDON, NW11 9PS   TEL: (0181) 458 9483
Lively pasta bar; over half the dishes are suitable for vegetarians and these are clearly
marked on the menu. Much of the pasta is freshly home-made .
OPEN ALL YEAR (ex. for 3 summer wks) NO SMOKING. V STD. CHILDREN. LICENSED. L. & D £12 -15.

W1

COUNTRY LIFE VEGETARIAN BUFFET, 1B HEDDON ST, W1
TEL: (0171) 434 2922   V EXC. NO SMOKING.

Mildred's Wholefood Cafe and Take-Away

58 GREEK ST, LONDON, W1V 5LR   TEL: (0171) 494 1634
Acclaimed vegetarian and wholefood restaurant serving very reasonably priced meals.
OPEN 12 NOON - 11 P.M.   NO SMOKING.   V STD.   LICENSED.   CHILDREN WELCOME.

Ming

35-36 GREEK ST, LONDON, W1V 5LN   TEL: (0171) 437 0292
OPEN 12 - 11.45.   N/S PART OF RESTAURANT.   V STD. LICENSED.   CHILDREN WELCOME.

THE ROYAL ACADEMY RESTAURANT, BURLINGTON HOUSE, PICCADILLY.
TEL: (0171) 287 0752   OPEN 10 - 5.30 DAILY. SUNDAY BRUNCH A SPECIALITY 11.45 - 2.45.   V STD.   NO
SMOKING.   LICENSED.   EXCELLENT DISABLED ACCESS.

W2

SEASONS VEGETARIAN RESTAURANT, 22 HARCOURT ST, W2
TEL: (0171) 402 5925   V, VE EXC.   N/S PART OF RESTAURANT, UPSTAIRS. LICENSED.

W C 1

V **GREENHOUSE VEGETARIAN RESTAURANT, 16 CHENIES ST.**
TEL: (0171) 637 8038   NO SMOKING.   V. EXC.   DISABLED: 'BY PRIOR ARRANGEMENT'.

Wagamama

4 STREATHAM ST, LONDON, WC1A 1TB   TEL: (0171) 323 9223   FAX: (0171) 323 9224
Highly acclaimed Japanese noodle bar.
NO SMOKING.   OPEN ALL YEAR (ex. Bank Holidays).   V STD.   CHILDREN WELCOME.   LICENSED.

W C 2

BRIXTONIAN BACKYARD, 4 NEAL'S YARD, COVENT GARDEN, WC2 9DP
TEL: (0171) 240 2769 V STD. NO SMOKING. LICENSED.

THE CANADIAN MUFFIN CO., 5 KING ST, COVENT GARDEN, WC2E 8HN
TEL: (0171) 379 1525 V STD.   NO SMOKING.   CHILDREN WELCOME.

V *Food For Thought*

31 NEAL ST, LONDON, WC2H 9PA   TEL: (0171) 836 0239   FAX: (0171) 379 1249
One of London's most popular vegetarian restaurants and has been serving excellent
meat-free fare since 1974. In Covent Garden.
OPEN 12 - 8.   NO SMOKING.   V, VE EXC.   CHILDREN WELCOME.

THE NATIONAL GALLERY RESTAURANT, TRAFALGAR SQUARE, WC2N 5DN
TEL: (0171) 389 1760   75% N/S (SEP. ROOM).   V STD.   LICENSED.   DISABLED ACCESS.   CHILDREN.

S W 1

CAFÉ FIGARO, 6 LOWER REGENT ST, LONDON
V STD. NO SMOKING.

V **WILKINS NATURAL FOOD, 61 MARSHAM ST, SW1 P3DP**
TEL: (0171) 222 4038   V, VE EXC.   NO SMOKING.   DISABLED ACCESS.   CHILDREN WELCOME.

V **THE WREN AT ST JAMES'S, 35 JERMYN ST, SW1Y 6JD**
TEL: (0171) 437 9419   V, VE EXC.   NO SMOKING.   DISABLED ACCESS.

S W 6

V **WINDMILL WHOLEFOODS, 486 FULHAM RD, SW6 5NH**
TEL: (0171) 385 1570   V, VE EXC.   NO SMOKING.   LICENSED.   DISABLED ACCESS.   CHILDREN WELCOME.

S W 7

NATURAL HISTORY MUSEUM, CROMWELL RD, SW7 5BD
TEL: (0171) 938 8149   V STD. NO SMOKING.   LICENSED.   DISABLED ACCESS.   CHILDREN WELCOME.

S W 9

Brixtonian

11 DORRELL PLACE, BRIXTON, LONDON, SW9 3PL   TEL: (0171) 978 8870
V STD. NO SMOKING. LICENSED. DISABLED ACCESS TO DOWNSTAIRS. CHILDREN

E 2

V *Cherry Orchard Vegetarian Restaurant*

241 GLOBE RD, LONDON, E2   TEL: (0181) 980 6678
OPEN Mon, Thurs, Fri 11-4, Tues, Wed, 11-7.   V, VE STD.   NO SMOKING.   DISABLED ACCESS.   CHILDREN.

E 17

V *Gannets Vegetarian Café & Restaurant*

458 HOE ST, WALTHAMSTOW, LONDON, E17 9AH   TEL: (0181) 558 6880
Wholefood & vegetarian restaurant using organic & unsprayed products wherever possible.
The café & restaurant menus have daily specials depending on seasonal availability of
products.
V EXC. OPEN: Café: Tues.-Fri. 10-4; Sat. 9-5. Restaurant: Thurs.-Sat. 7 (last orders 10 p.m.).   NO SMOKING.   WHEELCHAIR
ACCESS.   CHILDREN WELCOME.   LICENCE PENDING (BYO).

Berkshire & Buckinghamshire

ACCOMMODATION

MILTON KEYNES

CHANTRY FARM, PINDON END, HANSLOPE, MILTON KEYNES, BERKS.
Old farmhouse built of Northamptonshire Stone. Swimming pool and trout lake.
TEL: (01908) 510269 OPEN ALL YEAR.   V STD, S.D. B/A. NO SMOKING.   DISABLED ACCESS.   CHILD-
REN WELCOME. PETS B/A. BEVERAGES & T.V. IN ROOMS.   B. & B. FROM £12.50.

READING

ABBEY HOUSE HOTEL, 116 CONNAUGHT RD, READING, BERKS, RG3 2UF
TEL: (01734) 590549 OPEN ALL YEAR. V STD. EN SUITE, TV & BEVERAGES.

NEALS FARM, WYFOLD, READING, RG4 9JB
Spacious Georgian farmhouse in a rural and peaceful setting. The delicious home-cooked
food is all prepared from fresh, often home-produced ingredients.
(01491) 680258 OPEN ALL YEAR ex. Xmas.   V, S.D. B/A.   NO SMOKING.   CHILDREN WELCOME.   PETS
B/A. BEVERAGES IN ROOMS.   T.V. IN LOUNGE.   B. & B. AROUND £20.

St Hilda's Guest House

24 CASTLE CRESCENT, READING, BERKS, RG16 6AG   TEL: (01734) 568296
St Hilda's is a large family-run guest house which stands very close to the town centre in
Reading. It is very cosy and welcoming - there is central heatingthroughout - and although
breakfast is the only meal available, there are a number of good eating places in the town
to which you host, Mrs Hubbard, will gladly direct you; snacks may also be prepared.
Vegetarian and diabetics by arrangement.
OPEN ALL YEAR.   V, S.D. B/A.   NO SMOKING. BEVERAGES & COLOUR TV IN ROOMS. B. & B. FROM £15-20

RESTAURANTS

NEWBURY

CHAOS CAFÉ, WINDSOR ARTS CENTRE, ST LEONARDS ROAD, WINDSOR.
TEL: (01753) 859421 V STD.   N/S 50%. CHILDREN WELCOME.

THE CURIOUS CAT, 5 INCH'S YARD, MARKET ST, NEWBURY, BERKS.
TEL: (01635) 35491 V & FRESH FISH A SPECIALITY. NO SMOKING.   LICENSED.   CHILDREN (high chairs).

READING

CHEZ FONTANA, 3 QUEEN'S WALK, READING, BERKS.
TEL: (01734) 504513   V STD.   OPEN 12 - 2.30, 7 - 11.   N/S SEPARATE AREA.   LICENSED. CHILDREN WELCOME.

SRI BANGKOK, 183 OXFORD RD, READING, BERKS. TEL: (01734) 598925
Thai restaurant with beautiful decor. Many Thai vegetable dishes available.

SAVERNAKE

SAVERNAKE FOREST HOTEL, SAVERNAKE, BERKS. TEL: (01672) 810206
Fine organic English cuisine.
V STD.   N/S AREA.   LICENSED.

Hertfordshire

ACCOMMODATION

BISHOP'S STORTFORD

THE COTTAGE , 71 BIRCHANGER LN, BIRCHANGER, BISHOP'S STORTFORD
17th C. Grade II listed building with large garden. Good access Stanstead airport.
TEL: (01279) 812349   OPEN ALL YEAR.   NO SMOKING.   V B/A.   LICENSED.   DISABLED ACCESS.   CHILDREN
WELCOME.   SOME EN SUITE.   BEVERAGES & TV IN ROOMS.   CREDIT CARDS.   B. &. B. AROUND £35.

HERTFORD

THE HALL HOUSE, BROAD OAK END, OFF BRAMFIELD RD, HERTFORD.
Charming country home built around a 15th C. Hall House timber frame; attractive wooded
gardens; excellent cuisine prepared from fresh produce. Heated pool.
TEL: (01992) 582807   OPEN ALL YEAR.   NO SMOKING.   V, S.D. b'fast, but not dinner, B/A.   SOME EN SUITE ROOMS.
BEVERAGES & T.V. IN ROOMS.   ACCESS, VISA, MASTERCARD.   B. &. B. £30 - 45

RICKMANSWORTH

6 Swallow Close

NIGHTINGALE ROAD, RICKMANSWORTH, HERTS, WD3 2DZ   TEL: (01923) 720069
Charming guest house in a quiet cul-de-sac just ½ hr's tube ride from central London (the
underground station is nearby). All food is home-cooked - including the bread and preserves
- and there are home-grown vegetables and home-laid eggs!
OPEN ALL YEAR.   NO SMOKING.   V B/A.   OVER 5S ONLY.   B. &. B. FROM £17.

ST ALBANS

The Squirrels

74 SANDRIDGE RD, ST ALBANS, HERTS, AL1 4AR   TEL: (01727) 840497
ETB Approved Listed. Edwardian terrace house within 10 mins walk of St Albans town
centre & 20 mins mainline station with frequent trains to London. Imaginative breakfasts.
OPEN mid Jan.-mid Dec.   V, S.D. B/A.   NO SMOKING.   EN SUITE, TV & BEVERAGES IN ROOM.   B. & B. Dblr £27.50,
Sgl £17.50.

TRING

ROSE & CROWN HOTEL, HIGH ST, TRING, HERTS, HP23 4BN
TEL: (01442) 824071   OPEN ALL YEAR.   30% N/S DINING R & BEDRS.   V, S.D. B/A.   LICENSED.   DISABLED ACCESS.
CHILDREN WELCOME.   EN SUITE, TV & BEVERAGES IN ROOMS.   CREDIT CARDS.   B. & B. AROUND £45.

RESTAURANTS

BERKHAMSTEAD

COOKS DELIGHT, 360-364 HIGH ST, BERKHAMSTEAD, HP4 1HU
TEL:(01442) 863584   V, VE, MACROB. STD.   NO SMOKING.   LICENSED.   CHILDREN WELCOME.   ACCESS, VISA.

HEMEL HEMPSTEAD

THE GALLERY RESTAURANT, THE OLD TOWN HALL, HIGH ST, HP1 3AE
TEL: (01442) 232416   V STD.   NO SMOKING.   CHILDREN WELCOME.   LICENSED.   CREDIT CARDS.

ST ALBANS

Kingsbury Watermill Waffle House

ST MICHAELS ST, ST ALBANS, HERTS, AL3 4SJ   TEL: (01727) 853502
Freshly baked waffles served with tasty toppings; many organic ingredients are used
including organically-grown, stone-ground flour & free-range eggs.
OPEN Tues.-Sat. 11-6, Sun. 12-6. closes 5pm winter.   V STD.   CHILDREN WELCOME.

Oxfordshire

ACCOMMODATION

ABINGDON

FALLOWFIELDS, SOUTHMOOR WITH KINGSTON BAGPUIZE, ABINGDON
Beautiful 17th C. house in 12 acres; food prepared from home-grown ingredients.
TEL: (01865) 820416 OPEN Apr. - Sept.   V, S.D. B/A.   N/S DINING R.   LICENSED.   OVER 10S ONLY.   PETS
B/A. MOST ROOMS EN SUITE. BEVERAGES & TV IN ROOMS.   ACCESS, VISA. B. & B. AROUND £35.

BANBURY

WROXTON HOUSE HOTEL, WROXTON ST MARY, NR BANBURY.
All food prepared from fresh, local produce (some home-grown); bread is home-baked.
TEL: (01295) 730777 OPEN ALL YEAR.   V, S.D. B/A.   N/S DINING R & PART OF BAR.   LICENSED.   CHILDREN
WELCOME. P ETS B/A.   EN SUITE, TV & BEVERAGES IN ROOMS.   CREDIT CARDS.   B. & B. AROUND £50.

HENLEY-ON-THAMES

JENNIFER BOWER, 4 COLD HARBOUR CL., HENLEY. TEL; (01491) 575297
OPEN June - Sept. V STD. NO SMOKING. CHILDREN WELCOME. B. & B. AROUND £15.

MRS J LOVE, 30 VALLEY RD, HENLEY, OXON. TEL; (01491) 573191
OPEN Dec. - Oct. V STD. OVER 10s WELCOME. EN SUITE AVAIL. B. & B. AROUND £15.

OXFORD

Combermere House
11 POLSTEAD RD, OXFORD, OXON, OX2 6TW   TEL: (01865) 56971
Family-run guest house; quiet tree-lined road off Woodstock Rd; residential North Oxford.
OPEN ALL YEAR.   V, S.D. B/A.   N/S DINING R.   CHILDREN WELCOME. DISABLED ACCESS: 'to ground floor &
dining room'.   PETS B/A. EN SUITE, BEVERAGES & T.V IN ROOMS.   CREDIT CARDS. B. & B. FROM £22.

COTSWOLD HOUSE, 363 BANBURY RD, OXFORD, OX2 7PL
Charming, comfortable and highly acclaimed guest house in North Oxford.
TEL: (01865) 310558 OPEN ALL YEAR. NO SMOKING.   V STD, S.D. B/A. (breakfast only).   OVER 6S ONLY.   EN
SUITE, BEVERAGES & TV IN ROOMS.   B. & B. AROUND £26.

THE DIAL HOUSE, 25 LONDON RD, HEADINGTON, OXFORD, OX3 7RE
Elegant half-timbered house in beautiful gardens just a mile from Oxford city centre.
TEL: (01865) 69944 OPEN ALL YEAR ex. Xmas.   V B'FAST STD.   N/S DINING R. & BEDRS.OVER 6S ONLY.
PETS B/A.   EN SUITE, BEVERAGES & TV IN ROOMS.   B. & B. AROUND £26.

Earlmont Guest House
322-324 COWLEY RD, OXFORD, OXON, OX4 2AF   TEL: (01865) 240236
Non-smoking main house with all rooms en suite. Standard smokers'rooms in annexe.
OPEN Jan 1 - Dec. 15.   N/S MAIN HOUSE.   V, VE, S.D. B/A.   OVER 5s ONLY.   BEVERAGES & TV IN ROOMS.
CREDIT CARDS.   B. & B. FROM £18 Std, £22.50 en suite.

Morar Farm
WEALD ST, BAMPTON, NR. OXFORD, OX18 2HL TEL: (01993) 850162 FAX: (01993) 851738
Spacious stone-built farm house. Plentiful food features lots of wholesome items such as
home-made preserves and home-baked bread.
OPEN Jan. - early Dec. NO SMOKING. V, S.D. B/A.   OVER 6S ONLY. 2 ROOMS EN SUITE. BEVERAGES IN
ROOMS. T.V. IN LOUNGE. CREDIT CARDS. B. & B. AROUND £19.

Mount Pleasant Hotel
76 LONDON RD, HEADINGTON, OXFORD, OX3 9AJ   TEL & FAX: (01865) 62749
The Mount Pleasant Hotel is a small family-run hotel which stands in the shopping area of
Headington but is within easy reach of the main shops and colleges of Oxford. Mr and Mrs
Papamichael are especially welcoming hosts and will do all they can to make you feel at
home: the food is excellent - Greek, English and Continental dishes are all home-cooked
from fresh ingredients - and special diets can be catered for by arrangement. Accommodation is in comfortable bedrooms - each of which has en suite facilities - and there is a safe
car park for guests'use.

OPEN ALL YEAR. V, S.D., B/A. N/S ex. bar. LICENSED. CHILDREN. EN SUITE & BEVERAGES IN BEDROOMS.
CREDIT CARDS.   B. & B. FROM £35

RANDOLPH HOTEL, BEAUMONT ST, OXFORD, OX1 2LN TEL: (01865) 247481
Well-known Oxford landmark; first-rate meals are served in the excellent restaurant.
OPEN ALL YEAR. V STD, S.D. B/A. N/S 60% OF DINING R & SOME BEDR. LICENSED. DISABLED ACCESS.
CHILDREN. PETS B/A. EN SUITE, TV & BEVERAGES IN ROOMS. B. & B. AROUND £75.

Westwood Country Hotel

HINKSEY HILL TOP, OXFORD, OXON, OX1 5BG   TEL: (01865) 735408 FAX: (01865) 736536

The Westwood Country Hotel now has a 'nature wild life' which was opened by David Bellamy and gives some indication of the fact that this charming small hotel, located just 3 miles from Oxford, boasts an exceptional abundance of wildlife in its 3 acres of grounds: woodpeckers, nightingales, badgers, foxes and, if you are lucky, deer have all been spotted in and around the 400 acres of woodland which surround the hotel grounds - which is a testament to the peace and tranquillity to be found at Westwood. The bedrooms are exceptionally comfortable & well-appointed & the food (served on lace tablecloths in a beamed dining room) is exceedingly good; the cosy bar welcomes walkers from the footpaths that radiate from the front door. *Winner of 1991 Daily Mail Award for Tourism for All.*
OPEN ALL YEAR ex. Xmas.   V, S.D. B/A.   N/S DINING R & T.V. LOUNGE.   LICENSED.   DISABLED ACCESS.
CHILDREN WELCOME.   EN SUITE, BEVERAGES & T.V. IN ROOMS.   CREDIT CARDS.   2-NIGHT COUNTRY
BREAKS FROM £51, 7 NIGHTS £266.

WINDRUSH GUEST HOUSE, 11 IFFLEY RD, OXFORD TEL: (01865) 247933
Family-run guest house near Magdalen Bridge. Healthy Eating Award. Non-smokers preferred. Coaches to and from London airport.
OPEN ALL YEAR. V B/A. N/S DINING R. CHILDREN. TV & BEVERAGES. B. & B. AROUND £20.

TOWERSEY

UPPER GREEN FARM, MANOR RD, TOWERSEY, OXON, OX9 3QR
Very comfortable farmhouse accommodation. Peacefully quiet.
TEL: (01884) 212496 OPEN ALL YEAR.   V, S.D. B/A. NO SMOKING. 2 GROUND FLOOR BEDROOMS, BUT
NO ROOM FOR WHEELCHAIRS. MOST ROOMS EN SUITE. BEVERAGES & TV IN ROOMS.

WOODSTOCK

GORSELANDS, BODDINGTON LANE, NR LONG HANBOROUGH, NR WOOD-STOCK, OX8 6PU TEL: (01993) 881202
Rural Cotswold stone house with oakbeams and flagged floors in 1 acre of grounds between Oxford & Woodstock. Breakfast & evening meal, using fresh local produce, on request.
OPEN Apr. - Nov. V, S.D. B/A.   NO SMOKING. CHILDREN WELCOME.   1 EN SUITE ROOM. BEVERAGES &
SATELLITE T.V. IN LOUNGE.   B. & B. AROUND £16.

RESTAURANTS

ABINGDON

THAME LANE HOUSE, 1 THAME LANE, CULHAM, ABINGDON, OX14 3DS
TEL: (01235) 524177 NO SMOKING. V B/A BEFORE BOOKING. LICENSED.   CHILDREN: OVER 3s.

CHIPPING NORTON

Nutters Healthy Lifestyle Centre

10 NEW ST, CHIPPING NORTON, OX7 5LJ   TEL: (01608) 641995
Wholefood restaurant & therapy centre. Excellent home-made food. Galettes & crêpes a speciality. Vegetarian, vegan and fish dishes.
NO SMOKING. 40 SEATS.   OPEN 9 A.M. - 10 P.M.   PRICES 'REASONABLE'.   V STD, VE, DIAB, COEL. & OTHER
S.D. ON REQUEST.   LICENSED.   CHILDREN WELCOME.

OXFORD

BETJEMAN'S AT BETJEMAN & BARTON LTD, 90 HIGH ST, OXFORD
TEL: (01865) 241855   NO SMOKING . V STD.   CHILDREN WELCOME.

BROWN'S, 5 - 11 WOODSTOCK RD, OXFORD, OX2 6HA
N/S PART OF RESTAURANT.   V STD.   CHILDREN WELCOME (HIGHCHAIRS AVAILABLE).   LICENSED. WHEEL-
CHAIR ACCESS.   CREDIT CARDS.

Café MOMA

MUSEUM OF MODERN ART, 30 PEMBROKE ST, OXFORD, OX1 1BP   TEL: (01865) 722733
Café MOMA is a pleasant eating place which specialises in serving vegetarian food
although meat dishes are also available.
OPEN Tues. - Sat. 10 am - 5 pm, Late night opening, Thurs., Sun. 2 - 5 pm.   NO SMOKING.   80% V. STD.   LICENSED.
DISABLED ACCESS.   CHILDREN WELCOME.

St Aldate's Coffee House

94 ST ALDATE'S, OXFORD, OXON, OX1 1BP   TEL: (01865) 245952
'Place of Christian Hospitality and Intellectual Refreshment for all who come within its
walls' Absolutely delicious food.
OPEN 12 - 2 for hot food, 10 - 5 for cold snacks.   NO SMOKING.   PRICES: VARIOUS.   V STD.   DISABLED ACCESS:
'yes, but toilets difficult'.   CHILDREN WELCOME.

Central England

Gloucestershire

ACCOMMODATION

BOURTON ON THE WATER

DIAL HOUSE HOTEL, BOURTON ON THE WATER, GL54 2AN
Centrally situated in Bourton on the Water this 17th C. house has an acre of lovely garden;
inglenook fireplaces and oakbeams; excellent cuisine.
TEL: (01451) 22244 OPEN ALL YEAR. N/S DINING R & SOME BEDRS.   V, S.D. B/A. LICENSED. DISABLED
ACCESS. EN SUITE, BEVERAGES & TV IN ROOMS. ACCESS, VISA.   B. & B. AROUND £36.

CHELTENHAM

Charlton Kings Hotel

LONDON RD, CHARLTON KINGS, CHELTENHAM, GLOS, GL52 6UU   TEL: (01242) 231061
Beautifully refurbished hotel just 2 miles from the centre of Cheltenham, in an acre of
lawned gardens. Excellent food.
OPEN ALL YEAR. V STD. N/S DINING R & SOME BEDRS. LICENSED. DISABLED ACCESS. CHILDREN &
PETS B/A.   EN SUITE, TV & BEVERAGES IN ROOMS. ACCESS, VISA, MASTERCARD. B. & B. AROUND £32.

Hallery House Hotel

48 SHURDINGTON RD, CHELTENHAM SPA, GL53 0JE   TEL: (0242) 578450

Hallery House is a lovingly-restored listed Victorian
building which function as a small, family-run hotel
with a welcoming, relaxed and informal atmosphere.
There are sixteen light, airy bedrooms   - each with
individual furnishings and lots of character - and
there is an elegant dining room and comfortable
lounge; guests may choose to while away an hour or
two on the patio in sunny weather, and the grounds
include lots of space for parking. Hallery House food
is fresh, healthy and simple, prepared from the best
local produce to imaginative and tasty recipes; tradi-
tional or continental breakfasts are provided and the evening meal would typically feature
a choice of dishes such as Aubergine Gateaux, home-made Gnocchi with Basil and
Parmesan, Casserole of Vegetables with red rice Risotto followed by Chocolate Brulée or
Tangy Lemon Torte. Hallery House is within walking distance of Cheltenham town centre,
and within a short drive are all the charms of the Cotswolds.
OPEN ALL YEAR.   V, S.D. B/A. N/S DINING R. & SOME BEDROOMS. LICENSED.   CHILDREN & PETS WELCOME.
EN SUITE MOST ROOMS. BEVERAGES, T.V. & SATELLITE IN ROOMS. VISA, AMEX, MASTERCARD. B. & B. FROM
£20.

NORTHFIELD, CIRENCESTER RD, NORTHLEACH, CHELTENHAM, GL54 3JL
Detached family home set in large gardens overlooking open countryside. Principally a bed
and breakfast, packed lunches and evening meals are available by arrangement and fresh,
home-grown produce - including free-range eggs - are used wherever possible in cooking.
TEL: (01451) 60427 OPEN ALL YEAR. NO SMOKING. V, S.D. B/A. LICENSED. CHILDREN WELCOME. EN
SUITE & BEVERAGES IN ROOMS. T.V. IN LOUNGE. B. & B. FROM £15.

PRESTBURY HOUSE, THE BURGAGE, PRESTBURY, CHELTENHAM, GL52 3DN
Georgian manor house in secluded grounds in pretty village of Prestbury. Elegantly
appointed with chandeliered dining room and four-posters in some of the bedrooms.
TEL: (01242) 529533 OPEN ALL YEAR. V, VE, DIAB STD. S.D. B/A.   N/S Part dining r & bedrs. LICENSED.
DISABLED ACCESS: 3 specially equipped rooms'. CHILDREN. EN SUITE, TV & BEVERAGES IN ROOMS.

STRETTON LODGE, WESTERN RD, CHELTENHAM, GLOS, GL50 3RN
Beautiful late Victorian house, quietly situated in central Cheltenham. Healthy b'fast
options (yoghurt, fruit) and evening meal (by arrangement) cooked from fresh produce.
TEL: (01242) 528724 V B/A. OPEN ALL YEAR. NO SMOKING. LICENSED. C HILDREN WELCOME. EN
SUITE, TV & BEVERAGES IN ROOMS. ACCESS, VISA.   B. & B. AROUND £30.

WYCK HILL LODGE B. & B.,WYCK HILL, CHELTENHAM, GL54 1HT
Early Victorian building with extensive views over the Vale of Bourton. Excellent b'fasts.
TEL: (01451) 830141 O V STD. S.D. B/A. EN SUITE, TV & BEVERAGES. B. & B.AROUND £23.

CHIPPING CAMPDEN
THE COTSWOLD HOUSE HOTEL, CHIPPING CAMPDEN, GL55 6AN
Beautifully restored 17th C. country house elegantly furnished with antiques & paintings
to complement its period features. Lovely garden, open fires, excellent cuisine.
OPEN ALL YEAR ex. Xmas. V S.D. B/A. N/S DINING R.   LICENSED. OVER 8S WELCOME.   EN SUITE, TV
& ROOM SERVICE.   CREDIT CARDS.   B. & B. AROUND £45.

CIRENCESTER
RAYDON HOUSE HOTEL, 3 THE AVENUE, CIRENCESTER, GL7 1EH
Small family hotel close to town centre. Good food prepared from fresh, local produce
TEL: (01285) 653485 OPEN ALL YEAR. V STD, S.D. B/A. LICENSED. CHILDREN WELCOME. GROUND
FLOOR ROOMS. DOGS B/A. EN SUITE, TV & BEVERAGES IN ROOMS.   B. & B. AROUND £20.

The Wild Duck
DRAKES ISLAND, EWEN, CIRENCESTER, GLOS, GL7 6BY   TEL & FAX: (0285) 770310
15th C. Cotswold inn in small country village close to Cirencester Park & Cotswold Water
Park. Rooms have DD phone, 2 rooms 4-poster overlooking the garden. Oak-panelled
residents' lounge.
V, ORG, WH, STD., VE, S.D. BA. LICENSED. CHILDREN WELCOME. PETS ON REQUEST. EN SUITE, TV &
BEVERAGE-MAKING IN BEDROOMS. CREDIT CARDS. B. & B. FROM £32.50.

CLEARWELL
Tudor Farmhouse Hotel
CLEARWELL, NR COLEFORD, GLOW, GL16 8JS   TEL: (01594) 833046 FAX: (01594) 837093

Tudor Farmhouse is a 13th C. building which is the
home of Richard and Deborah Fletcher. It is a beautiful house which has retained many of its original
features including oak beams, wall panelling and a
large inglenook fireplace in the lounge. The Fletchers aim is to offer the highest possible standards
of service and hospitality: guesta are accomodated
in very comfortable rooms - luxury rooms are also
available - and the food is stupendous, a typical
evening menu featuring Filo Pastry Strudel with
Egg and Spinach, followed by a Ragout of Courg-
ettes, Wild Mushrooms and Potatoes topped with
Asparagus Cream and Avocado; a delicious selection of home-made desserts would complete the meal. The Forest of Dean is a beautiful partof the world to choose for a country
break: the Fletchers have a comprehensive choice of special weekends - some with an
emphasis on walking - and will do all they can to help you make the most of your stay.
OPEN ALL YEAR.   V, ORG, STD. VE, S.D., B/A. NO SMOKING. LICENSED.   CHILDREN.   PETS IN COTTAGE.
EN SUITE, TV & BEVERAGES IN ROOMS. CREDIT CARDS.   B. & B FROM £24.50.

GILBERT'S, GILBERT'S LN, BROOKTHORPE, NR GLOUCESTER, GL4 0UH
Beautiful listed building with organic farm.
TEL: (01452) 812364   V, VE STD. S.D. B/A. ORG EXC. CHILDREN WELCOME.   EN SUITE & BEVERAGES.   B. & B.
FROM £21.

KILCOT

ORCHARD HOUSE, ASTON INGHAM RD, KILCOT, NR NEWENT, GL18 1NP
Beautiful Tudor-style country home in 5 acres of peaceful grounds. Delicious and imaginative fare: prepared from only fresh produce.
TEL: (01989) 82417 OPEN ALL YEAR. NO SMOKING. V, S.D. B/A. LICENSED. OVER 12S ONLY.   EN SUITE &
BEVERAGES IN ROOMS. CREDIT CARDS. B. & B. AROUND £20.

MINCHINHAMPTON

The Owl House

MARKET SQUARE, MINCHINHAMPTON, GL6 9BW TEL: (01453) 886378   MOBILE: (0850) 152683
The Owl House is a charming Grade II listed period stone house which stands close to the 12th C. parish church at the head of the market square in Minchinhampton; it enjoys southerly views over the unspoilt heart of this former market town. Accommodation is in comfortable rooms, each of which have been equipped with a range of helpful facilities including radio alarms, dressing gowns, colour TVs and hairdryers; there is an excellent restaurant (Michelin listed) just 20 yards away. You are surrounded by beautiful Cotswold countryside - ideal for walking and cycling - and Minchinhampton Common itself is administered by the National Trust. Excellent touring centre.
OPEN ALL YEAR.   NO SMOKING.   S.D. B/A.   CHILDREN & WELL-BEHAVED PETS WELCOME.   TV & BEVER-
AGES IN ROOMS.   B. & B. FROM £15.

PAINSWICK

UPPER DOREY'S MILL, EDGE, NR PAINSWICK, GLOS, GL6 6NF
18th C. Cotswold stone mill house in tranquil valley; beams & woodburning stoves.
OPEN ALL YEAR. NO SMOKING. V, S.D. B/A. (b'fast only). C HILDREN WELCOME. EN SUITE & BEVER-
AGES IN ROOMS.   T.V. IN LOUNGE. B. & B. AROUND £20.

RUARDEAN

THE LAWN, RUARDEAN, GLOS, GL17 9US   TEL: (01594) 543259
18th C. Grade II listed building, formerly village gaol. Good provision for vegetarians.
TEL: (01452) 812459 OPEN ALL YEAR ex. Xmas. NO SMOKING. V, S.D. B/A. OVER 8S ONLY. EN SUITE,
BEVERAGES & T.V.

ST BRIAVELS

CINDERHILL HOUSE, ST. BRIAVELS, GL15 6RH
14th C. building with oakbeams, inglenook fireplaces & bread oven, nestling in hillside.
Home-cooked food from fresh, local produce. Also two self-catering cottages.
TEL: (01594) 530393 OPEN ALL YEAR. N/S ex. in sitting room. V, S.D. B/A. LICENSED.   CHILDREN
WELCOME.   EN SUITE & BEVERAGES IN ROOMS.   B. & B. AROUND £23.

STROUD

BURLEIGH COTTAGE, BURLEIGH, MINCHINHAMPTON, STROUD.
Charming cottage with splendid views. Healthy b'fast options (fruit, yoghurt, etc.).
TEL: (01453) 884703 OPEN ALL YEAR.   NO SMOKING.   V, S.D. B/A. EN SUITE. BEVERAGES & TV. IN
BEDROOMS.

REDDINGS, BURLEIGH, STROUD, GL5 2PH TEL: (01453) 882342
Comfortable, spacious house standing in 5 acres of gardens and paddocks splendidly set with mature trees. Healthy food a speciality.
OPEN ALL YEAR ex. Xmas.   S.D. B/A.   LICENSED.   CHILDREN WELCOME.

TETBURY

CALCOT MANOR, NR TETBURY, GLOS, GL8 8YJ
Beautiful manor converted from a farmhouse; lovely gardens with outdoor heated pool.
Individually styled bedrooms and excellent meals prepared from fresh, local produce.
TEL: (01666) 890391 OPEN ALL YEAR. N/S DINING R.   V, DIAB STD. S.D. B/A. LICENSED. OVER 12S.   EN
SUITE & TV IN ROOMS. ROOM SERVICE. B. & B. AROUND £75.

TEWKSBURY

PUCKRUP HALL HOTEL, PUCKRUP, TEWKSBURY, GLOS, GL20 6EL
Grand Regency house providing superb accommodation and excellent cuisine.
TEL: (01684) 296200   OPEN ALL YEAR.   V STD, S.D. B/A. N/S DINING R.   LICENSED.   CHILDREN
WELCOME.   EN SUITE & T.V. IN ROOMS.   CREDIT CARDS.   B. & B. FROM £69.50.

WOTTON UNDER EDGE

COOMBE LODGE VEGETARIAN B. & B., WOTTON UNDER EDGE, GL12 7NB
ETB 2 Crowns Commended. Grade II listed Georgian house 1 acre of gardens Free-range
eggs, local mushrooms and wholemeal bread. Good vegetarian food.
TEL: (01453) 845057   OPEN ALL YEAR ex. Xmas & New Year.   NO SMOKING.   V EXC.   CHILDREN: OVER 3S ONLY.
BEVERAGES & T.V. IN ROOMS.   B. & B. AROUND £20.

RESTAURANTS

BRIMSCOMBE

Yew Tree Tea Rooms
WALLS QUARRY, BRIMSCOMBE, STROUD, GLOS, GL5 2PA   TEL & FAX: (01453) 883428
This Cotswold stone-built dwelling was once a 16th C. ale house, and access to the Tea
Rooms is through what once was the barley door. Freshly brewed coffee, cakes, scones,
rolls, soup and sandwiches. Fit-to-Eat Award.
V, S.D. STD. VE B/A.   NO SMOKING.   L. AROUND £2.   S.D.   CHILDREN WELCOME.

The Baytree
REGENT ARCADE, CHELTENHAM, GLOS, GL50 1JZ   TEL: (01242) 516229
Pleasantly furnished café in busy, modern Regent Arcade in the centre of Cheltenham.
Vegetarian dishes always available & a wide range of beverages including speciality teas.
50% N/S.   V STD.   DISABLED ACCESS.   CHILDREN.

GLOUCESTER

The Undercroft Restaurant
CHURCH HOUSE, COLLEGE GREEN, GLOS, GL1 5ER   TEL: (01452) 307164
Lovely restaurant and coffee shop. The food is first-rate. Everything is freshly prepared on
the premises, including the delicious cakes, and there are some good vegetarian options.
OPEN 10 - 5.   N/S 2 DINING Rs.   V STD.   LICENSED.   DISABLED ACCESS.   CHILDREN.

STROUD

The Ragged Cot Inn
HYDE, CHALFORD, NR STROUD, GL6 8PE   TEL: (01453) 884643/731333
16th C. 'olde worlde' inn, tastefully decorated, in the heart of the Cotswolds; friendly
personal service, good home-made food in no-smoking area; 3 years holder of 'Fit to Eat'
Award.
L./D. AROUND £7-£10.   N/S RESTAURANT.   V STD.   LICENSED.   WHEELCHAIR ACCESS.   CHILDREN: OVER 14S
ONLY.   CREDIT CARDS.

TEWKSBURY

The Abbey Tea Rooms
59 CHURCH ST, TEWKSBURY, GL20 5RZ   TEL: (01684) 292215
Pleasant 'old world' tea rooms located in 15th C. building offering range of snacks, lunches
& afternoon teas. Home-cooked foods a speciality, including excellent cakes.
OPEN 10.30 - 5.30, MAR. TO NOV.   L. AROUND £3.50.   NO SMOKING.   V, WEIGHT WATCHERS STD.   LICENSED.
DISABLED ACCESS.   CHILDREN WELCOME.

Herefordshire

FOWNHOPE

THE BOWENS COUNTRY HOUSE, FOWNHOPE, HEREFORDSHIRE.
TEL: (01432) 860430 OPEN ALL YEAR. V STD. EN SUITE, TV & BEVERAGES IN ROOMS. B. & B. AROUND £19.

HAY-ON-WYE

THE HAVEN, HARDWICKE, HAY-ON-WYE, HERE, HR3 5TA
Early Victorian vicarage in 2 acres of mature gardens and paddocks 2m from Hay on Wye.
All food prepared from fresh, often home-grown, ingredients. Open air pool.
TEL: (014973) 254 OPEN Mar. - Nov. N/S Ex. in library. V, S.D. B/A. LICENSED. 1 GROUND FLOOR EN
SUITE ROOM. CHILDREN. PETS B/A. MOST ROOMS EN SUITE. BEVERAGES & TV. B. & B. AROUND £19.

THE OLD POST OFFICE, LLANIGON, HAY-ON-WYE, HERE.
TEL: (01497) 820008 OPEN DURING SEASON. V STD. NO SMOKING. BEVERAGES. B. & B. £12 - 17.

HEREFORD

Grafton Villa

GRAFTON, NR HEREFORD, HR2 8ED TEL: (01432) 268689
Farmhouse of character in 1 acre of lawns & garden; panoramic views; superb home-cook-
ing with fresh, organic vegetables & local produce.
OPEN ALL YEAR. NO SMOKING. V S.D. B/A. CHILDREN WELCOME. PETS B/A. EN SUITE TWIN &
DOUBLE ROOMS. BEVERAGES & TV IN ROOMS. B. & B. AROUND £20.

UPPER NEWTON FARM, KINNERSLEY, HEREFORD. TEL: (01544) 327727
Recently renovated 17th C. farmhouse. 4-poster bedroom.
OPEN ALL YEAR. V STD. NO SMOKING. CHILDREN WELCOME.

LEDBURY

Wall Hills Country Guest House

HEREFORD RD, LEDBURY, HEREFORDSHIRE, HR8 2RP TEL: (01531) 632833
Elegant Georgian mansion in its own lovely gardens on the hill slopes overlooking Ledbury.
AA QQQ. ETB 3 Crown Commended.
OPEN ALL YEAR ex. Xmas. N/S DINING R & BEDR. V, S.D. B/A. LICENSED. CHILDREN WELCOME. EN SUITE,
BEVERAGES IN ROOMS. T.V. LOUNGE. B. & B. from £24.

LEOMINSTER

Highfield

IVINGTON RD, NEWTOWN, LEOMINSTER, HR6 8QD TEL: (01568) 613216
ETB 2 CRowns Commended. Elegant Edwardian house. Excellent food "lovingly prepared
from fresh, seasonal produce" (including home-made brioches served for breakfast).
OPEN ALL YEAR. N/S DINING R & BEDRS. LICENSED. CHILDREN B/A. PRIVATE BATH/EN SUITE ALL
ROOMS. BEVERAGES. TV LOUNGE. B. & B. AROUND £20.

THE HILLS FARM, LEYSTERS, LEOMINSTER, HERE.
TEL: (01568) 87 205 OPEN Mar. - Oct. V STD. EN SUITE. B. & B. £19 -20

KIMBOLTON COURT, KIMBOLTON, LEOMINSTER, HERE., HR6 0HH
Charming stone-built farmhouse in 1 acre of partially wild garden 3m. from town; home-
made produce includes bread, preserves, marmalade & organically grown vegetables.
TEL: (01568) 87259 OPEN ALL YEAR ex. Xmas & New Year. N/S BEDRS & DINING R. V, S.D. B/A. CHILDREN
WELCOME. EN SUITE. BEVERAGES IN ROOMS. T.V. LOUNGE. B. & B. AROUND £16.

LOWER BACHE FARM, KIMBOLTON, NR LEOMINSTER
17th C. stone farmhouse; home produce includes free-range eggs & organic vegetables.
TEL: (01568) 87304 OPEN ALL YEAR ex. Xmas. N/S DINING R. V, S.D. B/A. LICENSED. OVER 8S ONLY.
EN SUITE, BEVERAGES IN SUITES. T.V. B. & B. AROUND £20.

RATEFIELD FARM, KIMBOLTON, LEOMINSTER, HR6 0JB
18th C. house forming part of a 110 acre livestock farm in a secluded position less than a
mile from Kimbolton. Home-produce used in cooking and home-baked bread and rolls.
TEL: (01568) 2507 OPEN Mar. - Mid Feb. N/S DINING R & BEDR. V, DIAB, COAL, B/A. LOW-FAT STD.
CHILDREN WELCOME. PETS B/A. BEVERAGES. T.V. IN LOUNGE. AMEX. B. & B. AROUND £16.

MUCH BIRCH

THE OLD SCHOOL, MUCH BIRCH, NR HEREFORD, HR2 8HJ
ETB 2 Crown Commended. Comfortable, converted Victorian school with a lovely large garden and fantastic views. Really good home-made food. Marvellous walking country. TEL: (01981) 540006 OPEN ALL YEAR.   V, VE, DIAB, S.D. B/A. N/S DINING R. & BEDR. CHILDREN WELCOME. EN SUITE. BEVERAGES IN ROOMS. T.V. IN LOUNGE. B. & B. FROM £15.

ROSS ON WYE

Brook House

LEA, NR ROSS ON WYE, HERE., HR9 7JZ   TEL & FAX: (01989) 750710

Brook House is a fine Grade II listed Queen Anne building standing on the site of a medieval hospice for weary travellers! Now extensively - and sympathetically - renovated, Brook House offers quite exceptionally comfortable accommodation to guests: all bedrooms have been furnished in keeping with the period details of the house's architecture, and there are many family antiques in the public rooms. The emphasis at Brook House is on comfort and good food; accordingly there is a very friendly and relaxed atmosphere and your hosts will always find time to chat to help you plan your stay. Breakfast is stupendous: the cinnamon bread and muffins are home-made and the bacon, sausages and eggs (free-range of course!) represent the best of local produce. Evening meals are imaginative and tasty, and snacks can be provided for late arrivals. Lea is a pleasant Herefordshire village just 4 miles from Ross on Wye on the Gloucester road; you are perfectly placed therein for visiting both the Wye Valley and the Forest of Dean.
OPEN ALL YEAR. N/S ex. in lounge (where it is discouraged). V STD, S.D. B/A. OVER 7S ONLY. PETS B/A. EN SUITE SHOWER 2 ROOMS & BATHROOM 1 ROOM. BEVERAGES & TV IN ROOMS. B. & B. FROM £15.50.

Edde Cross House

EDDE CROSS ST, ROSS ON WYE, HR9 7BZ   TEL: (01989) 565088

This delightful Georgian Grade II listed town house with its charming walled garden stands in a convenient position in Ross on Wye overlooking the river. It has a very friendly and warm atmosphere - a bit like staying in a house with friends - and all bedrooms have been comfortably furnished to a very high standard with extensive use of mellow old pine and have excellent facilities, including a welcome tray and a hairdryer. Breakfast is the only meal available at Edde Cross but it is a meal with lots of options including three different fish dishes, an extensive choice for vegetarians, and a continental alternative for lighter appetites.
OPEN Feb. - Nov. NO SMOKING. S.D. B/A. CHILDREN: OVER 10S. EN SUITE/PRIVATE BATH, BEVERAGES & TV IN ALL ROOMS. B. & B. FROM £21.

Linden House

14 CHURCH ST, ROSS ON WYE, HEREFORDSHIRE, HR9 5HN   TEL: (01989) 65373

Linden House is a comfortable, friendly, informal Georgian town house run by the resident proprietors and standing in a quiet street opposite St Marys church, just off the market square. This no-smoking house provides excellent traditional and vegetarian breakfasts (which include home-made jams and marmalades) in a cosy, beamed dining room. The bedrooms are comfortably furnished - many have brass beds - and each is equipped with a TV and tea and coffee making facilities; en suite rooms are available. There is a very wide choice of excellent eating places within a two or three minute walk of Linden House, and visitors with cars enjoy safe, on-street parking.
OPEN ALL YEAR. NO SMOKING. V, S.D. B/A. OVER 8S ONLY. SOME EN SUITE ROOMS. BEVERAGES & T.V. IN ROOMS. B. & B. FROM £17.

Pengethley Manor Hotel
NR. ROSS ON WYE, HERE, HR9 6LL TEL: (01989) 87211
Splendid country house in 15 acres of stunning English countryside. Exceptional cuisine
prepared from fine, fresh, local ingredients; much of the herbs, fruit and vegetables used
in cooking have been culled from the Pengethley estate.
V, VE STD. DIAB, S.D. B/A. OPEN ALL YEAR. LICENSED. DISABLED ACCESS. CHILDREN WELCOME. PETS B/A.
EN SUITE. BEVERAGES & T.V. IN ROOMS. CREDIT CARDS. D., B. & B. AROUND £70.

ULLINGSWICK

The Steppes Country House Hotel
ULLINGSWICK, HERE, HR1 3JG TEL: (01432) 820424
Listed 17th C. building beamed ceilings, inglenook fireplaces & tiled floors. Candlelit
5-course evening meal prepared from the finest fresh ingredients.
OPEN ALL YEAR. N/S MOST PUBLIC ROOMS. V, S.D. B/A. LICENSED. DISABLED: 'NOT FOR WHEEL-
CHAIR BOUND'. OVER 12S. PETS B/A. EN SUITE, BEVERAGES & T.V. IN ROOMS. B. & B. AROUND £37.

RESTAURANTS

HAY-ON-WYE

OSCARS BISTRO, HIGH TOWN, HAY-ON-WYE
TEL: (01497) 821193 V STD. OPEN 7 DAYS. LICENSED.

HEREFORD

CLOISTERS WINE BAR, 24 HIGH ST, ROSS-ON-WYE, HERE.
TEL: (01989) 67717 V STD. LICENSED. CHILDREN WELCOME.

THE MOSS COTTAGE BAR & RESTAURANT, FOLEY ST, HEREFORD.
TEL: (01432) 275642 V STD 9one vegetarian dish avail. daily). LICENSED. CHILDREN WELCOME.

'NUTTERS', CAPUCHIN YARD, OFF CHURCH ST, HEREFORD
Vegetarian restaurant.
NO SMOKING. V STD. LICENSED. WHEELCHAIR ACCESS. CHILDREN WELCOME.

LEOMINSTER

APPLE TREE RESTAURANT, VICTORIA ST, LEOMINSTER.
V STD.

GRANARY COFFEE HOUSE, 6 SOUTH ST, LEOMINSTER, HERE.
V STD. CHILDREN WELCOME.

OLIVE BRANCH, 3 CHURCH ST, LEOMINSTER, HERE.
V STD. CHILDREN WELCOME.

Shropshire

BRIDGNORTH

THE OLD VICARAGE HOTEL, WORFIELD, BRIDGNORTH, WV15 5JZ
Magnificent Edwardian house in 2 acres. The candlelit dinner is based around the availa-
bility of fresh, regional produce, changes daily and virtually everything is home-made,
including the bread, ice-cream, sorbets and preserves (plus vegetarian options).
TEL: (017464) 497 OPEN ALL YEAR. V, S.D. B/A. N/S DINING R & SOME BEDRS. LICENSED. RAMPS & SPECIAL
SUITE FOR DISABLED. CHILDREN WELCOME. EN SUITE, BEVERAGES & TV IN ROOMS. B. & B. AROUND £40.

CHURCH STRETTON

Mynd House Hotel
LITTLE STRETTON, CHURCH STRETTON, SHROP, SY6 6RB   TEL: (01694) 722212
Small Edwardian house hotel and restaurant with wonderful hill views. The candlelit
restaurant (open to non-residents) features an excellent fixed price 4-course Table d'hote
or an à la carte menu (both offer imaginative dishes and good meat-free options). Organic
wines.

OPEN Mar. - Dec.   N/S DINING R & BEDRS.   V B/A.   organic french wines available.   LICENSED. CHILDREN
WELCOME.   PETS.   EN SUITE, TV & BEVERAGES IN ROOMS.   B. & B. FROM £25

CLEOBURY MORTIMER

The Redfern Hotel

CLEOBURY MORTIMER, SHROPS., DY14 8AA   TEL: (01229) 270395

Standing in tree-shaded main street alongside half timbered and 18th century houses. b'fast
served in roof-top conservatory. English food made from organic, wholefood ingredients.
OPEN ALL YEAR.   V STD.S.D. B/A.   LICENSED.   CHILDREN WELCOME.   PETS B/A.   EN SUITE, TV &
BEVERAGES.   CREDIT CARDS.   B. & B. FROM £30.

THE OLD RECTORY, HOPESAY, CRAVEN ARMS, SY7 8HD

17th century rectory; home-grown/local produce
TEL: (015887) 245   V S.D. B/A.   NO SMOKING.   EN SUITE, TV, BEVERAGES.   B & B AROUND £30

CRAVEN ARMS

THE ELMS FARM, CHURCH BANK, CLUN, CRAVEN ARMS, SHROPS.

Small hill farm providing home-grown fruit, vegetables and home-baked bread.
TEL: (01588) 640665   V STD. NO SMOKING.   CHILDREN WELCOME.   B. & B. AROUND £15.

LUDLOW

Corndene

CORELEY, LUDLOW, SHROPSHIRE, SY8 3AW   TEL: (01584) 890324

ETB 2 Crowns. Corndene is a house of great charm, the
original part of which dates from the 18th C.; it stands amidst
2 acres of lovely gardens, some distance from any main road,
and has lovely views over woods and farms. Accommodation is in very comfortable twin-bedded rooms, three of
which are on the ground floor and have full wheelchair
access; additionally there is a pleasant sitting room with an
open fire, colour T.V., games, books and level access to the
terrace. The food is tasty, wholesome and home-cooked:
special diets - such as vegetarian - are catered for very
competently if prior notice is given, and packed lunches can
be provided on request. Corndene is situated 7 miles East of
Ludlow and 4 miles North of Tenbury Wells on the South
side of Titterstone Clee Hill; as such it is a perfect base from
which to explore the attractions of the lush, countryside
immortalised in A.E. Housman's poem, The Shropshire Lad.

OPEN ALL YEAR ex. Xmas & New Year.   NO SMOKING.   V, S.D. B/A.   "TOURISM FOR ALL": CATEGORY 1 DISABLED
ACCESS.   CHILDREN WELCOME.   EN SUITE & BEVERAGES IN ROOMS.   T.V. LOUNGE.   B. & B. FROM £18.50.

Dinham Weir Hotel

DINHAM BRIDGE, LUDLOW, SHROP, SY8 1EH   TEL: (01584) 874431

À la carte or table d'hote menu served in candlelit restaurant includes a vegetarian option.
OPEN ALL YEAR.   V STD, S.D. B/A.   LICENSED.   OVER 5S ONLY.   EN SUITE, BEVERAGES & T.V. IN
ROOMS.   B. & B. AROUND £32.

The Feathers at Ludlow

BULL RING, LUDLOW, SY8 1AA   TEL: (01584) 875261   FAX: (01584) 876030

Described by the New York Times as 'the most handsome inn in the world', the Feathers
at Ludlow has a deserved international reputation as a famous and historic hotel. With a
magnificent half-timbered front elevation and a richly decorated interior, the Feathers is a
splendid venue for a banquet, a conference, a honeymoon or a simple lunch. There are 40
luxuriously appointed bedrooms (10 have four posters), and comfortable public rooms. The
food is excellent: the à la carte menu in the Housman Restaurant offers a range of dishes,
from the simple to the exotic, to suit all tastes, and there is always a good selection of
vegetarian dishes such as Spinach Roulade with Ricotta Cheese and Tomato Sauce or
Courgette and Stilton Pie.
OPEN ALL YEAR.   N/S PART OF DINING R.   V, STD., S.D. B/A.   LICENSED.   DISABLED ACCESS. CHILDREN
WELCOME.   EN SUITE, BEVERAGES & TV IN ROOMS.   CREDIT CARDS.   B. & B. FROM £50. D £20.

MINSTERLEY

Cricklewood Cottage

PLOX GREEN, MINSTERLEY, SHROPSHIRE, SY5 OHT TEL: (01743) 791229
18th C. cottage which is beautifully situated at the foot of the Stiperstones Hills
OPEN ALL YEAR.   V, S.D. B/A.   NO SMOKING.   EN SUITE & BEVERAGES.   T.V. IN LOUNGE.   B. & B FROM £13

OSWESTRY

April Spring Cottage

NANTMAWR, OSWESTRY, SHROP, SY10 9HL   TEL: (01691) 828802
Situated down a peaceful country lane with no passing traffic, the cottage stands amidst an
acre of garden which is a mass of flowers and herbs in summer. Wholesome and delicious
food featuring home-grown vegetables and home-produced eggs. Vegetarians are more than
welcome - please let your host know when booking.
OPEN ALL YEAR.   V, DIAB B/A.   N/S DINING R & BEDRS.   OVER 8S ONLY.   BEVERAGES IN ROOMS.
T.V. IN LOUNGE.   B. & B. AOUND £18.

SHREWSBURY

ABBOTS MEAD, ST JULIAN FRIARS, GREYFRIARS BRIDGE, SHREWSBURY
TEL: (01743) 235281 OPEN ALL YEAR.   V STD. LICENSED.   EN SUITE, TV & BEVERAGES .   B. & B. FROM £22.

Frankbrook

YEATON LANE, BASCHURCH, SHREWSBURY SY4 2HZ   TEL: (01939) 260778
Peaceful country house; interesting garden, in lovely countryside. Home-grown produce.
OPEN ALL YEAR.   V, S.D. B/A.   NO SMOKING.   CHILDREN.   BEVERAGES.   T.V. IN LOUNGE   B. & B. FROM
£32.50.

THE LION, WYLE COP, SHREWSBURY, SHROP, SY1 1UY
Now a Forte Heritage hotel, The Lion dates from the 14th century.
TEL: (01743) 353107 OPEN ALL YEAR.   N/S DINING R.   V, VE STD.   S.D. B/A.   LICENSED.   CHILDREN
WELCOME. PETS B/A.   EN SUITE, TV & BEVERAGES IN ROOMS.   CREDIT CARDS.   B.& B. AROUND £45.

The Old House

RYTON, DORRINGTON, SHROP, SY5 7LY TEL: (01743) 73585
17th C. manor house in 2 acres of superb gardens. 6m South of Shropshire.
OPEN ALL YEAR.   V, VE STD. S.D. B/A.   NO SMOKING.   CHILDREN WELCOME.   EN SUITE & BEVERAGES
IN ROOMS.   T.V. LOUNGE.   B. & B. AROUND £20.

MERVALE HOUSE, 66 ELLESMERE RD, SHREWSBURY, SHROP, SY1 2QP
TEL: (01743) 243677 OPEN ALL YEAR.   V STD.   TV & BEVERAGES IN ROOMS.

TELFORD

THE COTTAGE, LYDBURY NORTH, SHROP, SY7 8AU
Cottage guest house in village. Home-grown vegetables and herbs used in cooking.
TEL: (015888) 224 OPEN ALL YEAR.   V, S.D. B/A.   CHILDREN.   EN SUITE. T.V.   B. & B. AROUND £16.

RESTAURANTS

CHURCH STRETTON

Acorn Wholefood Restaurant Coffee House

26 SANDFORD AVE, CHURCH STRETTON, SY6 6BW   TEL: (01694) 722495 FAX: (01694) 722495
Small family run business, recommended in many good food guides; all fare, except bread,
is made on the premises from wholefood ingredients. Excellent food; efficient service.
OPEN 9.30 - 5.30 Winter & 10 - 6 Summer, Sun. & Bank Hols, Closed 2 Weeks Feb. & nov.   V, VE, S.D. STD.   N/S 75%
RESTAURANT (SEP. ROOM).   CHILDREN WELCOME.

CRAVEN ARMS

The Sun Inn

CORFTON, DIDDLEBURY, NR CRAVEN ARMS.   TEL & FAX: (01584) 861239
Charming old 17th C. pub in beautiful countryside. Real ales. Home-made vegetarian
meals.

OPEN 11 - 3 & 11 P.M. WEEKDAYS.   12 - 2.30 & 7 - 10.30 SUNDAYS.   N/S RESTAURANT.   V STD.   CHILDREN & PETS WELCOME.   DISABLED ACCESS.

LUDLOW

Ⅴ **HARDWICKS RESTAURANT, 2 QUALITY SQUARE, LUDLOW.**
Excellent vegetarian and wholefood restaurant.
TEL: (01584) 876470   33 SEATS. N/S 65% OF RESTAURANT.   V STD.   LICENSED.   CHILDREN WELCOME.

OSWESTRY

BEATRICE'S CAFÉ BISTRO, 8 BEATRICE ST, OSWESTRY, SHROP.
Light or full lunches. Evening meals. Vegetarian standard.

ROGUES BAR-BRASSERIE, ENGLISH WALLS, OSWESTRY, SHROP.
Superb cuisine presented with flair. Vegetarian options.

SHREWSBURY

CARLTON'S COFFEE HOUSE, 1 FISH ST, SHREWSBURY, SHROP.
V MENU.   NO SMOKING.   LICENSED.

Ⅴ *The Good Life*
BARRACKS PASSAGE, WYLE COP, SHREWSBURY, SHROPSHIRE.   TEL: (01743) 350455
Restaurant in 14th C. building. Fresh vegetables and fruit, wholemeal flour, free-range eggs and demerara sugar are used to prepare quiches, nut loaves, cheeses and salads as well as a variety of tempting desserts and puddings; beverages (many caffeine-free) also available.
OPEN 9.30 - 3.30 (4.30 Sat.)   N/S IN 1 ROOM.   V EXC.   LICENSED.   DISABLED ACCESS.   CHILDREN WELCOME.

Staffordshire

ACCOMMODATION

BURTON-ON-TRENT

The Edgecote Hotel
179 ASHBY RD, BURTON ON TRENT, DE15 0LB   TEL: (01283) 68966
Attractive family-run hotel situated on the A50 Leicester road. Breakfast features cereals, yoghurt, fresh fruit and fruit juice follow by a cooked breakfast or a lighter Continental option with home-baked rolls and croissants; dinner has imaginative vegetarian options.
OPEN ALL YEAR.   V, S.D. B/A.   N/S DINING R, BEDRS. LICENSED.   CHILDREN WELCOME.   PETS B/A.
SOME EN SUITE ROOMS.   BEVERAGES & T.V. IN ROOMS.   B. & B. FROM £16.50, D. £9.

LEEK

Choir Cottage & Choir House
OSTLERS LANE, CHEDDLETON, NR LEEK, STAFFS, ST13 7HS   TEL: (01538) 360561
Small 17th C. stone-built cottage and Choir House is just 20 years old and was built on what was originally the cottage herb garden. Some rooms have four-posters.
OPEN ALL YEAR ex. Xmas.NO SMOKING.   V, S.D. B/A.   CHILDREN WELCOME.   EN SUITE, BEVERAGES & T.V. IN ROOMS.   B. & B. FROM £20.

PETHILLS BANK COTTAGE, BOTTOMHOUSE, NR LEEK, ST13 7PF
18th century Derbyshire stone farmhouse. B'fast includes fresh fruits & home-made jam.
TEL: (01538) 304277/304555   OPEN Mar. - Dec.   V, S.D. B/A.   NO SMOKING. OVER 5S.   EN SUITE, BEVER-AGES & TV.   B. & B. AROUND £20.

WARRINGTON HOUSE, 108 BUXTON RD, LEEK, ST13 6EJ   TEL: (01538) 399566
Good varied menu with fresh home-made bread.
OPEN ALL YEAR.   V STD.   CHILDREN WELCOME.   TV & BEVERAGES.   B. & B. £16 - 20.

THE WHITE HOUSE, GRINDON, NR LEEK, STAFFS, ST13 7TP
South-facing 17th C. house with uninterrupted views; stone mullions and oak beams. Breakfast features home-baked bread and preserves and free-range eggs from the village.
TEL: (01538) 304250   OPEN ALL YEAR ex. Xmas & New Year.   V, S.D. B/A.   N/S ex. lounge.   CHILDREN: OVER 10S ONLY.   EN SUITE, BEVERAGES & TV IN ROOMS.   B. & B. AROUND £20.

STOKE-ON-TRENT

FAIRVIEW GUEST HOUSE, 1 VICARAGE ROW, ALTON, STOKE.
TEL: (01538) 702086 V, S.D. B/A. CHILDREN & PETS. TV & BEVERAGES IN ROOMS. B. & B. AROUND £16.

HAYDEN HOUSE HOTEL, HAYDEN ST, BASFORD, STOKE-ON-TRENT, ST4 6JD
Large Victorian house retaining the period charm and features of the original building.
TEL: (01782) 711311 V, VE STD. DIAB, S.D. B/A. LICENSED. DISABLED ACCESS. CHILDREN WELCOME.
EN SUITE, BEVERAGES & T. V. IN ROOMS. B. & B. AROUND £36.

Wedgewood Memorial College

STATION RD, BARLASTON, STOKE-ON-TRENT, STAFFS, ST12 9DG TEL: (01782) 372105
Pleasant, well-appointed adult education college offering comfortable accommodation
with excellent quality home-cooked food, including an imaginative repertoire of vegetarian
dishes.
OPEN ALL YEAR. V, VE STD., S.D. B/A. N/S DINING R. LICENSED. WHEELCHAIR ACCESS. CHILDREN.
BEVERAGES IN ROOMS. B. & B. £12.50, D. £6.

WOLVERHAMPTON

Moors Farm and Country Restaurant

CHILLINGTON LN., CODSALL, NR WOLVERHAMPTON (0902) 842330
Moors Farm is a working livestock farm which uses traditional methods exclusively. All
food is home-cooked from organically home-grown and wholefood ingredients wherever
possible, and vegan and other special dietary requirements can be accommodated with
notice. Booking essential.
V, VE, DIAB, S.D. B/A. N/S PART OF RESTAURANT. LICENSED. OVER 4S ONLY. EN SUITE, BEVERAGES &
T.V. IN ALL ROOMS.

RESTAURANTS

LEEK

BILBERRIES, 7A STANLEY ST, LEEK.   TEL: (01538) 398162
V STD. CHILDREN WELCOME. NO SMOKING.

STOKE-ON-TRENT

THE RADDLE INN, QUARRY BANK, NR TEAN, STOKE-ON-TRENT.
TEL: (01889) 26 278 V STD. CHILDREN WELCOME. LICENSED.

WATERHOUSES

The Old School Restaurant

STAFFORDSHIRE PEAK ARTS CENTRE, CAULDON LOWE, NR WATERHOUSES, ST10 3EX TEL:
(01538) 308431
The Staffordshire Peak Arts Centre is housed in the atmospheric setting of a converted old
moorlands village school. The restaurant serves some tasty home-cooked vegetarian
options.
NO SMOKING. V, VE STD. S.D. B/A. LICENSED. DISABLED ACCESS. CHILDREN WELCOME.

Warwickshire

HENLEY IN ARDEN

IRELANDS FARM B. &B., IRELANDS LN, HENLEY IN ARDEN, B95 5SA
Spacious Georgian farmhouse in 220 acres of unspoilt countryside. Self-catering available.
Wholesome and delicious farmhouse breakfast each morning.
TEL: (01564) 792476 OPEN ALL YEAR ex. Xmas & New Year. V, S.D. B/A. N/S DINING R & BEDRS. PETS
B/A. SOME EN SUITE ROOMS. BEVERAGES & T.V. IN ROOMS. B. & B. AROUND £18.

OXHILL

NOLANDS FARM & COUNTRY RESTAURANT, OXHILL, CV35 0RJ
Working arable farm in a tranquil valley just off the main A422. All food prepared from
fresh ingredients. Self-catering also available.
TEL: (01926) 640309 FAX: (01926) 641662 OPEN ALL YEAR.   V B/A. N/S DINING R, SITTING R & LOUNGE.
WHEELCHAIR ACCESS.   OVER 7S.   EN SUITE, TV & BEVERAGES IN ROOMS.   B. & B. AROUND £17.

ROYAL LEAMINGTON SPA

Agape

26 ST MARY RD, ROYAL LEAMINGTON SPA , WARWICKS.
Pleasant guest house on the southern edge of town & within easy walking distance of its
many attractions. Warm, friendly atmosphere. BTA member. Home-made jams for b'fast.
TEL: (01926) 882896 OPEN ALL YEAR. NO SMOKING. V, S.D. B/A   OVER 5S.   EN SUITE, TV & BEVER-
AGES. B. & B. FROM £200.

THE WILLIS, 11 EASTNOR GROVE, ROYAL LEAMINGTON SPA, CV31 1LD
Lovely, spacious Victorian town house with a pretty garden set in a quiet cul-de-sac just
a short walk from the centre of Leamington Spa; English or continental breakfast.
TEL: (01926) 425820 OPEN ALL YEAR. V, S.D. B/A. NO SMOKING. CHILDREN WELCOME. PETS B/A. EN
SUITE IN ONE ROOM. BEVERAGES IN ROOMS. T.V IN SOME BEDROOMS. B. & B. FROM £15.

RUGBY

CARLTON HOTEL, RAILWAY TERR., RUGBY, CV21 3HE
 TEL: (01788) 543076 OPEN ALL YEAR. V STD. CHILDREN. SUITE, TV & BEVERAGES IN ROOMS.

HIGH HOUSE, THE GREEN, BROADWELL, NR RUGBY, CV23 8HD
TEL: (01926) 812687 OPEN ALL YEAR. V STD. CHILDREN WELCOME. BEVERAGES & TV. B. & B. FROM £16.

The School House Guest House

BOURTON ON DUNSMORE, NR RUGBY, CV23 9QY TEL: (01926) 632959
ETB 3 Crown Commended. Beautifully converted village school. Home-cooked food made
from fresh ingredients (including free-range eggs); vegetarians & diabetics welcome.
OPEN Jan. - DeC. V, DIAB B/A. N/S DINING R. CHILDREN B/A. 1 EN SUITE ROOM. BEVERAGES & TV IN ROOMS.
B. & B.AROUND £23.

SHIPSTON-ON-STOUR

LONGDON MANOR, SHIPSTON-ON-STOUR, CV36 4PW TEL: (01608) 82235
14th C. manor house. Home-grown & organic produce used when possible.
OPEN Mar. - Nov. V B/A. CHILDREN. EN SUITE, TV & BEVERAGES. B. & B. AROUND £37.

STRATFORD UPON AVON

Ashburton Guest House

27 EVESHAM PL, STRATFORD UPON AVON. CV37 6HT. TEL: (01789) 292444 FAX: (01789)
415658
Small, friendly guest house in a Victorian terrace 10 mins walk from the town centre. 6-dish
Japanese b'fasts (Japanese rice, miso soup with vegetables, home-made tofu, spinach and
sesame-seed roll, stir-fried Japanese radish and Japanese pickles). Many Japanese dishes
are naturally vegetarian and can be chosen for the evening meal.
OPEN ALL YEAR ex. XmaS.   V, VE STD. ORG, WH WHEN AVAIL. N/S PUBLIC ROOMS. CHILDREN
WELCOME. EN SUITE SHOWERS (BUT NO W.C. EN SUITE). BEVERAGES & TV IN ROOMS. B. & B. AROUND
£20.

BRETT HOUSE, 8 BROAD WALK, TRATFORD, CV37 6NS
TEL: (01789) 266374   OPEN ALL YEAR.   V BFAST STD.   BEVERAGES IN ROOMS.   TV.

Parkfield

3 BROAD WALK, STRATFORD-UPON-AVON, WARWICKS, CV37 6HS   TEL: (01789) 293313

Parkfield is an elegant Victorian house which is quietly situated in the peaceful 'old town' part of Stratford. Bedrooms are all warm, comfortable and centrally heated, and have been equipped with a range of helpful amenities including TV, hot-drink facilities and an easy chair. Your hosts offer a delicious breakfast which includes pancakes and vegetarian sausages in addition to the more traditional English breakfast fare: everything is free-range, home-made and organic wherever possible and unrefined sugar, wholemeal bread and low-fat milk are all available. Travellers by car will be glad to know that they can leave their car safely at Parkfield without having to worry about parking in town: it is just a few minutes' pleasant walk along the river from Parkfield to the Royal Shakespeare Theatre or to the centre of Stratford-upon-Avon.
OPEN ALL YEAR.   V, VE, S.D. STD.   NO SMOKING.   CHILDREN WELCOME.   EN SUITE, TV & BEVERAGES IN ROOMS.   CREDIT CARDS.   B. & B. £17-22.

SALAMANDER GUEST HOUSE, 40 GROVE RD, STRATFORD-UPON-AVON.
TEL/FAX: (01789) 205728 OPEN ALL YEAR.   V, DIAB STD.   CHILDREN WELCOME.   EN SUITE AVAILABLE.   D. £8.

WARWICK

THE CROFT, HASELEY KNOB, WARWICK, CV35 7NL TEL: (10926) 484 447
ETB 3 Crowns Commended. Large family house/smallholding in picturesque village. Delicious food with home-produce: eggs, vegetables, home-made jam and marmalade.
OPEN ALL YEAR.   V, S.D. B/A.   NO SMOKING.   DISABLED ACCESS: 'GROUND FLOOR BEDROOM BUT NOT SUITABLE FOR WHEELCHAIRS'.   CHILDREN WELCOME.   PETS B/A.   SOME EN SUITE ROOMS.   BEVERAGES & TV IN ROOMS.   B. & B. AROUND £18.

Northleigh House

FIVE WAYS RD, HATTON, NR WARWICK, WARWICKSHIRE, CV35 7HZ   TEL: (01926) 484203

ETB 3 Crowns Highly Commended. This small, country house, set in the quiet of rural Warwickshire, is really rather a special place: from its beautiful furnishings (all rooms have been individually designed with colour coordinating linen and upholstery) to its glorious setting amidst private gardens and open fields (several rooms have views), Northleigh House is, as its proprietor endeavours to make it, an exceptionally nice small hotel. Service is an important feature of a stay at Northleigh, where nothing seems to be too much trouble to your hostess (a laundry service, an extra hot water bottle, shoe-cleaning equipment...just ask and it's there). The food is first-rate - breakfasts are freshly prepared to suit individual requirements and evening meals or supper trays are available on request (although guests might want to sample the many fine restaurants in the area).
OPEN ALL YEAR ex. Xmas & Jan.   NO SMOKING.   V, S.D. B/A.   CHILDREN WELCOME.   PETS B/A.   EN SUITE, TV & BEVERAGES IN ROOMS.   CREDIT CARDS.   Singles from £28, Double from' £40.

RESTAURANTS

RUGBY

GOLDEN LION OF EASENHALL, NR RUGBY.
16th C. Free House. Choice of vegetarian meals.
TEL: (01788) 832878   V STD.   CHILDREN WELCOME.   LICENSED.

SUMMERSAULT, 27 HIGH ST, RUGBY, WARWICKS.
Vegetarian restaurant. Fresh cream gateaux a speciality.
TEL: (01788) 543223   V EXC.   CHILDREN WELCOME.

West Midlands

ACCOMMODATION

BIRMINGHAM

ASHDALE HOUSE HOTEL, 39 BROAD RD, ACOCKS GREEN, BIRMINGHAM
Victorian house. Free-range and organic breakfasts.
TEL: (0121) 706 3598 OPEN ALL YEAR. V STD. CHILDREN WELCOME. TV 7 BEVERAGES. B. & B. AROUND £24.

COVENTRY

Westwood Cottage

WESTWOOD HEATH RD, WESTWOOD HEATH, COV., CV4 8GN TEL/FAX: (01203) 471084
One of 4 sandstone cottages built in 1834 and set in rural surroundings; pleasingly
renovated and retaining many period features.
OPEN ALL YEAR ex. Xmas. N/S DINING R, BEDRS & LOUNGE. V, S.D. B/A. DISABLED ACCESS. CHILDREN
WELCOME. SOME EN SUITE ROOMS. BEVERAGES IN RECEPTION. T.V. IN LOUNGE. B. & B. FROM £18.

FILLONGLEY (Nr COVENTRY)

MILL FARMHOUSE, MILL LN, FILLONGLEY, NR COVENTRY, CV7 8EE
Peace and tranquillity in country residence in idyllic countryside. Good home-cooking.
TEL: (01676) 41898 OPEN ALL YEAR. V. S.D. B/A. EN SUITE, TV & BEVERAGES. B. & B. AROUND £23.

SUTTON COLDFIELD

New Hall

WALMLEY ROAD, SUTTON COLDFIELD, B76 8QX   TEL: (0121) 378 2442
The oldest moated manor house in England. First-rate food .
OPEN ALL YEAR. N/S DINING R. V, S.D. B/A. LICENSED. DISABLED ACCESS. CHILDREN: OVER 7S
ONLY. EN SUITE, TV & BEVERAGES IN ROOMS.

Standbridge Hotel

138 BIRMINGHAM ROAD, SUTTON COLDFIELD, W. MIDLANDS, B72 1LY   TEL: (0121) 354 3007
The Standbridge Hotel is a converted family house of great character which stands in
substantial mature gardens just a short distance from the 2,400 acre Sutton Park yet just
one mile from the town centre. The food is excellent: the proprietors received the Heartbeat
Award for their comprehensive selection of healthy food choices, and special diets are
catered for competently and sympathetically: the breakfast menu offers a hearty choice
and each meal is prepared from fresh, wholesome ingredients such as free-range eggs,
Greek yoghurt, Edam cheese, bananas and honey; wholemeal toast, home-made marmalade
and freshly brewed coffee (or tea, including herbal) complete the meal.
OPEN ALL YEAR. N/S DINING R. V, S.D. B/A. LICENSED. OVER 5S. EN SUITE SHOWERS IN MOST ROOMS.
BEVERAGES & T.V. IN ROOMS. ACCESS, VISA. B. & B. FROM £20.

RESTAURANTS

BIRMINGHAM

WILD OATS, 5 RADDLEBARN ROAD, SELLY OAK TEL: (0121) 471 2459
V, VE EXC. OPEN 12 - 2, 6 - 9. NO SMOKING. DISABLED ACCESS. CHILDREN.

COVENTRY

Ryton Organic Gardens and Restaurant

RYTON ON DUNSMORE, COVENTRY, CV8 3LG   TEL: (01203) 303517 FAX: (01203) 639229
There are 10 acres of beautiful gardens at Ryton Organic Gardens and it is a wonderful day
out for the family (there is an excellent children's area). The commitment to organic
growing extends to the restaurant in which almost all of the home-cooked food is organically grown, (much on site), and the menu features at least 6 vegetarian and 1 vegan dish
daily. The shop sells a wide range of organic food, wine, books, gifts and garden products.
OPEN ALL YEAR ex. Xmas. NO SMOKING. V, WH, ORG, VE, S.D. STD. CHILDREN WELCOME. WHEELCHAIR
ACCESS. GUIDE DOGS WELCOME (shade & water provided for others).

Worcestershire

ACCOMMODATION

BEWDLEY

V SHADES OF GREEN VEG. REST. & B. & B., THE GLEBE HOUSE, UPPER
ARLEY, BEWDLEY.
TEL: (012997) 311 OPEN ALL YEAR. V, VE EXC. NO SMOKING. CHILDREN WELCOME.

BROADWAY

Cusacks Glebe

SAINTBURY, NR BROADWAY, WORCESTERSHIRE, WR12 7PX   TEL: (01386) 852210
An ancient 14th C. cruck cottage farmhouse in beautiful gardens and paddocks. Rural area
of outstanding natural beauty. 2 beautiful bedrooms, antique furnishings & four-posters.
OPEN Jan.15 - Dec. 15.   NO SMOKING.   V STD, VE, S.D. B/A.   OVER 10s WELCOME.   EN SUITE, TV & BEVERAGES
IN ROOMS.   B. & B. FROM £24.50.

The Old Rectory

CHURCH ST, WILLERSEY, NR BROADWAY, WORCS., WR12 7PN   TEL: (01386) 853729
Splendid 17th C. rectory, built of mellow Cotswold stone, in lovely garden. Oak beams
and quaint stone-built fireplaces. Breakfast is a generous feast and vegetarian or continen-
tal options are available for meat-free or lighter appetites.
OPEN ALL YEAR.   V b'fasts STD. N/S ex. smoking lounge.   CHILDREN: OVER 8S ONLY. EN SUITE, BEVER-
AGES & SATELLITE T.V. IN ROOMS.   ACCESS, VISA.   B. & B. AROUND £37.

EVESHAM

Evesham Hotel

COOPER'S LANE, OFF WATERSIDE, EVESHAM. TEL: (01386) 765566
Ex-Tudor farmhouse; 2 acre gardens. Fabulous vegetarian options. Indoor-heated pool.
V STD. S.D. B/A.   OPEN ALL YEAR.   LICENSED.   WELL BEHAVED CHILDRENWELCOME.   PETS WELCOME
but not in public rooms.   EN SUITE, BEVERAGES & TV IN ROOMS.   CREDIT CARDS.   B. & B. AROUND £40.

GREAT MALVERN

Holdfast Cottage Hotel

WELLAND, NR MALVERN, WORCS, WR13 6NA   TEL: (01684) 310288
17th C.cottage. Imaginative dishes prepared from fresh, local produce.
OPEN ALL YEAR.   N/S DINING R & BEDRS.   V STD. S.D. B/A. LICENSED.   DISABLED: 'two steps into
building'.   CHILDREN WELCOME. EN SUITE, TV & BEVERAGES IN ROOMS.   B. & B. AROUND £36.

Oakwood

BLACKHEATH WAY, MALVERN, WORCS, WR14 4DR   TEL: (01684) 575508
ETB 3 Crown Highly Commended. Beautiful, detached Victorian residence in 4 acres of
grounds on the S.W. slopes of the Malvern Hills. Cordon Bleu cuisine.
OPEN ALL YEAR. NO SMOKING. V, S.D. B/A. LICENSED. CHILDREN WELCOME. MOST ROOMS EN SUITE.
BEVERAGES & TV IN ROOMS.   B. & B. AROUND £20.

THE RED GATE, 32 AVENUE RD, GREAT MALVERN, WR14 3BJ
Family-run hotel with country home atmosphere. Home-made food & vegetarian options.
 TEL: (01684) 565013   N/S DINING R . V, S.D. B/A.   LICENSED.   OVER 6S.   B. & B. AROUND £25

KIDDERMINSTER

COLLINGDALE HOTEL, 197 COMBERTON RD, KIDDERMINSTER.
Beautifully maintained Georgian buildling. Special diets catered for.
TEL: (01562) 515460 OPEN ALL YEAR. V STD. S.D. B/A. CHILDREN WELCOME. EN SUITE. B. & B. £16 - 26.

MALVERN WELLS

THE COTTAGE IN THE WOOD HOTEL, HOLYWELL RD, MALVERN WELLS
Twice voted the hotel with the best view in England. Good vegetarian options.
TEL: (01684) 573487 OPEN ALL YEAR. N/S DINING R.   V STD. LICENSED.   CHILDREN & PETS WEL-
COME. EN SUITE, BEVERAGES & TV IN ROOMS.   CREDIT CARDS.   B. & B. FROM £48.50.

WORCESTER

UPTON HOUSE, UPTON SNODSBURY, WORCESTER, WR7 4NR
12th C. village manor house. Antiques, log fires, beamed bedrooms. Own eggs & fruit.
TEL: (01905) 381226 OPEN ALL YEAR ex Xmas. V, VE, S.D. B/A. EN SUITE, TV & BEVERAGES. B. & B. FROM £33.

RESTAURANTS

BEWDLEY

V **SHADES OF GREEN VEG. REST. & B. & B., UPPER ARLEY, BEWDLEY.**
For further details, please see under entry in accomodation section.

DROITWICH

HOP POLE INN, FRIAR ST, DROITWICH, WORCS. TEL: (01905) 770155
Queen Anne building. Vegetarian dish of the day available.

THATCH RESTAURANT (Webbs Garden Centre), A38, WYCHBOLD, DROITWICH
Good, wholesome food. Vegetarian dish of the day. Clean food award. Fresh baked bread.

GREAT MALVERN

V **BRIEF ENCOUNTER VEG. RESTAURANT, THE STATION, GREAT MALVERN**
All dishes prepared to order. Special gourmet evenings.

WORCESTER

HODSON'S COFFEE HOUSE, 100 HIGH ST, WORCESTER, WORCS.
Clean Food Award, National Heartbeat Award. Excellent Coffee House and Patisserie,
with lovely *al fresco* dining area. Interesting selection of dishes, including 'platters', which
are exceedingly generous platefuls of hearty fare.
TEL: (01905) 21036 V STD. 50% N/S. LICENSED. DISABLED ACCESS. CHILDREN WELCOME.

East Anglia

Cambridgeshire

ACCOMMODATION

CAMBRIDGE

Arundel House Hotel
53 CHESTERTON RD, CAMBRIDGE, CB4 3AN   TEL: (01223) 367701

The Arundel House Hotel is privately owned
and has been converted from a fine terrace of
Victorian houses - modernisation has, thankfully, impaired neither the interiors nor the
facade. Health is taken very seriously at the
Arundel where, every year since the start of
the scheme, they have won the city's Clean
Kitchen Award and for 7 successive years
have added the Heartbeat award to their list
of accolades. The hotel's reputation for providing some of the finest food in the area at
a reasonable cost is matched by a something-
for-everyone policy in which guests can
choose from an à la carte, table-d'hote, exclusively vegetarian or (for parents) an ex-
tensive children's menu. Bar meals are also available. Additionally, it is just a short walk
across the river bridge to the city centre and all its fascinating historic landmarks.

OPEN ALL YEAR EX. Xmas.   V STD, S.D. B/A.   N/S MOST D.R. & 50% BEDROOMS.   LICENSED.   CHILDREN WELCOME.   EN SUITE MOST ROOMS.   CREDIT CARDS.   BEVERAGE, TV, DD PHONE, RADIO, HAIRDRYER ALL BEDROOMS.   B. & B. FROM £28.50.

BELSAR LODGE, 155 RAMPTON RD, WILLINGHAM, CAMBRIDGE, CB4 5JF
Guest house serving good food: everything home-made including bread & soups.
TEL: (01954) 60359 OPEN ALL YEAR.   V, VE, S.D. B/A.   ORG STD.   WH WHEN AVAIL.   DISABLED ACCESS. CHILDREN WELCOME. PETS B/A.   BEVERAGES & TV IN ROOMS.   B. & B. AROUND £17.

Bon Accord House

20 ST. MARGARET'S SQ, (Off Cherry Hinton Rd), CAMB., CB1 4AP   TEL: (01223) 411188/246568
Situated down a quiet cul-de-sac on a good bus route to Cambridge city centre. Breakfast only, but there is a wide variety of options.
OPEN ALL YEAR ex. Xmas.   NO SMOKING.   V, S.D. B/A.   CHILDREN WELCOME.   1 EN SUITE ROOM. BEVERAGES & TV IN ROOMS.   VISA, MASTERCARD.   B. & B. AROUND £20.

The Willows

102 HIGH STREET, LANDBEACH, CAMBRIDGE, CB4 4DT   TEL: (01223) 860332
The Willows is a beautiful Georgian farmhouse which is pleasantly situated in the small village of Landbeach just off the A10 and just three miles north of the historic city of Cambridge. There are two comfortable guest rooms in which up to six people can be easily accommodated and as your hostess, Mrs Wyatt, welcomes children and can also accommodate some pets by arrangement, The Willows is the ideal family holiday destination. For everyone's added comfort and enjoyment smoking is banned throughout the house.
OPEN ALL YEAR ex Xmas.   NO SMOKING.   V B/A.   PETS B/A.   CHILDREN WELCOME.   1 GROUND FLOOR ROOM.   BEVERAGES.   T.V. IN ROOMS.   B. & B. FROM £15.

ELY

Springfields

ELY ROAD, LITTLE THETFORD, ELY, CB6 3HJ   TEL: (01353) 663637   FAX: (01353) 663130

English Tourist Board De Luxe Award. Springfields is a lovely large home set in an acre of beautiful landscaped gardens and orchard in which guests are invited to wander and sit awhile to enjoy the tranquillity of the setting and (in summer) to smell the roses! The guest accommodation is housed in a separate wing and consists of three double rooms which have each been tastefully furnished and appointed with many delightful touches and everything you could wish to make your stay a happy and memorable one; all rooms have wash hand basins. Breakfast is served in a pleasant dining room in which guests sit around a large table to enjoy together the delicious, freshly prepared food. Springfields is set in a very quiet location yet is only two miles from historic Ely with its famous cathedral, Oliver Cromwell's house (he lived here from 1637 to 1644) and many other buildings of great architectural and historic interest, and of course it is a perfect base from which to explore the changeless beauty of the Fens!
OPEN ALL YEAR, EX. DEC.   V B/A.   NO SMOKING.   EN SUITE ROOMS AVAILABLE.   BEVERAGES & T.V. IN ALL ROOMS.   B. & B. FROM £20.

HUNTINGDON

Mrs Sue Rook

38 HIGH ST, HEMINGFORD GREY, HUNTINGDON   TEL: (01480) 301203
ETB 1 Crown Approved. Quiet, modern detached house with large garden. Good home-cooking is prepared from fresh produce (including free range eggs); organically home-grown fruit & veg.; vegetarians, vegans and diabetics by arrangement.
OPEN Jan - Nov.   NO SMOKING.   V, S.D. B/A.   BYO WINE.   OVER 10S ONLY.   BEVERAGES IN ROOM.   TV LOUNGE.   B. & B. AROUND £18.

PETERBOROUGH

CHESTERTON PRIORY, PRIORY GARDENS, CHESTERTON
Victorian gothic former rectory in 2 acres.
TEL: (01733) 230085 OPEN 2 Jan. to 24 Dec.   N/S DINING R & 3 BEDRS.   S.D. B/A.   LICENSED.   OVER 10S ONLY.   EN SUITE, BEVERAGES & TV IN ROOMS.   B. & B. AROUND £30.

RESTAURANTS

CAMBRIDGE

BROWNS RESTAURANT, 23 TRUMPINGTON STREET, CAMBRIDGE
TEL: (01223) 461655   V STD.   N/S 45% OF RESTAURANT.   LICENSED.   DISABLED ACCESS.   CHILDREN.

Hobbs Pavilion Restaurant

PARK TERRACE, CAMBRIDGE, CB1 1JH   TEL: (01223) 67480
Located in the pavilion of a cricket ground. Excellent vegetarian options since 1978.
SEPARATE ROOM FOR SMOKERS.   3-course meal £7.95 (£12.25 inc. side salad, coffee & .25 L plonk).   OPEN 12 - 2.15,
7 - 9.45.   V, VE, STD.   S.D. B/A.   LICENSED.   CHILDREN.

Kings Pantry

9A KINGS PARADE, CAMBRIDGE, CB2 1SJ   TEL: (01223) 321551
First-rate vegetarian restaurant located in the heart of Cambridge.
V, VE EXC.   NO SMOKING.   LICENSED.   CHILDREN WELCOME.   CREDIT CARDS.

PETERBOROUGH

PETERBOROUGH CATHEDRAL SHOP, 24 MINSTER PRECINCTS
TEL: (01733) 555098   OPEN 10 - 4.   NO SMOKING.   V.   CHILDREN WELCOME (HIGH CHAIR AVAIL.)

PUBS

CAMBRIDGE

The Cambridge Blue

85/87 GWYDIR ST, CAMBRIDGE, CB1 2LG   TEL(01223) 61382
19th C. terrace pub in side street off Mill Road. Real ale (Nethergate).
V STD.   N/S 1 BAR.   WHEELCHAIR ACCESS.   CHILDREN WELCOME in conservatory & garden (model railway in latter).

Essex

ACCOMMODATION

CHELMSFORD

Boswell House Hotel

118 SPRINGFIELD RD, CHELMSFORD, CM2 6LF TEL: (01245) 287587
Beautifully converted 19th C. town house now a charming small hotel; fresh food.
OPEN ALL YEAR ex. Xmas.   V, S.D. B/A.   N/S DINING R, SITTING R & 9 BEDRS.   LICENSED.   DISABLED
ACCESS: GROUND FLOOR BEDROOMS and just one step at the hotel entrance.   CHILDREN WELCOME.   EN
SUITE, BEVERAGES & TV IN ROOMS.   CREDIT CARDS.   B & B AROUND £32.

South Lodge Hotel

196 NEW LONDON RD, CHELMSFORD, CM2 0AR TEL: (01245) 264564 FAX: (01245) 492827
Family-run hotel within easy reach of the town centre and the A12. Vegan family member.
OPEN ALL YEAR.   N/S PART DINING R. & SOME BEDR.   V, VE STD.   LICENSED.   CHILDREN WELCOME.   EN SUITE,
TV & BEVERAGES IN ROOMS.   CREDIT CARDS.   B. & B. FROM £27.50.

COLCHESTER

Gill Nicholson

14 ROMAN ROAD, COLCHESTER, ESSEX, CO1 1UR   TEL: (01206) 577905
Spacious Victorian town house in a quiet square near the centre of Colchester. The full,
home-cooked English breakfast features a number of home-made items including the bread,
jam and lemon curd, and some healthy, vegetarian and low-cholesterol options, such as
muesli, prunes and low-fat yoghurt.

OPEN ALL YEAR ex. Xmas week.   NO SMOKING.   V, S.D. STD.   CHILDREN B/A.   1 ROOM EN SUITE.
BEVERAGES & TV IN ROOMS.   B & B AROUND £17.

FORDHAM

KINGS VINEYARD, FOSSETTS LN, FORDHAM, NR COLCHESTER, C06 3NY
Large detached house, on southfacing slope amongst gentle rolling countryside.
TEL: (01206) 240377 OPEN ALL YEAR.   V STD.   NO SMOKING. CHILDREN WELCOME. PRIVATE BATH-
ROOM AVAILABLE. BEVERAGES & T.V.   AMEX. B. & B. AROUND £18.

SOUTHEND-ON-SEA

Strand Guest House

165 EASTERN ESPLANADE, SOUTHEND-ON-SEA, ESSEX, SS1 2YB   TEL: (01702) 586611
Small, family-run guest house on the Thorpe Bay sea front. Healthy breakfast options.
OPEN Apr-Nov.   V B/A. N/S DINING R & 1 BEDR.   V B/A.   CHILDREN WELCOME. MOST ROOMS EN SUITE.
TV & BEVERAGES IN ROOMS.   B. & B. FROM £16.

THAXTED

Piggot's Mill

WATLING LANE, THAXTED, ESSEX, CM6 2QY   TEL: (01371) 830379
A range of traditional Essex barns, retaining many original features, now a farmhouse
standing in mediaeval village of Thaxted; lovely garden; very good breakfast.
OPEN ALL YEAR.   N/S DINING R & BEDR.   V, S.D. B/A.   OVER 12S ONLY. EN SUITE, BEVERAGES & TV IN
ROOMS.   B. & B. FROM £19.50.

RESTAURANTS

CASTLE HEDINGHAM

RUMBLES CASTLE RESTAURANT, ST JAMES ST, CASTLE HEDINGHAM
TEL: (01787) 61490   OPEN ALL YEAR.   V STD.   N/S DINING R, ALLOWED IN COFFEE LOUNGE & BAR AREA.
LICENSED.   DISABLED ACCESS.   CHILDREN WELCOME.

CHELMSFORD

Scott's

THE STREET, HATFIELD PEVEREL, CHELMSFORD, ESSEX, CM3 2DR   TEL: (01245) 380161
OPEN Mon.-Sat., 7 until late by booking.   NO SMOKING.   V.   LICENSED.   DISABLED ACCESS.

Farmhouse Feast

THE STREET, ROXWELL, CHELMSFORD, ESSEX, CM1 4PB   TEL & FAX: (01245) 248 583
Charming restaurant housed in a late 15th C. building. First-rate home-cooked food
prepared from fresh ingredientsx. Excellent vegetarian options; indeed Farmhouse Feast
has hosted some exclusively vegetarian events.
OPEN ALL YEAR, including Xmas Day. GOURMET EVENINGS LAST FRI. IN MONTH.   75% N/S (ON SEPARATE
FLOOR).   ORG, WH, V, VE S.D. B/A. LICENSED.   DISABLED ACCESS.   CHILDREN WELCOME.

DUNMOW

RUMBLES COTTAGE RESTAURANT, BRAINTREE RD, FELSTED, DUNMOW
TEL: (01371) 820996   OPEN ALL YEAR.   GUINEA PIG MENU £12.50, À LA CARTE £16.50-£19.50.   SEPARATE
DINING RS FOR NON-SMOKERS B/A. V STD. LICENSED. DISABLED ACCESS. CHILDREN WELCOME.

WALTHAM ABBEY

PAPGINO'S, 24A SUN ST, WALTHAM ABBEY, ESSEX. TEL: (01992) 714305
OPEN 7 DAYS. V STD. LICENSED.

PUBS & WINE BARS

CHELMSFORD

SEABRIGHTS BARN, GALLEYWOOD RD, GT BADDOW, NR CHELMSFORD
TEL: (01245) 478033 OPEN MON. TO SAT. 12 - 2, 6 - 11, SUN. 12 - 10. N/S CONSERVATORY FAMILY ROOM. V STD.
S.D. B/A.   WHEELCHAIR ACCESS. GOOD FACILITIES FOR CHILDREN. ACCESS, VISA.

Norfolk

ACCOMMODATION

BLAKENEY

Flintstones Guest House

WIVETON, BLAKENEY, NORFOLK, NR25 7TL   TEL: (01263) 740337

Flintstones Guest House is a charming single storey residence set in picturesque surroundings near to the village green in the quiet village of Wiveton one mile from the sea at Cley and Blakeney. It has been beautifully furnished throughout - the bedrooms have each been very comfortably appointed - and a friendly and relaxed atmosphere prevails. Food is of the good old-fashioned British variety and is served in good old-fashioned quantities, too: a typical evening meal would feature fresh grapefruit followed by Roast Chicken with all the trimmings and a home-made dessert such as Sherry Trifle; tea and coffee would complete the meal. The area is perfect for walkers and birdwatchers: the heathland at Salthouse and Kelling have stunning scenery, and the North Norfolk Coastal Path passes nearby.

OPEN ALL YEAR.   NO SMOKING.   V, S.D. B/A.   LICENSED.   CHILDREN WELCOME.   PETS B/A.   EN SUITE, BEVERAGES & T.V. IN ROOMS.   B. & B. FROM £16.

CASTLE ACRE

THE OLD RED LION, BAILEY STREET, CASTLE ACRE, PE32 2AG

Brick & flintstone building with private rooms or dormitories. Wholefood & vegetarian meals or self-catering. Courses; a retreat for artists, writers or 'seekers after solace.'

TEL: (01760) 755557   OPEN ALL YEAR.   NO SMOKING.   V, DIAB, GLUTEN-FREE, YEAST-FREE, DAIRY-FREE, S.D. B/A.   LICENSED (RESTAURANT) & BYO WINE.   CHILDREN WELCOME.   PETS B/A.

DEREHAM

Travellers Cottage

HORNINGTOFT, DEREHAM, NORFOLK. TEL: (01328) 700205

Delicious vegetarian meals are served in the cottage style kitchen with its wood-burning stove; everything is home-made including the bread, rolls & yoghurt; home-grown fruit & vegetables are served in season (including fresh strawberries at breakfast); substantial snack suppers are available or there are good meat-free meals to be had at nearby restaurants; tea, coffee and home-made cakes and biscuits are also available.

OPEN April - Oct.   VSTD. S.D. B/A.   WH STD. ORG WHEN AVAIL.   CHILDREN.   B. & B. FROM £14. D. £5.

DISS

'Strenneth'

OLD AIRFIELD RD, FERSFIELD, DISS, IP22 2BP TEL: (0379) 688182   FAX: (0379) 688260

This family-run 17th C. former farmhouse stands in a lovely lawned garden close to the market town of Diss; it has been renovated to a very high standard indeed while retaining the period features of the building (oak beams, casement windows, open fires, window seats) and the bed-rooms are decorated and furnished with taste and style and have en suite facilities and colour TVs (most of them are on the ground floor); one of the Executive rooms has a magnificent four poster bed and 'Pharaoh' bath. There is an especially attractive lounge which has been furnished with period furniture to harmonise with the heavily beamed ceilings and walls. The food is of a very high standard: special diets can be catered for and local produce is used extensively by the chef-owner. Diss is a charming town and is central to most of East Anglia's tourist attractions.

OPEN ALL YEAR.   N/S PART OF DINING R & 1 LOUNGE.   V, S.D. (NOT VE) B/A.   LICENSED.   PETS WELCOME. EN SUITE, BEVERAGES & TV IN ROOMS.   CREDIT CARDS.   B. & B. FROM £22. D. £13.

DOWNHAM MARKET

THE DIAL HOUSE, RAILWAY RD, DOWNHAM MARKET, PE38 9EB
Large, local 'Carr Stone' Georgian House; lots of health foods at breakfast.
TEL: (01366) 388358 OPEN ALL YEAR. V, VE, COEL., LOW-FAT, LOW-SUGAR, DIAB, S.D. B/A. N/S BEDRS
& MOST PUBLIC AREAS. CHILDREN WELCOME. EN SUITE. BEVERAGES & T.V.

FAKENHAM

MANOR FARMHOUSE, STIBBARD RD, FULMODESTONE, NR FAKENHAM,
ETB 1 Crown Commended. Lovely white-painted Georgian farmhouse; lots of home-pre-
pared food (including icecream) from fresh or home-produce, including free-range eggs.
TEL: (0132 878) 353 OPEN ALL YEAR. NO SMOKING. V, S.D. B/A. ACCESS, VISA. B. & B. AROUND £20.

FELMINGHAM

FELMINGHAM HALL COUNTRY HOUSE HOTEL, FELMINGHAM, NR28 OLP
16th C. mansion which has been sumptuously furnished and appointed; 17th C. candlelit
dining room; French & British cuisine prepared from fresh, often home-grown, produce.
TEL: (01692) 69631 OPEN ALL YEAR. N/S DINING R & BEDRS. LICENSED. CHILDREN: OVER 12S ONLY.
EN SUITE, BEVERAGES & T.V. IN ROOMS. B. & B. AROUND £40

HOLT

THE BLAKENEY HOTEL, BLAKENEY, NR HOLT, NORFOLK, NR25 7NE
Hotel overlooking the harbour of Blakeney. All food home-cooked from fresh ingredients.
Heated indoor pool, snooker, games room, spa bath, sauna, mini gym and a hair salon.
TEL: (01263) 740797 OPEN ALL YEAR. V STD. VE, DIAB, S.D. B/A. LICENSED. DISABLED ACCESS.
CHILDREN WELCOME. EN SUITE, TV & BEVERAGES IN ROOMS.

KINGS LYNN

CORFIELD HOUSE, SPORLE, NR SWAFFHAM, KINGS LYNN, PE32 2EA
Lovely period detached house which has been beautifully furnished and maintained.
TEL: (01760) 23636 OPEN Easter - Dec. NO SMOKING. V, DIAB B/A. LICENSED. SOME DISABLED ACCESS.
CHILDREN WELCOME. PETS B/A. EN SUITE & T.V. IN ROOMS. CREDIT CARDS. B. & B. AROUND £20.

THE TUDOR ROSE, ST NICHOLAS ST, KINGS LYNN, NORFOLK, PE30 1LR
15th C. beamed inn; food prepared from fresh local produce; very good vegetarian options.
TEL: (01553) 762824 OPEN ALL YEAR. N/S DINING R. V STD, S.D. B/A. LICENSED. CHILDREN WEL-
COME. PETS B/A. EN SUITE, BEVERAGES, T.V. IN ROOMS. CREDIT CARDS. B. & B. AROUND £40.

NEATISHEAD

Regency Guest House
NEATISHEAD, NR NORWICH, NR12 8AD TEL: (01692) 630233
Lovely 18th C. house in the unspoilt village of Neatishead on the Norfolk Broads;
beautifully furnished rooms (all decorated with Laura Ashley fabrics & wallcoverings).
Exceptionally generous breakfasts; good vegetarian options.
OPEN ALL YEAR. N/S DINING R & ALL PUBLIC AREAS. V, S.D. B/A. CHILDREN WELCOME. PETS B/A. SOME
ROOMS EN SUITE. BEVERAGES & T.V. IN ROOMS. B. & B. FROM £18.

NORWICH

The Almond Tree Hotel and Restaurant
441 DEREHAM RD, COSTESSEY, NORWICH, NR5 OSG TEL: (01603) 748798/749114
Very comfortably appointed small hotel on the main A47 Dereham Road; excellent meals
prepared from fresh, local produce.
OPEN ALL YEAR. N/S DINING R. V, DIAB, S.D. B/A. LICENSED. EN SUITE, TV & BEVERAGES. B. & B. AROUND
£45.

Grey Gables Country House Hotel and Restaurant
NORWICH RD, CAWSTON, NORWICH, NR10 4EY TEL: (01603) 871259
Formerly Brandiston Rectory, this beautiful house offers fine food prepared from fresh
ingredients and served by candlelight. Wine list includes some 200 items.
OPEN ALL YEAR. N/S DINING R. V CHOICE STD. S.D. B/A. LICENSED. SOME DISABLED ACCESS.
OVER 5S ONLY. MOST ROOMS EN SUITE. BEVERAGES & T.V. IN ROOMS. B. & B. AROUND £27.

Welbeck House

BROOKE, NORWICH, NORFOLK, NR15 1AT   TEL: (01508) 550292

Quiet Georgian farmhouse 7m S. of Norwich offering comfortable B. & B.for non-smokers.
OPEN ALL YEAR.   NO SMOKING.   V, S.D. B/A.   OVER 12S & PETS.   BEVERAGES IN ROOMS.   B. &B. £16 - 20.

SLOLEY

Cubitt Cottage

LOW ST, SLOLEY, NR NORWICH, NR12 8HD   TEL: (01692) 538295

Cubitt Cottage is a delightful little 18th C. building which stands in an acre of pretty gardens in which (Mrs Foulkes tells me) there are nearly 100 varieties of old-fashioned rose; the summer scent is intoxicating and a terrace leads out from the oak-beamed dining room where (weather permitting) breakfast is served to guests. As well as being a rose-grower, Mrs Foulkes also cultivates (organically) a wide variety of vegetables and this produce is used in the preparation of her excellent evening meals, in which a typical menu would feature Cashew and Cream Cheese Pâté, Vegetable Croustade and home-made Apricot Icecream.
OPEN ALL YEAR.   NO SMOKING.   V, VE, DIAB, GLUTEN-FREE S.D. ON REQUEST.   CHILDREN WELCOME.
BEVERAGES IN ROOMS.   T.V. IN LOUNGE.   B. & B. AROUND £21.

SNETTISHAM

ROSE AND CROWN INN, OLD CHURCH RD, SNETTISHAM, NORFOLK.

14th C. free house offering real ales and home-cooked fare.
TEL; (01485) 451382 OPEN ALL YEAR.   V STD.   CHILDREN.   EN SUITE, TV & BEVERAGES.   B. & B. FROM £16.

THETFORD

IVY COTTAGES, BLACKMOOR ROW, SHIPDHAM, THETFORD, IP25 7PU

2 beautiful 16th C. Norfolk cottages in an acre of pretty gardens. One cottage self-catering. Excellent b'fast of free-range eggs. Fresh organic vegetables may be delivered.
TEL: (01362) 820665 OPEN ALL YEAR.   V, S.D. B/A.   CHILDREN WELCOME.   PETS B/A.   BEVERAGES IN ROOMS.
T.V. IN SOME ROOMS & LOUNGE.   B. & B. AROUND £16.

WALTON HIGHWAY

Stratton Farm

WEST DROVE NORTH, WALTON HIGHWAY, WEST NORFOLK, PE14 7DP   TEL: (01945) 880162

Ranch-style bungalow set amidst 22 acres of grassland which supports a prize-winning herd of Short-horn cattle. Breakfast features free-range eggs, home-made marmalade, and goat's milk if required. Use of the heated swimming pool and fitness gym.
OPEN ALL YEAR.   V, DIAB B/A.   NO SMOKING.   DISABLED ACCESS.   OVER 5S ONLY.   EN SUITE, TV &
BEVERAGES IN ROOMS.   B. & B. AROUND £20.

WENDLING

Greenbanks Country Hotel & Restaurant

SWAFFHAM RD, WENDLING, NORFOLK, NR19 2AR TEL: (01362) 687742

ETB 3 Crowns., Highly Commended. Greenbanks is a charming 18th C. family-run hotel which stands amidst 9 acres of lakes and meadows in the heart of Norfolk's delightful countryside. It has been sympathetically restored and retains its original character in the elegant dining room and en suite bedrooms.All the food is home-prepared from fresh local produce wherever possible, and most recipes, including many vegetarian specialities, are created by the Chef proprietor. You are just 5 miles from the quaint Market towns of Dereham and Swaffham, and just 20 mins drive from Norwich. Golf, fishing and walking are all available in the area.
OPEN ALL YEAR.   V, VE, S.D., WH ORG STD.   N/S DINING R.   CHILDREN WELCOME.   PETS B/A.   LICENSED.
EN SUITE, TV & BEVERAGES IN ROOMS.   B. & B. FROM £21.

WORSTEAD

Geoffrey the Dyer House

CHURCH PLAIN, WORSTEAD, NORTH WALSHAM, NR28 9AL   TEL: (01692) 536562

17th C. listed building of unique character. Oak beams and inglenook fireplace.
OPEN ALL YEAR.   NO SMOKING.   V, S.D. ON REQUEST.   CHILDREN WELCOME.   PETS B/A.   EN SUITE,
BEVERAGES & TV IN ROOMS.   B. & B. AROUND £19.

RESTAURANTS

DISS

THE WAFFLE HOUSE, MARKET PLACE, DISS
Family restaurant offering good food at reasonable prices. Menu includes dishes prepared from organic meat and produce, as well as a choice of vegetarian and vegan dishes; delicious home-made cakes and scones are baked on the premises daily.
TEL; (01379) 650709　70% N/S (separate area).　V STD.　WHEELCHAIR ACCESS.　PARTY BOOKINGS.

GREAT YARMOUTH

LANES BISTRO, NO. 3, ROW 75, HOWARD ST SOUTH, GT YARMOUTH
TEL: (01493) 330622　NO SMOKING.　V STD.

NORWICH

THE ASSEMBLY HOUSE, 12 THEATRE ST, NORWICH, NR2 1RQ
TEL: (01603) 626402　NO SMOKING.　V STD.　LICENSED.　DISABLED ACCESS.　CHILDREN WELCOME.

BAGLEY'S BARN, 3 BAGLEY'S COURT, POTTERGATE, NORWICH.
Good restaurant offering excellent meat-free fare.
TEL: (01603) 626763　V STD.

BEDFORD'S, NO 1 OLD POST OFFICE YARD, BEDFORD ST, NORWICH.
Bedford's Brasserie offers a range of tasty vegetarian and vegan dishes.
TEL: (01603) 666869　V, VE STD.　LICENSED.

HECTOR'S HOUSE, 18 BEDFORD ST, NORWICH.　TEL: (01603) 622836
Good choice of food ranging from snacks to full meals.　Excellent vegetarian options.

THE LARDER, 19 BEDFORD ST, NORWICH.　TEL: (01603) 622641
V STD.　NO SMOKING.　CHILDREN WELCOME.

LLOYD'S OF LONDON ST RESTAURANT, 66 LONDON ST, NORWICH
TEL: (01603) 624978　50% N/S　V STD.　CHILDREN WELCOME, 'BUT NOT THE VERY YOUNG'.

Pizza One Pancakes Too!

24 TOMBLAND, NORWICH, NORFOLK, NR3 1RF　　TEL; (01603) 621583
Exceptionally popular pizza restaurant. Good vegetarian options.
OPEN 12 - 11.　N/S 60% RESTAURANT.　L. AROUND £5.85.　V STD.　LICENSED.
DISABLED ACCESS.　CHILDREN WELCOME.　CREDIT CARDS.

LA TIENDA, 10 ST GREGORY'S ALLEY, NORWICH, NR2 1ER
TEL: (01603) 629122　NO SMOKING.　V, VE, DIAB & GLUTEN-FREE AVAIL.　LICENSED.　CHILDREN.

The Treehouse Restaurant

14 DOVE ST, NORWICH, NORFOLK　TEL: (01603) 763258
The Treehouse Restaurant is situated above Rainbow Wholefoods in the centre of Norwich. A co-operatively owned establishment, it is renowned for its excellent vegetarian cooking. Vegan, gluten-free and sugar-free meals are always available, as are organic wines and beverages. Hours sometimes vary so please phone ahead.
48 SEATS.　OPEN 10 a.m. - 5 p.m. plus some evenings.　NO SMOKING.　L. under £5, D. £5 - £10.　V, VE, SUGAR-FREE AND GLUTEN-FREE STD.　CHILDREN WELCOME (HIGH CHAIRS AVAILABLE).

THE WAFFLE HOUSE, 39 ST GILES ST, NORWICH, NR2 1JN
Half the toppings are vegetarian; organic vegetables and free-range eggs have been used.
TEL: (01603) 612790　V STD.　N/S FIRST FLOOR & 60% DOWNSTAIRS.

WELLS-NEXT-THE-SEA

THE MOORINGS RESTAURANT, 6 FREEMAN ST, WELLS-NEXT-THE-SEA,
The Moorings Restaurant is in a charming old building a short walk from the beach at Wells-next-the-Sea. Good vegetarian options.
TEL: (01328) 710949　NO SMOKING　V STD.　LICENSED.　DISABLED ACCESS.　CHILDREN

Suffolk

ACCOMMODATION

ALDEBURGH

Uplands Hotel

VICTORIA RD, ALDEBURGH, SUFFOLK, 1P15 5DX   TEL: (01728) 452420 FAX: (01728) 454872

The Uplands Hotel is a family-run hotel and was formerly the home of Elizabeth Garrett Anderson, the first woman doctor and lady mayor of Aldeburgh. The hotel consists of 20 bedrooms, 12 in the main building and 8 in ground-floor rooms overlooking the gardens. The gardens recently won an Ashley Courtenay award and are filled with trees, shrubs, a herb garden, a rockery and pond area, and a 300 year old mulberry tree - all lovingly tended by the proprietors themselves. Breakfast and dinner are served in the restaurant overlooking the garden; the menu changes daily and all food is freshly prepared and cooked using many local specialities. Vegetarian and specail diets are catered for and special requests satisfied wherever possibe; the hotel is licensed and drinks may be enjoyed in the bar or by the log fire in one of the lounges.

OPEN ALL YEAR ex Xmas & New year.   V STD, S.D. B/A.   N/S DINING R & BEDRS.   LICENSED.   EN SUITE, TV & BEVERAGES I N ROOMS.   CREDIT CARDS.   B. & B. AROUND £30.

BURY ST EDMUNDS

CONEY WESTON HALL, CONEY WESTON, NR BURY ST EDMUNDS
Family owned & run country house. Good vegetarian food.
TEL: (0135921) 441 OPEN Feb. to Dec. V STD. S.D. B/A. N/S DINING R & BEDRS. LICENSED.   CHILDREN WELCOME. EN SUITE. BEVERAGES ON REQUEST. T.V. LOUNGE.   B. & B. AROUND £35.

HAMILTON HOUSE, 4 NELSON RD, BURY ST EDMUNDS, IP33 3AG
Elegant Edwardian villa situated in a quiet cul de sac offering accommodation of a very high standard. Home-made bread at breakfast. Italian, French and Spanish spoken.
TEL: (01284) 702201 OPEN ALL YEAR. NO SMOKING. V, S.D. B/A.   CHILDREN WELCOME.   2 EN SUITE ROOMS. BEVERAGES & TV IN ROOMS.   CREDIT CARDS.   B. & B. AROUND £20.

CAVENDISH

WESTERN HOUSE, HIGH ST, CAVENDISH, SUFFOLK, CO10 3AR
16th C. house in rambling gardens. Vegetarian owners.
TEL: (01787) 280550 OPEN ALL YEAR.   V STD. S.D. B/A. CHILDREN. BEVERAGES.   B & B AROUND £17.

FRAMLINGHAM

Shimmens Pightle

DENNINGTON RD, FRAMLINGHAM, SUFFOLK, IP13 9JT   TEL: (01728) 724036
E.T.B Listed Commended. B. & B. set in an acre of landscaped garden. Ground floor rooms with wash basins. Home-made preserves. Convenient for countryside & coast.
OPEN ALL YEAR ex. Xmas Day.   V, S.D. B/A.   NO SMOKING.   DISABLED ACCESS.   OVER 5s ONLY.
BEVERAGES.   T.V. LOUNGE.   B. & B. FROM £16.50.

HADLEIGH

Ash Street Farm

ASH STREET, SEMER, NR HADLEIGH, IP7 6QZ TEL: (01449) 741493
Fine early 15th C. farmhouse stands in a Domesday-recorded hamlet in pretty countryside in the Brett Valley. All food home-prepared from fresh produce including the home-made preserves and wholemeal bread; eggs are fresh from the farm hens.
OPEN ALL YEAR. N/S DINING R & BEDRS.   V, S.D. B/A. CHILDREN WELCOME. PETS B/A. 1 EN SUITE IN ROOM. BEVERAGES IN ROOMS. T.V. LOUNGE.   B. & B. FROM £14. D. £8.50.

HALESWORTH

Broad Oak Farm

BRAMFIELD, NR HALESWORTH, SUFFOLK.   TEL: (01986) 784232
Lovely farmhouse offering bed and breakfast, near the Heritage Coast. 8m. Southwold.
OPEN ALL YEAR.   N/S DINING R.   V S.D. B/A.   CHILDREN WELCOME.   PETS B/A. 1 ROOM EN SUITE.   BEVER-
AGES.   T.V.   B. & B. FROM £14.

IPSWICH

HILL FARM HOUSE, BURY RD, HITCHAM, IPSWICH. IP7 7PT
18th C. farmhouse and adjoining 15th C. cottage set in large grounds overlooking the gently
rolling countryside of South Suffolk.
TEL: (01449) 740651 OPEN Mar. - end Oct.   V, S.D. B/A.   CHILDREN WELCOME.   PETS B/A.   EN SUITE, TV &
BEVERAGES IN ROOMS.   B. & B. AROUND £16. D. £11.

Pipps Ford

NORWICH RD, NEEDHAM MARKET, IPSWICH, SUFFOLK, H IP6 8LJ   TEL: (01449) 760208   FAX:
(01449) 760561

Pipps Ford is a beautiful, half-timbered 16th C.
farmhouse which was built on the site of a Stone-
age battleground on a beautiful stretch of the
River Gipping amidst several acres of rambling
garden surrounded by farmland. Peace and rest
are the key ingredients at Pipps Ford - together
with the exceptionally nourishing food: only organic and wholefood ingredients are used in
cooking - including the herbs - and the extensive
breakfast menu includes waffles, cinnamon toast, crumpets and croissants as well as goose
egg omelettes, additive-free bacon and sausages ... the list is apparently endless; evening
meals (available by arrangement) are similarly imaginative, and vegetarians can be accommodated by arrangement. Bedrooms have been decorated with style and flair (there is a
4-poster, a French Provincial and a Victorian brass bed), and there is also a cottage in the
grounds which has been converted to accommodate four further guest rooms.
OPEN mid-Jan - mid Dec.   V, S.D. B/A.   N/S DINING R & BEDRS. LICENSED.   DISABLED ACCESS. OVER 5s ONLY.
EN SUITE & BEVERAGES IN ROOMS.   T.V. IN LOUNGE.   B. & B. FROM £25.

REDHOUSE, LEVINGTON, IPSWICH, OP10 OLZ TEL: (01473) 659670
Early Victorian farmhouse; 3 acres gardens, fields and trees. Views over river estuaries.
OPEN Mar. - Nov.   V B/A.   CHILDREN.   BEVERAGES IN ROOMS.   B. & B. AROUND £16.

WOODBRIDGE

Church Cottage

SAXTEAD, SUFFOLK. TEL: (01728) 724067
17th century family cottage with low ceilings. Half an hour to coast. Organic garden.
OPEN Easter - Nov.   V, VE EXC. S.D. B/A.   NON SMOKING HOUSE in practice though not banned.   CHILDREN
WELCOME.   PETS B/A.   BEVERAGES.   T.V. IN FAMILY SITTING ROOM.   B. & B. AROUND £15.

Old School

SAXTEAD, WOODBRIDGE, SUFFOLK, IP13 9QP TEL: (01728) 723887
Pleasantly renovated, but not over-heated or over-fussy, school house offering excellent
vegetarian & vegan cuisine prepared from home-grown and wholefood ingredients.
OPEN ALL YEAR.   V EXC. VE STD. NO SMOKING. S.D. B/A.   CHILDREN WELCOME.   PETS B/A. 2 EN
SUITE ROOMS. BEVERAGES.   B. & B. AROUND £12.

RESTAURANTS

BURY ST EDMUNDS

BEAUMONT'S, BRENTGOVEL ST, BURY ST EDMUNDS.   TEL: (01284) 706677
Vegetarian restaurant upstairs.

THE SANCTUARY, HATTER ST, BURY ST EDMUNDS. TEL: (01284) 755875
Varied menu with a vegetarian choice.

HADLEIGH

THE SPINNING WHEEL, 117/119 HIGH ST, HADLEIGH, IP7 5EJ
TEL: (01473) 822175   V, S.D. STD.   OPEN 12 - 2, 7 - 11. N/S 50% OF RESTAURANT. LICENSED. CHILDREN.

IPSWICH

BROADWALK CAFÉ BAR, 9 BUTTER MARKET, IPSWICH. TEL: (01473) 219376
Imaginative international menu. Plenty of vegetarian dishes available.

CAFÉ MARNO, 14 ST NICHOLAS ST, IPSWICH, SUFFOLK.
Freshly cooked vegetarian food. One vegan option daily.
TEL: (01473) 253106   V, VE STD.

ORWELL HOUSE, ORWELL PLACE, IPSWICH.
Excellent restaurant. Vegetarian menu available.
TEL: (01473) 230254 V STD. LICENSED.

LOWESTOFT

HAMPERS SANDWICH BAR & BUTTERY, 11A GROVE RD, LOWESTOFT, NR32 1EB
TEL: (01502) 500316   OPEN 10 - 4.   V STD. NO SMOKING. CHILDREN WELCOME.

East Midlands

Derbyshire

ACCOMMODATION

ALKMONTON

DAIRY HOUSE FARM, ALKMONTON, LONGFORD, DERBY, DE6 3DG
ETB 3 Crowns Commended. Picturesque farmhouse on working dairy farm in Peak District. Home-produced food.
TEL: (01335) 330359 OPEN ALL YEAR. NO SMOKING. V, S.D. B/A. LICENSED.   OVER 5S WELCOME. 3 EN SUITE ROOMS. BEVERAGES.   T.V. LOUNGE. B. & B. FROM £14.50.

ASHBOURNE

THE MANSE VEGETARIAN & VEGAN GUEST HOUSE, WETTON, ASHBOURNE, DE6 2AF
Small guest house with lovely views.
TEL: (0133527) 259 OPEN ALL YEAR ex. Xmas & New Year. V EXC. MAINLY VE. NO SMOKING. CHILDREN WELCOME. PETS B/A. 1 EN SUITE ROOM. BEVERAGES.   T.V. IN SITTING ROOM. B. & B. AROUND £15

THE OLD CHAPEL, WETTON, NR ASHBOURNE, DE6 2AE TEL: (0133527) 378
Converted chapel now a luxurious country house offering a very high standard of accommodation. The proprietor is a 'dedicated Gourmet Cook'.
OPEN Feb. - Nov.   V, S.D. B/A. N/S DINING R & BEDRS.   CHILDREN: OVER 7S ONLY.   PETS B/A.   EN SUITE & BEVERAGES IN ROOMS. T.V.   B. & B.AROUND £30.

BASLOW

CAVENDISH HOTEL, BASLOW, DERBYSHIRE, DE4 1SP   TEL: (01246) 582311
Splendid 18th C. building on Chatsworth Estate.
OPEN ALL YEAR.   V STD. S.D. B/A.   N/S DINING R.   LICENSED. CHILDREN WELCOME. EN SUITE, BEVERAGES & T.V. IN ROOMS.   CREDIT CARDS.   B. & B. AROUND £42.

BELPER

Dannah Farm Country Guest House

BOWMANS LANE, SHOTTLE, NR BELPER, DE56 2DR TEL: (01773) 550273 / 550630 FAX: (01773) 550590

ETB 3 Crown Highly Commended, AA QQQQQ Premier Selected, Finalists '92 Alternative Farmer Of The Year. Dannah Farm is an attractive Georgian building serving a 128 acre mixed farm on the beautiful Chatsworth Estate. The accommodation is very comfortable, and there is a superb 4-poster suite available. Joan Slack is very interested in (and knowledgeable about) healthy food and uses wholefood ingredients where possible in cooking. Muesli, yoghurt and fruit are always available at breakfast and the imaginative evening menu might feature Spinach and Cottage Cheese Filo, followed by Earl Grey Sorbet, Seafood Pie and a delicious dessert such as Stuffed Apple Pancakes with Cream. Joan recently opened her highly acclaimed non-residential restaurant, The Mixing Place, on the Dannah Farm site, offering the same superlative food; the excellence of her achievements have been recognised by the English Tourist Board (Dannah Farm is 3 Crown Highly Commended) and she has won the National Award for Farm Catering. Lots to see and do in the area which is, incidentally, excellent for walking.

OPEN ALL YEAR ex. Xmas. N/S BEDRS & DINING R. V STD. S.D. B/A. LICENSED. CHILDREN WELCOME. EN SUITE, BEVERAGES & T.V. CREDIT CARDS. B. & B. FROM £26, D. £15.

BUXTON

ALPINE GUEST HOUSE, HARDWICK MOUNT, BUXTON, SK17 6PS

Comfortable, friendly guest house near to the station and all amenities; good, wholesome food. Your landlady is a vegetarian but you can choose either traditional or vegetarian fare.
TEL: (01298) 26155 OPEN ALL YEAR. NO SMOKING. V STD. S.D. B/A. CHILDREN WELCOME. BEVERAGES IN ROOMS & ON LANDING. T.V. IN ROOMS. B. & B. AROUND £16.

BIGGIN HALL, BIGGIN-BY-HARTINGTON, BUXTON, SK17 0DH

Beautiful 17th C. Grade III listed, stone-built house in 8 acres of spacious grounds in the National Park; self-catering apartments also available; fresh, local produce used in cooking; b'fast features home-made brioches, croissants, jams and marmalades.
TEL: (01298) 84451 OPEN ALL YEAR. V, S.D. B/A. N/S DINING R & SITTING R. LICENSED. CHILDREN welcome for b. & b. but over 12s only for dinner. PETS B/A. EN SUITE, BEVERAGES & T.V.

Coningsby Guest House

6 MACCLESFIELD ROAD, BUXTON, DERBYSHIRE, SK17 9AH   TEL: (01298) 26735
Elegant Victorian house. Meals prepared from *fresh* produce wherever possible.
OPEN ALL YEAR ex. Xmas. NO SMOKING. V, S.D. B/A. EN SUITE. BEVERAGES & TV. B. & B. AROUND £22.

POPPIES, BANK SQUARE, TIDESWELL, BUXTON, DERBYSHIRE, SK17 8LA

3 letting rooms & restaurant with excellent choice of home-cooked vegetarian dishes.
TEL: (01298) 871083 OPEN ALL YEAR. V, VE STD. COEL. & S.D. B/A. N/S PART OF DINING R. WHEELCHAIR ACCESS TO RESTAURANT. CHILDREN WELCOME. PETS B/A. 1 EN SUITE ROOM. TV & BEVERAGES IN ROOMS. B. & B. FROM £13.80 - 17.50.

Westminster Hotel

21 BROAD WALK, BUXTON, DERBYSHIRE, SK17 6JR   TEL: (01298) 23929
Small, friendly family hotel in an enviable position overlooking the Pavilion Gardens. The food is good, traditional home-cooking using fresh, local ingredients wherever possible.
OPEN Feb. - Nov. & Xmas. N/S DINING R. V, S.D. B/A. LICENSED. CHILDREN WELCOME. EN SUITE, TV & BEVERAGES IN ROOMS. B. & B. AROUND £23.

CHESTERFIELD

SHEEPLEA COTTAGE FARM, BASLOW RD, EASTMOOR, CHESTERFIELD

Lovely old stone cottage set in 22 acres of garden and farmland just 2 miles from Chatsworth and Baslow village; beautiful moorland views.
TEL: (01246) 566785 OPEN Mar. - Oct. inc. V STD. S.D. B/A. NO SMOKING. CHILDREN: OVER 12S ONLY. PETS B/A. BEVERAGES & TV IN ROOMS. B. & B. AROUND £14.

DOVEDALE

THE IZAAK WALTON HOTEL, DOVEDALE, NR ASHBOURNE
Beautiful 17th C. stone-built ex-farmhouse where Izaak Walton stayed while collecting
material for 'The Compleat Angler.' Very comfortably furnished. Very good food.
TEL: (0133 529) 555 OPEN ALL YEAR.   N/S PART OF DINING R & SOME BEDRS.   V STD, S.D. B/A.   CHILD-
REN. PETS B/A. EN SUITE, TV & BEVERAGES IN ROOMS.   CREDIT CARDS.   B. & B. AROUND £45.

MATLOCK

DERWENT HOUSE, KNOWLESTON PL, MATLOCK, DERBYS., DE4 3BU
Charming 17th C. Grade II listed house built of Derbyshire gritstone in a secluded setting
near Hall Leys Park. 5 comfortable bedrooms are each named after Derbyshire rivers.
TEL: (01629) 584681 OPEN ALL YEAR ex. Xmas & New Year.   NO SMOKING. V STD. CHILDREN WELCOME.
PETS B/A. 1 ROOM EN SUITE. TV & BEVERAGES IN ROOMS. B. & B. AROUND £18.

Lane End House

GREEN LANE, TANSLEY, DERBYSHIRE, DE4 5FJ   TEL: (01629) 583981
Small Georgian farmhouse set behind Tansley village green near to the church and with
open fields and green hills to the rear. Bathrobes, current magazines, tapes, fresh fruit and
flowers in bedrooms. All food home-made - including the soups and pâtés - and vegetables
are nearly always steamed; fromage frais - or yoghourt - is served as an accompaniment to
the delicious desserts.
OPEN ALL YEAR. V, S.D. B/A. NO SMOKING. LICENSED. DISABLED ACCESS: 2 STEPS AT FRONT DOOR.
CHILDREN WELCOME. PETS B/A. EN SUITE, BEVERAGES & TV IN ROOMS. B. & B. AROUND £25.

SHERIFF LODGE HOTEL, 51 DIMPLE ROAD, MATLOCK, DE4 3JX
Quiet and elevated position, overlooking town & country. Home-cooking; free-range eggs.
TEL: (01629) 582973 OPEN ALL YEAR. V STD. VE, S.D. B/A.   N/S BEDRS & DINING R.   LICENSED.
CHILDREN WELCOME. PETS B/A. MOST ROOMS EN SUITE. BEVERAGES & TV. B. & B. AROUND £25.

Woodside

STANTON LEES, MATLOCK, DERBYSHIRE.   TEL: (01629) 734320
Woodside is a comfortable family home which stands amidst landscaped gardens in the
Peak District National Park; surrounded by ancient moors and woodland which are teeming
with wildlife, there are panoramic country views from many of the rooms. Accommodation
is in either a double or a twin-bedded room, both with private facilities, and there is a
comfortable lounge with a TV. Guests are treated to a full English breakfast and an evening
meal is available by arrangement. Home-grown organic produce is used when available in
cooking. The visitor's book testifies to the warmth of the welcome, the deliciousness of the
food and the beauty of the location - many entries represent repeat visits.
OPEN Easter - Oct. inc.   V ON REQUEST. WH, ORG STD.   NO SMOKING.   CHILDREN WELCOME. EN
SUITE, TV & BEVERAGES IN RS. B. & B. £16.

RESTAURANTS & PUBS

BAKEWELL

GREEN APPLE, DIAMOND COURT, WATER STREET, DE4 1EW
Charming little restaurant converted from five old cottages & retaining beamed ceilings
and the exposed stone walls. Home-prepared food
TEL: (01629) 814404 V STD. NO SMOKING.   LICENSED.   DISABLED ACCESS.   CHILDREN.

BELPER

**THE MIXING PLACE, DANNAH FARM COUNTRY GUEST HOUSE, DANNAH
FARM, BOWMANS LANE, SHOTTLE, NR BELPER, DE5 2DR**
For further details please see under the entry in the accommodation section.

CHESTERFIELD

THE HOUSE OF YORK, 26 THE GREEN, HASLAND, NR CHESTERFIELD
TEL: (01246) 211241 V STD. N/S SEPARATE DINING R. LICENSED. CHILDREN WELCOME.

ROYAL OAK INN, HIGH STREET, BARLBOROUGH, CHESTERFIELD
TEL: (01246) 810425 V STD. N/S SEPARATE SECTION. LICENSED. CHILDREN ALLOWED.

DERBY

ORCHARD RESTAURANT, 21 FRIARGATE, DERBY, DERBYS.
TEL: (01332) 40307 MAINLY VEGETARIAN. N/S MOST OF RESTAURANT. LICENSED. CHILDREN WELCOME.

QUATTIES RESTAURANT, 109 NORMANTON ROAD, DERBY, DERBYS.
TEL: (01332) 368701 V STD. NO SMOKING. LICENSED. WELL-BEHAVED CHILDREN WELCOME.

TICKNALL

Daisy's Tearoom

THE OLD COACH HOUSE, HAYES FARM, TICKNALL, DERBYS, DE7 1JZ   TEL: (01332) 862696
Situated in the coach house of a lovely large Georgian farmhouse in lovely informal gardens
with antiques showroom to the rear of the tea room. Lace tablecloths, fresh flowers, gentle
background music all create a peaceful ambience. Excellent food.
OPEN 10.30 - 5.30. V STD. S.D. B/A. NO SMOKING. CHILDREN WELCOME.

Leicestershire

ACCOMMODATION

BROUGHTON ASTLEY

THE OLD FARMHOUSE, OLD MILL RD, BROUGHTON ASTLEY, LE9 6PQ
18th C. farmhouse overlooking fields in a quiet position at the back of the village.
TEL: (01455) 282254 V, VE, DIAB, S.D. B/A WH STD. N/S. CHILDREN. BEVERAGES. B. & B. AROUND £20.

LEICESTER

BELMONT HOUSE HOTEL, DE MONTFORT ST, LEICESTER, LE1 7ER
Elegant hotel forming part of the Victorian conservation area of New Walk in the centre of
Leicester; very comfortable accommodation, excellent service and first-class cuisine.
TEL: (0116) 254 4773 OPEN ALL YEAR.   V STD. N/S 1 LOUNGE & SOME BEDRS. LICENSED. DISABLED
ACCESS. CHILDREN. PETS B/A. EN SUITE, BEVERAGES & T.V. IN ROOMS. B. & B. AROUND £78.

RICHARD'S BACKPACKER'S HOSTEL, 157 WANLIP LN., BIRSTALL, LEIC.
Small, independent hostel catering for cyclists, backpackers and young tourists. Stand B
city bus station to hostel's nearest stop: Windmill Ave, Birstall. Fresh vegetarian food daily.
TEL: (0116) 267 3107 OPEN ALL YEAR.   V, VE STD. S.D. B/A. N/S. BYO WINE. OVER 5S. B. & B. FROM £8.

LUTTERWORTH

Highcross House

HIGHCROSS, LUTTERWORTH, LE17 5AT   TEL: (01455) 220840 FAX: (01455) 682316
Highcross House is a 16th C. Grade II listed building standing at the historic crossing of

Fossways and Watling Street - the Roman
Centre of England. Your hosts offer an exceptionally thoughtful and memorable welcome
to guests: flowers and refreshments are ready
to greet you on your arrival, and additional
services, such as the provision of a picnic
basket, are available on request. Rooms are
tastefully decorated and beautifully furnished
- there is a genuine antique four-poster, en
suite with double jacuzzi and spa bath in one,
and another room with a half Tester bed - and
the imaginative menu, prepared from fresh,
local produce, is usually arranged by prior
notice with guests and changes daily. Highcross caters for both the tourist and business
traveller, but also offers excellent facilities for small conferences or special family occa-
sions. There is much to see and do in the locality including diving at Stoney Cove, the
country's foremost diving centre, or walking the Fosse.
OPEN ALL YEAR. NO SMOKING. V, S.D. B/A. LICENSED. DISABLED ACCESS. CHILDREN WELCOME. PETS
B/A. EN SUITE SOME ROOMS. BEVERAGES & T.V. ALL ROOMS. B. & B. FROM £20.

WHEATHILL FARM, CHURCH LANE, SHEARSBY, LUTTERWORTH, LE17 6PG
Traditional Leicestershire-built Grade II listed farmhouse standing in a large garden. Beams & inglenook fireplaces. Food cooked from fresh home-grown vegetables & free-range eggs.
TEL: 0116) 247 8663 OPEN ALL YEAR.   V B/A.   N/S DINING R, LOUNGE & BEDRS.   CHILDREN WELCOME.
GROUND FLOOR ROOM HAS PRIVATE FACILITIES.   BEVERAGES.   T.V. IN LOUNGE.   B. & B. AROUND £17

OAKHAM

RUTLAND COTTAGE, 5 CEDAR ST, BRAUNSTON-IUN-RUTLAND, OAKHAM.
Beautiful semi-self-catering cottages (breakfast is served in the house).
TEL: 901572) 722049 OPEN ALL YEAR. V, S.D. B/A. N/S. CHILDREN. EN SUITE, BEVERAGES & TV. B. & B. £16-20.

WHIPPER IN HOTEL, THE MARKET PL., OAKHAM, RUTLAND, LE15 6DT
TEL: (01572) 756971   OPEN ALL YEAR.   V STD, S.D. B/A. ORG, WH ON REQUEST. LICENSED. DIS-ABLED ACCESS.   CHILDREN.   PETS B/A.   EN SUITE.   BEVERAGES & T.V.   B. & B. AROUND £70

UPPINGHAM

GARDEN HOTEL, HIGH ST WEST, UPPINGHAM, LE15 9QD
Charming small hotel with large walled garden in which meals, drinks and barbeques are served in summer; all food prepared from fresh ingredients; home-baked bread.
TEL: (01572) 822352   OPEN ALL YEAR.   N/S 66% OF DINING R, & FIRST FLOOR. V, DIAB ON REQUEST. S.D. B/A. LICENSED. CHILDREN WELCOME.   PETS B/A.   EN SUITE. BEVERAGES   B. & B.AROUND £45.

The Lake Isle Hotel

16 HIGH EAST, UPPINGHAM, LEICS, LE15 9PZ   TEL: (01572) 822951
This small personally run restaurant and town house hotel is situated in the centre of the pretty market town of Uppingham, dominated by the famous Uppingham Public School and close to Rutland Water. The entrance to the hotel is reached via a quiet yard hung with flowering baskets. The bedrooms are each named after a wine-growing region in France and guets will find fresh fruit, mineral water, and a decanter of sherry. Excellent meals are served in the intimate restaurant and all dishes are prepared from fresh produce. There is an extensive wine list of 300 items, including half bottles, and special wine meetings are held 4 times a year.
OPEN ALL YEAR.   V STD. VE, DIAB. S.D. B/A. ORG/WH WHEN AVAIL. LICENSED.   CHILDREN & PETS WELCOME.
ALL ROOMS EN SUITE.   BEVERAGES.   T.V.   CREDIT CARDS.   B. & B. FROM £29 dbl, £39 sgl.

RESTAURANTS & PUBS

ASHBY-DE-LA-ZOUCH

Staunton Stables Tea Room

THE FERRERS CENT., STAUNTON HAROLD, NR ASHBY-de-la-ZOUCH, LE6 5RU TEL: (01332) 864617
Converted stable block. Home-made cakes, pastries and lunches. Cream teas and Hovis teas are served every afternoon. Home-made cakes, home-made preserves.
OPEN 10.30 - 5.   V STD.   NO SMOKING.   DISABLED ACCESS.   CHILDREN WELCOME.

LEICESTER

PARSONS GALLERY, 399 RATBY LN, KIRBY MUXLOE, LEICESTER, LE9 9AQ
TEL: (0116) 239 3534   V STD.   NO SMOKING.   ONLY WELL-BEHAVED CHILDREN WELCOME.

THE GOOD EARTH, 19 FREE LANE, LEICESTER, LE1 1JX
TEL: (0116) 262 6260   V, VE EXC.   N/S 50% OF RESTAURANT (SEPARATE FLOOR).   LICENSED.

LOUGHBOROUGH

The Greenhouse

27/29 BIGGIN ST (FIRST FLOOR), LOUGHBOROUGH, LE11 1UA   TEL: (01509) 262018
Vegetarian & vegan café. Open for evening meals B/A. A wid range of dishes from world cuisines. All fresh ingredients, mainly organic & home-cooked from bread to ice cream
V EXC.   NO SMOKING.   LICENSED.   CHILDREN WELCOME.

Lincolnshire

ACCOMMODATION

CASTLE BYTHAM

Bank House

CASTLE BYTHAM, NR GRANTHAM, LINCS, NG33 4SQ   TEL: (01780) 410523
English Tourist Board de Luxe. Bed and Breakfast of the Year in the Middle England Best of Tourism Awards Superbly appointed and comfortable private home. Menus feature healthy, home-made foods.
OPEN ALL YEAR.   V, S.D. B/A.   NO SMOKING.   EN SUITE, TV & BEVERAGES.   B. & B. AROUND £22.

EAST BARKWITH

THE GRANGE, TORRINGTON LNE, EAST BARKWITH, LN3 5RY
ETB 2 Crowns De Luxe. Welcoming Georgian farmhouse in extensive grounds with herb beds and lawn tennis courts; the spacious bedrooms have views of the farm and gardens.
TEL: (01673) 858249   OPEN ALL YEAR.   V, DIAB, S.D. B/A.   N/S BEDRS & MOST PUBLIC AREAS.   CHILDREN WELCOME.   ALL ROOMS EN SUITE.   B. & B. AROUND £20.

NORTH ORMSBY

ABBEY FARM, NORTH ORMSBY, NR LOUTH, LINCS, LN11 0TJ
TEL: (01472) 840272 OPEN Mar. - Oct.   V, DIAB, S.D. B/A. ORG WHEN AVAIL. CHILDREN WELCOME.   PETS B/A.   BEVERAGES IN ROOMS.   T.V. LOUNGE.   B. & B. AROUND £18.

NORTH THORSEBY

THE HEN HOUSE, HAWERBY HALL, NORTH THORESBY, DN36 5QL
Handsome Georgian manor house surrounded by gardens, fields & woods for women to come 'for holidays, short breaks or to unwind'. Wonderful food & numerous good walks.
TEL: (01472) 840278 OPEN ALL YEAR.   V, S.D. B/A.   N/S ex. in small bar area.   LICENSED.   DISABLED ACCESS.   CHILDREN WELCOME.   SOME EN SUITE ROOMS.   T.V.   D., B.& B. AROUND £36.

SLEAFORD

THE MALLARDS HOTEL, EASTGATE, SLEAFORD, LINCS.
Grade II listed building; excellent food made from fresh, local produce. Many local walks.
TEL: (01529) 303062 OPEN ALL YEAR.   V, DIAB STD.   N/S PART DINING R.   LICENSED.   DISABLED ACCESS.   CHILDREN WELCOME.   TV, EN SUITE & BEVERAGES IN ROOMS.   B. & B. AROUND £27.

SPALDING

GUY WELLS FARM, WHAPLODE, SPALDING, LINCS, PE12 6TZ
Lovely Queen Anne family home on a flower farm. Fresh and wholesome food; home produce includes vegetables and free range eggs.
TEL: (01406) 422239 OPEN ALL YEAR.   V, S.D. ON REQUEST.   NO SMOKING.   BEVERAGES.   TV.   B. & B. FROM £18.

RESTAURANTS

GRANTHAM

CLAIRE'S CONCOCTIONS, 15A BRIDGE ST, GRANTHAM, NG31 9AE
Vegetarian restaurant serving 'imaginative and healthy cuisine'.
TEL: (01476) 76981 V EXC. S.D. B/A.   N/S IN 2 ROOMS. LICENSED. DISABLED ACCESS.   CHILDREN.

SLEAFORD

BUMBLES BISTRO, 7 HANDLEY COURT MEWS, SOUTHGATE, SLEAFORD
TEL: (01529) 413996 V STD. NO SMOKING. V STD. LICENSED. DISABLED ACCESS.   CHILDREN WELCOME.

Northamptonshire

ACCOMMODATION

DAVENTRY

BAREWELL FIELDS, 1, PRESTIDGE ROW, MORETON PINKNEY, DAVENTRY,
Comfortable country home. Wholesome food made with home-grown produce.
TEL: (01295) 76 754 OPEN Jan. - Nov. V, S.D. B/A. N/S DINING R & BEDRS. OVER 5S ONLY. BEVERAGES
IN ROOMS. B. & B. AROUND £18.

NORTHAMPTON

WESTONE MOAT HOUSE, ASHLEY WAY, WESTON FAVELL, NORTHAMPTON.
Magnificent mansion; excellent cuisine.
TEL: (01604) 406262 OPEN ALL YEAR. V STD, S.D. B/A. N/S PART OF DINING R & SOME BEDR. LICENSED.
DISABLED ACCESS. CHILDREN WELCOME. EN SUITE, TV & BEVERAGES. B. & B. AROUND £70.

RESTAURANTS

BRIGSTOCK

HILL FARM HERBS, PARK WALK, BRIGSTOCK, NORTHANTS, NN14 3HH
TEL: (01536) 373694 NO SMOKING. WHEELCHAIR ACCESS. CHILDREN WELCOME.

TWYWELL

THE OLD FRIAR, TWYWELL, NR KETTERING, NN14 3AH TEL: (01832) 2625
V STD. N/S 1 DINING AREA. LICENSED. WHEELCHAIR ACCESS. CHILDREN.

Nottinghamshire

NEWARK

THE APPLETON HOTEL, 73 APPLETONGATE, NEWARK, NG24 1LN
Pleasant small hotel; à la carte menu with fresh produce used in cooking.
TEL; (01636) 71616 OPEN ALL YEAR. V STD. NO SMOKING. LICENSED. CHILDREN WELCOME. EN
SUITE, BEVERAGES, T. V. & PHONE IN ROOMS. B. & B. AROUND £28.

THE GRANGE HOTEL, 73 LONDON RD, NEWARK, NOTTS, NG24 1RZ
Victorian property in residential area surrounded by trees. Immaculate refurbished en suite
bedrooms. Good choice of b'fasts. Candle-lit restaurant. Home-cooked food.
TEL: (01636) 703399 FAX: (01636) 702328 OPEN ALL YEAR. V STD. VE, DIAB, S.D. B/A. N/S BEDRS. & DINING R.
CHILDREN WELCOME. LICENSED. CREDIT CARDS. B. & B. AROUND £27.

NOTTINGHAM

THE LUCIEVILLE HOTEL, 349 DERBY RD, NOTTINGHAM, NG7 2DZ
Executive-class hotel exclusively for non-smokers. Vegetarian choices on menu.
TEL: (0115) 978 7389 FAX: (0115) 979 0346 OPEN ALL YEAR. V STD. NO SMOKING. LICENSED.
DISABLED ACCESS. EN SUITE, T.V., BEVERAGES & HAIRDRYER IN ROOMS. B. & B. AROUND £53.

St Andrews Hotel

310 QUEENS RD, BEESTON, NOTTINGHAM. TEL & FAX: (0115) 925 4902
Private hotel forming good base for visits to Sherwood and Derbyshire. Indoor Tennis
Centre, Helmpier Point Watersports & Donington Race Track nearby.
OPEN ALL YEAR. V, VE, B/A. N/S DINING R. & EN SUITE ROOMS. CHILDREN & PETS WELCOME. EN SUITE,
TV & BEVERAGES IN MOST ROOMS. TV IN LOUNGE. B. & B. FROM £15 - £26.50.

REDMILE

PEACOCK FARM REST. & G.H., REDMILE, NOTTS, NG13 0GQ
280 year old farmhouse with views of the castle. Excellent vegetarian dishes.
TEL: (01949) 42475 OPEN ALL YEAR. V, VE, WH STD. DIAB B/A. CHILDREN WELCOME. LICENSED. WHEEL-
CHAIR ACCESS. EN SUITE, TV & BEVERAGES IN ROOMS. B. & B. £19.50 - 42.

RESTAURANTS

CALVERTON

Painters Paradise Restaurant

PATCHINGS FARM ART CENTRE, OXTON RD, CALVERTON, NG14 6NU TEL: (0115) 965 3479
Unique enterprise on 38 acre rural site consisting of a conversion of farm buildings in which
are housed two galleries; art, pottery and textiles studios; a gift shop, and a restaurant.
OPEN 9 A.M. TO 10 P.M. (GARDENS CLOSE AT 6 P.M.).   V, DIAB & ADDITIVE-FREE DIETS STD/B/A.   NO
SMOKING.   LICENSED.   DISABLED ACCESS.   CREDIT CARDS.

NEWARK

Gannets Café/Bistrot

35 CASTLEGATE, NEWARK, NOTTS, NG24 1AZ   TEL: (01636) 702066
Grade II listed Georgian building overlooking the castle on the main road through Newark.
Morning coffee, lunches and afternoon teas in the downstairs café throughout the week (a
garden room extension is planned for completion by March '95) with a choice of wonderful
home-made cakes and 'adventurous' salads (made from more than 25 ingredients). Bistrot
lunches and dinners are prepared by Colin White, who used to be head chef at the Sharrow
Bay Hotel,Everything on the menu has been home-made from fresh (always) and additive-
free (wherever possible) ingredients.
CAFÉ OPEN 9.30 - 4.30 DAILY. BISTROT OPEN TUES. TO SAT., 12 NOON - 2.30 & 6.30 - 9.30 V STD. NO SMOKING.
LICENSED.   CHILDREN WELCOME.

NOTTINGHAM

MAXINE'S SALAD TABLE, 56-58 UPPER PARLIAMENT ST, NOTTINGHAM.
Vegetarian restaurant serving home-made food; good vegan options.
TEL: (0115) 947 3622 75 SEATS. OPEN 9A.M. - 5P.M. 75% N/S (SEP. ROOM).   V, VE STD. LICENSED. CHILDREN
WELCOME.

Cumbria & the North West

Cumbria

ACCOMMODATION

ALSTON

The Miners Arms

NENTHEAD, ALSTON, CUMBRIA   TEL: (01434) 381427
Pub with restaurant & accommodation. Excellent meat-free fare. Owner has written cook
book.
V, VE, S.D. STD.   N/S DINING R.   OPEN ex. Xmas Day.   LICENSED.   CHILDREN & PETS WELCOME.   TV IN
ROOMS.   BEVERAGES AVAILABLE.   B. & B. £12, D. B. & B. £15.

AMBLESIDE

CHAPEL HOUSE HOTEL, KIRKSTONE ROAD, AMBLESIDE, LA22 9DZ
Originally two 16th C. cottages, this small family hotel overlooks the village and fells;
excellent food prepared by top hotel experienced chef.
TEL: (015394) 33143 OPEN Mar. - Oct.   N/S DINING R & BEDRS.   V, S.D. B/A.   LICENSED.   CHILDREN
WELCOME.   SOME EN SUITE ROOMS.   D., B. & B. AROUND £30.

GREY FRIAR LODGE, CLAPPERSGATE, AMBLESIDE, LA22 9NE
19th C. lodge in woodland. Excellent food: home-baked bread & home-made chocolates.
TEL: (015394) 33158 OPEN MOST OF YEAR.   V, LOW-FAT, WH B/A.   N/S DINING R & BEDROOMS.   LICENSED.
OVER 12s ONLY.   EN SUITE, TV & BEVERAGES IN ROOMS.   D., B. & B. AROUND £32.

Horseshoe Hotel

ROTHAY RD, AMBLESIDE, CUMBRIA   TEL: (015394) 32000

Pleasant hotel near the centre of Ambleside; magnificent mountain views. Superbly appointed and with separate lounge for smokers. All food home-made from fresh ingredients.
OPEN ALL YEAR.   V STD. LOW-FAT & SOME S.D. B/A.   N/S DINING R, BAR, SOME BEDRS & OTHER PUBLIC
AREAS.   LICENSED.   DISABLED ACCESS TO GROUND FLOOR; REST. BARS & LOUNGE.   CHILDREN WELCOME.
PETS B/A.   MOST ROOMS EN SUITE.   BEVERAGES & T.V. IN ROOMS.   B. &. B. AROUND £34.

Rothay Garth Hotel

ROTHAY ROAD, AMBLESIDE, CUMBRIA, LA22 0EE   TEL: (015394) 32217
OPEN ALL YEAR.   N/S ex. in bar.   V STD.   S.D. B/A.   LICENSED.   DISABLED ACCESS.   CHILDREN WELCOME.
PETS B/A.   EN SUITE, T.V. & BEVERAGES IN BEDROOMS.   ACCESS, VISA.   B. & B. FROM £32.

Windlehurst Guest House

MILLANS PARK, AMBLESIDE, CUMBRIA, LA22 9AG   TEL: (015394) 33137

Windlehurst is an elegant Victorian house which stands on a peaceful road in Ambleside in its own lovely garden, overlooking open fields and the Cumbrian fells. It has been very comfortably furnished and guests dine on delicious breakfasts (yoghurts and fresh fruit are also available). You are within easy reach of Ambleside (there is private parking at Windlehurst) and of course all the amenities and activities which Lakeland provides are within easy reach. Your hosts are very welcoming and will do all they can to make your stay happy and enjoyable.
OPEN JAN. - OCT. inc.   V STD, VE, DIAB., B/A.   NO SMOKING.   CHILDREN (family Rooms). DOGS B/A.   2 EN SUITE
ROOMS (WITH TV).   BEVERAGES IN ROOMS.   B. & B. FROM £14.

Yewfield Guest House

HAWKSHEAD HILL, HAWKSHEAD, AMBLESIDE, CUMBRIA, LA22 0PR   TEL: (015394) 36765

ETB 2 Crown Commended. Situated in 25 acres of its own grounds, this impressive house with its Gothic architecture was formerly an award-winning hotel; it stands in an elevated position with panoramic views over the Vale of Esthwaite. Although now a private residence, it is a peaceful retreat in the heart of the Lakes and there are a few letting rooms for bed and breakfast on a vegetarian basis. The double and twin rooms are appointed to a very high standard, and each has an en suite bath and shower, colour TV, radio and beverage-making facility; there is a lounge and library area for guests' use. Breakfast is a wholefood continental buffet and includes fresh fruits, mueslis, cereals, home-baked breads, toast, preserves, coffee and teas. Although Yewfield does not serve an evening meal, there are two vegetarian restaurants within a few miles of the house.
OPEN ALL YEAR.   NO SMOKING.   V EXC, VE, S.D, ORG, WH STD.   OVER 10s WELCOME.   EN SUITE, TV &
BEVERAGES IN ROOMS.   B. & B. FROM £22.50.

APPLEBY-IN-WESTMORLAND

Appleby Manor Hotel

ROMAN RD, APPLEBY-IN-WESTMORLAND, CA16 6JB   TEL: (07683) 51571

Comfortable hotel set in private wooded grounds; swimming pool, sauna and solarium avail. All food prepared from fresh ingredients.
OPEN ALL YEAR.   V STD; DIAB., S.D. B/A.   LICENSED.   DISABLED ACCESS GOOD: SOME GROUND FLOOR
BEDROOMS AVAIL.   CHILDREN WELCOME.   EN SUITE, BEVERAGES & TV IN BEDROOMS.

THE FRIARY, BATTLEBARROW, APPLEBY IN WESTMORLAND, CA16 6XT

Georgian House with grounds built on the site of a 12th C. Carmelite Friar; log fires in winter; hypnosis therapy offered for smokers, also aromatherapy and reflexology.
TEL: (017683) 52702 OPEN ALL YEAR.   CORDON VERT V, VE, DEMI-VEG., ARTHRITIC, GLUTEN-FREE, S.D.
B/A.   NO SMOKING. LICENSED.   OVER 6S ONLY.   EN SUITE & BEVERAGES.   T.V.   B. & B. AROUND £20.

ARNSIDE

STONEGATE GUEST HOUSE, THE PROMENADE, ARNSIDE

Vegetarian owner. All food freshly cooked.
TEL: (01524) 761171   OPEN ALL YEAR.   V, VE, S.D. STD. (vegetarian owner).   NO SMOKING.   CHILDREN
WELCOME.   PETS B/A.   TV & BEVERAGES IN ROOMS.   B. & B. AROUND £20.

BOWNESS ON WINDERMERE

BLENHEIM LODGE, BRANTFELL ROAD, BOWNESS-ON-WINDERMERE

Lovely Lakeland stone house peacefully situated against National Trust lands just minutes from the lake & shops. Food is "an art form": only fresh, local produce is used in cooking.
TEL: (015394) 43440 OPEN ALL YEAR. V, VE, S.D. B/A. N/S MOST AREAS. LICENSED. OVER 6S ONLY. EN SUITE, TV & BEVERAGES IN ROOMS. CREDIT CARDS.

BUTTERMERE VALLEY

Pickett Howe

BRACKENTHWAITE, BUTTERMERE VALLEY, CUMBRIA, CA13 9UY TEL: (01900) 85444

After a successful first few year at Pickett Howe, a '17th C. Lakeland statesman's long house' David and Dani Edwards, (ex of the highly acclaimed Low Hall) are looking forward to welcoming a second season of guests to their lovely home in the beautiful Buttermere Valley. With characteristic flair and meticulous attention to detail the Edwards have clearly taken great pleasure in decorating and furnishing their lovely home: bedrooms are individually styled and Laura Ashley fabrics, lace bedspreads, and elegant furniture (the bedsteads are restored Victorian) recreate the 17th & 18th centuries while power showers and whirlpool baths wash away the cares of the 20th; the original features, such as mullioned windows, flagged floors and oak beams have been retained and add to Pickett Howe's already considerable charm. Dani's culinary skills are as exceptional as ever; and the 5-course evening menu includes such delights as Spiced Apple Soup, Fennel, Lemon and Walnut in a Gougère Pastry Ring and Juniper Pudding. Crystal, candlelight and chamber music all combine to provide the all important sense of occasion which is the hallmark of dining in the Edwards' home.
OPEN MAR. TO NOV. NO SMOKING. VEGETARIAN & MEAT DISHES STANDARD. MOST OTHER SPECIAL DIETS BY ARRANGEMENT. LICENSED. CHILDREN: OVER 10S WELCOME. EN SUITE & TEA/COFFEE IN BEDROOMS. T.V. ON REQUEST. D., B. & B. FROM £45. ETB THREE CROWNS DE LUXE.

CALDBECK

HIGH GREENRIGG HOUSE, NR CALDBECK

Carefully restored stone-built 17th C. farmhouse at the foot of the Caldbeck Fells. Flagged floor, exposed beamsand open fires in cooler weather. Wholesome and imaginative food prepared from fresh produce served in beamed dining room.
TEL: (016998) 430 S.D. B/A. N/S DINING R, BEDRS & T.V. LOUNGE. LICENSED. DISABLED ACCESS. CHILDREN WELCOME. PETS B/A. EN SUITE. BEVERAGES IN T.V. LOUNGE. B. & B. AROUND £20.

CARLISLE

BESSIESTOWN FARM, CATLOWDY, PENTON, CARLISLE, CA6 5QP

Charming farmhouse with beamed ceilings & log fires; food is prepared with imagination and flair from fresh, and where possible, local ingredients.
TEL: (01228) 77219 OPEN ALL YEAR. V, S.D. B/A. N/S ex bar. LICENSED. CHILDREN WELCOME. EN SUITE & BEVERAGES IN ROOMS. T.V. LOUNGE. B. & B. FROM £18.50.

Cumbria Park Hotel

32 SCOTLAND RD, CARLISLE, CA3 9DG

Hotel standing in magnificent gardens. The food is wholesome and delicious: everything has been home-cooked from fresh ingredients, and there are always vegetarian options.
TEL: (01228) 22887 FAX: (01228) 514796 OPEN ALL YEAR. NO SMOKING IN PART OF DINING ROOM, SOME BEDROOMS & SOME PUBLIC AREAS. LICENSED. WHEELCHAIR ACCESS. CHILDREN WELCOME. EN SUITE, TV & TEA/COFFEE IN ROOMS. CREDIT CARDS. B. & B. FROM £49.

New Pallyards

HETHERSGILL, CARLISLE, CUMBRIA TEL: (01228) 577308

Modern country farmhouse with a converted barn, cottages and a new, purpose-built bungalow, which offers award-winning holiday accommodation to guests. (Esther Rantzen and the That's Life team stayed here while filming recently). Visitors can stay in either the

comfortably furnished farmhouse (and be treated to a first-rate breakfast each morning - the proprietors are the winners of a Salon Culinaire award for the Best Breakfast in Britain), or to self-cater in the other farm buildings (all units have been furnished and equipped to a very high standard).
OPEN ALL YEAR. V, VE, S.D. B/A. SEPARATE N/S FACILITIES. CHILDREN WELCOME. PETS B/A. EN SUITE & TV MOST ROOMS. BEVERAGES ALL ROOMS.

THE WARREN GUEST HOUSE, 368 WARWICK ROAD, CARLISLE, CUMBRIA
The Warren Guest house is near to Hadrian's Wall and Carlisle town centre. The proprietors specialise in the use of *fresh* produce in cooking; meals are delicious and wholesome.
TEL: (01228) 33663/512916 OPEN ALL YEAR. V, VE, S.D. B/A. LOW-FAT COOKING. N/S BEDRS & PART OF DINING R. CHILDREN WELCOME. EN SUITE, BEVERAGES & TV IN ROOMS. HAIRDRYERS & IRONING. B. & B. AROUND £20.

CONISTON

BEECH TREE, YEWDALE ROAD, CONISTON, CUMBRIA, LA21 8DB
Exclusively vegetarian. A Victorian house full of character standing in its own grounds at the foot of the Old Man of Coniston. Beautiful walks from door.
TEL: (015394) 41717 OPEN ALL YEAR. HEALTH FOOD, V, VE, S.D. STD. NO SMOKING. BABIES & OVER 6S ONLY. PETS B/A. SOME EN SUITE ROOMS. BEVERAGES IN ROOMS. T.V. IN LOUNGE. B. & B. FROM £14.

CONISTON LODGE, SUNNY BROW, CONISTON, CUMBRIA, LA21 8HH
High standard of accommmodation and comfort. Fresh local ingredients used in cooking.
TEL: (015394) 41201 OPEN ALL YEAR. ex Xmas. V, DIAB B/A. NO SMOKING. LICENSED. CHILDREN: OVER 10S ONLY. EN SUITE, TV & BEVERAGES IN ROOMS. ACCESS, VISA, MASTERCARD, EUROCARD. B. & B. AROUND £30.

GLENRIDDING

Moss Crag Guest House
GLENRIDDING, CUMBRIA, CA11 0PA   TEL: (017684) 82500

Moss Crag, a family-run guest house, is a charming stone-built house situated opposite Glenridding Beck in the heart of the Lake District hills and fells. Just 300 yards away is the hauntingly beautiful Lake Ullswater and, although you can fish, sail, canoe or windsurf thereon, it is best enjoyed (I feel) by just looking at it - perhaps the fishermen have got it right. Freshly prepared food is a feature of a stay at Moss Crag where a typical evening menu would feature Parton Bree (Crab Soup) followed by Beef and Noodle Bake or Spinach and Leek Pancakes and a delicious home-made dessert such as Citrus Condé or Coffee Fudge Pudding. Morning coffee, light lunch and afternoon tea are also served.
OPEN Feb. - Nov. inc. NO SMOKING. V, S.D. DIAB B/A. LICENSED. CHILDREN WELCOME. EN SUITE IN SOME ROOMS. BEVERAGES & T.V. IN ROOMS. B. & B. FROM £15.50 - 19.50. D., B. & B. FROM £28 - 32. ALL INCLUSIVE D., B. & B. BREAKS AVAILABLE FROM NOV. TO MARCH INCL., EX DEC., JAN. 10% REDUCTION ON B. & B. ONLY FOR WEEKLY STAY IN SUMMER.

GRANGE-OVER-SANDS

GRAYTHWAITE MANOR, FERNHILL RD, GRANGE-OVER-SANDS, LA11 7JE
Elegant and tranquil hotel, exceptionally well-appointed; fresh flowers and antiques; cuisine prepared from fresh, local ingredient.
TEL: (015395) 32001 OPEN ALL YEAR. V, S.D. B/A. N/S DINING R. LICENSED. DISABLED ACCESS. CHILDREN WELCOME. EN SUITE, BEVERAGES & TV IN ROOMS. VISA, MASTERCARD. D., B. & B. AROUND £42.

Prospect House Hotel
KENTS BANK RD, GRANGE-OVER-SANDS, LA11 7DJ TEL: (015395) 32116
Prospect House Hotel has 7 spacious bedrooms which are centrally heated and have been comfortably equipped with brand new beds and duvets; the hotel also has a cosy, well-stocked residents' bar with 12 different table wines, (including some organic Scottish wines) together with real ale and malt whiskies. The food is excellent: meals are imaginative and prepared from fresh produce (there is a vegetarian option by arrangement).
OPEN ALL YEAR. V STD, DIAB B/A. N/S DINING R. LICENSED. CHILDREN: OVER 6S ONLY. DOGS B/A. 6 EN SUITE ROOMS. TV & BEVERAGES IN ROOMS. B. & B. AROUND £17, D., B. & B. AROUND £25.

GRASMERE

Lancrigg Vegetarian Country House Hotel

EASEDALE, GRASMERE, CUMBRIA, LA22 9QN   TEL: (015394) 35317   FAX: (015394) 35058

It is now almost 10 years since a chance stay at Lancrigg inspired me to compile the first edition of *The Healthy Holiday Guide*. Happily (and unsurprisingly) Robert and Janet Whittington have continued to go from strength to strength in their provision of quite exceptional vegetarian hospitality. The house itself, set in 27 acres of gardens overlooking Easedale, has been converted from the Westmorland farm it originally was (a favourite haunt of the Wordsworths) and has been charmingly decorated - the sitting room with large, floral prints and ample armchairs, and the dining room with beautiful reproduction and period furniture, polished oak floor and prints by the lakeland artist W. Heaton Cooper. Accommodation is in beautiful and comfortably appointed rooms, one of which has a four-poster bed and a whirlpool bath. The 5-course evening menu is prepared from local organic produce (some home-grown) and would typically feature Greek Marinated Vegetables with Feta Cheese and wholemeal toast, followed by Spinach Soup, Savoury Stuffed Vine Leaves and a choice of desserts, such as Sticky Toffee and Date Pudding (digestion is enhanced by the gentle background music of Telemann and Vivaldi).
OPEN ALL YEAR.   V EXC. VE, S.D. B/A.   N/S LOUNGE & DINING R.   LICENSED.   DISABLED ACCESS. CHILDREN WELCOME.   PETS B/A.   MOST ROOMS EN SUITE (WHIRLPOOL BATH AVAILABLE).   BEVERAGES & TV IN ROOMS.   CREDIT CARDS.   D., B. & B. AROUND £40.

MICHAEL'S NOOK, GRASMERE, NR AMBLESIDE, CUMBRIA, LA22 9RP

Charming 19th C. house furbished with owner/antique dealer's collection of English rugs, prints, furniture and porcelain. Elegant, gracious - yet homely. Excellent cuisine.
TEL: (019665) 496 OPEN ALL YEAR.   V, S.D. B/A.   N/S DINING R.   LICENSED.   CHILDREN B/A.   EN SUITE & TV IN ROOMS.   ROOM SERVICE.   CREDIT CARDS.   D., B. & B. AROUND £80.

OAK BANK HOTEL, BROADGATE, GRASMERE, CUMBRIA, LA22 9TA

Small family run hotel in Grasmere: all meals are prepared from the finest of fresh ingredients by a Cordon Bleu trained chef. Special suite with spa bath available.
TEL: (015394) 35217   OPEN Feb. - Dec.   V, S.D. B/A.   N/S DINING R.   LICENSED.   CHILDREN WELCOME. PETS B/A.   EN SUITE, BEVERAGES & TV IN ROOMS.   ACCESS, VISA.   B. & B. AROUND £30.

WHITE MOSS HOUSE, RYDAL WATER, GRASMERE, CUMBRIA, LA22 9SE

18th C. house once owned by Wordsworth by Rydal water. Award-winning cuisine.
TEL: (019665) 295 OPEN Mar. - Nov.   V, S.D. B/A.   N/S DINING R.   LICENSED.   DISABLED ACCESS.   CHILDREN WELCOME.   EN SUITE & T.V. IN ROOMS.   D. , B. & B. AROUND £65.

HAWKSHEAD

Silverholme

GRAYTHWAITE, HAWKSHEAD, CUMBRIA, LA12 8AZ   TEL: (015395) 31332

Set in an elevated position on the West side of Lake Windermere, this unique Georgian mansion house, stands in its own lovely grounds and is approached by a long azalea and rhododendron lined drive. Retaining most of its original features, the beautifully proportioned rooms have been furnished in traditional style and the atmosphere is particularly welcoming and relaxing. Each of the large, comfortable, centrally heated bedrooms have mahogany beds, en suite facilities and enjoy spectacular views of the lake. Meals are served in a charming dining room overlooking the colourful gardens and lake, and there is also an elegant lounge with a log fire. Close to the picturesque village of Hawkshead, Silverholme is an ideal base from which to explore the charms of the Lakes.
OPEN ALL YEAR.   V STD.   NO SMOKING   BYO WINE.   EN SUITE & BEVERAGES IN ROOMS.   B. & B. FROM £19.50, D. £9.50

KESWICK

CHAUCER HOUSE HOTEL, AMBLESIDE ROAD, KESWICK

A strong emphasis on home-cooking and baking (including bread, jams and chutneys).
TEL: (017687) 72318 OPEN Easter - Dec. inc.　V STD. S.D. B/A.　WH STD.　N/S DINING R & LOUNGE.
LICENSED.　OVER 4S.　MOST ROOMS EN SUITE.　BEVERAGES & TV IN ROOMS.　B. & B. AROUND £25.

Claremont Housee

CHESTNUT HILL, KESWICK, CUMBRIA, CA12 4LT　TEL: (017687) 72089

Claremont house is a renovated 19th C. manor house which has been superbly equipped
with every modern comfort to provide accommodation of a very high order. Your hosts,
Hilda and Geoff Mackerness, are Associate Members of Cumbria Fine Foods, and as such
endeavour to ensure that all produce used in cooking is local and fresh. Breakfast is a feast
of fruit juice, yoghurt, muesli, cereals and fresh fruit, and the bread and croissants are
home-baked with local flour. The 5-course evening meal is prepared from seasonal produce,
and vegetarians are conscientiously catered for (all food is prepared without the use of
animal fats); special vegetarian dishes can be served on request.
OPEN ALL YEAR.　V STD, VE, S.D. B/A.　ORG, WH STD.　N/S DINING R.　LICENSED.　OVER 10s WELCOME.　EN
SUITE, TV & BEVERAGES IN ROOMS.　B. & B. AROUND £22.

COTTAGE IN THE WOOD, WHINLATTER PASS, CUMBRIA.

17th C. former coaching house in pine forest with superb views of Skiddaw Range.
TEL: (017687) 78409 OPEN Mar. To Nov.　V, S.D. B/A.　ORG, WH ON REQUEST.　NO SMOKING.　LICENSED.
CHILDREN WELCOME. PETS B/A.　EN SUITE & BEVERAGES IN ROOMS.　B. & B. AROUND £30.

Dalegarth House Country Hotel

PORTINSCALE, KESWICK, CUMBRIA, CA12 5RQ　　TEL: (017687) 72817

Spacious, Edwardian property in a sunny elevated position, amidst nearly an acre of
gardens 1m from Keswick. The food is wholesome, delicious and home-cooked; packed
lunches are also available on request.
OPEN ALL YEAR. NO SMOKING. V B/A. LICENSED. CHILDREN: OVER 5S ONLY. EN SUITE, TV & TEA/COFFEE-MAK-
ING IN BEDROOMS.　ACCESS, VISA. B. & B. FROM £24. D., B.& B. £35.

ⅴ Orchard House

BORROWDALE ROAD, KESWICK, CUMBRIA, CA12 5DE　　TEL: (017687) 72830

This exclusively vegetarian guest house is just two minutes' walk from the centre of
Keswick. The evening meal is a set, daily-changing 4-course dinner prepared by your host
and hostess, Jan and Mike Ryder (Jan is a Cordon vert cook); there is a good choice of
organic wines and beers to choose from, too. Keswick is an ideal base for exploring the
Northern Lakelands and within a short drive are historic homes, stone circles and watermills.
OPEN ALL YEAR.　NO SMOKING.　V Exc, VE & S.D. B/A.　LICENSED.　CHILDREN WELCOME.　DOGS B/A.　SOME
EN SUITE ROOMS.　BEVERAGES IN ROOMS.　T.V. IN SEPARATE LOUNGE.　B. & B. from £19.50. D. £10.　Open to
non-residents for dinner.

RICHMOND HOUSE, 37/39 ESKIN STREET, KESWICK　TEL: (017687) 73965

ETB 2 Crowns. Small, friendly personally run guest house a few minutes walk from the
centre of Keswick. Fresh, local produce used wherever possible.
OPEN ALL YEAR.　V, VE, ADDITIVE-FREE, S.D. B/A.　NO SMOKING.　LICENSED.　CHILDREN WELCOME.
MOST ROOMS EN SUITE.

Willow Cottage

BASSENTHWAITE, NR KESWICK, CUMBRIA, CA12 4QP　TEL; (017687) 76440

Rurally situated B. & B. in converted barn. B'fast features muesli, dried fruit compôte, fresh
fruit salad, yoghurt, free-range eggs, home-made marmalade and honey.
OPEN ALL YEAR.　V, S.D. B/A.　WH STD.　MOSTLY N/S.　OLDER CHILDREN WELCOME.　EN SUITE & BEVERAGES
IN ROOMS.　B. & B. £16 - 17.

KIRBY LONSDALE

ⅴ Lupton Tower Vegetarian Country House Hotel

NR. KIRKBY LONSDALE, CUMBRIA, LA6 2PR　　TEL: (015395) 67400

Magnificent house offering exclusively vegetarian fare and standing in its own grounds
amidst the beautiful open countryside. Everything home-cooked from fresh produce.
OPEN ALL YEAR ex. Xmas.　V EXC. NO SMOKING.　LICENSED.　CHILDREN WELCOME.　PETS B/A.　MOST
EN SUITE ROOMS.　BEVERAGES IN ROOMS.　B. & B. AROUND £16.

KIRKBY STEPHEN

ANNEDD GWYN, 46 HIGH ST, KIRKBY STEPHEN, CUMBRIA, CA17 4SH
This late Victorian home is run along 'green' lines, with home-cooked wholefoods & a relaxing, healthy environment. Meditation room & guest lounge.
TEL: (017683) 72302 OPEN Jan. 7 - Dec. 22.   NO SMOKING. V STD. BEVERAGES.   TV ON REQUEST. CHILDREN & PETS WELCOME. B. & B. AROUND £15.

Chestnut House

CROSBY GARRETT, KIRKBY STEPHEN, CUMBRIA, CA17 4PR   TEL: (017683) 71230

Chestnut House is situated in the secluded village of Crosby Garrett in the upper Eden Valley, 4 miles from Kirkby Stephen. Bound to the west by the mountains of the Lake District and to the east by the Pennines, the Eden Valley has been referred to as Cumbria's best kept secret. Chestnut House is a traditional cottage with two large bedrooms, each with a double and single bed. Both rooms have washbasins and night storage heaters; there is a separate bathroom with shower. Downstairs you can relax in a comfortable sitting room listening to classical music and warming yourself by the open log fire. Delicious vegetarian and vegan meals, prepared from fresh wholefood produce (some organically home-grown), are served in the dining room. As far as possible everything is home-made, including the bread which is baked from stone-ground flour from a local watermill. There is a wide selection of beverages including herb and fruit teas available at no extra charge. Your hosts, who are keen cyclists and walkers, will do all they can to help make your stay a happy and memorable one.
OPEN ALL YEAR.   NO SMOKING.   V & VE EXC.   ORG WH WHEN AVAILABLE.   CHILDREN WELCOME.   PETS B/A. BEVERAGES ALWAYS AVAILABLE. TV IN LOUNGE. B. & B. FROM £15, D. £9.

MILNTHORPE

EILDAN, 129 CHURCH STREET, MILNTHORPE CUMBRIA, LA7 7DZ
Home-baked bread and free-range eggs.
TEL: (015395) 63311   V, VE, S.D. B/A. NO SMOKING. CHILDREN. BEVERAGES. T.V. 1 BEDROOM.

MOSEDALE

MOSEDALE HOUSE, MOSEDALE, CUMBRIA.
An emphasis on home-made and home-grown provision: vegetables, fruit, produce (such as eggs), home-baked bread and rolls. Vegetarians welcome.
TEL: (017687) 79371 OPEN ALL YEAR.   V, S.D. B/A. NO SMOKING.   DISABLED ACCESS. CHILDREN WELCOME. PETS B/A. 4 EN SUITE ROOMS. BEVERAGES IN ROOMS. T.V. B. & B. AROUND £21.

PENRITH

Croft House

NEWTON REIGNY, PENRITH, CUMBRIA, CA11 0AY TEL: (01768) 65435
Peaceful, friendly haven with spacious gardens with views. Good, wholesome food.
OPEN ALL YEAR. V STD. NO SMOKING. CHILDREN & PETS. EN SUITE, TV, BEVERAGES. B. & B. FROM £18.

Fair Place Wholefood & Vegetarian Guest House,

FAIR PLACE, WATERMILLOCK, NR PENRITH, CUMBRIA, CA11 0LR   TEL: (017684) 86235
Handsome rag-stone building in secluded grounds 200 yards past Watermillock Church. Exclusively vegetarian and vegan B. & B., serving only the best and freshest of free-range and 'whole' breakfasts. Bedrooms are all en suite (and have very comfortable beds).
OPEN FEB. TO NOV.   NO SMOKING. V, VE STD, S.D. B/A. ORG/WH. CHILDREN. PETS B/A.   EN SUITE. BEVERAGES & T.V. IN BEDROOMS.   B. & B. FROM £19.

NUNNERY HOUSE, STAFFIELD, KIRKOSWALD, PENRITH, CA10 1EU
Small, country house hotel in splendid grounds with beautiful walks. Bedrooms all have views and meals prepared from fresh, local produce are served in a panelled dining room.
TEL: (0176 883) 537 OPEN Mar. - Jan. inc.   V, S.D. B/A.   NO SMOKING. LICENSED. DISABLED ACCESS TO DINING R. CHILDREN WELCOME. PETS B/A. 7 EN SUITE ROOMS. BEVERAGES & TV IN ROOMS.   B. & B. AROUND £30.

Prospect Hill Hotel

KIRKOSWALD, PENRITH, CUMBRIA, CA10 1ER   TEL: (01768) 898 500

This cosy little huddle of farm buildings, nestling together on a green, unspoilt and ever so peaceful hillside overlooking the splendid Eden Vale, has been lovingly restored by its owners, John and Isa Henderson, to provide a most charming and comfortable hotel which retains the traditional features of the original buildings (low-beamed ceilings, sandstone walls). It offers a taste of "18th century England with 21st century amenities". The culinary emphasis is on freshly prepared traditional fare using the best of local ingredients (bread comes fresh from the Melmerby and Lazonby bakeries) and a typical evening menu would feature Wine and Nut Paté with Wholemeal Herb Bread followed by Courgette Roulade and a selection of desserts (including home-made ice-cream!) The vegetarian menu is being continually updated with new and interesting dishes. Prospect Hill Hotel is convenient for visiting Hadrians Wall by car and Tullie House by train; the Settle to Carlisle railway passes through Lazonby, 2 miles away. The surrounding area offers excellent opportunities for walking (there are many magnificent riverside walks) and energetic cycling, and local maps, wellingtons and wet-weather gear are all available from your hosts for a small charge. Incidentally there is a super new ground floor unit for families at just £73 for 4 people.

OPEN ALL YEAR. V STD. S.D. B/A. LICENSED. CHILDREN WELCOME. SORRY NO DOGS. MOST ROOMS EN SUITE. TV IN LOUNGE. BEVERAGES IN ROOMS. B. & B. FROM £22

THE WHITE HOUSE, CLIFTON, NR PENRITH, CUMBRIA TEL: (01768) 65115
Beautiful 18th C. farmhouse in the village of Clifton; home-grown produce in cooking.

Woodland House Hotel

WORDSWORTH STREET, PENRITH, CA11 7QY TEL: (01768) 864177 FAX: (01768) 890152
An elegant and spacious licensed private hotel with a large car park, just five minutes walk from the centre of the town. All rooms are en suite and all have tea/coffee making facilities and a colour T.V. The meals are delicious and have been prepared from the best of fresh and local produce and, with notice, special dietary requirements can be catered for. There is a large library of maps and books for walkers, nature-lovers and sightseers and the proprietors will gladly help you plan your stay. Woodland House Hotel is an ideal centre for exploring the Lake District, Northern Pennines, Borders, Eden Valley, and is a perfect spot for an overnight stop on journeys to and from Scotland.

OPEN ALL YEAR.   NO SMOKING. V, S.D. B/A.   RESIDENTIAL LICENCE.   CHILDREN WELCOME. EN SUITE, BEVERAGES & T.V. IN ROOMS.   B. & B. FROM £20.

SEDBERGH

Oakdene Country Hotel

GARSDALE RD, SEDBERGH, CUMBRIA, LA10 5JN   TEL: (015396) 20280   FAX: (015396) 21501

Oakdene is a splendid Victorian house which retains many of its original features such as the fine pitch pine staircase, stained glass windows, gas light fittings, marble fireplaces and a wood-panelled bath in one of the bedrooms. Centrally heated and pleasantly furnished throughout in traditional style, there is a comfortable sitting room and bar (both with open fires), and each of the six guest bedrooms has views of the fells. The service is professional and friendly, the food simple, healthy and freshly prepared, and a typical evening menu always features some tasty vegetarian options such as Watercress Soup or Mushroom Paté followed by Spinach Filo Pie or Penne Pasta with Spicy Aubergine Sauce; desserts are home-made. Sedbergh is a relatively undiscovered part of Cumbria and offers holiday-makers in search of peace, tranquillity and good walks some of the finest scenery in the country in both the Lake District and the Yorkshire Dales National Parks; outdoor pursuits available locally include

horse-riding, fishing, cycling and golf. For guests arriving by car there is ample (inconspicuous) parking and for those arriving by train there is free collection from the station.
OPEN Feb. - Dec. inc.   V STD, S.D. B/A.   N/S DINING R., HALL, SITTING R. & 4 BEDRS.   CHILDREN WELCOME.   EN SUITE, TV & BEVERAGES IN BEDROOMS.   LICENSED.   ACCESS, DINERS, VISA, AMEX.   B. & B. £25 - 30, D. £12.50.

CROSS KEYS HOTEL, CAUTLEY, SEDBERGH, CUMBRIA, LA10 5NE
16th C. inn with beamed ceilings, flagged floors, mullion windows and log fires. All food prepared from fresh ingredients; home-baked bread.
TEL: (015396) 20284 OPEN Easter - NEw Year.   V, DIAB, S.D. B/A.   NO SMOKING.   CHILDREN WELCOME.   1 EN SUITE ROOM. BEVERAGES IN ROOMS.   B. & B. AROUND £24.

ULVERSTON

APPLETREE HOLME FARM, BLAWITH via ULVERSTON, CUMBRIA.
Exquisite farmhouse with beautiful gardens and views; welcoming log fires. Stupendous fare prepared from garden vegetables, home-laid free-range eggs and local dairy produce. Breakfast features porridge with Jersey cream & goat's milk yoghurt.
TEL: (01229) 885618 OPEN ALL YEAR.   V, S.D. B/A.   N/S ex. 1 lounge.   LICENSED.   EN SUITE, TV & BEVERAGES IN ROOMS.   D., B. & B. AROUND £52

Lonsdale House
11 DALTONGATE, ULVERSTON, LA12 7AD   TEL: (01229) 582598   FAX: (01229) 581260
20 bedroom Georgian house in centre of Ulverston with walled garden. Good selection of vegetarian dishes.
OPEN ALL YEAR. V STD, VE, S.D. B/A.   N/S DINING R.B   LICENSED.   CHILDREN & PETS.   CREDIT CARDS.   EN SUITE, TV & BEVERAGES IN ROOMS. B. & B. £27.50 - 40.

WINDERMERE

☙ *The Archway*
13 COLLEGE ROAD, WINDERMERE, CUMBRIA, LA23 1BU   TEL: (015394) 45613

This guest house is the one about which I received the most readers' recommendations when I was compiling the second edition of the guide. A small, 'impeccable' Victorian guest house furnished tastefully throughout with antiques, paintings and fresh flowers allows its reputation, nevertheless, to rest (and rest soundly) on the high standard of its cuisine: the best of fresh local ingredients are brought together in imaginative and nutritionally thoughtful menus (the breakfast fare offers everything from freshly squeezed fruit or vegetable juice to home-made spicy apple griddle cakes; bread, of course, is wholemeal and home-baked), while the 3-course evening menu includes a wine recommendation, and a tipple of home-made lemonade!
OPEN ALL YEAR.   NO SMOKING.   V, VE & DIAB STD.   LICENSED.   OVER 12S ONLY.   EN SUITE IN 5 ROOMS.   BEVERAGES & T.V. IN BEDROOMS.   CREDIT CARDS.   B. & B. FROM £22 - 25.

HAZEL BANK, HAZEL STREET, WINDERMERE, CUMBRIA.
Handsome Victorian residence 2 mins from Windermere; home-made, healthy cuisine .
TEL: (019662) 5486   V B/A.   NO SMOKING.   BYO WINE.   GOOD DISABLED ACCESS, inc. ground-floor bedroom.   OVER 7S ONLY.   EN SUITE & BEVERAGES.   T.V. IN LOUNGE.   B. & B.AROUND £18.

KIRKWOOD GUEST HOUSE, PRINCE'S ROAD, WINDERMERE, LA23 2DD
Attractive stone-built guest house peacefully 1 mile Lake Windermere. The breakfast is first-rate: a range of options are offered - including a menu for vegetarians.
TEL: (015394) 43907 OPEN ALL YEAR.   V STD. S.D. B/A.   N/S DINING R.   CHILDREN WELCOME.   PETS B/A. 5 EN SUITE ROOMS. BEVERAGES & TV IN ROOMS.   CREDIT CARDS.   B. & B. AROUND £20.

RESTAURANTS

AMBLESIDE

☙ HARVEST VEGETARIAN RESTAURANT, COMPSTON ROAD, AMBLESIDE,
Freshly prepared vegetarian food. Photographic exhibitions of Lakeland Landscapes.
TEL: (015394) 33151/33762   V, VE, GLUTEN-FREE STD.   NO SMOKING.   LICENSED.   DISABLED ACCESS.

V **WILF'S CAFE, 5 LAKE RD, AMBLESIDE, CUMBRIA, LA22 0AB**
Wholefood café with vegetarian and vegan choices situated above White Mountain.
TEL: (015394) 34749   NO SMOKING.   LICENSED.   DISABLED ACCESS.   CHILDREN WELCOME.

V **ZEFFIRELLI'S, AMBLESIDE, CUMBRIA.**
V EXC. NO SMOKING.   CHILDREN WELCOME.

CARLISLE

FANTAILS, THE GREEN, WEATHERHALL, CARLISLE, CUMBRIA.
TEL: (01228) 60239 V STD. N/S 1 SECTION.   LICENSED. CHILDREN WELCOME.

HUDSON'S COFFEE SHOP, TREASURY COURT, FISHER ST, CARLISLE
Centrally located café serving wide range of home-made meals and snacks.
TEL: (01228) 47733 V STD. NO SMOKING. LICENSED. DISABLED ACCESS.   CHILDREN WELCOME.

COCKERMOUTH

V **QUINCE AND MEDLAR, 13 CASTLEGATE, COCKERMOUTH, CA13 9EU**
VSUK Best Vegetarian Restaurant '89 & Vegetarian Living Best Vegetarian Restaurant '91.
TEL: (01900) 8235792 V STD. NO SMOKING. LICENSED. CHILDREN: OVER 5S ONLY

DENT

The Hop Bine Restaurant

DENT CRAFTS CENTRE, HELMSIDE, DENT, CUMBRIA. TEL: (015875) 400
Beautiful converted farm building (also housing the Dent Crafts Centre) serving a wide
range of delicious home-prepared food including cakes, pastries and teas. D B/A.
V STD. NO SMOKING. LICENSED. DISABLED ACCESS.   CHILDREN WELCOME.

KENDAL

Waterside Wholefoods

KENT VIEW, KENDAL, CUMBRIA. TEL: (01539) 729743
Day-time restaurant & shop serving fresh food; organic ingredients wherever possible.
V, VE EXC. S.D. B/A. NO SMOKING. DISABLED ACCESS: 'EXCELLENT'.   CHILDREN WELCOME.

Grange Bridge Cottage Tea Shop

GRANGE IN BORROWDALE, NR KESWICK, CUMBRIA, CA12 5OQ   TEL: (017687) 77201
An 18th C. beamed cottage by the bridge over the River Derwent at Grange in the beautiful
Borrowdale Valley. Delicious food - much of it home-prepared.
OPEN April - Oct. 11.30 am - 7 pm   V STD. NO SMOKING. DISABLED ACCESS.   CHILDREN WELCOME.

THE WILD STRAWBERRY, 54 MAIN STREET, KESWICK, CUMBRIA.
Friendly, cosy tea room with green slate floors & wooden beams; excellent range of
delicious home-made snacks & meals; speciality coffees & teas; vegetarian options.
TEL: (017687) 7439970 V, S.D.STD. NO SMOKING. WHEELCHAIR ACCESS, BUT NO TOILET FACILITIES.

KIRKBY LONSDALE

V **LUPTON TOWER VEG. G.H. & REST., LUPTON, NR KIRKBY LONSDALE**
For full details please see under entry in accommodatin section.

MEWS COFFEE HOUSE, MAIN STREET, KIRBY LONSDALE, CUMBRIA.
TEL: (01468) 71007 V STD. N/S 1 SEPARATE DINING R.   LICENSED. DISABLED ACCESS. CHILDREN.

KIRKBY STEPHEN

THE OLD FORGE BISTRO, 39 NORTH RD, KIRBY STEPHEN, CA17 4RE
Converted 17th C. smithy specialising in vegetarian & wholefood plus traditional fare.
TEL: (017683) 71832 V, WH STD. NO SMOKING. LICENSED. DISABLED ACCESS.   CHILDREN.

THE LORTON VALE

THE BARN, NEW HOUSE FARM, LORTON, COCKERMOUTH, CA13 9UU
The Barn is situated on the B5289 between Lorton and Loweswater in the beautiful Lorton
Vale. It offers a wide range of delicious lunches and teas are served therein.
TEL: (01900) 85404 V STD. NO SMOKING.

Cheshire & Manchester

ACCOMMODATION

HOLMES CHAPEL

HOLLY LODGE HOTEL, 70 LONDON ROAD, CW4 7AS
Large Victorian house in the centre of Holmes Chapel. Excellent food.
TEL: (01477) 37033 OPEN ALL YEAR. V STD. VE, S.D. B/A. LICENSED. DISABLED ACCESS. CHILDREN WELCOME. PETS B/A. EN SUITE, TV & BEVERAGES. CREDIT CARDS. B. & B. AROUND £36.

KNUTSFORD

Longview Hotel and Restaurant

51-55 MANCHESTER RD, KNUTSFORD, CHESHIRE, WA16 0LX   TEL: (01565) 632119

This charming small hotel overlooking the common in the historic market town of Knutsford, offers a true haven for the holiday-maker or business man or woman visiting Cheshire. The present owners have refurbished the hotel - but have done so with care to ensure that the elegance and character that it enjoyed in former Victorian times has been retained. The culinary standard is very high indeed: all food is prepared from fresh ingredients wherever possible and cooked on the premises; and the vegetarian selection is excellent (the hotel is included in *The Vegetarian Good Food Guide*). A typical dinner menu would feature perhaps Greek Salad, followed by Chicken Louchow (chicken in sauce with an Oriental influence) or, from the vegetarian menu, Vegetable Florina, tasty vegetables with a red wine sauce, topped with feta cheese sauce. A 'Vegetarian Medley' is also available, giving diners the chance to sample a little of each of the vegetarian dishes on the menu; you can complete your meal from a selection of tempting desserts.
OPEN ALL YEAR. V STD. S.D. B/A. LICENSED. CHILDREN WELCOME. PETS B/A. MOST ROOMS EN SUITE. BEVERAGES & TV IN ROOMS. CREDIT CARDS. B. & B. AROUND £32.

TOFT HOTEL, TOFT ROAD, KNUTSFORD, WA16 9EH
16th C. farmhouse. Vegetarian emphasis, including separate restaurant.
TEL: (01565) 3470 OPEN ALL YEAR. V STD. NO SMOKING. LICENSED. CHILDREN: OVER 10S ONLY. EN SUITE & TV IN 6 ROOMS. BEVERAGES IN ROOMS. CREDIT CARDS B. & B. AROUND £17.

NANTWICH

Rookery Hall

WORLESTON, NR NANTWICH, CW5 6DQ   TEL: (01270) 610016
Splendid Georgian hall - converted to a hotel & conference centre - in 200 acres including 28 acres of gardens and wooded parkland. High standard of service, decor and cuisine.
OPEN ALL YEAR. N/S DINING R. V, VE, S.D., B/A. LICENSED. DISABLED ACCESS. CHILDREN WELCOME. EN SUITE & SATELLITE TV IN ROOMS. ROOM SERVICE.

RESTAURANTS

BURY

The Ramsbottom Victuallers Company Ltd

16-18 MARKET PLACE, RAMSBOTTOM, BURY TEL: (01706) 825070
The award-winning Village Restaurant has been established for 8 years and is renowned for its 6-course celebration dinners (no choice, but no disappointment either!), while "The Ramsbottom Victuallers Supper Room" provides simple 3-course evening meals.
NO SMOKING. V, S.D. B/A. LICENSED. SOPHISTICATED CHILDREN WELCOME. ACCESS, VISA.

CHESTER

THE BLUE BELL RESTAURANT, 65 NORTHGATE STREET, CHESTER
Chester's only surviving mediaeval inn. High standard of service and excellent food.
TEL: (01244) 317758 V, S.D. STD. N/S ONE ROOM (13-15 SEATS). LICENSED. CHILDREN WELCOME.

MANCHESTER

CAFÉ GALLERY, CITY ART GALLERY, MOSLEY ST, MANCHESTER.
Specialising in home-cooking with a large vegetarian/vegan menu.
TEL: (0161) 236 5244 V STD. N/S AREA. CHILDREN WELCOME. CREDIT CARDS.

THE DRAWING ROOM, 254 MOSTON LN, MOSTON, MANCHESTER
Pre-war artefacts, open fire and music set the ambience. Excellent food.
TEL: (0161) 203 4967 OPEN ALL DAY. V STD. CHILDREN WELCOME. LICENSED.

THE GALLERY BISTRO, WHITWORTH ART GALLERY, OXFORD RD,.
TEL: (0161) 273 5651 NO SMOKING. V STD. LICENSED. DISABLED ACCESS. CHILDREN WELCOME.

V **THE GREENHOUSE VEGETARIAN REST., 331 GT WESTERN ST, RUSHOLME**
TEL: (0161) 224 0730 NO SMOKING. V, VE STD. WHEELCHAIR ACCESSS. CHILDREN 'if fully supervised'.

V *On the Eighth Day*
109 OXFORD ROAD, MANCHESTER, M1 7DU   TEL: (0161) 273 1850
On The Eighth Day celebrated 24 years as a non-smoking wholefood café in 1994.
Manchester's oldest cooperative continues to offer a daily changing menu of both vegan
and vegetarian food. Only 10 minutes from the city centre, it well deserves its reputation
for friendly service and the finest vegetarian cooking. The attached wholefood shop also
offers a wide selection of tasty take-away food and produce.   Outside catering service
available.
OPEN MON-FRI 10 A.M. - 7 P.M. SAT 10 A.M. - 4.30 P.M. NO SMOKING. V, S.D. STD. CHILDREN AND GUIDE
DOGS WELCOME. LICENSED.

SADDLEWORTH

V *Woody's Vegetarian Restaurant*
5 KING ST, DELPH, SADDLEWORTH, G.M.C. TEL: (01457) 871197
Vegetarian restaurant with a charming and elegant atmosphere. Excellent meat-free fare.
Woody's has been a 'Vegetarian Restaurant of the Year' finalist in 1989, 1990 and 1991.
NO SMOKING. V, VE EXC. LICENSED. DISABLED ACCESS. ACCESS, VISA.

Lancashire

ACCOMMODATION

BLACKPOOL

MAINS HALL COUNTRY HOUSE, MAINS LN, SINGLETON, NR BLACKPOOL.
Grade II listed country houses in 4 acres of private grounds. Excellent food prepared from
first-class seasonal ingredients. Good conference facilities. Private river frontage.
TEL: (01253) 885130 OPEN ALL YEAR. V, VE, DIAB, STD. S.D. B/A. N/S BEDRS. LICENSED. DISABLED
ACCESS. CHILDREN WELCOME. PETS B/A. EN SUITE, TV & BEVERAGES. B. & B. FROM £25.

RUSKIN HOTEL, ALBERT RD, BLACKPOOL, FY1 4PW TEL: (01253) 24063
First-rate food prepared from fresh, local ingredients and vegetarian option available.
OPEN ALL YEAR. V STD. S.D. B/A. LICENSED. DISABLED ACCESS. CHILDREN WELCOME. PETS B/A.
EN SUITE, TV & BEVERAGES IN ROOMS.

TREVINE HOTEL, 4 HAVELOCK ST, BLACKPOOL. TEL: (01253) 20897
OPEN ALL YEAR. V STD. CHILDREN. EN SUITE, TV & BEVERAGE. LICENSED. B. & B AROUND £50.

V **WILDLIFE HOTEL, 39 WOODFIELD RD, MID-SOUTH SHORE, BLACKPOOL**
Licensed family hotel adjacent to the promenade.
TEL: (01253) 46143 OPEN ALL YEAR. V, VE, EXC. NO SMOKING. CHILDREN. LICENSED. B. & B. AROUND £13.

CARNFORTH

KILNCROFT G. H., 15 MAIN ST, WARTON, CARNFRROTH, LA5 9NR
Family-run guest house and restaurant. Organically grown veg. from smallholding.
TEL: (01542) 735788 V STD. CHILDREN & PETS. EN SUITE, TV & BEVERAGES. B. & B. AROUND £17.

THIE-NE-SHEE, MOOR CLOSE LN, OVER KELLET, CARNFORTH, LA6 1DF
Bungalow with superb views of Lake District, mountains and Morecambe Bay. Near to Steamtown Carnforth and Leighton Moss R.S.P.B. Nature Reserve. Healthy breakfasts!
TEL: (01524) 735882 OPEN ALL YEAR ex. Xmas & New Year. V, S.D. B/A. NO SMOKING. CHILDREN WELCOME. ROOM SERVICE. T.V. B. & B. FROM £12.

Willowfield Hotel

THE PROMENADE, ARNSIDE, VIA CARNFORTH, LANCS, LA5 0AD TEL: (01524) 761354
Willowfield Hotel is a small, family-run hotel, which is beautifully situated immediately overlooking the Kent Estuary towards the Lakeland hills. All bedrooms are well furnished and have wash basins, central heating, electric blankets and shaver points (some have en suite showers), and the comfortable lounge and spacious dining room both overlook the estuary, as do most of the bedrooms. Willowfield Hotel is an ideal base for exploring South Cumbria and North Lancashire.
OPEN ALL YEAR. NO SMOKING. S.D. B/A. CHILDREN WELCOME. PETS B/A. TABLE LICENCE. SOME EN SUITE ROOMS. TV & BEVERAGES IN ROOMS. B. & B. FROM £18.

CHORLEY

SHAWHILL HOTEL, GOLF AND COUNTRY CLUB, PRESTON RD, WHITTLE-LE-WOODS, CHORLEY, PR6 7PP
TEL: (012572) 69221 OPEN ALL YEAR. V, VE, DIAB STD. S.D. B/A. LICENSED. CHILDREN WELCOME. PETS B/A. EN SUITE, TV & BEVERAGES IN ROOMS. B. & B. AROUND £42.

INGLETON

Bridge End Guest House

MILL LANE, INGLETON, NR CARNFORTH, LANCS, LA6 3EP TEL: (01524) 241413
Formerly a mill owner's Georgian home, this charming, listed guest house, stands on the River Doe by the Ingleton Waterfalls Walk. It has retained many period features and its patio cantilevers over the River Doe. Everything is home-cooked from fresh ingredients. You are just 3 minutes' walk from Ingleton village and are surrounded by the Yorkshire Dales National Park. Car park.
OPEN ALL YEAR. V, VE STD, S.D. B/A. ORG, WH WHEN AVAIL. LOW-FAT COOKING. CHILDREN & PETS WELCOME. EN SUITE, TV & BEVERAGES IN ALL ROOMS. B. & B. FROM £16, D. £8.50.

LYTHAM ST ANNES

Chadwick Hotel & Leisure Centre

SOUTH PROMENADE, LYTHAM ST ANNES, LANCS, FY8 1NP
The Chadwick is a family-run hotel and leisure complex which stands on a corner site commanding a beautiful sea front position. Accommodation is in comfortable rooms, many of which have sea views; there is a honeymoon suite with a four-poster bed. The food is excellent: everything is prepared from fresh produce wherever possible, and there are always two vegetarian options on the daily changing evening menu.
OEN ALL YEAR. V STD. VE, S.D. B/A. N/S DINING R. & LOUNGE. WHEELCHAIR ACCESS. LICENSED. CHILDREN WELCOME. EN SUITE, TV & BEVERAGES IN ROOMS. D. B. & B. FROM £35.

PRESTON

BRICKHOUSE HOTEL & RESTAURANT, CHIPPING, NR PRESTON
Charming 18th C. house; everything home-made including the bread and icecreams.
TEL: (01995) 61085 OPEN ALL YEAR. V, VE, DIAB & MOST S.D. STD. N/S PART DINING R. LICENSED. DISABLED ACCESS. CHILDREN WELCOME. EN SUITE, TV & BEVERAGES. B. & B. AROUND £26.

ROSSENDALE

SYKESIDE COUNTRY HOUSE HOTEL, HASLINGDEN, ROSSENDALE
A 19th C. country house convereted into award-winning hotel. Wonderful food.
TEL: (01206) 831163 OPEN ALL YEAR. V, S.D. B/A. N/S DINING R & BEDRS. V, S.D. B/A. LICENSED. DISABLED ACCESS. CHILDREN WELCOME. EN SUITE, TV & BEVERAGES. B. & B. AROUND £43.

SILVERDALE

LINDETH HOUSE, LINDETH RD, SILVERDALE, CARNFORTH, LA5 0TX
Pleasant country residence. Excellent English cuisine prepared from fresh, local produce
TEL: (01524) 701238 OPEN Feb. - Dec. V B/A. N/S DINING R BY REQUEST & BEDRS. LICENSED. DISABLED ACCESS. CHILDREN: OVER 12S. EN SUITE, BEVERAGES & T.V IN ROOMS. B. & B. AROUND £25.

SOUTHPORT

Ambassador Private Hotel

13 BATH ST, SOUTHPORT, LANCS, PR9 0DP   TEL: (01704) 543998

ETB 3 Crown Commended. The Ambassador Hotel occupies one of the most central positions in Southport adjacent to beautiful Lord Street, with its covered boulevard, elegant shops and the promenade. The en suite bedrooms are comfortably furnished and well-equipped with a range of amenities including a TV, radio alarm, hair dryer, a hospitality tray, (with various drinks and snacks), a shoe cleaner and a mending kit. Your host, Margaret Bennett, is a qualified chef and prepares tasty meals from fresh, seasonal produce: the breakfast menu is tremendous offering a wide variety of options including, in addition to the traditional English, cheese on toast or omelettes. There are many interesting places to visit including Martin Mere Wildfowl Sanctuary, Formby Red Squirrel Colony & Liverpool's Albert Dock & Maritime Museum. For the more energetic there is golf to be enjoyed at one of Southport's six courses, or the facilities of a leisure centre. There is a comfortable bar (not open to non-residents)where you will be entertained by the organist.

OPEN ALL YEAR Ex. Xmas. N/S DINING R & BEDRS. V, S.D. B/A. LICENSED. CHILDREN: OVER 5S ONLY. PETS WELCOME. EN SUITE, BEVERAGES & T.V IN ROOMS. CREDIT CARDS. B. & B. FROM £23.

RESTAURANTS

LANCASTER

LIBRA WHOLEFOOD RESTAURANT, 19 BROCK ST, LANCASTER
TEL: (01524) 61551 V, WH EXC. NO SMOKING. LICENSED. DISABLED ACCESS. CHILDREN WELCOME.

PRESTON

EAT FIT, 20 FRIARGATE, PRESTON, LANCS. TEL: (01772) 555855
V STD. 30% N/S. LICENSED. DISABLED: 'three shallow steps, which do not prohibit wheelchairs'

Yorkshire & Humberside

North Yorkshire

ACCOMMODATION

BEDALE

WATERSIDE, CRAKEHALL, BEDALE, N. YORKS, DL8 1HS
Modern house with an acre of mature gardens; home-cooked food prepared from organically grown vegetables, free range eggs and poultry.
TEL: (01677) 22908 OPEN ALL YEAR. V, S.D. B/A. N/S DINING RM, SUN LOUNGE, SITTING R & BEDR. CHILDREN WELCOME. 3 EN SUITE ROOMS. BEVERAGES & T.V. IN ROOMS. B. & B. AROUND £21.

DANBY

FOX & HOUNDS INN, BROOK LANE, AINTHORPE, NR DANBY, N. YORKS.
One of the oldest inns in the country and with an impressive guest list which has included Oliver Cromwell; all vegetarian, vegan and diabetic meals are home made from fresh ingredients wherever possible; excellent hand-pulled Theakstons ales.
TEL: (01287) 660218 OPEN ALL YEAR. V, VE STD. S.D. B/A. N/S PART OF DINING R. LICENSED. DISABLED ACCESS FOR DINING ONLY NOT TO BEDRS. CHILDREN WELCOME. BEVERAGES & TV IN ROOMS. B. & B. AROUND £18.

HARROGATE

V *Amadeus Vegetarian Hotel*

115 FRANKLIN RD, HARROGATE, HG1 5EN   TEL: (01423) 505151

Elegant Victorian house with luxurious en suite rooms. Superb vegetarian cuisine.
OPEN ALL YEAR ex Xmas. V EXC. VE, WH STD. SOME ORG & S.D. NO SMOKING. CHILDREN WELCOME.
PETS B/A. 4 EN SUITE ROOMS. TV & BEVERAGES IN ROOMS. B. & B. FROM £22. D £12.50.

Wharfedale House Hotel

28 HARLOW MOOR DRIVE, HARROGATE, N. YORKS, HG2 OJY   TEL: (01423) 522233

Wharfedale House is a quiet, comfortable spacious house which is beautifully situated overlooking the lovely Valley Gardens yet just a leisurely walk from the centre of the elegant spa town of Harrogate with its exhibition and conference centre. The house has been beautifully furnished and appointed and each of the en suite bedrooms has tea and coffee-making facilities and a colour T.V. Food is first-rate: the proprietors are trained chefs and will often prepare meals only after consultation with guests about their individual requirements and, having eschewed the idea of incorporating a potentially noisy bar onto the premises, they offer a much more civilised Licensed Bar Service in the comfortable lounge; lots of other helpful services are also available including babysitting, dry cleaning and free collection from the station. Situated twixt the Moors and the Dales, Harrogate is a perfect base from which to explore both of these regions, and additionally you are just 30 minutes' drive from York. Send for colour brochure to Tricia and Howard Quinn to receive details of special breaks, including Christmas and New Year.
OPEN ALL YEAR. N/S DINING R. V, S.D. B/A. LICENSED. CHILDREN WELCOME. PETS WELCOME B/A.
EN SUITE, BEVERAGES & TV IN ROOMS. B. & B. FROM £23.

HAWES

RIGG HOUSE WEST, APPERSETT, HAWES, DL8 3LR

Historic house. All food home-cooked & freshly prepared - including the bread.
TEL: (01969) 667712 OPEN ALL YEAR. N/S BEDRS. V & LOW FAT B/A. LICENSED. CHILDREN WEL-
COME. BEVERAGES ON REQUEST. T.V.

Simonstone Hall

HAWES, WENSLEYDALE, N. YORKS, DL8 3LY   TEL: (01969) 667255 FAX: (01969) 667741

Simonstone Hall, dating from 1733, has been restored and converted into a most comfortable owner-run country house hotel. The menu offers freshly prepared English dishes using an abundance of local produce. The English Tourist Board recently adjudged owner John Jeffryes the hotelier offering the warmest welcome to visitors and one of a select few to receive the RAC top award - the Blue Ribbon - for the last 5 years. The large, south-facing panelled drawing rooms are beautifully furnished with antiques and command uninterrupted views of upper Wensleydale. You are in excellent walking country, and only five minutes from the Pennine Way.
OPEN ALL YEAR. V & HEALTHY CHOICE STD. S.D. INC. GLUTEN-FREE & DIABETIC, B/A. SMOKING
EFFECTIVELY DISCOURAGED IN DINING R. LICENSED. DISABLED ACCESS. CHILDREN & DOGS AL-
WAYS WELCOME. EN SUITE, BEVERAGES & TV IN ROOMS. ACCESS, VISA. D. B. & B. FROM ABOUT £60
BUT PHONE FOR ANY SPECIAL OFFER DETAILS.

HELMSLEY

The Pheasant Hotel

HAROME, HELMSLEY, N. YORKS, YO6 5JG   TEL: (01439) 771241/770416

Delightful hotel created from existing village dwellings with a large garden & paddock, overlooking pond. Indoor heated swimming pool.
OPEN Mar. - Nov. N/S DINING R. V, S.D. B/A. LICENSED. DISABLED ACCESS. CHILDREN: OVER 12S
ONLY. PETS B/A. EN SUITE, TV & BEVERAGES IN ROOMS. D., B. & B. £49.50 - 60.

INGLETON

STORRS DALE, HAWES RD, INGLETON, LN. YORKS
Small guest house specialising in wholesome home cooking.
TEL: (01468) 41843 OPEN ALL YEAR. NO SMOKING.   V, S.D. B/A.   LICENSED. CHILDREN WELCOME.
BEVERAGES IN ROOMS. T.V.   B. & B. AROUND £17.

KIRKBYMOORSIDE

GEORGE AND DRAGON, MARKET PLACE, KIRKBY MOORSIDE, YO6 6AA
Exceptionally pleasant hostelry with log fires and excellent, home-cooked food.
TEL: (01751) 433334 OPEN ALL YEAR.   V STD. S.D. B/A.   EN SUITE, TV & BEVERAGES IN ROOMS LICENSED. B.
& B. £26 - 32.

LEYBURN

Greystone

PRESTON-UNDER-SCAR, NR LEYBURN, N. YORKS. TEL: (01969) 22042
Stone-built village house with superb views from bedrooms over Wensleydale Peace and
quiet. Excellent centre for walking. Only fresh produce used in cooking.
OPEN Mar. - OCt. V, VE, S.D. B/A.   N/S DINING R., BEDR & LOUNGE.   CHILDREN & PETS WELCOME. EN SUITE,
TV & BEVERAGES IN ROOMS.   B. & B. AROUND £14.

MALTON

NEWSTEAD GRANGE COUNTRY HOUSE, NORTON, MALTON, YO17 9PJ
Elegant Georgian country house retaining authentic features such as working shutters and
antique furniture; a log fire blazes in the lounge in cooler weather. Each bedroom is
individually styled with period furniture, paintings & prints. The hotel is set in 2 acres of
grounds with mature chestnut, copper beech and sycamore trees. All food has been prepared
from organically produced fruit and vegetables from the kitchen gardens wherever possible.
TEL: (01653) 692502 OPEN MID-FEB TO DEC. NO SMOKING. V, S.D. B/A. LICENSED. CHILDREN: OVER 12S
ONLY. EN SUITE, BEVERAGES & TV IN ROOMS. B. & B. FROM £26. D. £11.50.

MIDDLEHAM

MILLER'S HOUSE HOTEL, MARKET PLACE, MIDDLEHAM, WENSLEYDALE
Peaceful Georgian country house commanding splendid views from its elevated position
close to the cobbled village square of Middleham.
TEL: (01969) 22630   OPEN 1 Feb - 2 Jan. N/S DINING R. V STD, S.D. B/A.   LICENSED. OVER 10S ONLY.
EN SUITE, TV & BEVERAGES IN ROOMS. B. & B. AROUND £32.

NORTHALLERTON

SOLBERGE HALL HOTEL, NEWBY WISKE, NORTHALLERTON, DL7 9ER
Luxury hotel with an atmosphere of Victorian grandeur.
TEL: (01609) 77919 OPEN ALL YEAR.   V STD, S.D. B/A.   LICENSED.   DISABLED ACCESS.   CHILDREN
WELCOME. EN SUITE, BEVERAGES & T.V. B. & B. AROUND £40.

THE SUNDIAL HOTEL, DARLINGTON RD., NORTHALLERTON, DL6 2XF
Modern hotel in 3 acres of gardens and convenient for Teesside, the Moors and Dales.
TEL: (01609) 780525 OPEN ALL YEAR. V, VE & LOW-FAT STD. S.D. B/A. N/S PART DINING R. LICENSED.
DISABLED ACCESS. CHILDREN WELCOME. E N SUITE, TV & BEVERAGES IN ROOMS. ROOM AROUND £35.

PATELEY BRIDGE

MOORHOUSE COTTAGE, PATELEY BRIDGE, HG3 5JF TEL: (01423) 711123
Restored 18th century farmhouse in picturesque surroundings, overlooking Nidderdale.
OPEN Easter - Oct. inc.   V, S.D. B/A. NO SMOKING.   CHILDREN WELCOME. BEVERAGES & TV IN ROOMS.
B. & B. AROUND £15.

PICKERING

COSTA BECK HOUSE, 12 WESTGATE, PICKERING, N. YORKS.
Delightful Victorian house offering superb B. & B. accommodation. Vegetarian b'fasts.
TEL: (01751) 472380 OPEN ALL YEAR. V STD. NO SMOKING.   BEVERAGES & TV. B. & B. AROUND £16.

FOREST AND VALE HOTEL, MALTON RD, PICKERING, YO18 7DL
TEL: (01751) 472722 V STD.   CHILDREN & PETS.   LICENSED. EN SITE, TV & BEVERAGES IN ROOMS. B. & B.
AROUND £23.

Heathcote Guest House

100 EASTGATE, PICKERING, YO18 7DW   TEL: (01751) 476991

Heathcote Guest House is a lovely Victorian house retaining a number of original features including a magnificent mahogany staircase, a galleried landing and arched fireplaces (though there is central heating too). Situated in the charming town of Pickering on the edge of the North York Moors National Park, it is a perfect place from which to explore the Moors, Coast and Wolds. Bedrooms are comfortably furnished and have en suite or private facilities. Dinner is first-rate: a typical home-cooked evening menu featuring Stuffed Mushrooms, followed by Cheese and Lentil Loaf (with a selection of vegetables) and a dessert, such as Plum Pie with Ice Cream; freshly brewed coffee and mints would complete the meal.

OPEN JAN. - DEC. Ex Xmas.   V A SPECIALITY. S.D. B/A.   NO SMOKING.   3 EN SUITE ROOMS.   BEVERAGES & TV INROOMS.   CREDIT CARDS.   B. & B. FROM £18-21, D. £10.

RICHMOND

THE KINGS HEAD HOTEL, MARKET PLACE, RICHMOND, DL10 4HS

Elegant hotel overlooking cobbled market square. Meals cooked from fresh, local produce
OPEN ALL YEAR. V, VE STD. S.D. B/A. N/S DINING R. & SOME BEDR. LICENSED. DISABLED ACCESS. CHILDREN WELCOME. EN SUITE, BEVERAGES & T.V. IN ROOMS.

PEAT GATE HEAD, LOW ROW IN SWALEDALE, RICHMOND, DL11 6PP

300 year old house on an elevated south facing site overlooking river and dale; excellent food home-prepared from fresh produce
TEL: (01748) 86388. OPEN ALL YEAR. V STD, S.D. B/A. N/S DINING R, 1 SITTING R & BEDRS. LICENSED. GROUND FLOOR BEDROOM EN SUITE. OVER 5S. 3 EN SUITE ROOMS. BEVERAGES. T.V. LOUNGE. D., B. & B. AROUND £40.

Ridgeway Guest House

7 DARLINGTON RD, RICHMOND, N. YORKS, DL10 7BG TEL: (01748) 823801

1920's detached house in an acre of lovely gardens. A collection of furniture, clocks and china complement the house. Locally grown produce used where possible in cooking.
OPEN ALL YEAR. V B/A. NO SMOKING. LICENSED. CHILDREN & PETS B/A. EN SUITE & BEVERAGES-ROOMS. T.V. IN SITTING ROOM. B. & B. AROUND £20.

ROBIN HOODS BAY

Falconhurst Wholefood Guest House

MOUNT PLEASANT SOUTH, ROBINS HOODS BAY, N. YORKS. TEL: (01947) 880582

Double-fronted villa on the Bank Top of the village; all food home-cooked from fresh, sometimes organic, ingredients, including bread, yogurt, preserves and ice cream
OPEN Easter to Sept. NO SMOKING. V EXC. WH STD. CHILDREN & PETS B/A. BEVERAGES IN ROOMS. TV IN LOUNGE. B. & B. AROUND £19.

Meadowfield Bed & Breakfast

MOUNT PLEASANT NORTH, ROBIN HOOD'S BAY, NR WHITBY, YO22 4RE TEL: (01947) 880564

Delightful Victorian guest house, completely refurbished but retaining original character. Traditional, vegetarian and vegan options always available.
OPEN ALL YEAR. V, VE STD. N/S DINING R & ALL PUBLIC AREAS. CHILDREN WELCOME. BEVERAGES IN ROOMS. PORTABLE T.V. AVAILABLE. B. & B. FROM £13.

SCARBOROUGH

ALL SEASONS, 5 GRANVILLE RD, SCARBOROUGH, N. YORKS.
TEL: (01723) 361970 V STD. CHILDREN WELCOME. EN SUITE, TV & BEVERAGES. B. & B. AROUND £17.

Amber Lodge

17 TRINITY RD, SCARBOROUGH, YO11 2TD TEL: (01723) 369088

Edwardian house of great charm, peacefully situated in conservation area 10 mins walk from South bay. Fresh ingredients used in cooking. Separate vegetarian menu, tasty options.
OPEN Mar. - Oct. V STD. S.D. B/A. NO SMOKING. 5 EN SUITE ROOMS. BEVERAGES & TV IN ROOMS. CREDIT CARDS. B. & B. FROM £17, D. £7.

Avoncroft

CROWN TERRACE, SOUTH CLIFF, SCARBOROUGH, YO11 2BL   TEL: (01723) 372737

The Avoncroft is a comfortable, friendly, family-run hotel which stands in the centre of a Georgian terrace overlooking the Crown Gardens and within mintes walk of the beach., town centre, road and rail terminals. Bedrooms have been comfortably appointed with a range of helpful amenities, and hairdryers and irons are available on request; the hotel is licensed and there is a well-stocked bar in which to relax. The food is very good: all meals are prepared in plentiful quantities from fresh, local produce, and individual requirements - incuding vegetarian - are always catered for on the daily changing menu.

OPEN ALL YEAR.   V, VE, DIAB, STD. S.D. B/A.   LICENSED.   CHILDREN & PETS.   EN SUITE, TV & BEVERAGES. B. & B. FROM £20.

Bay Hotel

67 ESPLANADE, SCARBORO'. TEL: (01723) 501038

Magnificently situated overlooking the South Bay and the Spa, the Bay Hotel is a beautiful Victorian house which commands one of the finest views in Scarborough, from its fine castle and picturesque harbour on one side, to the sea-swept cliffs to Filey Brigg on the other. Guests at the Bay are accommodated in comfortable, centrally heated bedrooms - each with a private bathroom - and there is a pleasant, spacious lounge overlooking the sea and coastline. The food is delicious: traditional dishes are prepared from fresh, local produce and meals are served in a attractive dining room with views. Scarbrough is one of Britain's great seaside resorts - and as such has much to commend it; additionally you are within easy reach of York, Whitby and the North York Moors.

OPEN Mar. - Nov.   N/S DINING R., SOME BEDROOMS.   S.D. B/A. LICENSED.   CHILDREN & PETS WELCOME. EN SUITE, TV & BEVERAGES IN ROOMS.

EXCELSIOR HOTEL, 1 MARLBOROUGH ST, SCARBORO', YO12 7HG

Small private hotel on a corner of the North Bay. Much of the food is home made from fresh ingredients - including the bread, preserves, cakes, soups and sweets.

TEL: (01723) 360716 OPEN Easter to Oct.   S.D. B/A.   NO SMOKING.   CHILDREN WELCOME. BEVERAGES IN ROOMS.   T.V. IN LOUNGE.   B. & B. FROM £18.

Flower in Hand Guest House

BURR BANK, SCARBOROUGH, N. YORKS, YO11 1PN   TEL: (01723) 371471

The Flower in Hand, nestling beneath the castle walls and overlooking the harbour and South Bay, has for 150 years been a much-loved feature of Scarborough's Old Town. It is no longer a pub, but a warm and friendly B. & B. run by people who genuinely like people and is renowned for traditional sizzling Yorkshire breakfasts, as well as for the wide alternative choice offered to vegetarians and vegans.

OPEN ALL YEAR Ex. Xmas/New Year.   N/S DINING R.   V, S.D. B/A.   OVER 2S ONLY.   3 EN SUITE ROOMS. BEVERAGES & T.V. IN ALL ROOMS.   CREDIT CARDS.   B. & B. FROM £17.50.

Glywin Guest House

153 COLUMBUS RAVINE. SCARBOROUGH, YO12 7QZ   TEL: (01723) 371311

Glywin Guest House is a clean, comfortable establishment close to the sea front and all the attractions of Scarborough. The proprietors specialise in vegetarian cuisine although omnivores are also catered for.

OPEN ALL YEAR.   V SPECIALITY, S.D. B/A.   N/S DINING R.   CHILDREN WELCOME.   BEVERAGES & T.V. IN ROOMS. B. & B. FROM £13. D. £5.50.

'The Gypsy' Vegetarian Guesthouse

'RANWORTH', CHURCH RD, RAVENSCAR, SCARBOROUGH, YO13 0LZ   TEL: (01723) 870366

A Victorian house in the small, peaceful village of Ravenscar overlooking Robin Hood's Bay. Aromatherapy massages also available.

OPEN ALL YEAR.   V, WH EXC. S.D. B/A.   NO SMOKING.   CHILDREN WELCOME.   PETS B/A.   BEVERAGES IN ROOMS.   T.V. LOUNGE AND PORTABLE T.V. FOR BEDROOMS.   B. & B. FROM £14. D. £7.

HARCOURT HOTEL, 45 ESPLANADE, SCARBROUGH, YO11 2AY

TEL: (01723) 373930 V STD. CHILDREN WELCOME. EN SUITE & BEVERAGES IN ROOMS. B. B. AROUND £23.

LONSDALE VILLA HOTE, LONSDALE RD, SOUTH CLIFF, SCARBOROUGH.
TEL: (01723) 363383 V STD. CHILDREN & PETS. EN SUITE, TV & BEVERAGES. B. & B. AROUND £18.

MOSELEY LODGE, 26 AVENUE VICTORIA, SOUTH CLIFF, SCARBOROUGH,
TEL: (01723) 360564 V STD. CHILDREN WELCOME. EN SUITE AVAILABLE. B. & B. AROUND £17.

Selbourne Licensed Hotel

4 WEST ST, SOUTH CLIFF, SCARBOROUGH, N. YORKS, YO11 2QL   TEL: (01723) 372822

The Selbourne is a 14-bedroom family-run hotel which stands on Scarborough's South Cliff close to the Esplanade and within just a few minutes walk of the cliff lift to the sea. Each of the roomy bedrooms face either the front or overlook gardens to the side of the hotel; there is a well-stocked bar and spacious lounge for guests' use. Although not an exclusively vegetarian hotel, vegetarian, vegan and any special diet can be catered for by arrangement; packed lunches are also available. There are reductions for weekly bookings, senior citizens and children throughout the year.
OPEN early Jan - mid Dec.   V, VE, S.D. B/A.   CHILDREN WELCOME. LICENSED. EN SUITE, TV & BEVERAGES IN ROOMS. CREDIT CARDS. B. & B. FROM £18.25.

WREA HEAD HOUSE, WREA HEAD FARM, BARMOOR LANE, SCALBY
Beautifully appointed house with panoramic views of the sea and surrounding countryside, set on the edge of the North York Moors Nat. Park.
TEL: (01723) 375844 OPEN ALL YEAR. V, S.D. B/A. NO SMOKING. CHILDREN: OVER 8S ONLY.   EN SUITE, BEVERAGES & T.V. IN ROOMS. CREDIT CARDS. B. & B. AROUND £22.

SETTLE

Sansbury Place Vegetarian Guest House

50 DUKE ST, SETTLE, N. YORKS, BD24 9AS TEL: (01729) 823840
Sansbury Place is a spacious Victorian house with splendid views of the surrounding hills, and just a few minutes walk from the famous Settle to Carlisle railway. Your hosts offer a wide range of imaginative dishes prepared from fresh and wholefood ingredients (organic where possible). Guests are welcomed with a pot of tea and home-baking, and a typical evening meal would feature Mushroom and Walnut Pâté, folowed by Asparagus and Peanut Strudel and a delicious dessert such as Lemon and Blackberry Charlotte.
OPEN ALL YEAR. V EXC. VE, S.D. STD. CHILDREN WELCOME. TV IN LOUNGE. B. & B. FROM £16. D £9.

SKIPTON

BRIDGE END FARM, GRASSINGTON, THRESHFIELD, SKIPTON, BD23 5NH
A charming Dales cottage with beams, window seats & a spiral staircase; its large gardens run down to the river. Log fires. Interesting vegetarian dishes.
TEL: (01756) 752463 OPEN ALL YEAR. V, S.D. B/A. NO SMOKING. CHILDREN. T.V. MOST BEDROOMS. B. & B. FROM £18.

Devonshire Arms Country House Hotel

BOLTON ABBEY, SKIPTON, N. YORKS, BD23 6AJ   TEL: (01756) 710441 FAX: (01756) 710564

The Devonshire Arms is an historic hotel (hospitality has been offered on this site since the 17th C.) which stands in the heart of the Yorkshire Dales, midway between the east and west coasts. It has been carefully restored and extended, under the personal supervision of the Duchess of Devonshire, to create an hotel of great elegance, character and charm: a stone-flagged reception hall with an open log fire leads into handsome lounges furnished with antiques and family portraits from Chatsworth, and the recenty refurbished Burlington restaurant extends into the new, Georgian-style conservatory with its fine views over the lawned gardens to the hills and moors beyond. The food served therein is first-rate: a range of English and Continental dishes are prepared with imagination and flair, and a typical à la carte selection might feature Mille Feuille of Smoked Duck and Red Cabbage on a Raspberry Dressing followed by King Prawns Deep Fried in a Cinnamon Batter and Pan

Fried Loin of Venison served with a Confit of Cabbage, Bacon and Thyme Spatzle; the desserts are irresistible. Although history abounds, the old has been embraced by the new with the addition of a health, beauty and leisure club offering a full range of facilities. The extensive grounds include croquet lawns and a 9-hole putting green, and fly-fishing and clay-pigeon shooting may each be enjoyed locally.

OPEN ALL YEAR. V, S.D. B/A. N/S DINING R & BEDRS. LICENSED. DISABLED ACCESS. CHILDREN. PETS B/A. EN SUITE, BEVERAGES & TV IN ROOMS. ACCESS, VISA, AMEX, DINERS. B. & B. FROM £85.

Fox and Hounds

STARBOTTON, SKIPTON, N. YORKS, BD23 5HY   TEL: (01756) 760862   FAX: (01756) 760862

The Fox and Hounds is a 400 year-old stone building which has been a pub for 160 years in Starbotton, a small limestone village 15 miles north of Skipton, which is renowned for its spectacular walks. The cosy bar has a large stone fireplace, oak beams and a flagstone floor, and the walls are decorated with with old prints; hanging from the beams is a large collection of jugs along with an old still, and just off the main bar is a small dining room which is kept for non-smokers. There is a twin and a double guest bedroom at the pub. The food is excellent: everything is home-made from fresh ingredients, and home-baked bread is served with many of the starters. There s a wide variety of vegetarian choices and the dessert menu features home-made ice-creams; the cellar is well stocked with Theakstons ales and, during the summer months, there is a good choice of guest beers and malt whiskies.

OPEN MID FEB. - MID DEC. V, VE, S.D., WH, ORG STD. N/S PART DINING R. LICENSED. PETS IN BEDROOMS ONLY. EN SUITE, TV & BEVERAGES IN ROOMS. CREDIT CARDS. B. & B. £22.

Hilltop

STARBOTTON, NR SKIPTON, N. YORKS, BD23 5HY TEL: (01756) 760321

A 17th C. family home, Hilltop and its adjacent barn have been converted into a comfortable small guest house with spacious bedrooms and fine views of Wharfedale. The house has been very comfortably appointed: there are log fires in cooler weather and a cosy bar. Meals are prepared from fresh, local produce and there is always a vegetarian option if prior notice is given; there is an excellent choice of wines. You are an ideal spot for touring and there are numerous excellent walks nearby.

OPEN ALL YEAR. N/S ex in bar. V B/A. EN SUITE ROOMS. LICENSED.

WHITBY

COTE BANK FARM, EGTON RD, AISLABY, WHITBY, N. YORKS.

Substantial, stone-built 18th C. farmhouse with mullioned windows, log fires and period furniture in a sheltered position amidst a large garden enjoying wonderful country views. The food is wholesome and delicious: fresh produce is used wherever possible and, although this is primarily a B. & B., evening meals area available on request.

TEL: (01947) 85314 OPEN ALL YEAR ex. Xmas.   V, S.D. B/A.   NO SMOKING.   CHILDREN WELCOME. H & C, SHAVER POINTS & BEVERAGES IN ROOMS. T.V. IN LOUNGE.   AMEX.   B. & B. FROM £16. D. £9.

Falcon Guest House

29 FALCON TERRACE, WHITBY, N. YORKS, YO21 1EH   TEL: (01947) 603507

Guest house in quiet location 7 mins walk from town centre and harbour. Lounge with TV. Sunny breakfast room.

OPEN ALL YEAR. V, VE, STD. S.D. B/A. NO SMOKNG. CHILDREN WELCOME. BEVERAGES IN ROOMS. B. & B. FROM £13.

'THE LOW HOUSE', BAYSDALE, KILDALE, NR WHITBY, YO21 2SF

Small 18th century guest house surrounded by moorland near a river. Superb views.

TEL: (01642) 722880 OPEN Easter - Sept. V EXC. NO SMOKING. OVER 5S ONLY. B. & B., picnic lunch & D. FROM £25.

SHEPHERD'S PURSE VEGETARIAN HOTEL, 95 CHURCH ST, WHITBY.

Wholefood café serving a wide range of tasty and imaginative vegetarian dishes.

TEL; (01947) 820228 OPEN MOST OF THE YEAR. V EXC. VE STD. NO SMOKING. LICENSED. CHILDREN WELCOME.

1 WELL CLOSE TERRACE, WHITBY, N. YORKS, YO21 3AR

Vegetarian B. & B. family guest house.

TEL: (01947) 600173   OPEN MOST OF YEAR But subject to availability.   V STD.   NO SMOKING.   B. & B. AROUND £12.

Wentworth House

27 HUDSON ST, WEST CLIFF, WHITBY, YO21 3EP　TEL: (01947) 602433

Wentworth House is a beautiful 4-storey Victorian house which is conveniently situated just 5 minutes' walk from the harbour, beach and town centre of Whitby. The house is spacious and offers very comfortable centrally heated accommodation in its attractive guest bedrooms, some of which have en suite facilities. The food is wholesome and delicious: everything is freshly prepared (from organic ingredients wherever possible - including free-range eggs) and the proprietors specialise in wholefood vegetarian meals, although non-vegetarian dishes are also available; vegan and other special diets can be accommodated by arrangement and there is a good selection of reasonably priced organic wines. Whitby is a picturesque fishing town with a maze of cobbled streets and houses which huddle on the steep hillsides which sweep down to the harbour; it has much of historical interest to commend it, too, in its ancient abbey, the church of St Mary's & the places which commemorate one of its most famous sons, Cpt. James Cook.

OPEN ALL YEAR.　V/WH A SPECIALITY. S.D. B/A.　NO SMOKING.　LICENSED.　CHILDREN WELCOME. GROUND FLOOR EN SUITE ROOM WITH SUITABLE FITTINGS IN SHOWER ROOM.　3 EN SUITE ROOMS. BEVERAGES IN ALL ROOMS.　T.V. LOUNGE.　CREDIT CARDS. B. & B. FROM £15. D. £8.

YORK

BOWEN HOUSE, 4 GLADSTONE ST, HUNTINGTON RD., YORK YO3 7RF
Late Victorian town house, carefully decorated and furnished with antique and period furniture. Private car par. Close to city centre. Traditional English/vegetarian breakfasts.
TEL: (01904) 636881OPEN ALL YEAR.　V STD.　NO SMOKING.　CHILDREN WELCOME.　PETS B/A.　2 EN SUITE ROOMS.　BEVERAGES & TV IN ROOMS.　CREDIT CARDS.　B. &. B. FROM £18. reduced winter rates.

Byron House Hotel

THE MOUNT, YORK, YO2 2DD　　TEL: (01904) 632525　FAX: (01904) 639424
Byron House Hotel Is an elegant Georgian house which is beautifully situated on the Mount in York. The hotel is owned and run by Mr and Mrs Tyson whose aim is to provide a friendly atmosphere and personal service in relaxing surroundings: certainly the elegant proportions of the house help them to achieve a relaxing, gracious ambience - an effect which they have enhanced by their judicious use of furnishings and wallcoverings. The food is also excellent: meals are served in a charming dining room, and packed lunches can be provided on request. The hotel is licensed and the lounge bar is a particulary pleasant place to enjoy a pre-dinner - or post-dinner - drink. The hotel is about 10 minutes' walk from the city walls, the railway station and the race course and, as guests can enjoy private parking, you can forget about your car while you enjoy the charms of this historic city - a privelege which few visiting drivers can hope for!
OPEN ALL YEAR (ex. Xmas)　N/S DINING R. & SOME BEDROOMS.　V STD, VE, S.D., ORG, WH B/A.　CHILDREN & SOME PETS. LICENSED.　CREDIT CARDS　EN SUITE, TV & BEVERAGES IN ROOMS.

City Guest House

68 MONKGATE, YORK, N. YORKS, YO3 7PF
ETB 2 Crowns. Lovely Victorian terraced house just a few mins' walk from the city walls. There are vegetarian, vegan and continental options available.
TEL: (01904) 622483 OPEN ALL YEAR.　V STD. S.D. B/A.　NO SMOKING.　EN SUITE, TEA/COFFEE & T.V. IN ROOMS.　CREDIT CARDS.　B. & B. AROUND £16.

Dairy Wholefood Guesthouse

3 SCARCROFT RD., YORK, N. YORKS, YO2 1ND　TEL: (01904) 639367
A pleasant, tastefully renovated Victorian town house decorated and furnished throughout with plants and natural pine, with touches of Sanderson, Habitat and Laura Ashley. It enjoys full central heating and has a lovely enclosed courtyard. A full breakfast is served ranging from traditional British to wholefood/vegetarian. You are only 200 yards south of the mediaeval city walls, within easy walking distance of the many attractions of York city centre.
OPEN Feb. - Dec.　V, WH A SPECIALITY. S.D. B/A.　N/S DINING R & SITTING R.　CHILDREN WELCOME.　2 EN SUITE ROOMS.　BEVERAGES & TV IN ROOMS.　B. & B. AROUND £16.

Eastons

90 BISHOPTHORPE RD, YORK, YO2 1JS   TEL: (01904) 626646

Easton's

Fine Period Bed & Breakfast

Built in 1878 and originally a city wine merchant's residence, Easton's has been sympathetically restored in keeping with its period character; open fires blaze in the original fireplaces in cooler weather, and the William Morris decor and period furnishings have helped create a guest house with a very special ambience - at affordable prices. Accommodation is in individually designed bedrooms - each centrally heated and with every possible amenity - and the Victorian Sideboard breakfast menu offers an excellent choice of both traditional and vegetarian dishes. There is private parking at Eastons so you can explore York without worrying about car parks and traffic. The mediaeval city walls are just 250 yards away, while the Jorvik Centre, Clifford's Tower and the Castle Museum are all within strolling distance.

OPEN ALL YEAR (ex. Xmas).   NO SMOKING.   S.D. V.   OVER 4s WELCOME.   EN SUITE, TV & BEVERAGES IN BEDROOMS.   CREDIT CARDS.   B. & B. FROM £17.50.

Heworth Guest House

126 EAST PARADE, HEWORTH, YORK, YO3 7YG   TEL: (01904)

Pleasant guest house close to York city centre. Vegetarians & vegans very welcome.
OPEN ALL YEAR.   V, VE, S.D., ORG, WH STD.   N/S DINING R.   CHILDREN WELCOME.   PETS B/A.   1 EN SUITE ROOM.   TV & BEVERAGES IN ROOMS.   B. & B. £14.50 - 22.

THE LIMES HOTEL, 135 FULFORD RD, YORK.

Family-run hotel. Home-cooked meals and home-baking from wholefood ingredients.
TEL: (01904) 624548 OPEN ALL YEAR.   V B/A.   N/S ex. bar.   LICENSED.   CHILDREN WELCOME.   EN SUITE, TV & BEVERAGES IN ROOMS.   CREDIT CARDS.   B. & B. AROUND £28.

THE LODGE, EARSWICK GRANGE, EARSWICK, YORK, YO3 9SW

Modern family home in large, well-kept gardens, complete with paddock, free-range hens and apiary (fresh eggs and plenty of honey for breakfast!) in a lovely rural setting.
TEL: (01904) 761387 OPEN ALL YEAR.   V B'FAST OPTION, S.D. B/A.   NO SMOKING.   CHILDREN WELCOME. BEVERAGES.   T.V. LOUNGE.   B. &. B. FROM £13.

21 Park Grove

YORK, N. YORKS, YO3 7LG   TEL: (01904) 644790

Exclusively vegetarian B. & B. in spacious Victorian town house quietly situated in a residential area 10 mins. walk from the centre of York and the Minster. En suite accommodation. Organic food including home-made bread. 3 good vegetarian restaurants nearby.
OPEN ALL YEAR.   NO SMOKING.   V EXC, VE, S.D. STD.   EN SUITE & BEVERAGES IN ROOMS.   T.V. IN LOUNGE.   B. & B. FROM £16.

Papillon

43 GILLYGATE, YORK, N. YORKS, YO3 7EA   TEL: (01904) 636505

City centre guest house just 300 yards from York Minster. Private parking. High standards.
OPEN ALL YEAR Ex Xmas & New year.   N/S.   V B/A.   CHILDREN WELCOME.   MOST ROOMS EN SUITE. BEVERAGES & T.V. IN ROOMS.   B. & B. FROM £15.

Regency House

7 SOUTH PARADE, BLOSSOM ST, YORK, YO2 2BA   TEL: (01904) 633053

This charming Grade II listed Regency House was built in 1824 and stands in a private cobbled road just 6 minutes' walk from the railway station and less than 2 minutes' walk from Micklegate Archway and the city centre. The bedrooms have each been comfortably furnished (some have *en suite* facilities) and the dining room has an old Yorkshire Range and a low-beamed ceiling; the breakfast is excellent and some recent guests commented that it was the best they had had on their travels! You are within easy reach of a number of interesting places at Regency House including Whitby, Harrogate, Scarborough and the Yorkshire Moors and Dales. Parking & garaging avail.
OPEN Jan. - Mid-dec.   NO SMOKING.   V, DIAB, STD.   OVER 8S ONLY.   BEVERAGES & T.V. IN ROOMS. B. & B. FROM £15.50.

RESTAURANTS

HARROGATE

BETTY'S CAFÉ TEAROOMS, 1 PARLIAMENT ST, HARROGATE, HG1 2QU
TEL: (01423) 502746   V STD.   80% N/S LICENSED. CHILDREN VERY WELCOME.   ACCESS, VISA.

LOW HALL HOTEL & COACHHOUSE RESTAURANT, RIPON RD, KILLING-HALL, HARROGATE.
TEL: (01423) 508598   N/S RESTAURANT.   V, VE STD. S.D. B/A.   LICENSED.   DISABLED ACCESS.

ILKLEY

BETTY'S CAFÉ & TEA ROOMS, 32 - 34 THE GROVE, ILKLEY, N. YORKS.
TEL: (01943) 608029 V STD. 80% N/S. LICENSED.   DISABLED ACCESS to restaurant but not toilets.   CHILDREN.

KNARESBOROUGH

POLLYANNA'S TEA ROOM, JOCKEY LANE, HIGH ST, KNARESBOROUGH.
TEL: (01423) 869208   V STD. NO SMOKING. LICENSED.   DISABLED ACCESS. CHILDREN WELCOME.

NORTHALLERTON

BETTYS CAFÉ TEAROOMS, 188 HIGH ST, NORTHALLERTON, DL7 8LF
TEL: (01609) 775154 V STD.   70% N/S. LICENSED. DISABLED ACCESS BUT NOT TO TOILETS.   CHILDREN.

PICKERING

THE BLACKSMITH'S ARMS, AISLABY, PICKERING, YO18 8PE
TEL: (01751) 472182   V, VE STD.   N/S RESTAURANT. LICENSED. DISABLED ACCESS. CHILDREN WELCOME.

RICHMOND

THE KING'S HEAD HOTEL, RICHMOND, N. YORKS, DL10 4HS
For further details please see under entry in accommodation section.

RIPON

THE OLD DEANERY RESTAURANT, MINSTER RD, RIPON, HG4 1QS
V, DIAB STD.   NO SMOKING.   LICENSED.   DISABLED ACCESS.   CHILDREN WELCOME.

SCARBOROUGH

BONNET & SON, 38 HUNTRISS ROW, SCARBOROUGH, N. YORKS.
TEL: (01723) 361033 V STD. NO SMOKING. CHILDREN WELCOME.

SETTLE

CAR AND KITCHEN, SETTLE, N. YORKS, BD24 9EF
Family run business established in 1976; snacks & lunches from the finest fresh ingredients.
TEL: (01729) 823638 V STD.   NO SMOKING.   CHILDREN WELCOME.   CREDIT CARDS.

SKIPTON

DALES TEAPOT, ROPEWALK, ALBION SQUARE, SKIPTON.
TEL: (01756) 793416 NO SMOKING. V STD. LICENSED.   GOOD DISABLED ACCESS.

'HERBS', HEALTHY LIFE NATURAL FOOD CENTRE, 10 HIGH ST, SKIPTON.
TEL: (01756) 790619 NO SMOKING. V EXC, S.D. B/A.   CHILDREN'S PORTIONS.

WHITBY

Magpie Café

14 PIER RD, WHITBY, N. YORKS.   TEL: (01947) 602058
Excellent café overlooking the harbour at Whitby. All the food is fresh and the menu offers a choice of over 30 home made desserts as well as cakes, jam and chutney. Excellent vegetarian options. Children will love the food on their own menu with shortbread elephants, chocolate fish ice cream and jelly baby jelly!
98 SEATS. OPEN FEB - EARLY JAN. 80% NO-SMOKING. V, WEIGHT WATCHERS, DIAB. AND GLUTEN-FREE STD.
LICENSED.   EXCELLENT FACILITIES FOR CHILDREN, INCLUDING CHILDREN'S MENU.   VISA, MASTERCARD.

V **SHEPHERD'S PURSE VEGETARIAN RESTAURANT, 95 CHURCH ST, WHITBY.**
Wholefood café serving a wide range of tasty and imaginative vegetarian dishes.
TEL: (01947) 820228 OPEN MOST OF THE YEAR. V EXC. VE STD. NO SMOKING. LICENSED. CHILDREN
WELCOME.

YORK

BETTYS CAFÉ TEAROOMS, ST HELENS SQUARE, YORK, N. YORKS.
TEL: (01904) 659142 70% N/S. LICENSED. V STD. DISABLED ACCESS but not to toilets. CHILDREN.

V **THE BLAKE HEAD VEGETARIAN CAFÉ, 104 MICKLEGATE, YORK.**
TEL: (01904) 623767 N/S RESTAURANT. DISABLED ACCESS. CHILDREN'S PORTIONS.

Four Seasons Restaurant

45 GOODRAMGATE, YORK   TEL: (01904) 633787
15th C. half timbered restaurant - a culinary and architectural treat!
50% NO-SMOKING. V STD. LICENSED. CHILDREN WELCOME. CREDIT CARDS.

V ## Gillygate Wholefood Bakery

MILLERS YARD, YORK, N. YORKS, YO3 7EB   TEL: (01904) 610676
Wholefood vegetarian bakery, shop and café. Vegan food always available. Outside seating.
NO SMOKING.   V. EXC. DISABLED ACCESS. CHILDREN WELCOME.

THE GREENHOUSE CAFÉ, 12A CHURCH ST, YORK, N. YORKS, YO1 2BB
TEL: (01904) 629615 NO SMOKING. V STD. LICENSED. DISABLED ACCESS. CHILDREN WELCOME.

V **THE RUBICON, 5 LITTLE STONEGATE, YORK, N. YORKS.**
TEL: (01904) 676076   NO SMOKING. V EXC. BYO WINE. CHILDREN WELCOME.

TAYLORS IN STONEGATE, 46 STONEGATE, YORK, N. YORKS, YO1 2AS
Family run Tea Rooms and Coffee shop founded in 1886. Outstanding variety of teas and
coffees offered together with many Yorkshire and Continental specialities.
TEL: (01904) 622865 70% N/S. CHILDREN'S PORTIONS. ACCESS, VISA.

TREASURER'S HOUSE TEA ROOMS, MINSTER YARD, YORK, N. YORKS.
Tastefully furnished tea room in 17th C. Treasurer's House behind York Minster.
TEL: (01904) 624247/646757 OPEN DAILY APRIL - DEC. NO SMOKING.

THE YORK ARMS, HIGH PETERGATE, YORK, N. YORKS.
TEL: (01904) 624508 N/S UPSTAIRS DINING R (LUNCHTIME). V STD.

West Yorkshire

HALIFAX

COLLYERS HOTEL, BURNLEY RD, LUDDENDENFOOT, HALIFAX.
Sympathetically converted Victorian building overlooking the River Calder and with
magnificent views. The elegant restaurant features a wide selection of both imaginative
and traditional dishes (including vegetarian)prepared from the finest, seasonal produce.
TEL: (01422) 882624 OPEN ALL YEAR. V, S.D. STD. N/S SOME BEDRS. LICENSED. DISABLED ACCESS.
CHILDREN WELCOME. PETS B/A. MOST ROOMS EN SUITE. BEVERAGES & T.V. IN ROOMS.   B. & B.
AROUND £25.

HOLDSWORTH HOUSE HOTEL, HOLDSWORTH, HALIFAX, HX2 9TG
Beautifully preserved 17th C. house with panelling, open fireplaces.
TEL: (01422) 240024 V, S.D. B/A. N/S PART RESTAURANT. LICENSED. DISABLED ACCESS. EN SUITE &
T.V. IN ROOMS.

HEBDEN BRIDGE

HEBDEN LODGE HOTEL, NEW RD, HEBDEN BRIDGE, HX7 8AD
Excellent small hotel. Everything on the extensive and daily-changing menu is prepared
from fresh, seasonal produce.
TEL: (01422) 845272 OPEN ALL YEAR ex. Xmas. V STD. S.D. B/A. LICENSED. DISABLED ACCESS &
GROUND FLOOR ROOMS. CHILDREN WELCOME. PETS B/A.   EN SUITE, T.V., PHONES & BEVERAGES IN
ROOMS. B. & B. AROUND £39

HAWORTH

Ponden Hall

STANBURY, NR HAWORTH, W. YORKS, BD22 0HR   TEL: (01535) 644154

Ponden Hall is a listed Elizabethan farmhouse with a Georgian extension which is gloriously situated on the Pennine Way amidst rugged moors and farmland; it was reputed to be the Thrushcross Grange of Emily Bronte's *Wuthering Heights* (a little booklet about the literary link is published by the proprietors), but these days is a family home which, for the best part of this century, has offered comfortable hospitality to numerous travellers and walkers on the moors. The atmosphere is 'friendly and informal' and guests dine around a huge table (which seats 18) in the large oak-beamed dining room with its mullioned windows; the food is plentiful, fresh and home-cooked, and vegetarians and vegans can be catered for with advance notice. The guest rooms are beautiful: one is 16th C. and the other two were modernised at the time of the extension.

OPEN ALL YEAR ex. Xmas. V, S.D. B/A. FACILITIES FOR DISABLED. CHILDREN & PETS. B. & B. FROM £16.50. D. £9.

HOLMFIRTH

Holme Castle Country Hotel

HOLME VILLAGE, HOLMFIRTH, W. YORKS, HD7 1QG   TEL: (01484) 686764

Large Victorian house standing in a mature, walled garden with magnifcent views; beautifullly furnished & with many original features. Excellent vegetarian options with prior notice.

OPEN ALL YEAR. NO SMOKING.   WH, ORG, V VE, B/A. LICENSED.   CHILDREN.   EN SUITE ROOMS. T.V., RADIO ALARM, HAIRDRYER IN ROOMS. ACCESS, VISA, AMEX. B. & B. from £25 (reduced Fri. & Sun.) D. £19

WETHERBY

WOOD HALL, LINTON, WETHERBY, W. YORKS. TEL: (01937) 67271

Lovely Georgian house set in its own parkland, sumptuously furnished and with views.

OPEN ALL YEAR. N/S DINING R & BEDRS. V STD, S.D. B/A. LICENSED. DISABLED ACCESS. CHILDREN WELCOME. EN SUITE & TV IN ROOMS. B. & B. AROUND £56.

RESTAURANTS

HUDDERSFIELD

The Blue Rooms

9 BYRAM ARCADE, WESTGATE, HUDDERSFIELD, W. YORKS.   TEL: (01484) 512373

The Blue Rooms are situated in a beautiful, refurbished Victorian arcade in the heart of bustling Huddersfield. The proprietor has worked hard to create just the right kind of ambience - classical music, pleasing decor, an informal, friendly atmosphere - and as a consequence the café is exceedingly popular with a wide cross-section of Huddersfield folk, 'from lawyers to students to shoppers...' Pleasing ambience notwithstanding, the repeat visits are clearly a direct result of the dependably excellent food: everything is home-prepared daily from fresh, additive-free ingredients (including free-range eggs), and the mouth-watering menu features a wide range of tasty options including, in addition to tasty sandwiches, snacks and full meals, some wonderful hot French bread sand-

wiches, baked potatoes, pancakes and, to follow, delicious wholemeal cakes and puddings; vegan, gluten-free and vegetarian dishes are clearly denoted so on the menu. The Blue Rooms now has a high quality outside catering service for small parties to weddings, etc.
OPEN 10 - 5, Mon.- Sat.   V, WH., STD; VE, GLUTEN-FREE AVAIL.   N/S 80% RESTAURANT.   L. AROUND £3. LICENSED.   CHILDREN WELCOME.

ILKLEY

BETTYS CAFÉ TEA ROOMS, 32/34 THE GROVE, ILKLEY, LS29 9EE
TEL: (01943) 608029   V STD. 75% N/S.   LICENSED.   DISABLED ACCESS TO RESTAURANT BUT NOT TOILETS. CHILDREN WELCOME.   ACCESS, VISA.

MUFFINS, RAILWAY ROAD, ILKLEY, W. YORKS.
TEL: (01943) 817505   V STD.   NO SMOKING.   WHEELCHAIR ACCESS.   CHILDREN WELCOME.

LEEDS

Strawberry Fields Bistro & Wine Bar
159 WOODHOUSE LANE, LEEDS 2, W. YORKS.   TEL: (0113) 243 1515
Intimate friendly family-run bistro serving a wide variety of home-made vegetarian and meat dishes. Wine Bar upstairs.
V, VE STD., S.D. B/A. (phone first) 40 SEATS.   OPEN Mon. - Fri., 11.45 - 2.00, Mon. - Sat. 5.30 - 10.30 (last orders).   MAIN COURSE £4 - £10.   N/S 75% OF RESTAURANT.   DISABLED ACCESS, but not to toilets. CHILDREN.   CREDIT CARDS.

The North East

Cleveland

ACCOMMODATION

STOCKTON-ON-TEES

Swallow Hotel
JOHN WALKER SQUARE, STOCKTON-ON-TEES, TS18 1AQ   TEL: (01642) 679721

The Swallow Hotel at Stockton on Tees is a modern 4 star hotel right in the heart of the town centre. 50 of the 124 en suite bedrooms are totally smoke-free and each is equipped with a Satellite TV, direct dial phone, hairdryer, iron and trouser press. There are two restaurants: in the Portcullis both table d'hote and a la carte menus are available and, with a less formal atmosphere, the Matchmaker Brasserie (named after John Walker, the Stockton man who first came up with the bright idea of the match!), offers a range of meals and snacks. The Swallow Leisure club has an Egyptian theme and includes a heated pool, jacuzzi, sauna and steam room in addition to a minigym, climbing and cycling machines, rower and sunbeach area. There are conference and banqueting facilities for up to 300 delegates - each conference receives free use of overhead projector, flip charts and notepads - and the professional team can provide any additional equipment that you require. Free covered parking.
OPEN ALL YEAR.   N/S BOTH RESTAURANTS & IN SOME BEDROOMS.   V, S.D. B/A.   LICENSED.   DISABLED ACCESS.   CHILDREN WELCOME.   PETS B/A.   EN SUITE, BEVERAGES & TV IN ROOMS.   CREDIT CARDS.   B. & B. FROM £43.

RESTAURANTS

LOFTUS

THE TEA SHOPPE, 19 HIGH ST, LOFTUS, CLEVELAND, TS13 4HW
English Tea Rooms. Excellent vegetarian menu.
TEL: (01287) 643999 OPEN MOST DAYS. V STD. CHILDREN WELCOME. DISABLED ACCESS.

MIDDLESBOROUGH

Barneys

19 ST BARNABAS ROAD, LINTHORPE, MIDDLESBOROUGH, TS5 6JR   TEL: (01642) 826385
Heartbeat Award. Retail shop & café staffed by volunteers from St Barnabas Parish Church; all food cooked fresh on the premises; home-made soup, quiches & savoury dishes such as lasagne, Moussaka, vegetarian loaf, filled potatoes & salads. Sweets include gateaux, cheesecakes, fruit pies, fruit salad. Shop sells wide range of gifts, books & greeting cards.
20 SEATS. OPEN 11.30 - 4. L. FROM £1.   NO SMOKING. V STD.   DISABLED ACCESS.   CHILDREN ESPECIALLY WELCOME (PLAYING AREA PROVIDED).

Co Durham

ACCOMMODATION

BARNARD CASTLE

EAST MELLWATERS FARM, BOWES, BARNARD CASTLE, CO DURHAM.
17th C. farmhouse on working cattle/sheep farm. Home-made bread.
TEL: (01833) 28259 OPEN ALL YEAR. V STD. CHILDREN & PETS. BEVERAGES & TV.

BOWBURN

BOWBURN HALL HOTEL, BOWBURN, DH6 5NH
Beautifully appointed traditional-style hotel standing in 5 acres of gardens and woodlands;.
TEL: (0191) 3770311 OPEN ALL YEAR. V & LOW-FAT STD. S.D. B/A. LICENSED. CHILDREN WELCOME. EN SUITE & T.V. IN ROOMS. B. & B. AROUND £40.

CONSETT

Bee Cottage Farm

CASTLESIDE, CONSETT, CO DURHAM, DH8 9HW   TEL: (01207) 508224
Working farm close to the Northumberland/Durham border. Self-catering or breakfast.
OPEN ALL YEAR. V, S.D. B/A. WH ON REQUEST. NO SMOKING. DISABLED ACCESS. EN SUITE & BEVERAGES. B. & B. AROUND £18.

DURHAM

Bees Cottage Guest House

BRIDGE ST, DURHAM, CO DURHAM, DH1 4RT   TEL: (0191) 384 5775
Durham's oldest cottage in a central location close to cathedral & castle. Museums, university, river walks and shops all nearby. Private parking.
OPEN ALL YEAR. V, S.D. B/A. N/S DINING R & BEDRS. CHILDREN WELCOME. EN SUITE, TV & BEVERAGES IN ROOMS. B. & B. AROUND £20, SINGLE £25.

COLEBRICK, 21 CROSSGATE, DURHAM. TEL: (0191) 384 9585
Lovely whitewashed house, full of character half a mile from the city centre; magnificent views of the Cathedral. Healthy options at breakfast.
OPEN ALL YEAR. NO SMOKING. V S.D. B/A. DISABLED ACCESS: 'GOOD'. CHILDREN: OVER 4S ONLY. BEVERAGES & T.V. IN ROOMS. B. &. B. AROUND £18.

Ramside Hall Hotel

CARRVILLE, DURHAM, DH1 1TD   TEL: (0191) 386 5282
Splendid castellated building set in large grounds just of the A1(M)/A690. Luxuriously appointed bedrooms. Excellent home-cooking.
OPEN ALL YEAR. N/S B'FAST, IN PART OF CARVERY & IN SOME BEDRS. V, S.D. B/A. LICENSED. DISABLED ACCESS. CHILDREN WELCOME. EN SUITE, BEVERAGES & TV. B. & B. AROUND £80.

Royal County Hotel

OLD ELVET, DURHAM, DH1 3JN   TEL: (0191) 386 6821
The Royal County Hotel is a first-class 150-bedroomed hotel, which has been stylishly

appointed and beautifully furnished. It is in the luxury business-class category and therefore has a superb range of leisure amenities including an indoor swimming pool, a spa pool,
sauna, steam room, solarium and mini-gym. The bedrooms are very comfortable and have
excellent facilities, and some smoke-free rooms are available. A wide choice of menu is
served in the hotel's restaurants and these, too, have good smoke-free areas.
OPEN ALL YEAR. V MENU STD. VE, DIAB & S.D. ON REQUEST. LICENSED. DISABLED ACCESS. CHILD-
REN WELCOME. EN SUITE, BEVERAAGES & TV IN ROOMS. ACCESS, VISA, AMEX, DINERS, AIRPLUS. B.
& B. AROUND £85. Special w/e & summer breaks avail.

STANHOPE

HORSLEY HALL, EASTGATE, STANHOPE, CO DURHAM, DL13 2LJ
Large country house with panoramic views. Vegetarian evening meals available.
TEL: (01388) 517239 OPEN ALL YEAR. V STD. CHILDREN & PETS WELCOME. EN SUITE, TV & BEVERAGES.

TANTOBIE

THE OAK TREE INN, TANTOBIE, CO DURHAM.
Carefully restored manor house furnished with antiques; excellent food freshly cooked.
TEL: (01207) 235445 OPEN ALL YEAR. V, S.D. B/A. N/S PART OF DINING R & SOME BEDRS. LICENSED.
SOME DISABLED ACCESS. CHILDREN WELCOME. PETS B/A. EN SUITE, BEVERAGES & TV IN ROOMS.
B. &. B. AROUN D £18.

WEARDALE

PENNINE LODGE, ST JOHN'S CHAPEL, WEARDALE.
Commended country house by the River Wear.
TEL: (01388) 537247 OPEN Apr. - Sept. N/S DINING R. V, DIAB & LOW-FAT DIETS B/A. LICENSED. EN
SUITE. B. & B. AROUND £18.

FRIARSIDE FARM, WOLSINGHAM, CO DURHAM.
17th C. farmhouse with views; home-cooking - including bread; also self-catering.
TEL: (01388) 527361 V, DIAB B/A. LOW-FAT STD. N/S DINING R. OVER 5S ONLY. B. & B. AROUND £18.

RESTAURANTS

BARNARD CASTLE

V *'Priors'*

7 THE BANK, BARNARD CASTLE, CO. DURHAM, DL12 8PH   TEL: (01833) 638141
Excellent wholefood, vegetarian restaurant with organic wine list; craft shop & gallery.
OPEN Mon.-Fri. 10-5, Sat. 10-5.30, Sun: 12-5.   NO SMOKING.   V, VE, S.D. STD.   LICENSED.   CHILDREN
WELCOME.   CREDIT CARDS.

NEWCASTLE-ON-TYNE

RUPALI RESTAURANT, 6 BIGG MARKET, NEWCASTLE-ON-TYNE, NE1 1UW
Excellent restaurant specialising in Indian, Vegetarian, Tandoori & English cuisine.
TEL: (0191) 232 8629   N/S 50%   V STD.   LICENSED.   CHILDREN WELCOME.   CREDIT CARDS.

WILLINGTON

STILE RESTAURANT, 97 HIGH ST, WILLINGTON, NR CROOK, DL15 0PE.
Originally a mine-owner's country cottage and now with two beautiful conservatories
overlooking an attractive garden. Excellent home-prepared food from fresh, local ingre-
dients.
TEL: (01388) 746615   V STD, S.D. B/A.   N/S DINING R (28 SEATS), ALLOWED IN CONSERVATORY AREA.
LICENSED.   SOME DISABLED ACCESS: 'TWO STEPS.' CHILDREN WELCOME. ACCESS, VISA.

Northumberland

ACCOMMODATION

ALNMOUTH

The Grange

NORTHUMBERLAND ST, ALNMOUTH, NE66 2RJ   TEL: (01665) 830401

ETB 2 Crown Highly Commended. Heartbeat Award. 200 year-old stone-built house, formerly used as a granary, standing in large landscaped gardens overlooking the River Aln just 2 mins from the beautiful sandy beach. Excellent b'fast including fruit compôte.
OPEN Mar. - Nov. V B/A. NO SMOKING. CHILDREN: OVER 5S ONLY. SOME EN SUITE ROOMS. BEVERAGES & T.V. IN ROOMS.   B. & B. AROUND £20.

ALNWICK

BEAMISH COUNTRY HOUSE HOTEL, POWBURN, ALNWICK, NE66 4LL
Elegant Georgian-style building, originally a 17th C. farmhouse, set in 5 acres of gardens and woodlands; sumptuous furnishings and log fires; excellent Cordon Bleu cuisine.
TEL: (01665)78266 OPEN Feb. to Dec. V B/A. N/S DINING R. LICENSED. SOME DISABLED ACCESS. OVER 12S ONLY, YOUNGER B/A.   EN SUITE, BEVERAGES & TV IN ROOMS. D., B. & B. AROUND £47.

CHARLTON HOUSE, 2 AYDON GARDENS, SOUTH RD, ALNWICK.
ETB 3 Crowns Commended. Charming Victorian town house just 5 mins walk town centre. Exceptional home-cooking using home-grown produce.
TEL: (01665) 605185 OPEN MOST OF THE YEAR. V STD. EN SUITE, TV & BEVERAGES IN ROOMS. E.M. B/A.

CROSSHILLS HOUSE, 40 BLAKELAW RD, ALNWICK, NE66 1BA
ETB 2 Crown Commended. Comfortable home 10 mins just stroll from town. Superb b'fast menu includes veg. options.
TEL: (01665) 602518 OPEN MOST OF YEAR. V STD. EN SUITE, TV & BEVERAGES IN ROOMS.

TOWNFOOT FARM, TOWNFOOT, LESBURY, ALNWICK, NE66 3AZ
Beautiful farmhouse with garden overlooking the River Aln; comfortable accommodation & open fire; excellent wholefood menu prepared from home-grown produce.
TEL: (01665) 830755   OPEN Mar. - Oct. N/S DINING R & UPSTAIRS. V, S.D. B/A.   CHILDREN WELCOME. PETS B/A. BEVERAGES IN ROOMS. T.V. IN LOUNGE. B. & B. AROUND £19.

BARDON MILL

VALLUM LODGE HOTEL, MILITARY RD, TWICE BREWED, NR BARDON MILL, NE47 7AN
Delightful small hotel, warm and comfortable, set in open countryside by Hadrian's Wall. Good choice of fresh foods at all meals. Home-baking. All ground floor rooms.
TEL: (01434) 344248 OPEN Feb. - Nov. inc. V, S.D. B/A. N/S DINING R.   GROUND FLOOR ROOMS. LICENSED. CHILDREN & PETS WELCOME. EN SUITE ROOMS. TV. BEVERAGES. B. & B. AROUND £22.

BELLINGHAM

EALS LODGE, TARSET, BELLINGHAM, NE48 1LF
ETB 3 Crown Commended. 200-year-old former coaching inn on the shores of Kielder Water. Meals are prepared from fresh, local produce & high-fibre and low-fat alternatives available; lots of pasta and wholegrain rice dishes are also available as healthy options.
 TEL: (0434) 240269 OPEN ALL YEAR. V, DIAB STD. S.D. B/A. N/S DINNG R. & BEDRS. LICENSED. EN SUITE, BEVERAGES & TV IN ROOMS. B. & B. FROM £21.

IVY COTTAGE, LANEHEAD, BELLINGHAM, NR HEXHAM, NE48 1NT
Beautiful stone-built cottage, modernised yet retaining character (beamed ceilings, etc); spacious bedrooms with views; excellent food prepared from fresh, local produce.
 TEL: (01434) 240337 OPEN ALL YEAR. V, VE STD. S.D. ON REQUEST. N/S DINING R & BEDRS. BYO WINE. CHILDREN. PETS B/A. SOME EN SUITE ROOMS. BEVERAGES & T.V. IN ROOMS.   B. & B. AROUND £17.

LYNDALE GUEST HOUSE, BELLINGHAM, NE48 2AW
Attractive stone-built house in delightful village; meals are home-prepared from fresh produce wherever possible (including some home-grown fruit and vegetables in season).
TEL: (01434) 220361 OPEN ALL YEAR. V, S.D. B/A. WH ON REQUEST. N/S BEDRS & public areas ex. DINING R. CHILDREN WELCOME. BEVERAGES IN ROOMS.   T.V. ON REQUEST.   B. & B. AROUND £18.

WESTFIELD HOUSE, BELLINGHAM, NR HEXHAM, NE48 2DP
Lovely large 19th C. house approached by tree-lined drive (with glorious views); evening meals by arrangement prepared from fresh, local and (sometimes) home-grown produce.
TEL: (01434) 220340 OPEN ALL YEAR. NO SMOKING. V, S.D. B/A. CHILDREN WELCOME. PETS B/A.
SOME EN SUITE. BEVERAGES IN ROOMS. T.V. IN LOUNGE. B. & B. AROUND £19.

BERWICK-UPON-TWEED

ARISAIG GUEST H, 49 CHURCH ST, BERWICK-ON-TWEED, TD15 1EE
Attractive Georgian town house. Wholesome b'fast with vegetarian alternatives.
TEL: (01289) 330412 OPEN ALL YEAR. V STD. DOGS B/A.

THE ESTATE HOUSE, FORD, BERWICK-UPON-TWEED, TD15 2QG
Beautiful Edwardian country house in large, lawned gardens. The food is wholesome and tasty, home-cooked from fresh, local ingredients wherever possible.
TEL: (0189 082) 297 OPEN FROM April - Oct. 'OTHER TIMES ON REQUEST'. V, GLUTEN-FREE, S.D. B/A. N/S DINING
R. CHILDREN: OVER 5S ONLY. BEVERAGES IN ROOMS. T.V. IN LOUNGE. B. & B. AROUND £16.

'Tree Tops'
THE VILLAGE GREEN, EAST ORD, BERWICK-UPON-TWEED, TD15 2NS TEL; (01289) 330679
Spacious single storey house in a delightful setting facing out onto the village green. Delicious food is prepared from fresh, often garden-grown, produce.
OPEN Mar. to Oct. V STD. NO SMOKING. DISABLED ACCESS: 'YES, WITH HELPER: SINGLE STOREY
ACCOMMODATION WITH WIDE DOORS'. ALL ROOMS EN SUITE. BEVERAGES. T.V. B. & B. AROUND £20.

CORBRIDGE

CHANDLERS RESTAURANT, ANGEL INN, MAIN ST, CORBRIDGE, NE45 5LA
TEL: (01434) 712119 OPEN ALL YEAR. V, VE & DIAB STD. S.D. B/A. N/S PART DINING R. LICENSED.
DISABLED ACCESS. CHILDREN WELCOME. EN SUITE. BEVERAGES & TV. B. & B. AROUND £50.

CORNHILL-ON-TWEED

THE COACH HOUSE AT CROOKHAM, CROOKHAM, CORNHILL-ON-TWEED.
Reputedly the oldest cottage in north Northumberland; home-baked cakes & tea served on arrival; most food prepared from organically produced ingredients (including the wines).
TEL: (0189 082) 293 OPEN Mar. - Nov. N/S DINING R & LOUNGE. V STD. DIAB, S.D. B/A. LICENSED.
EXCELLENT DISABLED ACCESS. DOGS B/A. MOST ROOMS EN SUITE. BEVERAGES & TV IN ROOMS. B.
& B. AROUND £23.

GREENHEAD-IN-NORTHUMBERLAND

Holmhead Farm Licensed Guest House and Holiday Flat
HADRIAN'S WALL, GREENHEAD IN NORTHUMBERLAND, VIA CARLISLE CA6 7HY TEL:
(016977 47402)

ETB 3 Crown Commended 3 Keys Commended. AA QQQ. Holmhead Farm is a charming old house, which stands amidst pretty gardens (complete with stream) surrounded by the unspoilt and rugged beauty of the Northumberland countryside; it literally stands on Hadrian's Wall and is built from its stones. Understandably the views are quite spectacular. Accommodation is in four cosy and comfortable en suite bedrooms - each with lovely rural views - and there is a separate self-catering cottage for non-smokers in which the range of excellent amenities includes first-class facilities for disabled guests. Perhaps the best thing about a stay at Holmhead is the food: the proprietors boast correctly that their breakfast menu is the longest in the world: I have no reason to doubt them and wish I could do justice to the range of dishes on offer; suffice to say that if you are in Northumberland and wish to dine at 8 a.m. on a choice of English or Scottish porridge followed by Devilled Kidneys, waffles and Raspberry tea - Holmhead Farm would be your best bet. The evening meal lacks choice (most guests doubtless welcome a break from menu-reading) but does not lack quality: fresh, local ingredients are included in the imaginative and tasty 3-course meal, and guests dine together by candlelight at a large, oak

table in the cosy beamed dining room. *Winner of Heartbeat Award & Disabled Category 2 by Holiday Care Service.*
OPEN JAN 6TH - DEC. 20TH.   NO SMOKING.   V, S.D. B/A.   LICENSED.   DISABLED ACCESS TO HOLIDAY FLAT & GROUND FLOOR B. & B. (Nov. - Mar. the latter).   CHILDREN WELCOME.   ALL ROOMS EN SUITE.   BEVERAGES & TV IN LOUNGE.   ACCESS, VISA.   B. & B. FROM £21. D. £17

HALTWHISTLE

ASHCROFT GUEST HOUSE, HALTWHISTLE, NE49 0DA
Winners of Heartbeat Award. Victorian vicarage in private grounds in the quiet market town of Haltwhistle. Comfortably furnished bedrooms, one with a 4-poster. Healthy breakfast with lighter meal options.
TEL: (01434) 320213 OPEN ALL YEAR.   V B/A.   NO SMOKING.   CHILDREN WELCOME.   T.V. IN LOUNGE. B. & B. AROUND £16.

White Craig Farm

SHIELD HILL, HALTWHISTLE, NORTHUMBERLAND, NE49 9NW   TEL: (01434) 320565
Heartbeat Award. 17th C. croft-style farmhouse on a working farm where sheep - including some prizewinning rare breeds - and English Longhorn cattle are raised. Open fireplace, timber ceiling beams. Wholesome and delicious breakfast. S/C cottage also available.
OPEN ALL YEAR, ex. Xmas/New Year.   V, S.D. B/A.   NO SMOKING.   DISABLED ACCESS.   OVER 10S ONLY. EN SUITE, TV & BEVERAGES IN ROOMS.   B. & B. AROUND £20.

HAYDON BRIDGE

GEESWOOD HOUSE, WHITTIS RD, HAYDON BRIDGE, NE47 6AQ
Charming 19th C. stone-built house and garden through which flows the Langley Burn; good home-cooking with home-baked bread.
TEL: (01434) 684220   OPEN ALL YEAR.   V, LOW-FAT, GLUTEN-FREE, DIAB, S.D. B/A.   NO SMOKING. CHILDREN: OVER 10S ONLY.   PETS B/A.   T.V.   B. & B. AROUND £20.

HEXHAM

AMBER HOUSE, 2 WOODLANDS, CORBRIDGE RD, HEXHAM, NE46 1HT
Heartbeat Award. Good food a speciality.
TEL: (01434) 602148 OPEN ALL YEAR. V STD. CHILDREN. EN SUITE TV & BEVERAGES. B. & B. £16 - 18.

Croft House

SLALEY, HEXHAM, NORTHUMBERLAND   TEL: (01434) 673322
ETB 2 Crown Commended. Beautiful country house in lovely large garden. Excellent food everything is freshly prepared using low-fat cooking methods where possible.
OPEN ALL YEAR. NO SMOKING IN THE HOUSE. VEGETARIAN & OTHER DIETS STANDARD. EN SUITE & TEA/COFFEE-MAKING IN BEDROOMS. TV IN LOUNGE. B. & B. £35 DOUBLE.

Crowberry Hall

ALLENDALE, HEXHAM, NE47 9SR TEL: (01434) 683392
Crowberry Hall is run by John and Isabel Wentzel who especially welcome walkers (they have devised eight first-rate walks for guests). Wholefood and organic ingredients are used as much as possible in the preparation of the tasty meat-free dishes.
OPEN ALL YEAR. V STD, S.D. B/A.   NO SMOKING.   OVER 5S. SOME EN SUITE.   T.V.   B. & B. AROUND £15.

MIDDLEMARCH, HENCOTES, HEXHAM, NE46 2EB
Listed Georgian house overlooking the Sele and Abbey in the centre of Hexham.
TEL: (01434) 605003 OPEN ALL YEAR. V, S.D. B/A. N/S DINING R. & BEDRS. CHILDREN: OVER 10S ONLY. PETS B/A. SOME EN SUITE. BEVERAGES & TV IN ROOMS. B. & B. AROUND £23.

WEST CLOSE HOUSE, HEXTOL TERRACE, HEXHAM, NE46 2AD
Charming, detached 1920's residence in pretty, prize-winning gardens. The culinary emphasis is on wholefood cuisine, and only the finest products are used in cooking. The generous breakfast features a Wholefood Continental or Traditional English choice (all freshly cooked to individual requirements), and light snacks with home-made cakes, or packed lunches, can be provided on request.
TEL: (01434) 603307 OPEN ALL YEAR.   V, VE, GLUTEN-FREE & S.D. B/A.   N/S DINING R & BEDR & DISCOURAGED ELSEWHERE. OVER 2S ONLY.   EN SUITE.   BEVERAGES IN ROOMS. T.V. IN LOUNGE. B. & B. AROUND £18.

KIRKWHELPINGTON

THE OLD VICARAGE, KIRKWHELPINGTON, NE19 2RT
Beautiful Grade II listed Georgian vicarage in prize-winning village; free-range eggs and organically home-grown and wholefood fare.
TEL: (01830) 40319 OPEN Apr. to Oct. N/S DINING R & LOUNGE. V, S.D. B/A. CHILDREN WELCOME. PETS B/A. SOME EN SUITE ROOMS. BEVERAGES IN ROOMS. T.V. IN LOUNGE. B. & B. AROUND £14.

MORPETH

THE BAKERS CHEST, HARTBURN, MORPETH, NORTHUMBERLAND.
Beautiful stone-built house in delightful countryside in the charming village of Hartburn; comfortable accommodation and excellent food; beautiful walks through tranquil woods.
TEL: (01670) 72214 OPEN Easter - Oct. V, S.D. B/A. NO SMOKING. CHILDREN WELCOME. BEVERAGES. T.V. IN LOUNGE. B. & B. AROUND £16.

ROTHBURY

THROPTON DEMESNE FARMHOUSE, THROPTON, NE65 7LT
Victorian stone-built farmhouse with walled garden in an unspoilt dale; home-cooked food prepared from fresh, local ingredients.
TEL: (01669) 20196 OPEN ALL YEAR. V, S.D. B/A. NO SMOKING. CHILDREN WELCOME. EN SUITE, TV & BEVERAGES IN ROOMS. B. & B. AROUND £19.

SLALEY

RYE HILL FARM, SLALEY, NORTHUMBERLAND.
300-year-old stone farmhouse in 30 acres of working farm; self-catering & B. & B. (with D. by arrangement); log fires, home-cooking.
TEL: (01434) 673259 OPEN ALL YEAR. N/S DINING R & ALL BEDRS. V, S.D. B/A. LICENSED. CHILDREN WELCOME. PETS B/A. EN SUITE, TV & BEVERAGES IN ROOMS. B. & B. AROUND £18.

STOCKSFIELD

THE DENE, 11 CADE HILL RD, STOCKSFIELD, NE43 7PB
Edwardian house quietly situated and surrounded by beautiful gardens and woodland; spacious rooms furnished with antiques; good home-cooking (Northumbrian and oriental menus) prepared from garden produce.
TEL: (01661) 842025 OPEN ALL YEAR. V, S.D. B/A. N/S DINING R. & MOST OF HOUSE. CHILDREN WELCOME. EN SUITE, BEVERAGES & TV IN ROOMS. B. & B. AROUND £18.

Tyne & Wear

ACCOMMODATION

NEWCASTLE-ON-TYNE

'BYWELL', 54 HOLLY AVENUE, JESMOND, NEWCASTLE-ON-TYNE, NE2 2QA
Large, Victorian town house in a quiet residential cul-de-sac in the popular area of Jesmond, with its restaurants, bistros & wine bars.
TEL: (0191) 281 7615 OPEN ALL YEAR. V STD. S.D. B/A. NO SMOKING. CHILDREN. B.& B. FROM £16.50.

OTTERBURN

PERCY ARMS HOTEL, OTTERBURN, NE19 1NR
Fine country inn; food home-cooked from fresh ingredients.
TEL: (01830) 20261 OPEN ALL YEAR. V, VE, DIAB, S.D. STD. WH WHEN AVAIL. LICENSED. DISABLED ACCESS. CHILDREN WELCOME. PETS B/A. EN SUITE, TV & BEVERAGES. B. & B. AROUND £43.

RESTAURANTS

ALNWICK

BEAMISH COUNTRY HOUSE HOTEL, POWBURN, ALNWICK
TEL: (0166578) 266/544 N/S RESTAURANT. V STD. LICENSED. OVER 12S ONLY.

BAMBURGH

The Copper Kettle Tearooms

21 FRONT ST, BAMBURGH, NORTHUMBERLAND, NE69 7BW   TEL: (01668) 214315
One of a row of 18th C. cottages in the picturesque village of Bamburgh with its magnificent
castle overlooking the sea. With the exception of the bread and teacakes which are provided
by a local baker, the owners bake and prepare all the items on their extensive menu using
their own recipes and choosing only the finest ingredients: there is a very wide choice of
beverages (including eleven speciality teas and twenty-five herbal infusions).
28 SEATS PLUS 20 IN GARDEN.   OPEN MARCH TO OCT., 7 DAYS, USUALLY 10.30 - 5.30.   NO SMOKING
INDOORS.   V OFTEN AVAIL.   TABLE LICENCE.   WELL-BEHAVED CHILDREN WELCOME.

MORPETH

CHANTRY TEAROOM, 9 CHANTRY PLACE, MORPETH, NE61 1PJ
Pretty country-style tearoom with views of the old chantry building; all home-baking.
TEL: (01670) 514414   V STD. NO SMOKING.   LICENSED. SOME DISABLED ACCESS. CHILDREN WELCOME.

ROTHBURY

PIZZA KATERINA, HIGH ST, ROTHBURY.
TEL: (01669) 20691 OPENING HOURS vary according to season: phone & check first. V STD. CHILDREN WELCOME.

Channel Islands

GUERNSEY

La Favorita Hotel

FERMAIN BAY, GUERNSEY   TEL: (01481) 35666

La Favorita is an attractive hotel set amidst pleasant
gardens in the beautiful wooded valley which leads
down to Fermain Bay. It was once a privately owned
country house and, although it has been considerably extended and modernised, it retains the character (and of course magnificent sea views!) of its
former life. From the elegant drawing room with its
open fire to the intimate dining room with its lovely
garden views, everywhere there is an atmosphere of
peaceful tranquility and guests are encouraged to
relax, unwind and enjoy. The food is excellent: the
menu, which changes daily, is based around traditional English cooking (with some
imaginative Continental culinary excursions). A typical evening meal could feature Baked
Blue Brie with Mushroom Sauce, followed by Cream of Chicken Soup, Baked Sea Bream
with Tomato, and a delicious home-made dessert; there is a good vegetarian option on each
evening menu. A recent highly successful addition to La Favorita is its pleasant Coffee
Shop, overlooking the garden, in which light meals are served throughout the day, and an
indoor heated pool, spa and sauna.
OPEN MAR. TO NOV. N/S DINING R. V STD. LICENSED. 1 BEDROOM EQUIPPED FOR DISABLED GUESTS.
CHILDREN WELCOME: NAPPY-CHANGING ROOM. EN SUITE, TV & BEVERAGES IN ROOMS. VISA, AMEX,
MASTERCARD. B. & B. FROM £36.

MIDHURST HOUSE, CANDIE RD, ST PETER PORT, GUERNSEY
Elegant Regency town house which has been exceptionally well-restored; some bedrooms
overlook the lovely south facing garden; superb food prepared from fresh ingredients.
TEL: (01481) 724391 OPEN Easter to Oct. N/S DINING R. V, DIAB, COEL, ALLERGY-FREE B/A. LICENSED.
OVER 8S ONLY. EN SUITE, BEERAGES & TV IN ROOMS. D., B. & B. £32.

OLD GOVERNMENT HOUSE HOTEL, ANN'S PLACE, ST PETER PORT
Elegant building, sumptuously furnished, good food; sea views; swimming pool.
TEL: (01481) 724429 V, VE STD. DIAB, S.D. B/A.   OPEN ALL YEAR. LICENSED. CHILDREN WELCOME. EN
SUITE & TV IN ALL ROOMS. CREDIT CARDS. B. & B. FROM £58.

JERSEY

HINCHCLIFFE G.H., VICTORIA AVE, FIRST TOWER, ST HELIER, JERSEY
Small, family-run guest house with views of St Aubins Bay; health-watcher b'kfast.
TEL: (01534) 21574   OPEN Mar. to Oct. NO SMOKING SPECIAL DIETS BY ARRANGEMENT.   TEA/COFFEE-MAKING IN ALL ROOMS. T.V. IN LOUNGE. B. & B. FROM £16.50.

SARK

Beauvoir Guest House And Tea Shop
SARK, CHANNEL ISLANDS.   TEL: (01481) 832352 FAX: (01481) 832551

Situated at the centre of the island close to the Seigneurie, Beauvoir is a charming granite-built house, built at the turn of the century. It has recently undergone extensive renovations and now offers exceptionally comfortable accommodation and very good food; there is a charming tea garden (and indoor tea shop for those not inclined to al fresco dining) which specialises in home-baking and dishes prepared from organically home-grown fruit and vegetables. Resident guests at Beauvoir are really in for a treat: all meals have been home-cooked from fresh ingredients and the imaginative 5-course evening menu features such delights as home-made Smoked Mackerel Pate, followed by Orange Sorbet, home-made Brie and Herb Quiche and an irresistible dessert, such as home-made Chocolate Gateau; guests may also enjoy the benefits of a quiet lounge and a separate residents' bar. Sark is the smallest and, thankfully, the least developed of the Channel Islands: there are no street lights (bring a torch) and the beautiful sandy beaches are all reached by many steps or steep paths; this, combined with the fact that there is a short walk from the ferry to the guest house (although your luggage is taken by carrier) means that a holiday on Sark is best suited to those who find it easy to get about.
OPEN ALL YEAR. NO SMOKING. V, DIAB, LOW-CAL., GLUTEN-FREE, S.D. B/A. LICENSED. GROUND-FLOOR ROOMS WITH RAMPED ACCESS. OVER 10S ONLY. EN SUITE, BEVERAGES & TV IN ROOMS. B. & B. FROM £20, D. B. & B. FROM £30.

HOTEL PETIT CHAMP, SARK TEL: (01481) 832046
Charming hotel in unrivalled position on the west coast of the unique island of Sark. Restaurant renowned for good cuisine. Solar-heated swimming pool.
OPEN Apr. to Oct. N/S DINING R & 1 LOUNGE/LIBRARY. V, S.D. B/A. LICENSED. CHILDREN: OVER 7S ONLY. ALL ROOMS EN SUITE. CREDIT CARDS. HALF BOARD £35-46.

Scotland

Borders

ACCOMMODATION

DENHOLM

BARNHILLS FARMHOUSE, NR DENHOLM, ROXB'SHIRE, TD9 8SH
Beautiful ex-farmhouse set in a wild garden with orchard and vegetables; 3m from the nearest village; excellent vegan cuisine.
TEL: (0145 087) 577 OPEN ALL YEAR. V, WH EXC. NO SMOKING. CHILDREN. BEVERAGES. B. & B. AROUND £14.

HAWICK

KIRKTON FARMHOUSE, KIRKTON, HAWICK, ROXB'SHIRE, TD9 8QS
Spacious farmhouse surrounded by beautiful countryside offering a friendly welcome and good home-cooking; log fires in cooler weather; private sitting room with colour TV.
TEL: (01450) 72421 OPEN Mar. - Nov. V, S.D. B/A. CHILDREN WELCOME. BEVERAGES IN ROOMS. B. & B. AROUND £16.

Whitchester Christian Guest House & Retreat Centre

BORTHAUGH, HAWICK, ROXBURGHSHIRE, BORDERS, TD9 7LN   TEL & FAX: (01450) 77477
STB 3 Crown Commended. Taste of Scotland Member. Mid 19th C. manor standing in 3 acres of lawned garden and offering 'a place of rest, rehabilitation and peace' within a Christian context; beautifully furnished throughout and with lovely views; excellent cuisine prepared from fresh, often home-grown, produce.
OPEN Feb. - Dec.   V STD. S.D. B/A. N/S ex. in TV lounge.   DISABLED ACCESS. CHILDREN WELCOME. PETS B/A. EN SUITE IN 5 OF 10 ROOMS.   BEVERAGES IN ROOMS.   T.V. IN LOUNGE.   B. & B. FROM £13.20.

JEDBURGH

Froylehurst

FRIARS, JEDBURGH, ROXBURGHSHIRE, BORDERS, TD8 6BN   TEL: (01835) 862477
STB Highly Commended. AA QQQQ. Detached late Victorian house with lovely garden offering comfortable accommodation in tastefully decorated rooms; full Scottish breakfast.
OPEN Mar - Nov. N/S DINING R. V.   OVER 5S ONLY. BEVERAGES & T.V. IN ROOMS.   B. & B. FROM £15.

Harrietsfield House

ANCRUM, BY JEDBURGH, ROXBURGHSHIRE, BORDERS, TD8 6TZ   TEL: (01835) 830327

Harrietsfield House is a spacious and comfortable ex-farmhouse with a lovely garden set in beautiful countryside just 5 miles from Jedburgh. Breakfast is the only meal which is usually available at Harriets-field, but all food is prepared from wholefoods and, when possible, organically home-grown produce. Accommodation is in warm, comfortable rooms and there is an inviting lounge with a log fire in the evening as well as a cup of tea and home-baking. You are centrally situated in this part of the world for visiting all the Border towns and are just 44 miles from Edinburgh; golf, riding and fishing may all be enjoyed locally.
OPEN Easter/April - Oct. NO SMOKING. V, WH STD, S.D. B/A.   1 DOWNSTAIRS BEDROOM.   CHILDREN WEL-COME (at full tariff). PETS B/A. 2 EN SUITE ROOMS. TEA IN LOUNGE 9.30 PM.   T.V. IN LOUNGE. B. & B. FROM £16.

MELROSE

PRIORY VIEW, 15 PRIORS WALK, MELROSE
Beautiful detached house with pretty gardens in a quiet area 5 mins walk from town centre and the Abbey; all food prepared from fresh ingredients; home-cooking & home-baking
TEL: (01896 82) 2087 OPEN ALL YEAR. V, DIAB B/A. NO SMOKING. CHILDREN WELCOME. BEVERAGES IN ROOMS. T.V. B. & B. AROUND £14.

PEEBLES

DRUMMORE, VENLAW HIGH ROAD, PEEBLES, EH45 8RL
Beautiful modern farmhouse standing in peaceful, wooded surroundings with panoramic
views; all meals prepared from fresh ingredients.
TEL: (01721) 20336 OPEN Easter to Oct.   V, LOW-FAT DIETS B/A.   NO SMOKING.   CHILDREN B/A.   BEVER-
AGES IN ROOMS.   T.V.   B. & B. AROUND £15.

Kingsmuir Hotel

SPRINGHILL RD, PEEBLES, EH45 9EP TEL: (01721) 720151 FAX: (01721) 721795

Kingsmuir is a charming century old country
house which stands amidst leafy grounds on the
quiet, South side of Peebles looking across parkland to the River Tweed; indeed it is just 5
minutes' walk through the park to the High
Street. It is a family-run hotel and as such offers
friendly, efficient service: the bedrooms are exceptionally comfortable and there is a stylish
new lounge for guests' use; the modern refur-
bishments and additions have been sympathetically undertaken, but the original character of
the building is still clearly in evidence in the
other comfortable lounge and in the dining room. The food is excellent: everything is
prepared from fresh, local produce, and in addition to an imaginative evening à la carte
menu, there are some good choices for children and vegetarians on separate menus; the
Kingsmuir Hotel is "Taste of Scotland Recommended", incidentally. Peebles is a Royal
and Ancient Borough just 40 minutes' drive South of Edinburgh; there are many fine shops
in the city and in addition you are close to many stately homes and castles of historic interest.
OPEN ALL YEAR ex. Xmas day.   N/S DINING R & LOUNGE.   V STD.   LICENSED.   CHILDREN & DOGS
WELCOME. E N SUITE, TV & BEVERAGES IN ROOMS.   CREDIT CARDS.   B. & B. AROUND £30.

TWEED VALLEY HOTEL & RESTAURANT, WALKERBURN, BY PEEBLES
Lovely Edwardian country mansion standing in its own grounds; fresh food & home-grown
herbs used in cooking; activity courses & holidays throughout the year.
TEL: (0189687) 636 OPEN ALL YEAR.   V, S.D. B/A.   N/S DINING R. LICENSED.   CHILDREN WELCOME.
PETS B/A.   EN SUITE, TV & BEVERAGES IN ROOMS.   CREDIT CARDS.   B. & B. AROUND £49.

SELKIRK

TIBBIE SHIELS INN, ST MARY'S LOCH, SELKIRK, BORDERS, TD7 5NE
Situated on the tranquil shore of St Mary's Loch and named after its first owner of 1823,
the Tibbie Shiels inn has been offering hospitality to (some, very famous) guests for nearly
200 years; lots of character and excellent food.
TEL: (01750) 42231 OPEN ALL YEAR.   EXTENSIVE VEGETARIAN MENU.   1 N/S DINING R.   LICENSED.   DISABLED
ACCESS. CHILDREN.   BEVERAGES IN ROOMS.   T.V. IN LOUNGE.   B. & B. AROUND £17.

Dumfries and Galloway

ACCOMMODATION

The Rossan

AUCHENCAIRN, DUMFRIES & GALLOWAY, DG7 1QR   TEL: (01556) 640269

The Rossan is an early Victorian ex-manse standing
well back from the A711 in over an acre of beautiful
gardens between the Screel Hills and the sea; the
house itself overlooks Auchencairn Bay and there
are two lovely sandy beaches close by. Mrs Bardsley
has been welcoming guests - especially ornitholig-
ists and vegetarians - to her house for many years
now; she is keen to point out, however, that it is, first
and foremost, her (very welcoming) home; consequently, guests must make do with shared use of two
bathrooms, there is a cosy atmosphere and guests are

She is a dab hand at catering for special diets, too. STB listed & approved.
OPEN ALL YEAR ex. 2 weeks in Jan. V, GLUTEN-FREE, WH STD; VE, S.D. B/A. N/A DINING R & ALLOWED IN BEDRS AFTER 9 PM. WELL-BEHAVED DOGS FREE. BEVERAGES IN ROOMS. T.V. B & B AROUND £14.

KIRKCUDBRIGHT

Millburn House

MILLBURN ST, KIRKCUDBRIGHT, DUMF & GALL., DG6 4ED   TEL: (01557) 330926
Charming 19th C. white-painted, stone-built house of traditional design with lovely conservatory breakfast room; breakfast only.
OPEN ALL YEAR.   NO SMOKING.   V, S.D. B/A.   CHILDREN WELCOME AT FULL TARIFF.   EN SUITE & BEVERAGES IN ROOMS.   T.V. IN LOUNGE.   B & B FROM £20.

RESTAURANTS

NEW ABBEY

Abbey Cottage Coffees & Crafts

26 MAIN STREET, NEW ABBEY, DUMFRIES, DG2 8BY   TEL: (01387) 85377
Country restaurant in a charming setting next to Sweetheart Abbey, serving home-made meals; good vegetarian selection.
OPEN 10 - 5.30.   L. AROUND £4.   NO SMOKING.   V STD, S.D. B/A.   LICENSED.   CHILDREN WELCOME.
DISABLED ACCESS: 'WIDE DOORS, RAMP, DISABLED LOO'.

Edinburgh

ACCOMMODATION

Adam Guest House

2 HARTINGTON GARDENS, EDINBURGH, EH10 4LD TEL: (0131) 229 8664 FAX: (0131) 228 5807

Adam House is a family-run guest house which is situated in a quiet cul-de-sac (free from parking restrictions), just fifteen minutes' walk from the city centre and close to bus routes, shops, theatres and restaurants; Bruntsfield Links and The Meadows public parks are just a short walk away. The house has recently been completely refurbished by the present owners and all the rooms are now bright, comfortable and well-equipped with a T.V., hot drink facilities and wash hand basin; some have en suite facilities. The proprietors and staff offer warm hospitality and a very friendly service, and families and children are particularly welcome with reduced rates being available throughout the year.

OPEN ALL YEAR. NO SMOKING.   V, S.D. B/A.   CHILDREN WELCOME. PETS B/A.   SOME ROOMS EN SUITE.   BEVERAGES & T.V. IN ROOMS.   B. & B. FROM £17 PER PERSON.

HIGHFIELD GUEST HOUSE, 83 MAYFIELD RD, EDINBURGH, EH9 3AE
STB Commended. Small, friendly, guest house 10 mins drive from the city centre. The full cooked breakfast includes cereals, oatcakes, yoghurt, toast, home-made porridge.
TEL: (0131 667) 8717 OPEN ALL YEAR.   V, S.D. B/A.   NO SMOKING.   GROUND-FLOOR BEDROOM & SHOWER/ROOM/WC. CHILDREN WELCOME.   GUIDE DOGS B/A.   BEVERAGES IN ROOMS.   T.V. IN LOUNGE. B. & B. AROUND £15.

Sandeman

33 COLINTON RD, EDINBURGH, EH10 5DR   TEL: (0131) 447 8080
STB 2 Star Commended. Victorian family home near to the city centre. The breakfast menu features oat-cakes and home-made preserves (organic in the case of raspberry & strawberry) and a good choice of teas; organically home-grown fruits are also available in season.
OPEN Mar - Oct. (other times by arrangement).   V, S.D. B/A.   NO SMOKING.   CHILDREN WELCOME.   PETS B/A.
EN SUITE, TV & TEA/COFFEE IN ROOMS.   B. & B. FROM £20.

SAN MARCO GUEST HOUSE, 24 MAYFIELD GARDENS, EDINBURGH
STB 2 Crown Commended. Friendly, family-run guest house near the city centre on the
main A7 road South of the city. Vegetarians can be accommodated by arrangement.
TEL: (0131) 667 8982 FAX: (0131) 662 1945 OPEN ALL YEAR. V STD. S.D. B/A. CHILDREN WELCOME. PETS
B/A. 2 EN SUITE ROOMS. BEVERAGES & TV IN ROOMS. B. & B. AROUND £15.

Sandilands House

25 QUEENSFERRY RD, EDINBURGH. TEL: (0131) 332 2057
B. & B. situated 1m from city centre. Some en suite. Well-furnished, attractive rooms.
OPEN ALL YEAR. NO SMOKING. V, S.D. B/A. CHILDREN WELCOME. SOME EN SUITE; TV & BEVERAGES IN
ROOMS

STUDIO B. & B., 173 BRUNTSFIELD PL, EDINBURGH, EH10 4DG
Friendly, informal B. & B. in spacious apartment near to lovely walks and within easy
strolling distance of the city centre; varied, tasty food prepared from fresh ingredients.
TEL: (0131 229) 2746 OPEN ALL YEAR. V STD, S.D. B/A. NO SMOKING. CHILDREN WELCOME. BEVER-
AGES. B. & B. FROM £14.

Teviotdale House

53 GRANGE LOAN, EDINBURGH, EH9 2ER (031 667) 4376
Elegant, stone-built Victorian town house in quiet conservation part of Edinburgh; excep-
tionally well-appointed. Fresh produce used in cooking (including vegetables & herbs from
the organic kitchen garden) and there are also home-made scones, bread, jams, marmalade,
Scottish honey, Teviotdale Special (soaked apricots, pineapple, raisins, sultanas and
prunes) and Old Fashioned Porridge made from Pin Head Oatmeal and Wholegrain Wheat.
OPEN ALL YEAR. V, S.D. B/A. NO SMOKING. CHILDREN WELCOME. EN SUITE, BEVERAGES & T.V. IN
ROOMS. CREDIT CARDS (SURCHARGE). B & B. AROUND £28.

The Town House Guest House

65 GILMORE PLACE, EDINBURGH, EH3 9NU TEL: (0131) 229 1985

STB Highly Commended.The Town House is, as its name
suggests, a charming 3-storey Victorian town house which
was built in 1876 as the manse for the neighbouring church.
Today it has been beautifully renovated and sympathetically
decorated in order to provide every possible modern con-
venience while still retaining the style, and indeed the atmosphere, of a 19th C. building. Breakfast is the only meal to be
served at the Town House, but it is an exceeding generous
meal with lots of healthy options; there are, of course,
numerous first-rate eating places in Edinburgh. You are just
a mile from the city centre at the Town House but you are
also on a very good and direct bus route. Your hosts are very
friendly and welcoming and will gladly give you information
to help you plan your stay.
OPEN ALL YEAR. NO SMOKING. V, S.D. B/A. ALL ROOMS EN SUITE.
BEVERAGES & TV IN BEDROOMS. B. & B. FROM £20.

Turret Guest House

8 KILMAURS TERRACE, EDINBURGH, EH16 5DR TEL: (0131) 667 6704
The Turret is a small, family-run guest house which is quietly situated in a residential area
of the city near to the Royal Commonwealth Swimming Pool. The house has retained many
of its original Victorian features, including a large open wooden staircase, and each of the
bedrooms has been very comfortably furnished and tastefully decorated (one four-poster
room is available). Your hosts, Ian and Jackie Cameron, will do everything they can to
make your stay as enjoyable as possible, and are on hand to give helpful information to
help you plan your stay.
OPEN ALL YEAR ex Xmas. N/S DINING R. V STD, S.D. B/A. OVER 2s PREFERRED. SOME EN SUITE ROOMS.
BEVERAGES & TV IN ROOMS. B. & B. FROM £14.

RESTAURANTS

CHAPTER ONE, 57 GEORGE STREET, EDINBURGH, EH2 2JQ
Café located in general bookshop/newsagents in the centre of the city.
TEL: (0131) 225 4495 V STD. 75% N/S. CHILDREN WELCOME.

CORNERSTONE CAFÉ, ST JOHN'S CHURCH, PRINCES STREET, EDINBURGH
Vegetarian/vegan/wholefood cafe serving hot food, salads, snacks, cakes, etc.
TEL: (0131) 229 0212 NO SMOKING. DISABLED ACCESS difficult, but there is a ramp; toilet has wheelchair access'.

CRAWFORDS COUNTRY KITCHENS, 26/27 ST JAMES CENTRE, EDINBURGH
TEL: (0131) 556 3098 V, S.D. STD. N/S UPPER FLOOR. DISABLED ACCESS. CHILDREN WELCOME.

HELIOS FOUNTAIN, 7 GRASSMARKET, EDINBURGH, EH1 2HY
Excellent vegetarian/wholefood cafe with friendly atmosphere at the rear of book shop.
TEL: (0131) 229 7884   V, VE, SUGAR-FREE STD. NO SMOKING. DISABLED ACCESS.   CHILDREN WELCOME.

The Indian Cavalry Club
3 ATHOLL PLACE, EDINBURGH, EH3 8HP   TEL: (0131) 228 3282
The Indian Cavalry Club is a wonderful restaurant which won itself so many friends that it soon began to feel like a real club. It serves the kind of modern Indian cuisine favoured by the most exclusive circles of Delhi and Bombay: lighter and less fiery than traditional fare and rely on the finest, freshest ingredients. The main courses include vegetarian delicacies.
60 SEATS. OPEN 12 - 2.30, 5.30 - 11.30.   L. AROUND £10.   V STD, S.D. ON REQUEST.   N/S 25%.   LICENSED.
DISABLED ACCESS.   CHILDREN WELCOME.   CREDIT CARDS.

The Kalpna Restaurant
2-3 ST PATRICK SQUARE, EDINBURGH, EH8 9EZ   TEL: (0131) 667 9890
Widely recommended, award-winning Indian vegetarian restaurant, rated amongst the best in Britain, specialising in Indian vegetarian wholefood cuisine from the Gujarat region. The name Kalpna denotes a combination of 'imagination'and 'creation'and the logo is the elephant, which reminds diners that you do not have to eat meat to be big, strong and intelligent.
OPEN 12 - 2, 5.30 - 11.   NO SMOKING.   CHILDREN WELCOME.   WHEELCHAIR ACCESS.

Parrots
3-5 VIEWFORTH, EDINBURGH, EH10 4JD   TEL: (0131) 229 3252
Very popular restaurant - parrots abound - serving a wide range of dishes including good vegetarian options; excellent cooking; booking virtually essential.
OPEN Fri. & Sat. 5 - 11.30 P.M. (last orders), Sun. - Thurs. 6 - 11.30 P.M.   V STD.   NO SMOKING.   LICENSED.
DISABLED ACCESS.   CHILDREN WELCOME from 5 - 7 pm & at lunchtime functions.

PIZZA HUT (UK) LTD, 34-36 HANOVER STREET, EDINBURGH, EH2 2DR
TEL: (0131) 226 3652 V, VE STD. 66% N/S. LICENSED.   DISABLED ACCESS, 'not to toilet'. CHILDREN.

THE POTTING SHED, BRUNTSFIELD HOTEL, 69 BRUNTSFIELD PL
TEL: (0131) 229 1393 V STD.   N/S CONSERVATORY. LICENSED. DISABLED ACCESS. CHILDREN WELCOME.

THE QUEEN'S HALL, CLERK STREET, EDINBURGH
Excellent wholefood restaurant.
TEL: (031 668) 3456 V/WH STD. NO SMOKING.   LICENSED. DISABLED ACCESS: 'ramp/toilets etc.' CHILDREN.

"REEDS" RESTAURANT & COFFEE SHOP, 124 PRINCES STREET, EDINBURGH EH2 3AA
TEL: (0131) 225 6703 50% N/S V STD. LICENSED. DISABLED ACCESS. CHILDREN WELCOME.

Seeds Wholefood Café
53 WEST NICOLSON ST, EDINBURGH, EH8 9DB   TEL: (0131) 667 8729
V, WH EXC. NO SMOKING. CHILDREN WELCOME.

"THE STEDDING", 118 BIGGAR ROAD, EDINBURGH, EH10 7DH
TEL: (0131) 445 1128   V STD. 50% N/S LICENSED. DISABLED ACCESS. CHILDREN 'LIMITED'.

Fife

ACCOMMODATION

ABERDOUR

HAWKCRAIG HOUSE, HAWKCRAIG POINT, ABERDOUR, FIFE, KY3 0TZ
STB 2 Crown Highly Commended. Beautiful old white-painted ferryman's house over-looking the sea .All food is prepared from fresh local produce ('Taste of Scotland').
TEL: (01383) 860335 OPEN Feb. - Nov. V, DIAB B/A. NO SMOKING. BYO WINE. CHILDREN: OVER 8S ONLY. BOTH ROOMS EN SUITE & WITH TV. BEVERAGS ONREQUEST. B. & B. AROUND £19.

CULROSS

WOODHEAD FARM, CULROSS, FIFE.
Lovely old farmhouse standing in pretty garden in beautiful countryside. Home-grown, farm or local produce used in cooking.
TEL: (01383) 880270 OPEN ALL YEAR. V, S.D. B/A. NO SMOKING. CHILDREN WELCOME. BEVERAGES & T.V. IN ROOMS.   B. & B. AROUND £19.

CUPAR

GREIGSTON FARMHOUSE, PEAT INN, CUPAR, FIFE, KY15 5LF
16th/17th C. Laird's house; home-grown vegetables, soft fruits, milk & cream.
TEL: (01334) 840284 OPEN Mar. - Nov.   V B/A. NO SMOKING. DISABLED ACCESS. CHILDREN WEL-COME. PETS B/A. EN SUITE & BEVERAGES IN ROOMS.   T.V. IN LOUNGE. B. & B. AROUND £15.

FREUCHIE

Lomond Hills Hotel

LOMOND ROAD, FREUCHIE, KY7 7EY   TEL: (01337) 57329
White-painted hotel in the picturesque village of Freuchie. Candle-lit dinners reflect both Scottish and French influences. Small leisure centre.
OPEN ALL YEAR. N/S REST, 4 BEDROOMS, CONSERVATORY & LEISURE CENTRE. V STD. LICENSED. DIS-ABLED: "RESTAURANT & 1 BEDROOM ON GROUND FLOOR". CHILDREN WELCOME. EN SUITE, BEVERAGES & T.V. IN ROOMS.

GLENROTHES

Rescobie Hotel

VALLEY DRIVE, LESLIE, GLENROTHES, FIFE, KY6 3BQ TEL: (01592) 742143 FAX: (01592) 620231
harming small country house in 2 acres of lovely gardens; elegantly furnished. First-rate cuisine features international and traditionally Scottish dishes prepared from fresh, local produce. Excellent vegetarian options.
OPEN ALL YEAR ex. Xmas. V STD, S.D. B/A. LICENSED. CHILDREN WELCOME. EN SUITE, BEVERAGES & TV IN ROOMS.   ACCESS, VISA, AMEX, DINERS.   B. & B. AROUND £35.

ST ANDREW'S

Edenside House

EDENSIDE, ST ANDREWS, FIFE, KY16 9SQ   TEL: (01334) 838108   FAX: (01334) 838493
STB 2 Crown Commended. Edenside House enjoys a superb waterfront setting with fine

views of the estuary bird sanctuary /nature reserve yet it is within 2½ miles of historic St Andrews (5 minutes by car on A91). A listed former Scottish farmhouse predating 1775, now tastefully modernised, Edenside House offers a high standard of comfort to discerning guests and is non-smoking throughout. All nine double/twin rooms are furnished to 3 Crown Commended standard and have en suite facilities, colour TV and beverage tray (some are on the ground floor). Edenside House provides guaranteed parking within private grounds. The traditional and extensive break-fast menu includes fish dishes. Edenside Riding Stable is nearby. As well as the world-re-nowned Old Course and other five St Andrews courses, other fine tests of golf, including

Carnoustie, abound locally and we are happy to discuss your golf requirements at the time of booking. Contact Dr and Mrs Jim Mansell for brochure and booking.
OPEN ALL YEAR.   V, VE STD, SOME WH.   SOME S.D. B/A.   NO SMOKING.   OVER 12s WELCOME.   PETS B/A.
DISABLED ACCESS: SOME GROUND FLOOR ROOMS.   EN SUITE, BEVERAGES & TV IN ROOMS.   ACCESS, VISA.
B. & B. FROM £20.

LATHONES MANOR HOTEL, BY LARGOWARD, ST ANDREW'S, KY9 1JE
Splendidly renovated inn with open fires, exposed stone work and oak beams in the picturesque East Neuk of Fife; excellent cuisine.
TEL: (01334) 84494 OPEN Feb. - Dec.   V STD. S.D. B/A.   N/S DINING R.   LICENSED.   DISABLED ACCESS.
EN SUITE, BEVERAGES & TV IN ROOMS.   B. & B. AROUND £25.

Rufflets Country House

STRATHKINNESS LOW RD, ST ANDREWS, FIFE, KY16 9TX   TEL: (01334) 72594 FAX: (01334) 78703

Designed by Dundee architect Donald Mills and built in 1924, this outstanding country house stands in 10 acres of award-winning gardens and has been privately owned and personally managed by the same family since 1952. Over the years the house has been extended and refurbished, but all additions have been in keeping with the original building, and an overall atmosphere of gracious calm prevails: each of the spacious public rooms overlooks the magnificent gardens, and the 21 en suite bedrooms have been furnished to a very high standard and are equipped with a range of useful amenities including a direct dial phone; a cottage in the grounds has equally splendid accommodation for 3 further sets of guests. The food is excellent: everything is prepared from fresh, seasonal and local produce; indeed many of the vegetables, fruits and herbs come from the hotel's kitchen garden. This idyllic retreat offers the best of both worlds: a sense of rural tranquillity, yet the proximity to the world famous "Home of Golf", St Andrews.
OPEN Jan. - Dec.   V STD. DIAB. B/A.   N/S DINING R, PART OF BAR, SOME BEDR.   LICENSED.   CHILDREN
WELCOME.   EN SUITE, TV & BEVERAGES IN ROOMS.   CREDIT CARDS.

St Andrews Golf Hotel

40 THE SCORES, ST ANDREWS, FIFE, KY16 9AS.   TEL: (01334) 72611

Situated on the cliffs overlooking St Andrews Bay and links, and 200 metres from the 'old course', St Andrews Hotel is a tastefully modernised, listed Victorian building with comfortable bedrooms and elegant public rooms (including a charming oak-panelled restaurant). The food is excellent: everything is prepared from fresh, local sea-food, game and meats, and is complemented by a first-rate choice of wines; meals are served by candlelight in the aforementioned dining room or, if you prefer a more informal atmosphere, you could dine in Ma Bells basement bar and restaurant with its vast array of foreign and local beers. The hotel is owned and run by the Hughes family and specialises in providing golfing holidays for individuals and small groups.
OPEN ALL YEAR.   V, S.D. B/A.   N/A RESTAURANT.   LICENSED.
CHILDREN WELCOME.   PETS B/A.   EN SUITE, TV & BEVERAGES IN
ROOMS.   CREDIT CARDS .

Glasgow & Central

GLASGOW

Mrs J Freebairn-Smith

14 PROSPECT AVENUE, CAMBUSLANG, GLASGOW, G72 8BW   TEL: (0141) 641 5055

STB Listed Approved. Large Victorian villa standing in half an acre of lovely gardens.
OPEN ALL YEAR.   V B/A.   NO SMOKING IN PUBLIC ROOMS & SOME BEDROOMS.   V B/A.   CHILDREN
WELCOME.   PETS B/A   BEVERAGES & T.V. IN ROOMS.   B & B FROM £13.

Regent Guest House

44 REGENT PARK SQUARE, STRATHBUNGO, GLASGOW, G41 2AG   TEL: (0141) 422 1199

Charming 'B'listed Victorian terraced house at the quiet end of a busy street 2m from the
city centre & 1m from the Burrell Collection. Excellent breakfast menu features healthy
options such as fresh fruit and yoghurt. Good nearby restaurants.
OPEN ALL YEAR.   V, VE STD.   DIAB, S.D. B/A.   ORG, WH WHEN AVAIL.   N/S ex. 3 BEDRS.   CHILDREN
WELCOME.   PETS B/A.   BEVERAGES & TV IN BEDRS.   CREDIT CARDS.   B. & B. AROUND £25.

STIRLING

**MRS THELMA HARPER, 67 BURNHEAD ROAD, LARBERT, STIRLING TEL:
(01324) 553168**
Pleasant house in rural setting in close proximity to both Glasgow and Edinburgh.
OPEN ALL YEAR.   V, S.D. B/A.   NO SMOKING.   BEVERAGES IN ROOMS.   T.V. ON REQUEST.

MRS D MCLAREN, "ALLANDALE", 98 CAUSEWAYHEAD RD, STIRLING
Warm and friendly B. & B.
TEL: (01786) 65643 OPEN ALL YEAR.   NO SMOKING.   V, S.D. B/A.   CHILDREN WELCOME.   BEVERAGES
IN ROOMS.   T.V. LOUNGE.   B & B AROUND £16.

RESTAURANTS

GLASGOW

BURNBANK HOTEL, 67/85 WEST PRINCES STREET, GLASGOW
TEL: (0141) 332 4400 V, S.D. STD. NO SMOKING. LICENSED. DISABLED ACCESS. CHILDREN WELCOME.

CAFÉ JJ, 180 DUMBARTON ROAD, GLASGOW, G11 6XE
Small, family-run café offering a wide selection of home-made reasonably priced food.
TEL: (0141) 357 1881 V, S.D. STD. NO SMOKING. LICENSED. CHILDREN WELCOME.

THE COACH HOUSE, BALMORE, TORRANCE, GLASGOW, G64 4AE
Charitable enterprise offering home-baked snacks & cakes together with craft/gift shop.
TEL: (01360) 20742   V STD.   NO SMOKING.   CHILDREN WELCOME.

SHISH MAHAL RESTAURANT, 45-47 GIBSON STREET, GLASGOW
Excellent restaurant serving Western and Indian food.
TEL: (0141) 334 7899 V STD. N/S PART OF RESTAURANT.   LICENSED. DISABLED ACCESS.   CHILDREN.

STIRLING

BROUGHTON'S RESTAURANT, BLAIR DRUMMOND, STIRLING, FK9 4XE
TEL: (0786) 841897   V STD.   N/S RESTAURANT.   LICENSED.   DISABLED ACCESS.   CHILDREN LUNCH-
TIME.

Grampian

ACCOMMODATION

BALLATER

The Green Inn

9 VICTORIA ROAD, BALLATER, GRAMPIAN, AB3 5QQ   TEL: (013397) 55701

The Green Inn is a granite-built former temperance hotel which overlooks Ballater village green. All the food has been prepared on the premises and maximum use is made of local, fresh produce. Traditional Scottish specialities are a regular feature of the menu and a set vegetarian menu is also available. Desserts are particularly delicious and feature Sticky Toffee Pudding served with Citrus Fruits and a Whisky Butterscotch Sauce, or 'Crowdie Cake'- a blend of Crowdie Cheese, lemon and buttermilk served with Blairgowrie Fruit and Berries in a raspberry and red wine sauce. There is a wine list with items representing every region from Alsace to Australia & from Champagne to Chile.

OPEN ALL YEAR. V STD, S.D. B/A. N/S DINING R LICENSED. DISABLED ACCESS. CHILDREN WELCOME. EN SUITE, TV & BEVERAGES IN ROOMS. ACCESS, VISA. B. & B. AROUND £20.

MONALTRIE HOTEL, 5 BRIDGE SQUARE, BALLATER, GRAMPIAN.
Splendid 19th C. hotel on the Dee; cuisine prepared from fresh produce; Thai restaurant.
TEL: (013397) 55417 OPEN ALL YEAR. V, S.D. B/A. N/S RESTAURANT. LICENSED. DISABLED ACCESS. CHILDREN WELCOME. PETS B/A. EN SUITE, TV & BEVERAGES IN ROOMS.

BANFF

BANKHEAD CROFT, GAMRIE, BY BANFF, GRAMPIAN, AB45 3HN
TEL: (01261) 851584 OPEN ALL YEAR. V, VE, DIAB, S.D. B/A. WH STD. DISABLED ACCESS. CHILD-REN WELCOME. PETS B/A. BEVERAGES & T.V. IN ROOMS. CREDIT CARDS. B. & B. AROUND £14.

GLENLIVET

MINMORE HOUSE HOTEL, GLENLIVET, BALLANDALLOCH, AB3 9DB
Splendid house, individually furnished rooms; fresh flowers, log fires; good home-cooking from fresh, organic vegetables.
TEL: (01807) 590378 OPEN May - Nov. V, S.D. B/A. N/S ex. bar. LICENSED. CHILDREN WELCOME. PETS B/A. EN SUITE & BEVERAGS IN ROOMS. B. & B. AROUND £30.

HUNTLY

FAICH-HILL FARMHOUSE HOLIDAYS, GARTLY, HUNTLY, ABERDEENSHIRE
19th C. farmhouse; excellent home-cooking; prepared from fresh and farm produce. Twice winner of *Scottish Farmhouse of the Year*.
TEL: (01466) 720240 OPEN ALL YEAR. V, S.D. B/A. N/S ex. sun lounge. CHILDREN: OVER 4S ONLY. EN SUITE, BEVERAGES, RADIOS & ELECTRIC BLANKETS IN ROOMS. T.V. IN LOUNGE. B. & B. AROUND £17.

THE OLD MANSE OF MARNOCH, HUNTLY, ABERDEENSHIRE, AB54 5RS
Fine 19th C. country house in 3 acres of splendid gardens. All food home-prepared (including the after dinner mints) & only fresh produce (some organically home-grown) is used in cooking
TEL: (01466) 780873 OPEN ALL YEAR. V, VE, DIAB, S.D. B/A. N/S DINING R. LICENSED. CHILDREN: OVER 12S ONLY. DOGS WELCOME. EN SUITE & BEVERAGES IN ROOMS. T.V. IN LOUNGE.

KEITH

THE HAUGHS FARM GUEST HOUSE, KEITH
Beautiful and comfortable farmhouse with an interesting history; very well-appointed; home-cooking from fresh produce.
TEL: (01542) 882238 OPEN 1 Apr. - 15 Oct. V, DIAB, B/A. NO SMOKING. DISABLED ACCESS. CHILDREN WELCOME. 3 EN SUITE ROOMS. BEVERAGES & TV IN ROOMS. B. & B. AROUND £16.

MUIR OF ORD

The Dower House

MUIR OF ORD, ROSS-SHIRE, GRAMPIAN, IV6 7XN   TEL & FAX: (01463) 870090
Exceptionally comfortable accommodation & award-winning food.
OPEN ALL YEAR.   V B/A.   N/S DINING ROOM & SOME BEDROOMS.   LICENSED.   DISABLED ACCESS.

RESTAURANTS

ABERDEEN

Charles Michie Chemists

391 UNION STREET, ABERDEEN, GRAMPIAN.   TEL: (01224) 585312
Beautiful store with fresh and pretty coffee shop. Delicious home-prepared food. Open for
morning coffee, lunches and afternoon tea.
OPEN SHOP HOURS.   V, DIAB STD.   NO SMOKING.   DISABLED: 'STAFF HELP WITH WHEELCHAIRS'.

FOCHABERS

THE GALLERY, 85 HIGH ST, FOCHABERS, GRAMPIAN.
TEL: (01343) 820981 V STD. NO SMOKING.

FRASERBURGH

RITCHIES COFFEE SHOP, 30 CROSSS ST, FRASERBURGH, GRAMPIAN.
TEL: (01346) 2774 V STD. NO SMOKING.

Highlands

ACCOMMODATION

AULTBEA

MELLONDALE GUEST HOUSE, 47 MELLON CHARLES, AULTBEA.
Small, family-run guest house with garden overlooking Loch Ewe; home-cooked meals
prepared from fresh, local ingredients.
TEL: (01445) 731326 OPEN Mar. - Oct.   V, VE B/A.   NO SMOKING.   DISABLED ACCESS.   CHILDREN
WELCOME. 3 EN SUITE ROOMS.   BEVERAGES & TV IN ROOMS.

ORAN NA MARA, DRUMCHORK, AULTBEA, ROSS-SHIRE, IV22 2HU
Spacious, comfortable hill side guest house with stunning loch views from all rooms. Also
2 STB "Highly Commended" self-catering apartments.
TEL: (01445) 731394 OPEN Easter - Oct. inc.   V, VE STD.   NO SMOKING.   ALL ROOMS ON GROUND FLOOR.
OVER 8S WELCOME. PETS B/A.   WASH-HAND BASIN, BEVERAGES & T.V. IN ROOMS.   B. & B. AROUND £16.

BOAT OF GARTEN

AVINGORMACK, BOAT OF GARTEN, INVERNESS-SHIRE, PH24 3BT
Converted croft superbly situated on a hillside with magnificent views of the Cairngorms.
TEL: (01479) 831614 OPEN ALL YEAR.   V STD. NO SMOKING.   CHILDREN WELCOME.   BEVERAGES &
TV IN ROOMS. B. & B. AROUND £15.

Heathbank - The Victorian House

BOAT OF GARTEN, INVERNESS-SHIRE, HIGHLAND, PH24 3BD   TEL: (01479) 83234
OPEN Dec. - Oct.   V B/A.   N/S DINING R & BEDRS.   LICENSED.   CHILDREN ACCEPTED.   SOME EN SUITE ROOMS.
BEVERAGES IN ROOMS. T.V. LOUNGE.   B. & B. FROM £16, D.,B. & B. £28.

BRORA

ARD BEAG, BADNELLAN, BRORA, SUTHERLAND, KW9 6NQ
Small, comfortable former croft house with a homely atmosphere in a pleasant south-facing
garden. Good, wholesome, home-cooked food prepared from fresh garden produce where
possible; the delicious bread is home-baked.

TEL: (01408) 621398　OPEN May - Sept.　V, B/A.　N/S DINING R & BEDRS.　CHILDREN WELCOME.　BEVER-AGES IN ROOMS.　B. & B. AROUND £15.

SUMUNDAR VILLA, HARBOUR ROAD, BRORA, SUTHERLAND, KW9 6QF
Peaceful family home superbly situated at the mouth of the River Brora on the shores of the North Sea; home-baking; vegetarian household.
TEL: (01408) 621717　OPEN Feb. - Nov.　V, DIAB STD.　NO SMOKING.　DISABLED ACCESS.　CHILDREN WELCOME.　BEVERAGES & T.V. IN ROOMS.　B. & B. AROUND £16.

TIGH FADA (NON-SMOKERS HAVEN), GOLF ROAD, BRORA, KW9 6QS
Lovely spacious house peacefully situated in pleasant gardens with fine, uninterrupted views of the sea and hills; the garden gate leads to both the golf course and sandy beach. Cosily furnished; home-cooked wholesome food.
TEL: (01408) 621332　OPEN ALL YEAR.　V, S.D. B/A.　NO SMOKING.　CHILDREN WELCOME, 'NOT TOD-DLERS'.　PETS B/A.　BEVERAGES IN ROOMS.　B. & B. AROUND £15.

CORNHILL

Castle of Park

CORNHILL, BANFFSHIRE, HIGHLANDS, AB45 2AY　　TEL & FAX: (01466) 751667
16th C. castle in 16 acres of peaceful park & woods near Banffshire coast.　Restaurant is open to non-residents; choice of menus prepared from fresh produce. 4-poster available.
OPEN ALL YEAR.　V, VE STD.　DIAB, S.D. B/A.　ORG, WH WHERE POSSIBLE.　N/S DINING R.　LICENSED. CHILDREN WELCOME.　PETS B/A.　WHEELCHAIR ACCESS TO RESTAURANT ONLY.　TV IN SOME ROOMS.　EN SUITE & BEVERAGES IN ROOMS.　CREDIT CARDS.　B. & B. £22 - 38.　Special breaks available.

DORNOCH

DORNOCH CASTLE HOTEL, DORNOCH, IV25 3SD
Formerly the palace of the Bishops of Caithness, this imposing 15th/16th C. mansion offers exceptionally good accommodation & food.
TEL: (01862) 810216　OPEN ALL YEAR.　N/S DINING R.　V B/A.　LICENSED.　DISABLED ACCESS.　CHILD-REN WELCOME.　EN SUITE AVAIL.　BEVERAGES IN ROOMS.　T.V.　B. & B. FROM £28.

DULNAIN BRIDGE

Auchendean Lodge Hotel

DULNAIN BRIDGE, INVERNESS-SHIRE, HIGHLANDS, PH26 3LU　TEL & FAX: (01479) 851347

Visitors to Auchendean Lodge Hotel will feel that they have stepped back into another era. Beautifully appointed throughout with period antiques, furnishings and paintings which have been chosen to complement the building's many original Edwardian features, Auchendean Lodge has outstanding views across the River Spey and over the Abernethy Forest to the Cairngorm Mountains. Its owners, Eric Hart and Ian Kirk, have created an ambience of comfort, style and good service, which prevails in an atmosphere of informality and great friendliness. Both owners share the cooking and specialise in an imaginative cuisine (and some traditional Scottish dishes), which have been prepared not only from local and home-grown produce but from ingredients culled from the moors and woods (such as the wild mushrooms which Eric picks daily in late summer and autumn). Staying at Auchendean Lodge is an enjoyable and unique experience - and whether your strongest memories will be of the house, the food or the magnificent surroundings will be for you to decide.
OPEN ALL YEAR.　V, VE, S.D. B/A.　N/S DINING & SITTING R.　LICENSED.　DISABLED ACCESS.　CHILDREN WELCOME.　PETS B/A.　MOST BEDROOMS EN SUITE.　BEVERAGES & T.V. ALL ROOMS.　B. & B. FROM £21.

DURNESS

Port-na-Con House

PORT-NA-CON, LOCH ERIBOLL, BY ALTNAHARRA, LAIRG, SUTHERLAND, HIGHLAND, IV27 4UN.　TEL: (01971) 511367
Port-na-Con stands on the west side of Loch Eriboll, 6 miles east of Durness, and was built 200 years ago as a Custom House and harbour store. Completely renovated in 1984, it is now a comfortable, centrally heated guest house in which all bedrooms overlook the loch:

the first floor lounge and balcony have particularly impressive views and here guests can enjoy not only the scenery, but also the varied wild life, including seals, otters and birds. The food is the very best of Scottish fare, and the restaurant is open to non-residents by arrangement: all dishes are home-cooked from fresh, local ingredients and the à la carte menu might feature Salmon and Crab Terrine with home-made bread, followed by Roast Beef with fresh vegetables, and a delicious dessert, such as Chocolate & Orange Cheesecake.

OPEN mid mar. - OCt. inc. Restaurant open to non-residents by prior arrangement. NO SMOKING. V, S.D. B/A. LICENSED. CHILDREN & WELL-BEHAVED DOGS WELCOME. BEVERAGES IN ROOMS. ACCESS & VISA. D., B. & B. £27, SINGLE £33 (May - Sept inc. out of ain season single at standard rate.

ELGIN

MANSION HOUSE HOTEL, THE HAUGH, ELGIN, MORAY, IV30 1AW

Imposing Scottish mansion with picturesque riverside outlook in the ancient burgh of Elgin; excellent leisure facilities including sauna, Turkish bath, and gym.

TEL: (01343) 540728 OPEN ALL YEAR. V, VE STD. S.D. B/A. ORG, WH ON REQUEST. CHILDREN WELCOME. EN SUITE, TV & BEVERAGES IN ROOMS. B. & B. AROUND £60.

FORT WILLIAM

THE LODGE ON THE LOCH, ONICH, NR FORT WILLIAM, PH33 6RY

Beautiful hotel in spectacular setting on the shores of loch; tasteful furnishings; relaxed yet impeccable service.Outstanding Scottish cuisine; use of nearby pool & leisure club.

TEL: (01855) 821237 FAX: (01855) 821463 OPEN Xmas & New Year, Easter - Oct. V, S.D. STD. N/S DINING R. LICENSED. DISABLED ACCESS. CHILDREN & PETS WELCOME. EN SUITE, TV & BEVERAGES IN ROOMS.

MRS B GRIEVE, 'NEVIS VIEW', 14 FARROW DRIVE, CORPACH, FORT WILLIAM, INVERNESS-SHIRE, PH33 7JW

Beautiful architect-designed house on a small, quiet estate looking out with stupendous views to lochs and mountains. The food is excellent; fresh & local ingredients are used in the preparation of home-cooked cuisine; the vegetarian options are imaginative and tasty.

TEL: (01397) 772447 FAX: (01397) 772800 OPEN ALL YEAR. V STD. VE B/A. NO SMOKING. CHILDREN WELCOME. PETS B/A. BEVERAGES & TV IN ROOMS. B & B AROUND £14.

RHU MHOR GUEST HOUSE, ALMA RD, FORT WILLIAM.

Family-run, traditional & old-fashioned guest house in 1 acre of wild tree-shrouded garden on a hill behind town. Vegetarian proprietors. Tea & biscuits served. Dinner booked.

TEL: (01397) 702213 OPEN April - Sept. V STD. S.D. B/A. N/S DINING R & 1 LOUNGE. CHILDREN & PETS. B. & B. AROUND £15.

GLENFINNAN

THE STAGE HOUSE, GLENFINNAN, INVERNESS-SHIRE, PH37 4LT

17th C. coaching inn in picturesque glen at the head of Loch Shiel; beautifully renovated; excellent, imaginative cuisine prepared from fresh, local produce.

TEL: (01397) 722246 OPEN Mar. - Jan. N/S ex. 2 bars. V STD. LICENSED. OVER 5S ONLY. PETS B/A. EN SUITE, BEVERAGES & TV IN ROOMS. ACCESS, VISA. B. & B. FROM £25.95.

INVERGARRY

Glendale Vegetarian Guest House

MANDALLY ROAD, INVERGARRY, INVERNESS-SHIRE, HIGHLAND, PH35 4HP TEL: (01809) 501282

Glandale is a small but spacious guest house which stands amidst an acre of grounds on the outskirts of the pretty village of Invergarry; run by a mother-and-daughter team, Mary and Michelle Rivers, it has a very friendly atmosphere. Michelle is a trained vegetarian chef who has established a reputation for providing delicious, imaginative and nutritionally balanced meals. Home-grown organic herbs, fruits and vegetables

are often incorporated into cooking and free-range eggs, fresh produce and non-animal rennet cheese are always used. Accommodation is in comfortable family, twin or double rooms, and there is a large lounge with a TV books, maps and games for guests' use. All rooms are on the ground floor thus providing easy access for elderly and disabled guests. Glendale stands amidst beautiful countryside and is an excellent base for exploring the Highlands.
OPEN ALL YEAR ex Xmas & New Year. V, WH & ORG EXC. S.D. B/A N/S DINING R & SITTING R. LICENSED. CHILDREN WELCOME (UNDER 4S FREE). PETS B/A. 1 EN SUITE ROOM. BEVERAGES & TV (B/A) IN ROOMS. DISABLED ACCESS. T.V. LOUNGE. B. & B. FROM £15. D. £11 (3-course).

INVERNESS

ARDMUIR HOUSE HOTEL, 16 NESS BANK, INVERNESS, IV2 4SF
Charming stone-built house of character; excellent and imaginative home-cooking prepared from fresh ingredients.
TEL: (01463) 231151 OPEN ALL YEAR. V, S.D. B/A. N/S DINING R. LICENSED. DISABLED ACCESS. CHILDREN WELCOME. ALL ROOMS EN SUITE. BEVERAGES. T.V.

Glendruidh House
OLD EDINBURGH ROAD, INVERNESS, IV1 2AA TEL: (01463) 226499 FAX: (01463) 710745
Charming, unusual building in its own pleasant grounds overlooking Inverness, the Moray Firth and the Black Isle. Excellent food superbly prepared from fresh local produce.
OPEN ALL YEAR. V, S.D. B/A. NO SMOKING. LICENSED. DISABLED ACCESS: 'WITH ASSISTANCE; GROUND FLOOR ROOMS & WIDE DOORS'. CHILDREN WELCOME. EN SUITE, BEVERAGES & T.V. IN ROOMS. CREDIT CARDS. B. & B. £29 - 39.

GLEN MHOR HOTEL & RESTAURANT, 9-12 NESS BANK, INVERNESS
Beautiful large old country house overlooking the River Ness; excellent cuisine.
TEL: (01463) 234308 OPEN ALL YEAR ex. New Year. V STD. VE, S.D. B/A. ORG WHEN AVAIL/ON REQUEST. WH ON REQUEST. LICENSED. DISABLED ACCESS. CHILDREN WELCOME. PETS B/A. EN SUITE, TV & BEVERAGES IN ROOMS. CREDIT CARDS. D., B. & B. AROUND £49.

Hebrides
120A GLENURQUHART RD, INVERNESS, IV3 5TD TEL: (01463) 220062
Attractive family-run B. & B.1m from town on A82. Adjacent to leisure centre & Caledonian Canal.
OPEN ALL YEAR. NO SMOKING. S.D. B/A. CHILDREN WELCOME. EN SUITE, TV & BEVERAGES IN ROOMS. B. & B. £18 - 22.

SKY HOUSE, UPPER CULLERNIE, BALLOCH, INVERNESS IV1 2HU
Spacious, modern home in beautiful open countryside yet just 5 mins' drive from Highland capital and its airport; magnificent views across the Moray Firth; wholesome, fresh food.
TEL: (01463) 792582 OPEN ALL YEAR. V B/A. NO SMOKING. PETS B/A. SOME EN SUITE ROOMS. BEVERAGES & T.V. IN ROOMS. ACCESS, VISA. B. & B. FROM £18.

KINGUSSIE

THE CROSS, 25/27 HIGH STREET, KINGUSSIE, PH21 1HX TEL: (01540) 661166
'A Restaurant with Rooms'; excellent and imaginative home-prepared cuisine.
OPEN ALL YEAR ex 3 weeks, May/June, 5 weeks Nov/Dec. V B/A. N/S DINING R & BEDRS. LICENSED. ALL ROOMS EN SUITE. ACCESS, VISA. B & B AROUND £32.

HOMEWOOD LODGE, NEWTONMORE ROAD, KINGUSSIE, INVERNESS-SHIRE, PH21 1HD
Charming country house offering excellent accommodation; log fires & delicious dinners with home-made bread, scones & icecreams.
TEL: (01540) 661507OPEN ALL YEAR ex. Xmas. V, S.D. B/A. NO SMOKING. LICENSED. CHILDREN WELCOME. PETS B/A . EN SUITE & BEVERAGES IN ROOMS. T.V. IN LOUNGE. B. & B. AROUND £25.

The Royal Hotel
29 HIGH STREET, KINGUSSIE, INVERNESS-SHIRE, HIGHLAND, PH21 1HX TEL: (01540) 661898 FAX: (01540) 661061
Family-owned & run hotel in the quiet village of Kingussie; excellent cuisine prepared from fresh, local produce.
OPEN ALL YEAR. N/S DINING R, PART OF BAR & RECEPTION. V, S.D. B/A. LICENSED. DISABLED ACCESS. CHILDREN WELCOME. PETS B/A. EN SUITE , TV & BEVERAGES IN ROOMS. CREDIT CARDS. B. & B. FROM £26 D. £12.

KYLE OF LOCHALSH

CULAG, CARR BRAE, DORNIE, KYLE, ROSS-SHIRE, IV40 8HA (01599) 555341
Modern bungalow situated just outside Dornie village with spectacular views over Loch
Duich and Loch Alsh; exclusively vegetarian B. & B.
OPEN ALL YEAR. V, VE EXC. NO SMOKING. DISABLED ACCESS: 'GROUND FLOOR ONLY (BUNGALOW)'.
CHILDREN WELCOME. BEVERAGES IN ROOMS. B. & B. FROM £10.50.

KIRKBEAG, KINCRAIG, KINGUSSIE, INVERNESS-SHIRE, PH21 1ND
Beautiful 19th C. church converted into a family home and workshop. B. & B. & S/C. All
food has been home-prepared to guests' requirements from fresh, local ingredients.
TEL: (015404) 298 OPEN ALL YEAR. V, VE, S.D. B/A. WH ON REQUEST. CHILDREN. BEVERAGES. B. & B.
AROUND £16.

KYLESKU

Linne Mhuirich

UNAPOOL CROFT ROAD, KYLESKU, VIA LAIRG, SUTHERLAND, IV27 4HW TEL: (01971)
502227

STB 2 Crowns Commended. Fiona and Diar-
mid MacAulay welcome up to 6 non-smoking
guests to their modern croft house, which is
superbly situated on a hillside leading down to
the rocky shore of Loch Glencoul; its quiet,
peaceful, yet accessible position makes it an
excellent base for exploring the north-west
Highlands. Many guests return annually for the
comfort and attention, peace and the delicious
food (which is 'Taste of Scotland' recommended). Everything has been home-made
from fresh and local ingredients, and Fiona
specializes in preparing local fish and seafood
dishes; quiches, pates, tasty casseroles, delicious vegetarian dishes and tempting desserts
also feature on her menus (although there are also low-calorie choices for those with an
eye on the waistline!). There is no T.V. reception here - so nothing can interfere with after
dinner conversation or just sitting back and enjoying the spectacular views from the comfort
of the lounge (or perhaps browsing through the MacAulays' extensive collection of books).
OPEN May to Oct. V, LOW-FAT, HIGH-FIBRE DIETS B/A. NO SMOKING. BYO WINE. CHILDREN WEL-
COME. PETS B/A. 1 ROOM WITH PRIVATE BATHROOM. BEVERAGES IN ROOMS. B. & B. AROUND £19.

LAIRG

GNEISS HOUSE, INVERSHIN, BY LAIRG, SUTHERLAND, IV17 4ET
New bungalow standing in pretty garden amidst the glorious unspoilt Sutherland country-
side. B. & B. only but tea and home-made scones greet you on your arrival & breakfast is
a splendid repast with bowls of hot porridge.
TEL: (01549) 421282 OPEN ALL YEAR. V, S.D. B/A. NO SMOKING. PETS B/A. EN SUITE & BEVERAGES
IN ROOMS. T.V. IN LOUNGE. CREDIT CARDS. B. & B. AROUND £15.

INVERCASSLEY COTTAGE, ROSEHALL, BY LAIRG, SUTHERLAND
Charmingly renovated house in a beautiful rural setting complete with duck ponds.
Excellent b'fast & everything - including the bread - is home-made. Terrain bikes are for
hire and maps and packed lunches can be provided. Dinner by arrangement.
TEL: (01549) 441288 OPEN ALL YEAR. V STD. VE B/A. ORG, WH WHEN AVAIL. N/S BEDRS. DISABLED ACCESS.
CHILDREN WELCOME. PETS B/A. T.V. IN ROOMS. B. & B. AROUND £15.

LOCHCARRON

**LADYTREK SCOTLAND, 'FOXGLOVES', LEACANASHIE, LOCHCARRON,
WESTER ROSS, IV54 8YD TEL: (01520) 722238**
Award-winning walking holidays based in cosy Highland cottages offering leisurely
leader-accompanied walks into mountains using ancient drove tracks; excellent and im-
aginative home-cooked meals.
OPEN Easter to Oct. V, S.D. B/A. NO SMOKING. BEVERAGES. INCLUSIVE HOLIDAY RATES.

LOCHNESS-SIDE

THE FOYERS HOTEL, LOCHNESS-SIDE, INVERNESS, IV1 2XT
Comfortable Victorian country house hotel in pleasant grounds overlooking Loch Ness. All food freshly prepared by the chef-proprietor.
TEL: (01456) 486216   OPEN ALL YEAR.   V STD. VE, S.D. B/A.   NO SMOKING.   LICENSED.   CHILDREN WELCOME.   SOME EN SUITE ROOMS.   T.V. LOUNGE.   CREDIT CARDS.   B. & B. AROUND £30.

MUIR OF ORD

ORD HOUSE HOTEL, MUIR OF ORD, ROSS-SHIRE, IV6 7UH
Beautiful 17th C. country house standing in 25 acres of formal gardens and woodlands; elegantly furnished and appointed; excellent cuisine prepared from home-grown produce.
TEL: (01463) 870492 OPEN mid May. - mid Oct.   V, DIAB, B/A. ORG when avail. WH on request.   N/S DINING R ANNEXE. LICENSED.   CHILDREN.   PETS B/A.   EN SUITE & BEVERAGES.   T.V.   B. & B. AROUND £32.

THE DOWER HOUSE, MUIR OF ORD, ROSS-SHIRE, IV6 7XN
Nestling in 3 acres of mature grounds & converted to the *cottage orne* style in 1800, the Dower House offers exceptionally comfortable accommodation & award-winning food.
TEL & FAX: (01463) 870090 OPEN ALL YEAR.   V, S.D. B/A.   N/S DINING R & SOME BEDRS.   LICENSED. DISABLED ACCESS.   CHILDREN.   DOGS B/A.   EN SUITE & T.V.   CREDIT CARDS.   B. & B. AROUND £50.

NAIRN

CLIFTON HOTEL, VIEWFIELD STREET, NAIRN, NAIRN-SHIRE
Sumptuously appointed Victorian house; wonderful food cooked from fresh ingredients.
TEL: (01667) 53119 OPEN Mar. - Nov.   V STD.   S.D. B/A.   N/S IN T.V. ROOM & PART OF DINING AREA. CHILDREN WELCOME.   PETS B/A.   ALL ROOMS EN SUITE.   ACCESS, VISA.   B. & B. AROUND £45.

Dallaschyle

CAWDOR, NAIRN, HIGHLAND, IV12 5XS   TEL: (01667) 493422
Charming house offering excellent home-cooking prepared from fresh, local and some home-grown produce; home-baked cakes, biscuits, jams and marmalade. Large, peaceful garden. Evening tea & home-baking in lounge.
V, DIAB. B/A. ORG, WH WHEN AVAIL.   OPEN Apr - Oct. N/S BEDROOMS.   DISABLED: GROUND FLOOR BEDROOMS. CHILDREN WELCOME.   B. & B. FROM £14. D. FROM £9.50.

NEWTONMORE

CRAIGELLACHIE HOUSE, MAIN STREET, NEWTONMORE, PH20 1DA
Comfortable family home; excellent breakfast menu with lots of options. Dinner B/A.
TEL: (01540) 673360   OPEN ALL YEAR ex. Xmas.   V, VE STD. S.D. B/A.   NO SMOKING.   CHILDREN WELCOME.   PETS B/A.   BEVERAGES IN ROOMS.   T.V. IN LOUNGE.   B. & B. AROUND £17.

SPEAN BRIDGE

Old Pines

GAIRLOCHY ROAD, SPEAN BRIDGE, INVERNESS-SHIRE, PH34 4EG   (01397) 712324
STB 3 Crowns Commended. Home of great character in 30 peaceful acres with views of Aonach Mor, Ben Nevis. Log fires. Imaginative food prepared from fresh local ingredients.
OPEN ALL YEAR.   V, S.D. B/A.   NO SMOKING INDOORS.   BYO WINE.   DISABLED ACCESS: 'completely accessible; 3 specially adapted ground floor bedrooms.' CHILDREN WELCOME.   PETS B/A.   MOST ROOMS EN SUITE   BEVERAGES.   T.V. IN LOUNGE.   ACCESS, VISA, MASTERCARD.   D., B. & B. AROUND £39

STRATHPEFFER

Gardenside Guest House

STRATHPEFFER, ROSS AND CROMARTY, HIGHLANDS, IV14 9BJ   TEL: (01997) 421242

Gardenside is a charming 19th C. house set in a splendid situation surrounded by woodland and fields on the southwest side of the Victorian Spa village of Strathpeffer. Accommodation is in well-appointed rooms, some with views, and there is an inviting guest lounge. Meals are served in an attractive dining room: the 3-course dinner is prepared from fresh, local produce. Strathpeffer owes its existence to the discovery in the 18th C. of a nearby spring with healing waters. Formerly one of Britain's most elegant health resorts (the village is full of opulent and spacious turn of the century villas), it is currently undergoing a modest revival. If the waters are not enough to lure you to Strathpeffer, then its proximity to so many other of the Highland's tourist attractions surely will: head out from the village in a different direction each day and come across Inverewe Gardens, Drumnadrochit, Invergordon and Bonor Bridge.

OPEN 1 Mar. - 30 Nov. NO SMOKING. V, S.D. B/A. LICENSED. GROUND FLOOR ROOMS AVAIL. CHILDREN WELCOME. SOME EN SUITE ROOMS. BEVERAGES IN ROOMS. T.V. IN LOUNGE. B. & B. FROM £14.

TONGUE

Ben Loyal Hotel

TONGUE, SUTHERLAND, IV27 4XE TEL: (01847) 611216

The Ben Loyal Hotel is a white-painted building standing in a quite splendid location overlooking the waters of the Kyle of Tongue and the peaks of the mountain after which it has been named. The hotel has been designed with the seemingly sole intention of enabling guests to enjoy these quite stunning panoramas in almost every room: from the comfortably furnished lounge with its picture window to the beautifully appointed bedrooms (pine furniture, pretty fabrics, fourposters). Perhaps the best views can be had from the dining room, however - although here you will find that your loyalties are torn between relishing the view and savouring the food: only fresh, local produce - some of it home-grown - is used in the preparation of a largely traditional menu and the table d'hote meal could well feature home-made Lentil Soup followed by Supreme of Salmon in a Seafood Sauce (served with fresh vegetables) and a selection of good old-fashioned puddings, such as Bread and Butter Pudding. Ben Loyal is, as I have indicated, surrounded by quite breathtaking countryside; there are lots of lovely sandy beaches to wander along and the wildlife flourishes in abundance.

OPEN ALL YEAR. V, S.D. B/A. N/A DINING R. LICENSED. DISABLED ACCESS: 'partial, with assistance'. CHILDREN WELCOME. MOST ROOMS EN SUITE. BEVERAGES IN ROOMS. T.V. ON REQUEST. D., B. & B. AROUND £47.

ULLAPOOL

ALTNAHARRIE INN, ULLAPOOL, IV26 2SS TEL: (01854) 633230

Lovely old house on the shores of Loch Broom & reached by launch (6 trips daily); outstanding cuisine (chef rated among top few in the country - the others being in London).

OPEN Easter - late Oct. V, S.D. B/A. NO SMOKING. LICENSED. OVER 8S ONLY. PETS B/A. ALL ROOMS EN SUITE. D., B. & B. £125 - 145.

Tigh-Na-Mara (House by the Sea)

THE SHORE, ARDINDREAN, NR ULLAPOOL, LOCH BROOM, WESTER-ROSS, IV23 2SE TEL: (01854) 655282

A special guest house for special people! Tony invites you to share his secluded and idyllic home, a beautiful old house with lots of character and breathtaking views overlooking Loch Broom. The 30 foot lounge/dining room is warmed by a wood-burning stove and has a spiral stair leading up to just two romantic bedrooms and a wood-panelled bathroom (there is a new Honeymoon suite in the boatshed!). There is a gourmet Scottish vegetarian and vegan dishes which have been cooked on the range, and a typical evening meal might feature Roast Onion stuffed with Vegetarian Haggis followed by Sea-weed Roly-Poly served with Fennel Potatoes, Cauliflower and Date Salad and Kale in Garlic Butter; delicious desserts are based around organic fruit from the garden; full board is available but breakfast is enormous, packed lunches can be prepared on request, and the 4-course evening meal will satisfy the stoutest of appetites. You are blissfuly isolated at Tigh-na-Mara, so bring your own wine and wellies (Ullapool is 20 minutes'drive away and Inverness train, bus and air services an hour's drive), but your hosts have thought of everything to keep you happy in situ, including providing a babysitting service, transfers from Inverness (by helicopter if you so wish), and free use of boats, bikes and windsurfers.

OPEN FEB - NOV. V & other meat-free diets STD. NO SMOKING. CHILDREN WELCOME. BEVERAGES IN BEDROOMS. D., B. & B. FROM £28.50. (£179 p.w.)

RESTAURANTS

DORNOCH

DORNOCH CASTLE HOTEL, CASTLE ST, DORNOCH, IV25 3SD
TEL: (01862) 810216   V STD.   N/S RESTAURANT.   LICENSED.   DISABLED ACCESS. CHILDREN WELCOME.

GLENFINNAN

THE STAGE HOUSE, GLENFINNAN, INVERNESS-SHIRE, PH37 4LT
For full details please see under entry in accommodation section.

KYLE OF LOCHALSH

WHOLEFOOD CAFÉ, HIGHLAND DESIGN WORKS, PLOCKTON RD, KYLE OF LOCHALSH
TEL: (01599) 534388/534702   OPEN 12.30 - 3, 6.30 - 8.30. D. AROUND £11.   V, VE, EXC. DIAB & GLUTEN-FREE STD.
NO SMOKING.   LICENSED.   DISABLED ACCESS.   CHILDREN WELCOME.   ACCESS, VISA.

LOCHINVER

ACHINS BOOKSHOP AND COFFEE SHOP, INVERKIRKAIG, LOCHINVER.
Small coffee shop attached to book shop; open seasonally.
TEL: (01571) 844262   OPEN 10 - 5.   V STD.   NO SMOKING.   V STD.   DISABLED ACCESS.   CHILDREN.

NAIRN

CAWDOR CASTLE RESTAURANT, CAWDOR CASTLE, NAIRN, HIGHLAND,
Pleasant café/restaurant serving wide range of snacks & teas prepared in the castle kitchens.
TEL: (01667) 404615   V STD.   NO SMOKING. LICENSED.   DISABLED ACCESS.   CHILDREN WELCOME.

ULLAPOOL

CEILIDH PLACE, WEST ARGYLE ST, ULLAPOOL, HIGHLAND.
Pleasant café-bar, serving good range of vegetarian options.
TEL: (01854) 612103   V STD.   N/S RESTAURANT. CHILDREN WELCOME IN DINING AREAS ONLY.

Strathclyde

ACCOMMODATION

ARGYLL

The Anchorage

SHORE RD, ARDNEDAM, SANDBANK, ARGYLL, PA23 8QG   TEL: (01369) 5108

The Anchorage was built in the late 19th C. by a Victorian craftsman and stands along the coastal road, some 3 miles north of the town of Dunoon, on the banks of the Holy Loch. Your hosts, Dee and Tony Hancock offer an exceptionally friendly welcome to their beautiful home, and pride themselves on offering quality accommodation at a reasonable price. The bedrooms have been designed with comfort in mind: each has en suite facilities and a range of helpful amenities. All the delicious meals are prepared from fresh, local produce, and breakfast, lunch and dinner are served in a stylish dining room with a large panoramic window overlooking the loch; a typical evening meal would feature a choice of dishes such as Carrot and Lemon Soup followed by Scottish Salmon with fresh vegetables, and a home-made dessert; cheese, biscuits, coffee and mints would complete the meal. Although the beach is less than a stone's throw from the front door, there is a tranquil garden for you to enjoy. In Dunoon there are modern leisure facilities, and you are in an excellent place for exploring Argyll and the west coast of Scotland.
OPEN ALL YEAR. NO SMOKING. S.D. B/A. CHILDREN WELCOME. EN SUITE, TV & BEVERAGES IN ROOMS. B. & B. FROM £15 - 23.

AYR

Strathcoyle

HILLHEAD, COYLTON, AYR, STRATHCLYDE, KA6 6JR TEL: (01292) 570366

Detached bungalow with ground floor rooms. Private parking. on A70 4m east of Ayr.
OPEN Feb. - Nov.   V, VE, S.D. B/A. NO S MOKING.   CHILDREN WELCOME. BEVERAGES IN ROOMS. TV
LOUNGE. B. & B. £14 - 15, Single £16 - 18.

OBAN

ASKNISH COTTAGE, ARDUAINE, BY OBAN, ARGYLL, STRATH, PA34 4XQ

Small, modern house on hillside with views over islands Jura, Scarba, Shuna and Luing.
TEL: (01852) 200247 OPEN ALL YEAR. V, S.D. B/A. NO SMOKING. CHILDREN & PETS WELCOME. BEVER-
AGES IN ROOMS. T.V. IN LOUNGE. B. & B. AROUND £17.

PAISLEY

MYFARRCLAN GUEST HOUSE, 146 CORSEBAR ROAD, PAISLEY, PA2 9NA

STB 2 Crown de Luxe. Tastefully decorated house in quiet area 1m from town centre; some
rooms have microwaves for self-caterers; safe, quiet garden has children's play area.
TEL: (0141) 884 8285 OPEN ALL YEAR. V, LOW-FAT B/A. NO SMOKING. CHILDREN WELCOME. MOST
ROOMS EN SUITE. BEVERAGS & TV IN ROOMS. B. & B. FROM £22.50.

SEAMILL

Spottiswoode Guest House

SANDY RD, SEAMILL, WEST KILBRIDE, AYRSHIRE, STRATHCLYDE, KA23 9NN TEL: (01294)
823131

Built in 1896, Spottiswoode is a spacious Victorian home which has been tastefully
decorated and traditionally appointed by its present
owners who have taken care to retain the house's original charm and character. It stands just feet away from
the Firth of Clyde - the beautiful sea and island views
can be appreciated from the dining room, lounge and a
bedroom - and the surrounding countryside is both rich
in natural wildlife and also an ideal base from which to
explore Ayrshire and the nearby islands (Glasgow is
just 45 minutes away by train or car). Your hosts at
Spottiswoode, Christine and Jim Ondersma, are thor-
oughly committed to quality and guest satisfaction:
each of the guest bedrooms have been decorated to a very high standard and are equipped
with fluffy towels, reading materials, well-lit mirrors and other thoughtful touches. The
breakfast menu is another example of the Ondersmas' attention to detail: prepared with
minimum fat and salt, both Scottish and American specialities are offered, including
locally-made, additive-free sausages, free-range eggs, and home-made bread and yoghurts;
evening meals are creative and freshly prepared (24 hours notice, please). There is much
to enjoy *in situ* - a soak in the deep Victorian bath, afternoon tea on the lawn, games and
music at the fireside . . . There is no reason at all to move from base except, perhaps, to
enjoy a walk in the magnificent surrounding countryside or shore, or to enjoy a game of
golf arranged by your hosts.
OPEN ALL YEAR. V A SPECIALITY. S.D. B/A. .NON-SMOKERS ONLY. CHILDREN: OVER 10S. EN SUITE,
TV, BEVERAGES, HAIRDRYER IN ROOMS. CREDIT CARDS. B. & B. AROUND £18.

ST CATHERINE'S

ARNISH COTTAGE LOCHSIDE G.H., POLL BAY, ST CATHERINE'S, ARGYLL

Lovely house in conservation area midway between St Catherine's & Strachur. A truly
idyllic spot on a private road 20 ft from the lochside. A wealth of wildlife & peace.
TEL: (01499) 302405 OPEN ALL YEAR. V, S.D. B/A. NO SMOKING. EN SUITE & BEVERAGES IN ROOMS.
TV IN LOUNGE. B. & B. AROUND £19.

TURNBERRY

MALIN COURT, TURNBERRY, AYRSHIRE, STRATHCLYDE, KA26 9PB

Both residential and hotel accommodation in a modern, comfortable building set amidst
tranquil gardens. Beautifully equipped. Meals are prepared from fresh, local produce and
are served in a restaurant with breath-taking views of the Isle of Arran.

TEL: (01655) 331457 FAX: (01655) 31072 OPEN ALL YEAR.   V STD, S.D. B/A.   LICENSED.   CHILDREN WELCOME.   PETS B/A.   EN SUITE, TV & BEVERAGES IN ROOMS.   CREDIT CARDS.   B. & B. AROUND £55.

RESTAURANTS

ARGYLL

BRIDGE OF ORCHY HOTEL, BRIDGE OF ORCHY, ARGYLL, STRAT, PA36 4AD
TEL: (01838) 400208   N/S RESTAURANT.   V, DIAB, VE STD.   LICENSED.   CHILDREN WELCOME.

THE SMIDDY, SMITHY LANE, LOCHGILPHEAD, ARGYLL, STRATHCLYDE.
Vegetarian and seafood restaurant.
TEL: (01546) 603606   NO SMOKING.   V EXC.   CHILDREN WELCOME.   ACCESS, VISA.

PAISLEY

PAISLEY ARTS CENTRE, NEW STREET, PAISLEY, STRATHCLYDE, PA1 1EZ
TEL: (0141) 887 1010   N/S AREA.   V STD.   LICENSED.   DISABLED ACCESS.   CHILDREN WELCOME.

Tayside

ACCOMMODATION

ABERFELDY

DALCHIORLICH, GLENLYON, BY ABERFELDY, PERTHSHIRE, PH15 2PX
Remote sheep farm amidst in Scotland's longest glen; good home-cooking.
TEL: (01887) 866226 OPEN Mar. - Nov.   V, LOW-FAT STD.   N/S BEDROOMS.   CHILDREN WELCOME.   BEVERAGES IN ROOMS.   T.V. IN LOUNGE.   B & B AROUND £16.

FENDOCH, FORTINGALL, BY ABERFELDY, PERTHSHIRE, PH15 2LL
Warm welcome in peaceful village. Ideal touring centre. Good home-cooked food. Fishing, hill-walking & pony-trekking can be arranged.
TEL: (01887) 830322 OPEN ALL YEAR.   V, LOW-FAT, S.D. B/A.   CHILDREN & PETS WELCOME.   EN SUITE. T.V. & BEVERAGES IN ROOMS.   B & B AROUND £15.

BLAIRGOWRIE

DRYFESANDS G.H., BURNHEAD RD, BLAIRGOWRIE, PERTHSH., PH10 6SY
Spacious bungalow in pretty gardens on a hillside overlooking Blairgowrie; the wonderful food is freshly cooked to Cordon Bleu standards from local or home-grown ingredients.
TEL: (01250) 873417 OPEN ALL YEAR.   V, S.D. B/A.   NO SMOKING.   CHILDREN: OVER 10S.   EN SUITE & BEVERAGES IN ROOMS.   T.V. LOUNGE.   B & B AROUND £25.

BRECHIN

BLIBBERHILL FARMHOUSE, BRECHIN, ANGUS, DD9 6TH
18th C. farmhouse in peaceful surroundings; home-cooking includes jams & marmalade.
TEL: (01307) 830225 OPEN ALL YEAR.   V, S.D. B/A.   NO SMOKING.   MOST ROOMS EN SUITE.   BEVERAGES IN ROOMS.   B & B AROUND £15.

BROUGHTY FERRY

Invermark Hotel

23 MONIFIETH ROAD, BROUGHTY FERRY, DUNDEE, TAYSIDE, DD5 2RN TEL: (01382) 739430
The Invermark is a small privately run hotel conveniently situated in the Dundee suburb of Broughty Ferry; the furnishings are modern and attractive - there are two large public rooms which can comfortably host small functions, such as weddings or birthday parties - and all bedrooms have been tastefully furnished and appointed. The food is exceptionally good: only fresh produce is used in the cooking and, while breakfast is

the only meal which is usually available at Invermark, evening meals may be taken on request. Originally a fishing village, Broughty Ferry is now a bustling, residential city suburb; it still has lots of character: the seafront is guarded by a 15th C. castle, and the high street is full of interesting craft shops.

OPEN ALL YEAR.   NO SMOKING.   V, S.D. B/A.   RESTRICTED LICENCE.   CHILDREN WELCOME.   SOME EN SUITE ROOMS.   BEVERAGES & TV IN ROOMS.   B & B FROM £20.

CALLANDER

Brook Linn Country House

LENY FEUS, CALLANDER, TAYSIDE, FK17 8AU   TEL: (01877) 330103
OPEN Easter -Oct.   V B/A.   NO SMOKING.   LICENSED.   CHILDREN WELCOME.   PETS B/A.   EN SUITE, TV & BEVERAGES IN ROOMS. B & B FROM £18.   ·

ORCHARDLEA HOUSE, MAIN STREET, CALLANDER, FK17 8BG

Lovely house in grounds; good Scottish cooking from fresh and local produce.
TEL: (01877) 330798 OPEN May. To Oct.   V, LOW-FAT, DIAB B/A.   NO SMOKING.   DISABLED ACCESS: GROUND FLOOR BEDROOMS.   MOST ROOMS EN SUITE.   BEVERAGES.   T.V.   B & B AROUND £19.

ROSLIN COTTAGE GUEST HOUSE, LAGRANNOCH, CALLANDER, PER-THSHIRE, FK17 8LE   TEL: (01877) 330638

Beautiful 18th C. house on the outskirts of Callander; oak beams, exposed stone walls & open fireplace; home-grown vegetables, honey from home-based hives & free-range eggs from the hens used in cooking; home-made wine.
OPEN ALL YEAR.   V STD. S.D. B/A.   N/S ex. in lounge.   CHILDREN & PETS WELCOME.   BEVERAGES.   T.V. LOUNGE.   B. & B. AROUND £14.

CRIANLARICH

Portnellan Lodge Hotel

by Crianlarich, TAYSIDE, FK20 8QS TEL: (01838) 300284 FAX: (01838) 300332
Mid 19th C house in the wooded grounds of a private estate overlooking Glen Dochart. Delicious home-cooked food is prepared from fresh, local ingredients and, with sufficient advance notice, special requests can be undertaken (lunch boxes can also be prepared).
OPEN ALL YEAR.   V, S.D. B/A.   N/S BEDR, DINING R & DRAWING R.   LICENSED. CHILDREN UNDER 10 & VISITORS WITH PETS ACCOMMODATED IN LODGE SUITES.   EN SUITE, BEVERAGES, TV, VIDEO, RADIO, TROUSER PRESS & HAIRDRIER IN ROOMS.   CREDIT CARDS.   D., B. & B. AROUND £35.

CRIEFF

CAIRNLEITH, NORTH FORR, CRIEFF, TAYSIDE, PH7 3RT

Edwardian manse with walled garden and 4 acres of land with rare breeds; vegetarians welcome; mountain bikes for hire; very friendly.
TEL: (01764) 652080 OPEN ALL YEAR.   V B/A.   NO SMOKING.   CHILDREN WELCOME.   PETS B/A.   PRI-VATE BATHROOM. BEVERAGES IN ROOMS.   T.V. IN LOUNGE.   B & B AROUND £16.

DUNKELD

ORONSAY HOUSE, OAK ROAD, BIRNAM, DUNKELD, PH8 0BL

Elegant Victorian villa in an attractive garden near the River Tay; 3 bedrooms have hill views; home-made preserves, oatcakes, wholemeal bread and porridge at breakfast.
TEL: (01350) 727294 OPEN Apr. - Oct.   V, S.D. B/A.   NO SMOKING.   EN SUITE, TV & BEVERAGES IN ROOMS. B & B AROUND £18.

KILLIECRANKIE

DRUIMUAN HOUSE, KILLIECRANKIE, PH16 5LG

Elegant country house standing in private grounds. Excellent breakfast.
TEL: (01796) 473214 FAX: (01796) 472692OPEN Apr. - Oct.   V STD.   NO SMOKING.   CHILDREN WELCOME. EN SUITE, BEVERAGES & TV IN ROOMS.   B. & B. AROUND £20.

KINLOCH RANNOCH

Cuilmore Cottage

KINLOCH RANNOCH, TAYSIDE, PH16 5QB   TEL: (01882) 632218
18th C. stone croft nestling under wooded hills on the edge of village; log fires; home-cooking from organically home-grown vegetables & fruit; home-baked bread and free-range eggs.
OPEN Feb. - Nov.   V, S.D., B/A. NO SMOKING.   PETS B/A.   BEVERAGES IN ROOMS.   D. B. & B. from £40.

GLENRANNOCH HOUSE, KINLOCH RANNOCH, TAYSIDE.
Former manse standing in 1 acre of fruit and vegetable-producing gardens; views of
Schiehallion and Loch Rannoch; superb cuisine prepared from own and local produce.
TEL: (01882) 632307 OPEN ALL YEAR. V, S.D. B/A.   N/S ex. in lounge. CHILDREN WELCOME.   PETS B/A.
BEVERAGES ON REQUEST.   T.V. IN ROOMS.   B & B AROUND £15.

KIRRIEMUIR

Purgavie Farm

LINTRATHEN, KIRRIEMUIR, TAYSIDE.   TEL & FAX: (01575) 560213
Beatuful old stone-built farmhouse at the foot of Glen Islaall; food is home-prepared.
OPEN ALL YEAR.   V B/A.   N/S DINING R & BEDRS.   CHILDREN WELCOME.   PETS B/A.   2 EN SUITE ROOMS.
BEVERAGES IN ROOMS.   T.V.   B & B FROM £14.

LOCHEARNHEAD

Stronvar Country House Hotel

BALQUHIDDER, LOCHEARNHEAD, TAYSIDE, FK19 8PB TEL: (01877) 384688
Elegant 19th C. mansion on the shores of Loch Voil overlooking the Braes O'Balquhidder.
Guest rooms have spectacular views over the surrounding mountains and countryside;
OPEN Mar. to Oct.   V, DIAB B/A.   N/S DINING R & BEDRS.   LICENSED.   CHILDREN WELCOME.   EN SUITE,
TV & BEVERAGES IN ROOMS.   ACCESS, VISA.   B. & B. AROUND £30.

PITLOCHRY

BURNSIDE APARTMENTS, 19 WEST MOULIN RD, PITLOCHRY, PH16 5EA
STB 4 & 5 Crown Highly Commended. Beautifully converted Victorian building offering
award-winning serviced apartments with taste of Scotland coffee shop.
TEL: (01796) 472203 OPEN ALL YEAR.   V STD, S.D. B/A.   N/S COFFEE SHOP & SOME APARTMENTS.
LICENSED. DISABLED ACCESS. CHILDREN WELCOME. PETS B/A. EN SUITE BATHROOMS, TV & GAL-
LERY KITCHEN IN APARTMENTS.   ACCESS, VISA. AROUND £60 (2/3 PERSONS) DAILY.

Tigh-Na-Cloich Hotel

LARCHWOOD ROAD, PITLOCHRY, TAYSIDE, PH16 5AS   TEL: (0796) 472216

Scottish Tourist Board 3 Crowns Commended. Tigh-
Na-Cloich (Gaelic for 'house on the sentinel stone') is
a beautiful stone-built Victorian villa, southfacing and
peacefully situated in its own lovely gardens just a
short walk from the centre of Pitlochry. The house has
been completely refurbished in recent years with the
emphasis on creating a home atmosphere for guests.
The food is exceptionally good: everything is home-
made from the best, fresh local produce, and a typical
evening menu would feature Baked Brie in Filo Pastry
followed by Medallions of Venison with Wild Mushroom Sauce or Fillet of Salmon steamed with Aromates
and a delicious dessert suh as Hazelnut Parfait with
Plum Sauce. The proprietors are not only very helpful to those with special dietary needs,
but will even offer to cook a favourite dish for you on request! Pitlochry is Scotland's
premier inland tourist resort and as such offers something to every visitor, from sailing on
rivers and lochs or walking amidst the beautiful hill scenery to visiting the many woollen
mills, distilleries or craft centres in the region.
 OPEN MAR. - OCT.   NO SMOKING.   V, S.D. B/A.   LICENSED.   CHILDREN WELCOME.   EN SUITE
INALL TWIN/DBLE ROOMS.   BEVERAGES & T.V. IN ROOMS.   B & B FROM £22.

"Tom-na-Monachan" Vegetarian B. & B.

CUILC BRAE, PITLOCHRY, TAYSIDE.   TEL: (01796) 473744
Large family house quietly situated in an acre of wooded garden just 10 minutes walk from
both the railway station and shopping centre.
OPEN ALL YEAR.   V, VE, WH EXC. S.D. B/A.   NO SMOKING.   DISABLED ACCESS: '1 GROUND FLOOR
BEDROOM & BATHROOM. RAMP'. CHILDREN WELCOME.   BEVERAGES IN ROOMS.   B & B AROUND £18.

Western Isles

RESTAURANTS

ISLE OF ARRAN

GLENCLOY FARMHOUSE, BRODICK, ISLE OF ARRAN, KA27 8BZ
Farmhouse in peaceful glen; home-grown vegetables, free-range eggs.
TEL: (01770) 302351 OPEN 1 Mar. - 7 Nov.   V, VE, DIAB B/A. N/S ex. in BEDRS. CHILDREN WELCOME. 2 EN SUITE ROOMS. BEVERAGES IN ROOMS. B. & B. AROUND £32.

KILMICHAEL HOUSE, GLEN CLOY, BY BRODICK, ISLE OF ARRAN
Small historic mansion in 4 acres; organic and wholefood ingredients are used in cooking.
TEL: (01770) 302219 OPEN ALL YEAR.   V STD. N/S DINING R & BEDRS.   TABLE LICENCE. CHILDREN WELCOME. T.V. LOUNGE. B. & B. AROUND £15.

ISLE OF BUTE

"PALMYRA", 12 ARDBEG ROAD, ROTHESAY, ISLE OF BUTE, PA20 0NJ
Charming stone-built dwelling by the sea shore, in an acre of grounds.The food is oustandingly good.
TEL: (01700) 502929 OPEN ALL YEAR.   V, VE, DIAB, COEL, S.D. B/A.   N/S DINING R.   LICENSED. CHILDREN WELCOME. PETS B/A. EN SUITE, TV & BEVERAGES IN ROOMS.   B & B AROUND £20.

ISLE OF HARRIS

MINCHVIEW HOUSE, TARBERT, ISLE OF HARRIS, PA85 3DB
Guest house serving excellent home-cooking prepared from fresh produce.
TEL: (01859) 502140 OPEN ALL YEAR.   N/S DINING R & BEDRS.   V, S.D. B/A. B. & B. AROUND £15.

Scarista House

ISLE OF HARRIS, W ISLES, PA85 3HX   TEL: (01859) 550238 FAX: (01859) 550277

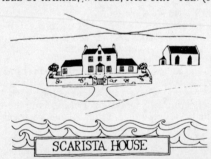

Situated on the magnificent Atlantic coast of Harris overlooking a 3-mile shell-sand beach, Scarista House is one of the most remote hotels in Great Britain. Furnished with antiques, it is a haven of tranquillity with peat fires (to supplement the central heating!), books and a large collection of baroque and classical music. Each of the 3 bedrooms has views - most over the sea. Your hosts pay particular attention to the freshness and integrity of the ingredients used in cooking: cheeses are obtained direct from farm or dairy, and all breads cakes, preserves and confectionary are homemade. Breakfasts are prepared with similar care and feature freshly squeezed juices & local puddings. Meals are served in a candlelit dining room with fine silverware and china chosen to complement the quality of the food.
OPEN Easter - mid. Oct.   N/S ex. 2 SITTING RS.   V, S.D. B/A. LICENSED.   DISABLED ACCESS: '4 BEDRS, DINING RS & LIBRARY ON GROUND FLOOR'.   CHILDREN: OVER 8S ONLY.   PETS B/A.   EN SUITE & BEVERAGES IN ROOMS. B. & B. AROUND £47.

ISLE OF IONA

Argyll Hotel

ISLE OF IONA, PA76 6SJ   TEL & FAX: (01681) 700334

This beautiful sea-facing hotel (the front lawn runs down to the shore and jetty) is one of the hotels about which I invariably receive a large number of recommendations throughout the year; guests comment on the peace and tranquility which seems to pervade the place - a sense doubtless partly attributable to the fact that the beautiful louges (with their open fires), spacious dining room and plant-filled sun lounge all look out over the Sound of Iona to the hills of Mull; external beauty recreating inner peace. I am sure that the excellence of the food is also an inexorable part of the lure of the place, too: wholefood and organically home-grown vegetables and produce are used in the preparation of excellent meals which would typically feature Hummus followed by Stuffed Peppers with Tahini Sauce, Lemon and Blackberry Sponge and a cheeseboard.

OPEN Easter - mid Oct. N/S DINING R. & LOUNGE. V, S.D. B/A. LICENSED. CHILDREN WELCOME. PETS BY ARRANGEMENT. EN SUITE 10 ROOMS. BEVERAGES IN ROOMS. ACCESS, VISA. B. & B. FROM £28, D. £17.

ISLE OF ISLAY

CEOL-NA-MARA, BRUICHLADDICH, ISLE OF ISLAY, PA49 7UN
Pleasantly situated house in small coastal distillery village overlooking Loch Indaal. Own & local produce used where possible in cooking.

TEL: (01496) 850419 OPEN ALL YEAR. V, VE, S.D. B/A. NO SMOKING. CHILDREN WELCOME. PETS B/A. TV IN LOUNGE. B & B AROUND £15.

ISLE OF LEWIS

BAILE-NA-CILLE, TIMSGARRY, ISLE OF LEWIS, PA86 9JD
Converted manse and stables on the shore at Timsgarry. The food is excellent: almost everything having been home-made - including the delicious bread - and from the wonderful breakfast (with its 'mighty but not compulsory Stornoway black pudding') to the exceedingly generous evening meal (lots of local produce, including trout, mackerel and salmon) you are wined and dined in truly splendid style.

TEL: (01851) 672241 OPEN mid-Mar. to mid-Oct. V, S.D. B/A. N/S DINING R, 2 SITTING RS & BEDRS. LICENSED. CHILDREN & PETS WELCOME. SOME ROOMS EN SUITE. BEVERAGES IN ROOMS. T.V. IN SITTING R B. & B. AROUND £26

ISLE OF MULL

Bellachroy Hotel

DERVAIG, ISLE OF MULL, PA75 6QW TEL: (01688) 400225/400314
Hotel at the head of picturesque village of Dervaig; fresh local produce used in cooking.

OPEN ALL YEAR. V, DIAB, S.D. B/A. LICENSED. CHILDREN WELCOME. PETS B/A. BEVERAGES & T.V. IN LOUNGES. B & B AROUND £20.

Bruach Mhor

FIONNPHORT, ISLE OF MULL, PA66 6BL TEL: (01681) 700276
Small modernised croft house standing alone on the slopes of Tor Mor half a mile from Iona Ferry; centrally heated & comfortable,. Wholesome home-cooked meals prepared from healthy, fresh ingredients; vegetarians & vegans especially welcome.

OPEN ALL YEAR. V STD. S.D. B/A. ORG WHEN AVAIL. WH ALMOST ALWAYS. CHILDREN WELCOME. BEVERAGES IN ROOMS. T.V. LOUNGE. B & B FROM £13.

DRUIMARD COUNTRY HOUSE, DERVAIG, ISLE OF MULL, PA75 6QW
STB Highly Commended. Award-winning country house hotel and restaurant. Excellent food prepared from fresh, local produce. 6 comfortable, well-furnished bedrooms.

TEL: (01688) 400345 OPEN Mar. to Oct. V STD. S.D. B/A. N/S RESTAURANT. LICENSED. CHILDREN WELCOME. PETS B/A. 4 EN SUITE ROOMS. BEVERAGES & TV. B. & B. AROUND £35.

DRUIMNACROISH, DERVAIG, ISLE OF MULL, PA75 6QW
Small, exclusive country house hotel in the beautiful Bellart Glen; home-grown fruit and vegetables; local produce used in cooking.

TEL: (01688) 400274 OPEN mid-Apr. - mid-Oct. V, S.D. B/A. N/S ex. in smoking lounge. LICENSED. DIS-ABLED ACCESS. OVER 12S. PETS B/A. EN SUITE, TV & BEVERAGES IN ROOMS. B. & B. AROUND £50

The Glenforsa Hotel

SALEN BY AROS, ISLE OF MULL, PA72 6JW TEL: (01680) 300377 FAX: (01680) 300535
Attractive Norwegian chalet-style hotel standing in 6 acres of secluded grounds overlooking Sound of Mull; excellent home-cooking using fresh produce & home-grown herbs.

OPEN ALL YEAR. N/S DINING ROOM. V STD. S.D. B/A. LICENSED. DISABLED ACCESS. CHILDREN WELCOME. PETS B/A. EN SUITE & BEVERAGES. T.V. LOUNGE. ACCESS, VISA, AMEX. B. & B. FROM £30.50.

KEEPER'S COTTAGE, TORLOISK, ULVA FERRY, ISLE OF MULL, PA74 6NH
Traditional stone-built cottage with garden and stream situated in a remote yet sheltered position close to a waterfall near the west coast of Mull; good home-grown food and good conversation!

TEL: (01688) 500265 OPEN ALL YEAR. V B/A. NO SMOKING. T.V. B & B AROUND £18.

Tigh an Allt
DERVAIG, ISLE OF MULL, PA75 6QR   TEL: (01688) 400247
STB 1 Crown Commended. Modern bungalow in secluded setting in grassy, wooded area. Wholefood ingredients used where possible in cooking. Wide choice of breakfasts and 3-course evening meal. Central heating.
OPEN ALL YEAR (ex Xmas). V, VE, S.D. B/A. WH STD. NO SMOKING. CHILDREN & PETS B/A. WHEELCHAIR ACCESS: 'reasonable'. BEVERAGES IN ROOMS. B. & B. £16, D. £9.

ULVA HOUSE HOTEL, TOBERMORY, ISLE OF MULL, PA75 6PR
Beautiful 19th C. house with lots of character; log fires, excellent food (including home-made chocolates) beautiful views.
TEL: (01688) 302044 OPEN Mar. - Oct.   V, VE, DIAB STD. S.D. B/A.   N/S DINING R.   LICENSED.   CHILDREN WELCOME.   PETS B/A.   SOME EN SUITE ROOMS.   BEVERAGES & TV IN ROOMS.   B. & B. AROUND £20.

ISLE OF RAASAY

ISLE OF RAASAY HOTEL, RAASAY, BY KYLE OF LOCHALSH, IV40 8PB
Renovated mansion with views; excellent home-cooking using fresh, local produce.
TEL: (01478) 660222/660226 OPEN Apr. - Oct.   V, DIAB B/A.   N/S DINING R & T.V. LOUNGE.   LICENSED. DISABLED ACCESS.   CHILDREN.   PETS B/A.   EN SUITE, BEVERAGES & TV.   B. & B. AROUND £30.

ISLE OF SKYE

Atholl House
DUNVEGAN, ISLE OF SKYE, IV55 8WA   TEL: (01470) 521 219   FAX: (01470) 521 481
Centrally situated in Dunvegan village, the Atholl has panoramic views of Macleods Tables & Loch Dunvegan. Comfortably furnished. Excellent food & wines; lounge & log fire.
OPEN Mar. - Dec.   N/S DINING R.   S.D. B/A.   LICENSED.   CHILDREN & PETS WELCOME.   EN SUITE, TV & BEVERAGES IN ROOMS.   B. & B. £18 - 28.

DUNRINGELL HOTEL, KYLEAKIN
Beautiful country house in 4 acres of secluded grounds; fresh food.
TEL: (01599) 534180 OPEN Mar. to Oct.   V, S.D. B/A.   N/S DINING R & 1 LOUNGE.   DISABLED ACCESS. CHILDREN WELCOME.   SOME EN SUITE ROOMS.   BEVERAGES IN ROOMS.   T.V. IN LOUNGE.   B. & B. AROUND £17.

JANET KERNACHAN, 4 LEPHIN, GLENDALE, ISLE OF SKYE
Small, modern crofthouse on 6 acre working croft; home-cooking from fresh, local produce including bread, cakes, soups and jams.
TEL: (01470) 511376 OPEN ALL YEAR EXCEPT OCT. N/S DINING ROOM. V, S.D. B/A. CHILDREN WELCOME. PETS B/A.   B. & B. FROM £10.50

SKYE ENVIRONMENTAL CENTRE GUEST HOUSE, HARAPOOL, BROADFORD
Wildlife holidays about the wildlife of skye based in a guest house overlooking the bay. All profits fromguest house and wildlife holidays go directly into wildlife conservation work & the centre's wildlife rehabilitation hospital.
TEL: (01471) 822487   OPEN ALL YEAR.   V STD.   S.D. B/A.   N/S DINING R.   LICENSED.   CHILDREN WELCOME.   PETS B/A.   BEVERAGES & TV IN LOUNGE.   B. & B. AROUND £19.

RESTAURANTS
The majority of hotels and guest houses on the Western Isles which are listed above are also open to non-residents for dinner. It is suggested that you phone in advance to check the evening meal arrangements for each establishment. We were unable to find any other restaurants or cafés in the Western Isles with good vegetarian options. If *you* can find any - do please let us know!

Clwyd

ACCOMMODATION

BODELWYDDAN

THE MANOR, FAENOL FAWR COUNTRY HOTEL, BODELWYDDAN, CLWYD
Beautiful 16th C. Grade II listed manor; Jacobean fireplace & panelled drawing room.
TEL: (01745) 591691 OPEN ALL YEAR. V, STD. N/S DINING R, SOME BEDRS & PART OF THE BAR.
LICENSED. DISABLED ACCESS. CHILDREN WELCOME. PETS B/A. EN SUITE, BEVERAGES & TV IN
ROOMS. B. & B. AROUND £30.

BRYNEGLWYS

CAE CRWN FARM, BRYNEGLWYS, CLWYD, LL21 9NF
Detached farmhouse peacefully situated; home-cooked meals & good vegetarian option.
TEL: (01490) 450243 OPEN ALL YEAR. V STD. NO SMOKING. CHILDREN WELCOME. PETS B/A. BEVER-
AGES. T.V. IN LOUNGE. B. & B. FROM £13.

Westwood Hotel

COED GORLLEWIN, 51 PRINCES DRIVE, COLWYN BAY, LL29 8PL TEL: (01492) 532078
WTB 3 Crowns. Taste of Wales. Comfortable, family-run guest house. Excellent veg.
options.
OPEN ALL YEAR. V, VE, S.D. B/A. ORG. WH. STD.N/S DINING R. CHILDREN & PETS WELCOME. LICENSED.
CREDIT CARDS. EN SUITE, TV & BEVERAGES IN ROOMS. B. & B. FROM £14, D. £6.

HANMER

Buck Farm

HANMER, CLWYD, SY14 7LX   TEL: (01948) 74339

This beautiful unspoilt half-timbered 16th C. farmhouse stands in eight acres of woodland and paddocks (alive with butterflies, wild flowers...) on the
A525 midway between Whitchurch and Wrexham.
It is appropriate that it should be situated straddling
two counties for the proprietors themselves have a
cosmopolitan background (Frances a Trinidadian of
Chinese ancestry, and Cedric a naturalized Canadian) which makes for great diversity in the culinary
styles to be sampled at Buck Farm: Spanish, African
and Indian influences combine with Frances' already wide culinary experience. The main nutritional influence, however, is that of healthy food
preparation: generous portions of simply cooked food prepared from fresh, local, wholefood and, where possible, organic ingredients make for very good dining indeed! Breakfast
is enormous (home-baked bread, fruit compote, etc.) and an evening meal might feature
Watercress or Sorrel Soup followed by Vegetable Croustade and warm Blackcurrant Cake
with Egg Custard. Food apart, Buck Farm is an exceptionally nice place to stay: beautifully
furnished (and with a little library and music facilities), friendly (your hosts will lend you
maps, guide books, cycle shelter, and offer a maildrop service for tourers), and with
excellent nearby walks (you can now follow footpaths directly from Buck Farm onto the
link betwn Offa's Dyke & the Sandstone Way).
OPEN ALL YEAR. NO SMOKING. V, S.D. B/A. DISABLED ACCESS TO DINING ROOM AND TOILETS. CHILD-
REN WELCOME. TEA/COFFEE ON REQUEST. T.V. IN LOUNGE. B. & B. FROM £13.50.

LLANGOLLEN

HILLCREST, HILL STREET, LLANGOLLEN, LL20 8EU   TEL: (01978) 860208
WTB 3 Crown Commended. Victorian house in an acre of gardens 3 mins from Llangollen.
OPEN ALL YEAR. V, S.D. B/A. NO SMOKING. 1 DOWNSTAIRS DOUBLE ROOM. CHILDREN WELCOME. EN
SUITE & BEVERAGES IN ROOMS. SEPARATE T.V. LOUNGE. B. & B. AROUND £21.

Dyfed

ACCOMMODATION

ABERYSTWYTH

GLYN-GARTH GUEST HOUSE, SOUTH ROAD, ABERYSTWYTH, SY23 1JS
WTB Highly Commended. A pleasantly appointed family-run guest house situated close to the South Promenade of Aberystwyth; wholesome food.
TEL: (01970) 615050 OPEN ALL YEAR ex. Xmas.   V, S.D. B/A.   N/S DINING R & SOME BEDRS.   CHILDREN WELCOME.   MOST ROOMS EN SUITE.   BEVERAGES & T.V. IN ROOMS.   B. & B. AROUND £17.

BONCATH

GWELFOR GUEST HOUSE, BLAENFFOS, BONCATH, DYFED, SA37 0HZ
WTB 2 Crowns. Guest house with panoramic views of the Preseli Hills. Wholesome traditional & vegetarian dishes; home-grown, local or organic produce used in cooking; great for country lovers, bird watchers, painters; ancient sites, golf, riding, water sports.
TEL: (01239) 831599 OPEN ALL YEAR.   V, VE STD.   S.D. B/A.   NO SMOKING IN THE HOUSE.   CHILDREN WELCOME.   PETS B/A.   SOME ROOMS EN SUITE.   BEVERAGES IN ROOMS.   T.V. IN LOUNGE.   B. & B. AROUND £18.

CARDIGAN

TRELLACCA GUEST HOUSE, TREMAIN, CARDIGAN, SA43 1SJ
Trellacca Guest House has been superbly converted from two slate and stone cottages; beautifully furnished with much handcrafted pine furniture and fittings; lovely rural setting.
TEL: (01239) 810730 OPEN ALL YEAR.   V, DIAB B/A.   N/S BEDRS & DINING-R.   CHILDREN WELCOME.   SOME ROOMS EN SUITE .   BEVERAGES.   T.V. IN LOUNGE & BEDR ON REQUEST.   B. & B. AROUND £16.

CAREW

Old Stables Cottage
CAREW, DYFED, SA70 8SL   TEL: (01646) 651889
Grade II listed stone cottage overlooking River Carew. Low beams and inglenook in lounge. Aga-cooked meals prepared from fresh produce; home-baked bread.
OPEN 10 Mar. - 30 Nov. V, S.D. B/A. NO SMOKING. OVER 5s WELCOME. EN SUITE, TV & BEVERAGES IN ROOMS.
B. & B. AROUND £25.

CRYMYCH

Felin Tygwyn Farm
CRYMYCH, DYFED, SA41 3RX TEL: (01239) 79603
Traditional earth and slate farmhouse at the foot of the Preseli Mountains, some 9 miles from Cardigan and Newport beach. There are beamed ceilings with bunches of home grown dried flowers, and an open fire in the lounge. The farmhouse forms part of an organic smallholding. Meals are prepared from home-grown vegetables, herbs or local produce.
OPEN ALL YEAR.   V, S.D. B/A.   NO SMOKING.   LICENSED.   CHILDREN WELCOME.   PETS B/A.   BEVERAGES.   T.V. LOUNGE.   D., B. & B. AROUND £20.

FISHGUARD

Coach House Cottage
GLENDOWER SQUARE, GOODWICK, FISHGUARD, DYFED, SA64 0DH   TEL: (01348) 873660

This traditional Pembrokeshire stone cottage stands in a secluded location by a mountain stream, yet is conveniently situated in the heart of the village of Goodwick, 1 mile from the centre of Fishguard and a few minutes' walk from the harbour and seafront. Centrally heated accommodation is provided for just two people in a prettily decorated bedroom, with beautiful hill and sea views (and almost exclusive use of the bathroom), and guests are also welcome to use the rest of the cottage including the large, eclectic collection of books, the lovely garden (with its sea views) or the sitting room with T.V. The proprietors specialise in providing delicious vegetarian, vegan and whole-

food fare (prepared with organic produce wherever possible), but light, 'snack'type meals can be provided in the evening for meat-eaters (there are several other good eating places within walking distance). Pembrokeshire is a beautiful county and is said to have the highest number of working craftsmen within its boundaries (including, incidentally your host, 'Max'Maxwell-Jones, who is a well-known local artist and calligrapher).
OPEN ALL YEAR.   V STD, S.D. B/A.   NO SMOKING.   BYO WINE.   CHILDREN WELCOME.   PETS B/A.   BEVER-AGES IN ROOMS.   T.V. IN LOUNGE.   B. & B. FROM £12. D. £8.50 & £6.

GELLIFAWR COUNTRY HOUSE, PONTFAEN, NR FISHGUARD, SA65 9TX

Beautiful country house once the centre of a 700 acre estate with many original farm buildings; excellent cuisine imaginatively prepared from fresh, local produce.
TEL: (01239) 820343 OPEN ALL YEAR.   V, STD. VE, DIAB, S.D. B/A.   LICENSED.   DISABLED ACCESS. CHILDREN WELCOME.   PETS B/A.   SOME EN SUITE ROOMS.   BEVERAGES ON LANDINGS.   T.V. IN LOUNGE.   B. & B. AROUND £23.

Glanmoy Country House Hotel

GOODWICK, FISHGUARD, PEMROKESHIRE, DYFED.   TEL: (01348) 872844

Luxurious Edwardian country house with large en suite rooms standing in 8 acres in a peaceful area. Chef-owner offers multi-choice menu with vegetaraian options. Library, classical music.
OPEN ALL YEAR.   V STD, S.D. B/A. N/S DINING R.   OVER 8s WELCOME.   DOGS IN 2 ANNEXE ROOMS.   LICENSED. EN SUITE, TV & BEVERAGES IN ROOMS.   CREDIT CARDS.   B. & B. £21 - 25.

Tregynon Country Farmhouse Hotel

GWAUN VALLEY, NR FISHGUARD, SA65 9TU   TEL: (01239) 820531   FAX: (01239) 820808

It is over a decade since Peter Heard decided to abandon the stress-filled London rat race for a more peaceful way of life in a Welsh farmhouse. A tremendous amount of renovation work had to be done on Tregynon but, with a lot of hard work and enthusiasm, the run-down farmhouse soon became a thriving Country Farmhouse Hotel which has won several awards and received much national acclaim. Much of the recognition is due not just to the wonderfully comfortable surroundings (winter evenings log fires in the inglenook fireplace in the oakbeamed lounge, beautiful bedrooms) but to the superlative quality of Jane's cuisine. Jane, co-author of 'Dining with Angels'(an anthology of food and verse), uses fresh produce - much of it local - wherever possible in the preparation of all meals. Free-range eggs, organic and unpasteurised cheeses, home-smoked bacon and gammon for non-vegetarians, are all part of the Tregynon gastronomic experience - as are the range of speciality additive-free breads and rolls. But Tregynon's surroundings provide the enduring lure for guests who return year after year...situated on the edge of the Gwaun Valley with its ancient oak forest, this beautiful part of the world is a haven for wildlife - badgers, buzzards and herons are regularly seen, whilst red kites and peregrine falcons are also spotted from time to time.
OPEN ALL YEAR.   V, STD S.D. ON REQUEST.   N/S RESTAURANT & BEDRS, DISCOURAGED ELSEWHERE. LICENSED. DISABLED ACCESS. CHILDREN WELCOME. EN SUITE, BEVERAGES & T.V. IN ROOMS.   B. & B. FROM £23.

HAVERFORDWEST

DRUIDSTON HAVEN, HAVERFORDWEST, DYFED.

Hotel and self-catering cottages standing in 20 acres of wild garden overlooking the sea; educational courses; excellent healthy food.
TEL: (01437) 781221 OPEN Feb. to Oct. plus Xmas.   V, WH STD.   VE, S.D. B/A.   LICENSED.   CHILDREN WELCOME. PETS B/A.   BEVERAGES.   B. & B. AROUND £25.

NEW QUAY

NANTERNIS FARM, NANTERNIS, NEW QUAY, DYFED, SA45 9RP

Small 8 acre farm set on a hillside with beautiful views; a stream runs by the farm along which a footpath leads to the sea just over a mile away.
TEL: (01545) 560181 OPEN Easter to end Sept.   V, S.D. B/A.   N/S BEDRS & DINING R.   CHILDREN WELCOME. BEVERAGES IN ROOMS.   T.V.   B. & B. AROUND £16.

Ty Hen Farm Country Hotel & Cottages
LLWYNDAFYDD, NEW QUAY, DYFED, SA44 6BZ   TEL: (01545) 560346

This charming stone-built farmhouse (Ty Hen means simply 'Old House') offers a very high standard of accommodation to guests and stands in spacious gardens in a peaceful location just 2 miles from the rocky cliffs and sandy beaches of the Cardiganshire coast. Health is a priority at Ty Hen where the generous breakfast features a number of very laudable items such as yoghurt, muesli and fresh fruit as well as a huge platter of bacon, eggs, mushrooms and anything else breakfasty you care to name. The restaurant offers a 4-course evening menu and specialises in fish and vegetarian options. The leisure centre at Ty Hen has an indoor heated pool where private lessons, particularly for adults, are available, and also contains a gymnasium, sauna, sunbed and skittles alley; further leisure facilities are planned. Stone-built self-catering cottages are also available.

OPEN ALL YEAR. NO SMOKING. V STD. S.D. B/A. LICENSED. DISABLED ACCESS. PETS B/A. CHILDREN WELCOME. EN SUITE, BEVERAGES & T.V. PLUS VIDEO CHANNEL IN ROOMS. VISA, MASTERCARD. B. & B. FROM £20.

RHYDLEWIS

BRONIWAN, RHYDLEWIS, LLANDYSUL, SA44 5PF
Cosy Victorian farmhouse 10 mins from Penbryn Beach. Part of a working organic farm (Member of the Soil Association), much of the delicious food been prepared from home-grown produce; vegetarian meals are a speciality

OPEN ALL YEAR. V, S.D. B/A. NO SMOKING. CHILDREN WELCOME. PETS B/A. 1 EN SUITE ROOM. BEVERAGES AVAILABLE. T.V. IN LOUNGE. B. & B. AROUND £15.

ROBESTON WATHEN

ROBESTON HOUSE HOTEL & RESTAURANTS, ROBESTON WATHEN (ON MAIN A40), PEMBROKESHIRE, SA67 8EU
Elegant, country house hotel in 5 acres of grounds. Log fires in winter. Acclaimed restaurant serves first-class meals prepared fresh produce.

TEL & FAX: (01834) 860392 & 861195 OPEN ALL YEAR.   V, S.D. B/A.   N/S DINING R.   LICENSED. CHILDREN IN BUTTERY ONLY. PETS B/A. EN SUITE, BEVERAGES & TV IN ROOMS.   B. & B. AROUND £26.

TREGARON

THE EDELWEISS COUNTRY GUEST HOUSE, PENUWCH, TREGARON, SY25 6QZ
Charming oak-beamed house in 1½ acres of grounds in the beautiful Ceridigion countryside.

TEL: (01974) 821601 OPEN ALL YEAR .   V, S.D. B/A.   NO SMOKING. BYO WINE. CHILDREN WELCOME. BEVERAGES SERVED 7 - 11. T.V. IN ALL BEDROOMS. B. & B. FROM £12-£14, £73 WEEKLY. B., B. & D. £17-£19.50, £111 WEEKLY. CARAVAN AROUND £120 WEEKLY. B. B. & D. 3-day specials £55 Sept. - June.

YSTRAD MEURIG

Hillscape Walking Holidays
BLAEN-Y-DDÔL, PONTRHYDYGROES, YSTRAD MEURIG, SY25 6DS   TEL: (01974) 282640
Blaen-y-Ddôl is an idyllic rural guest house: beautifully isolated and surrounded by lush, hilly countryside with footpaths radiating from the front door. Thus it is the perfect base for Hillscape Walking Holidays with its choice of 40 exclusive self-guided routes ranging from 5 - 20 miles and graded to suit all levels of fitness. The food is excellent, too: home-grown vegetables, herbs and fruits are used in the preparation of substantial and tasty vegetarian meals, and the delicious bread is also home-made. Cyclists and bird-watchers will also appreciate a stay at Blaen-y-Ddôl.

OPEN Mar. - Nov.   V, VE, S.D. B/A. NO SMOKING.   ACCOMPANIED OVER 11S WELCOME.   EN SUITE & BEVERAGES IN ROOMS.   D., B. & B. £29.50.

RESTAURANTS

LLANWRDA

Felin Newydd - the Mill at Crugybar

LLANWRDA, DYFED, SA19 8UE   TEL: (015585) 375

One of the last working watermills in Wales with converted milking parlour as tea shop. Almost all food home-made using the mill's renowned wholemeal flour whenever possible.

V STD. N/S INCLUDING MILL & CRAFT WORKSHOP. DISABLED ACCESS. CHILDREN WELCOME.

Glamorgan

ACCOMMODATION

CARDIFF

Annedd Lon Guest House

3 DYFRIG STREET, PONTCANNA, CARDIFF, SOUTH GLAMORGAN, CF1 9LR   TEL: (01222) 223349

Lovely Victorian guest house in a quiet close on Cathedral Road; interestingly furnished in keeping with the period.

OPEN ALL YEAR.   V, S.D. B/A.   NO SMOKING.   CHILDREN WELCOME.   SOME EN SUITE ROOMS. BEVERAGES & TV IN ROOMS.   B. & B. FROM £18.

RHOOSE

LOWER HOUSE FARM GUEST HOUSE AND COTTAGE, RHOOSE ROAD, RHOOSE, SOUTH GLAMORGAN, CF6 9ER

Lovely Georgian farmhouse with a nearby thatched cottage avail. to self-caterers. B & B.

TEL: (01446) 710010 OPEN ALL YEAR. V STD. NO SMOKING. CHILDREN WELCOME. PETS B/A. BEVERAGES. T.V. AVAILABLE.   B. & B. FROM £15. Cottage from £165 per week.

SWANSEA

THE BAYS GUEST HOUSE, 97 MUMBLES ROAD, MUMBLES, SWANSEA, WEST GLAMORGAN, SA3 5TW

Guest house with large gardens adjoining sea-front; recent winners of Health Award.

TEL: (01792) 404775 OPEN ALL YEAR. V, S.D. B/A.   NO SMOKING.   CHILDREN: OVER 10S ONLY.   1 EN SUITE ROOM. BEVERAGES & TV IN LOUNGE.   B. & B. AROUND £18.

Gwent

ACCOMMODATION

ABERGAVENNY

PENTRE HOUSE, BRECON RD, LLANWENARTH, ABERGAVENNY, NP7 7EW

WTB Farm & Guest House Award 1994. Small, pretty country house in lovely award-winning gardens; comfortably furnished; generous breakfasts with a variety of options.

TEL: (01873) 853435   OPEN ALL YEAR.   V, S.D. B/A.   N/S DINING R, & BEDRS.   CHILDREN & PETS B/A. BEVERAGES IN ROOMS. T.V. SITTING ROOM.   B. & B. FROM £15.

THORNTREES, GOVILON, ABERGAVENNY, GWENT, NP7 9BY

Beamed cottage idyllically situated in Brecon Beacons National Park. Panoramic views. S/C cottage available. Food cooked on Rayburn from free-range eggs, veg., fruit, Spring Water.

TEL: (01873) 831686 OPEN Easter - Nov. V B/A. NO SMOKING. SOME EN SUITE ROOMS. TV & BEVERAGES. B. & B. AROUND £18.

CAERLEON

Clawdd Farm

BULMORE ROAD, CAERLEON, GWENT, NP6 1QQ   TEL: (01633) 423250/421788
Edwardian farmhouse, set on 19 acres of hillside in the peaceful vale of Usk; excellent food
prepared from organic & wholefood ingredients.
V, VE, S.D. B/A. ORG & WH WHEN AVAIL./B/A.   OPEN ALL YEAR.   N/S PART DINING R. & SOME BEDROOMS.
BRING YOUR OWN WINE.   CHILDREN 'IF CONTROLLED'.   PETS B/A.   BEVERAGES & TV IN ROOMS.
CREDIT CARDS.   B. & B. FROM £15. D. £8.50.

NEWPORT

Anderley Lodge Hotel

216 STOW HILL, NEWPORT, GWENT, NP9 4HA   TEL & FAX: (01633) 266781
Award-winning family-run 19th C. hotel with spacious, elegant bedrooms; evening meal
by arrangement prepared from fresh produce.
OPEN ALL YEAR.   NO SMOKING.   NOT LICENSED, BUT WINE OFFERED WHEN AVAILABLE.   CHILDREN
WELCOME.   BEVERAGES, T.V. & SHOWERS IN ROOMS.   B. & B. FROM £15.

CHAPEL G.H., CHURCH RD, ST BRIDES, WENTLOOG, NR NEWPORT, NP1 9SN

Converted chapel in small country village adjacent to Elm Tree Restaurant; B. & B.
TEL: (06133) 681018 OPEN ALL YEAR.   V, S.D. B/A.   NO SMOKING.   CHILDREN WELCOME.   PETS B/A. 1
EN SUITE ROOM. BEVERAGES.   T.V. IN LOUNGE.   B. & B. AROUND £15.

The West Usk Lighthouse

ST BRIDES, WENTLOOGE, NR NEWPORT, GWENT, NP1 9SF   TEL: (01633) 810126/815860

The West Usk Lighthouse was built in 1821 by
James Walker, a Scottish architect, on the estuaries
of the rivers Usk and Severn; as you might imagine
it has quite magnificent views of the Bristol Channel
and stands on its own promontory. Its design is quite
extraordinary: 50 feet in diameter, the walls are 2
feet thick and the rooms are shaped like pieces of a
pie: there are 6 guest bedrooms and the dining room
is decorated in a nautical style; log fires blaze in the
lounge. A variety of courses are held at the lighthouse on a wide selection of themes; there is also an
amazing stress-release flotation tank for guests' use
(10 inches of water, a ton of Epsom salts and you!).
Breakfast is not the only meal to be offered at the Lighthouse; evening meals, however, are
available by arrangement.
OPEN ALL YEAR.   V, VE, S.D., B/A.   NO SMOKING.   CHILDREN WELCOME.   3 EN SUITE ROOMS.   BEVERAGES
IN ROOMS.   CREDIT CARDS.   B. & B. FROM £20.

TINTERN

The Old Rectory

TINTERN, GWENT, NP6 6SG   TEL: (01291) 689519
Lovely old house, once used as a rectory for the Church of St Mary's (now in ruins on the
hillside opposite the Abbey); own produce used in home-made cuisine.
OPEN ALL YEAR.   V, S.D. B/A.   N/S ex SITTING R.   CHILDREN.   PETS B/A. B. & B. AROUND £15.

Parva Farmhouse Hotel

TINTERN, GWENT, NP6 6SQ   TEL: (01291) 689411 FAX: (01291) 689557
17th C. former farmhouse nestled on the bank of the River Wye. Excellent food.
OPEN ALL YEAR.   V STD, VE, S.D. B/A.   CHILDREN & PETS WELCOME.   LICENSED. EN SUITE, TV & BEVERAGES
IN ROOMS.   B. & B. AROUND £29.

Valley House

RAGLAN ROAD, TINTERN, GWENT, NP6 6TH   TEL: (01291) 689652
Charming Georgian house opposite picturesque woods within a mile of Tintern Abbey.
Lovely en suite rooms. Numerous forest walks begin from the doorstep. Many places to
eat nearby which cater for vegetarians.
OPEN ALL YEAR.   N/S DINING R & BEDROOMS.   V, B/A.   PETS B/A.   EN SUITE, TV & BEVERAGES IN
BEDROOMS.   B. & B. FROM £15, D. £12.50.

USK

Ty-Gwyn Farm

GWEHELOG, USK, GWENT, NP5 1RT TEL: (01291) 672878
Charming award-winning house in beautiful rural setting with magnificent views. Excellent food prepared from fresh fruit & vegetables. Free-range eggs & home-made preserves at b'fast. Vegetarians welcome.
OPEN ALL YEAR. V STD. S.D. B/A. NO SMOKING. CHILDREN WELCOME. EN STEUI, TV & BEVERAGES IN ROOMS. B. & B. AROUND £10.

Gwynedd

ACCOMMODATION

ABERDOVEY

The Harbour Hotel

ABERDOVEY, GWYNEDD, LL35 0EB   TEL: (01654) 767250   FAX: (01654) 767078
The Harbour Hotel is a lovely, award-winning, Victorian hotel which stands on the seafront in the heart of the picturesque village of Aberdovey overlooking miles of golden sandy beaches. Owned and run by the resident proprietors, the Harbour Hotel has been beautifully restored and its furnishing and decor are of an exceptionally high standard; bedrooms are very comfortable and family suites are available (with separate children's and parents' bedrooms). Excellent, home-cooked food may be enjoyed in the Alacarte (*sic.*) Restaurant, and there is a family restaurant, 'Rumbles', which has good children's options; there is also a basement wine bar.
OPEN ALL YEAR.   V STD, S.D. B/A.   N/S DINING R, SITTING R & SOME BEDRS.   LICENSED.   PETS B/A.
CHILDREN WELCOME.   EN SUITE, BEVERAGES & TV IN ROOMS.   CREDIT CARDS.   B. & B. FROM £29.75.

One Trefeddian Bank

ABERDOVEY, GWYNEDD, LL35 0RU TEL: (01654) 767487
Lovely house in quiet, elevated position with stunning views over the Dovey Estuary.
OPEN Mar. - Oct. inc.   V, S.D. B/A.   NO SMOKING.   CHILDREN WELCOME.   BEVERAGES IN ROOMS.   T.V. IN LOUNGE AND BEDRS.   B. & B. FROM £13. D. £8.50.

BALA

PALÉ HALL HOTEL, LLANDDERFEL, BALA, LL23 7PS
Splendid country house & gardens; excellent cuisine prepared from fresh, local produce.
TEL: (01678) 530285 OPEN ALL YEAR. V, S.D. B/A. N/S DINING R & 1 guest lounge. LICENSED. DISABLED ACCESS. CHILDREN. PETS IN KENNELS. EN SUITE & TV. ROOM SERVICE. B. & B. AROUND £46.

BARMOUTH

LAWRENNY LODGE HOTEL, ABERAMFFRA ROAD, BARMOUTH, LL42 1SU
Stone-built house commanding a superb position overlooking the Mawddach Estuary and Barmouth Harbour; pleasingly furnished and offering very good freshly prepared food.
TEL: (01341) 280466 OPEN Mar. - Dec. V STD, S.D. B/A. N/S DINING R. LICENSED. CHILDREN. PETS B/A B. & B. AROUND £18.

PEN PARC GUEST HOUSE, PARK ROAD, BARMOUTH, LL42 1PH
Small guest house in a quiet location overlooking the bowling and putting green, and tennis court, 4 mins walk from the sea; a choice of vegetarian or traditional cuisine is served.
TEL: (01341) 280150 V STD, S.D. B/A. N/S. BYO WINE. BEVERAGES. T.V. B. & B. AROUND £16.

BANGOR

Rainbow Court

PENTIR, NR BANGOR, GWYNEDD, LL57 4UY   TEL: (01248) 353099
Excellent restaurant just outside Bangor (on B4366 at Caerhun turnoff), specialising in serving many, delicious original dishes. Vegetarian options are tasty and imaginative. Low/non alcoholic wines and beers are available or you are welcome to bring your own wine.

OPEN ALL YEAR.   V, S.D. B/A.   NO SMOKING.   BYO WINE.   CHILDREN B/A.   MOST ROOMS EN SUITE.
BEVERAGES & T.V. IN ROOMS.   CREDIT CARDS.   B. & B. AROUND £16.

BETWS-Y-COED

Ty'n-y-Celyn House

LLANRWST RD, BETWS-Y-COED, SNOWDONIA NATIONAL PARK, N. WALES, LL24 0HD   TEL:
(01690) 710202 FAX: (01690) 710800

Ty'n-y-Celyn is a large Victorian house which nestles in a quiet elevated position overlooking the picturesque village of Betws-y-Coed. It has been very comfortably furnished: there are 8 bedrooms - 3 of which are family rooms - and each has been tastefully refurbished with new beds and fitted furniture, together with a range of helpful amenities including TV, hairdryer, radio-cassette and tea-making facilities; most bedrooms have magnificent views of the Llugwy Valley, surrounding mountains or the Conwy River. Your hosts, Ann and Clive Muskus, will do all they can to make your stay a happy and comfortable one - including picking you up from the station if you are arriving by rail. Betws-y-Coed is a perfect touring base: it is in the heart of the Snowdonia National Park, yet is also within easy reach of the fine coastlines; in addition to walking and climbing, it is an excellent centre for other outdoor pursuits such as fishing (which can be arranged in the nearby streams, rivers and reservoirs) and horse riding.

OPEN ALL YEAR.   N/S DINING R.   V, S.D. B/A.   LICENSED.   CHILDREN & PETS WELCOME.   EN SUITE, TV
& BEVERAGES IN ROOMS.   B. & B. £20 - 22.

CAERNARFON

TY'N RHOS, SEION, LLANDDEINIOLEN, CAERNARFON, LL55 3AE

From the outside Ty'n Rhos is an unashamedly modern looking building, but inside it's everything you'd expect a *proper* Welsh farmhouse to be complete with Welsh Dressers, log fires, and bedrooms with cottagey windows which look out onto cottagey scenes. Until the advent of milk quotas Ty'n Rhos was a working dairy farm: these days the proprietors, Linda and Nigel Kettle, have turned their considerable energies into running a guest house (there's still enough of the Jersey herd left to provide milk, yoghurt and cream). The food is first-rate: organic and wholefood ingredients are used wherever possible to prepare delicious meals. Ty'n Rhos nestles at the foot of Snowdonia and is nearby to first-rate climbing 'for the serious minded'(and some energetic strolling, for the not-so-intent).

TEL: (01248) 670489 OPEN ALL YEAR.   V, VE, S.D. B/A.   ORG WHEN AVAIL. WH ON REQUEST.   N/S DINING
R.   LICENSED.   DISABLED ACCESS.   OVER 6s.   EN SUITE, TV & BEVERAGES.   B. & B. AROUND £24.

COLWYN BAY

Westwood Hotel

COED GORLLEWIN, 51 PRINCES DRIVE, COLWYN BAY, LL29 8PL TEL: 901492) 532078

WTB 3 Crowns. 'Taste of Wales'. Comfortable family-run guest house. Excellent veg. options.

OPEN ALL YEAR.   V, VE, S.D. B/A.   ORG, WH STD.   N/S DINING R.   CHILDREN & PETS WELCOME.   LICENSED.
CREDIT CARDS.   EN SUITE, TV& BEVERAGES IN ROOMS.   B. & B. FROM £14, D. £6.

CONWY

CASTLE HOTEL, HIGH STREET, CONWY, GWYNEDD, LL32 8DB

A coaching house in the 19th C. (some parts of the building date from the 15th C.) this superbly converted hotel offers very comfortable accommodation and excellent cuisine.

TEL: (01492) 592324 OPEN ALL YEAR.   V, STD. S.D. B/A.   N/S DINING R.   LICENSED.   CHILDREN WEL-
COME.   PETS B/A.   EN SUITE, BEVERAGES & TV IN ROOMS.   CREDIT CARDS.   B. & B. AROUND £39.

The Old Rectory

LLANSANFFRAID GLAN CONWY, NR CONWY, LL28 5LF TEL: (01492) 580611 FAX: (01492)
584555

There has been a rectory on this beautiful site on the Conwy Estuary with its spectacular views from Conwy Castle to Snowdonia, for the last 5 centuries. The cuisine is exceptionally good: the finest local produce is used to prepared dishes of imagination and flair.

OPEN Feb. - Dec.   V, S.D. B/A.   NO SMOKING.   LICENSED.   OVER 10S ONLY.   EN SUITE & TV IN ROOMS.
ROOM SERVICE.   ACCESS, VISA.   D, B. & B. AROUND £62.

CRICIETH

MURIAU, CRICIETH, GWYNEDD, LL52 0RS   TEL: (01766) 522337
Lovely granite-built house, part 17th and part 19th C., in small coastal town of Cricieth.
OPEN ALL YEAR.   V, S.D. B/A.   NO SMOKING.   CHILDREN WELCOME.   BEVERAGES IN ROOMS.   T.V. IN
LOUNGE.   B. & B. AROUND £14.

Dolmelynllyn Hall

GANLLWYD, DOLGELLAU, GWYNEDD, LL40 2HP   TEL & FAX: (01341) 440273

Dolmelynllyn Hall dates from the 16th C. although several spates of subsequent rebuilding have made for an eclectic building whose style reflects that of three different architectural periods. It stands amidst 3 acres of formal terraced gardens the whole surrounded by 1200 acres of National Trust owned mountains, forest and river: you can walk for miles without crossing a road or encountering a car - bliss! Your hosts, father and daughter Jon Barkwith and Jo Reddicliffe, have refurbished their home in splendid style: each of the en suite bedrooms has a different decorative theme, and the conservatory bar and elegant lounge with wonderful valley views are relaxing venues for pre-prandial drinks (or post-prandial chats). Meals are served in a charming dining room: Jo is responsible for the cooking (traditional British, with imagination), and the comprehensive wine list has over a hundred items.
NO SMOKING   OPEN Feb. - Nov.   S.D. B/A.   OVER 10s & PETS B/A.   LICENSED.   EN SUITE, BEVERAGES
& TV IN ROOMS.   B. & B. £40 - 50; Sgle £45 - 52.50; D. £22.50; Special Breaks avail.

DOLGELLAU

BONTDDU HALL HOTEL, BONTDDU, NR DOLGELLAU, LL40 2SU
Built in 1873 as a country mansion for the sister of Joseph Chamberlain; 14 acres of landscaped gardens and rhododendron forest; best local and home-grown produce is used in cooking.
TEL: (01341 49) 661 OPEN Easter - Oct.   V, S.D. B/A.   N/S LOUNGE, 50% OF DINING R & SOME BEDRS.
LICENSED.   CHILDREN WELCOME.   PETS B/A.   EN SUITE, BEVERAGES & TV.   B. & B. AROUND £29.

Penmaenuchaf Hall

PENMAENPOOL, DOLGELLAU, GWYNEDD, LL40 1YB   TEL & FAX: (01341) 422129
It would be difficult to imagine a more beautiful and idyllic situation than the one enjoyed by this lovely country manor hotel which nestles in the foothills of Cader Idris overlooking the famous Mawddach Estuary. Upon entering the hall you are instantly transported back to an age of gracious living: the oak panelling, exquisite furnishings, fresh flowers and blazing log fires encourage a feeling of relaxation and well-being. Lulled thus into a condition of happy anaesthesia with respect to 20th C. concerns, the most stressful decision you are likely to have to make is whether your choice of afternoon tea will spoil your appetite for the superb evening meal: the food is fabulous and not to be missed, an evening menu choice perhaps featuring Tomato Consommé with Corriander, Madeira and Herb Dumplings followed by Pan-fried Pork with Apple and Rosemary and some outstandingly irresistible desserts (Apricot Soufflé on an Orange Caramel Sauce, Mille Feuille of Chocolate on a Compote of Cherries). Vegetarian choices are always included on the menu and other diets can be accommodated by arrangement.
OPEN ALL YEAR.   N/S DINING R, 2 LOUNGES & BEDROOM.   V STD. S.D. B/A.   LICENSED.   CHILDREN.   EN
SUITE, TV & BEVERAGES IN ROOMS.   CREDIT CARDS.   B. & B. FROM £47.50.

HARLECH

ARIS GUEST HOUSE, PEN-Y-BRYN, HARLECH, LL46 2SL
Modern detached house set above the village of Pen-y-Bryn with magnificent views of Harlech Castle and Cardigan Bay; garden and local produce.
TEL: (01766) 780409 OPEN ALL YEAR.   V, VE, S.D. B/A.   NO SMOKING.   CHILDREN WELCOME.   PETS
B/A.   BEVERAGES IN ROOMS.   T.V. IN ROOMS.   B. & B. AROUND £15.

HOTEL MAES-Y-NEUADD, TALSARNAU, NR HARLECH, LL47 6YA
This ancient Welsh manor house standing on a wooded mountainside in 8 acres of landscaped grounds, is a gracious blend of 14th, 16th, 18th and 20th C. additions and has played host to travelling bards for centuries (many lines in Welsh literature bear witness to its hospitality). Now less bard-like travellers may also linger and enjoy this beautiful old

house with its exposed stone-work, elegant dining room with stupendous views and woodburning stoves; bedrooms are individually styled - many with a pleasing medley of antique and contemporary craftmanship - and look out over mountain or sea views. The food is tremendous: home-grown vegetables and herbs are culled daily from the kitchen garden to be used in the making of stupendous meals.
TEL: (01766) 780200 OPEN ALL YEAR ex. 2 weeks mid-Dec.   V, S.D. B/A.   N/S DINING R.   LICENSED. DISABLED ACCESS. CHILDREN & PETS B/A. EN SUITE. T.V. CREDIT CARDS. B. & B. AROUND £55.

Tremeifion Vegetarian Country Hotel

TALSARNAU, NEAR HARLECH, GWYNEDD, LL47 6UH   TEL: (01766) 770491

Charming house, with beautiful views of Portmeirion, the estuary and the wonderful mountains of Snowdonia; individually styled bedrooms; everything is home-baked and much of the organic produce comes fresh from the garden. Tremeifion is a wonderful base from which to explore the many scenic attractions of North Wales from the beautiful mountains and hills to the safe sandy beaches of the estuary.
OPEN ALL YEAR.   V, VE EXC. other meat-free S.D. B/A.   NO SMOKING. LICENSED.   CHILDREN WELCOME. PETS B/A. SOME EN SUITE ROOMS. BEVERAGES IN ROOMS. T.V. IN LOUNGE. D., B. & B. AROUND £30.

LLANDUDNO

BRIN-Y-BIA LODGE HOTEL, CRAIGSIDE, LLANDUDNO, LL30 3AS

Charming hotel in walled grounds on the Little Orme overlooking the town and the sea. Excellent meals carefully prepared from the finest of fresh, local produce.
TEL: (01492) 549644 OPEN ALL YEAR ex. Xmas & New Year.   V, S.D. B/A.   N/S DINING R.   LICENSED. CHILDREN. PETS B/A. EN SUITE, TV & BEVERAGES. ACCESS, VISA, AMEX. B. & B. AROUND £27.

THE GRAFTON HOTEL, PROMENADE, CRAIG-Y-DON, LLANDUDNO, GWYNEDD, LL30 1BG

Pleasant hotel on quieter part of promenade; excellent vegetarian meal options.
TEL: (01492) 876814 OPEN Feb. to Nov. NO SMOKING IN DINING ROOM & SOME BEDROOMS. VEGETARIAN BY ARRANGEMENT. LICENSED. DISABLED ACCESS. CHILDREN WELCOME. PETS BY ARRANGEMENT. EN SUITE, TEA/COFFEE & TV IN BEDROOMS. CREDIT CARDS. B. & B. FROM £15.50.

PLAS MADOC HOTEL, 60 CHURCH WALKS, LLANDUDNO, LL30 2HL

Family-run hotel at the foot of the Great Orme with magnificent views over Llandudno and the wonderful mountains of Snowdonia; fresh local ingredients used in cooking; vegetarian and other special diets by arrangement.
TEL: (01492) 876514 OPEN ALL YEAR.   V, S.D. B/A.   N/S DINING R & BEDRS.   LICENSED.   CHILDREN WELCOME. EN SUITE, BEVERAGES & TV IN ROOMS. B. & B. FROM £15.

LLWYNGWRIL

PENTRE BACH, LLWYNGWRIL, GWYNEDD, LL37 2JU

A former manor house, Pentre Bach is splendidly situated in a secluded position and has wonderful views of the sea and the mountains. There is a great emphasis on the use of healthy produce and guests can also buy free-range eggs, organic fruit and vegetables and preserves, all produced on the premises.
TEL: (01341) 250294 OPEN ALL YEAR ex. Xmas.   V STD, S.D. B/A.   NO SMOKING.   CHILDREN WELCOME. EN SUITE, TV & BEVERAGES IN ROOMS. B. & B. AROUND £20.

MAENTWROG

The Old Rectory Hotel

MAENTWROG, LL4 14HN   TEL: (0176 685) 305

The Old Rectory stands in its own grounds in the delightful Vale of Ffestiniog in the village of Maentwrog bounded on one side by the River Dwyryd which meets the sea at Tremadog Bay. It is a lovely old building - over 200 years old, and with a wealth of interesting features including some quite extraordinary chimneys! The house has been comfortably decorated with taste and style and there is a very good restaurant, open to non-residents, in which delicious freshly-prepared meals are served, such as home-made Lentil and Coriander Soup followed by a special dish of sweet potatoes, sweetcorn, peas, coriander, coconut and cumin (there is a strong African and Eastern influence in the Old Rectory kitchen!) and a delicious dessert such as home-made Bramley Apple Pie; many

dishes are suitable for vegetarians and vegans and traditional Italian dishes are a speciality, too. the area boasts many attractive features including the beach at Black Rock which is not only one of the safest for children, but also has the added advantage of being a 'drive-on' beach.
OPEN ALL YEAR. V, VE, DIAB. STD; S.D. B/A. ORG./WH. WHEN AVAIL. OPEN ALL YEAR. LICENSED. CHILDREN WELCOME. PETS B/A. EN SUITE, BEVERAGES IN ALL BEDROOMS. T.V. CREDIT CARDS. B. & B. FROM £16.

PORTMEIRION

THE HOTEL PORTMEIRION, PORTMEIRION, GWYNEDD, LL48 6ET
Beautiful hotel based around a Victorian villa in the Italianate village of Portmeirion; open air pool; fresh produce used in French-based menu.
TEL: (01766) 770228 OPEN ALL YEAR. V, S.D. B/A. N/S DINING R. LICENSED. CHILDREN WELCOME. EN SUITE & TV IN ROOMS. ROOM SERVICE. CREDIT CARDS. B. & B. AROUND £40.

TALYLLYN

MINFFORDD HOTEL, TALYLLYN, TYWYN, GWYNEDD, LL36 9AJ   TEL: (01654) 761665
17th C. Drover's Inn; real fires, beautifully furnished and appointed bedrooms and excellent food prepared on kitchen Aga: all meals are prepared from fresh, local produce
OPEN Mar. - Dec. V B/A. N/S DINING R, SITTING R & BEDRS. LICENSED. CHILDREN between ages of 3 and 12 accepted. EN SUITE & BEVERAGES IN ROOMS. ACCESS, VISA, DINERS. D., B. & B. AROUND £45.

TRAWSFYNYDD

Old Mill Farmhouse

FRON OLEU FARM, TRAWSFYNYDD, SNOWDONIA NATIONAL PARK, LL41 4UN TEL: (01766) 540397
Traditional built 18th C. Welsh farmhouse with inglenooks; fresh home-cooked food a speciality; own produce; free-range eggs, used in cooking. *Winner of Holiday Care Award Nov. '93.*
OPEN ALL YEAR. V, S.D. B/A. N/S IN ALL PUBLIC AREAS. BYO WINE. DISABLED ACCESS. CHILDREN WELCOME. PETS B/A. EN SUITE, TV & BEVERAGES IN ROOMS. D, B. & B. weekly £160.

TRIFRIW

CRAFNANT GUEST HOUSE, MAIN STREET, TREFRIW, LL27 0JH
Detached Victorian residence; candlelit dinners (traditional or vegetarian) have been prepared from fresh ingredients including some home-grown salad vegetables.
TEL: (01492) 640809 OPEN ALL YEAR. V A SPECIALITY. S.D. B/A. NO SMOKING. CHILDREN WELCOME. PETS B/A. SOME EN SUITE ROOMS. BEVERAGES & T.V. IN ROOMS.

TYWYN

Glenydd Guest House

OFF PIER RD, TYWYN, GWYNEDD, LL36 0AN TEL: (01654) 711373
Glenydd guest house is a charming modernised Edwardian house which stands in a private road just 200m from the beach and station, and 300m from the Talyllyn Steam Railway. Accommodation is in comfortably furnished, centrally heated rooms, and the delicious home-cooking is prepared from fresh, organic produce, much of it home-grown. Glenydd is an excellent base for touring: there are several good, sandy beaches nearby, and of course climbing in Snowdonia.
OPEN ALL YEAR. V STD. S.D. B/A. NO SMOKING. CHILDREN WELCOME. PETS B/A. BEVERAGES IN ROOMS. B. & B. £12.50, D. £8.

GREENFIELD HOTEL & REST, HIGH ST, TYWYN, GWYNEDD, LL36 9AD
Centrally sitated hotel within a few mins walk of the sea. Excellent vegetarian options.
TEL: 901654) 710354 OPEN Jan. - Nov. V STD. VE, S.D. B/A. CHILDREN. EN SUITE, TV & BEVERAGES. B. & B. AROUND £20.

RESTAURANTS

ANGLESEY

BODEILIO CRAFT CENTRE, BODEILIO, TALWRN, NR LLANGEFNI, ANGLE-SEY, GWYNEDD.
TEL: (01248) 722535 V STD. NO SMOKING. LICENSED. CHILDREN WELCOME. CREDIT CARDS.

BANGOR

RAINBOW COURT, PENTIR, NR BANGOR, GWYNEDD, LL57 4UY
Excellent restaurant in central Bangor specialising in tasty, imaginative vegetarian options.
TEL: (01248) 353099 OPEN ALL YEAR. V STD. S.D. B/A. NO SMOKING. BYO WINE.

LLANBERIS

Y BISTRO, 43-45 HIGH ST, LLANBERIS, GWYNEDD, LL55 4EU
Restaurant at the foot of Mount Snowdon serving meals prepared from fresh produce.
V STD, VE, S.D. B/A. N/S DINING R. DISABLED ACCESS. CHILDREN WELCOME.

LLANGEFNI

THE WHOLE THING, 5 FIELD ST, LLANGEFNI, GWYNEDD.
Wholefood restaurant and coffee shop above wholefood shop.
TEL: (01248) 724832 OPEN Mon. - Fri. V EXC. WH STD. NO SMOKING. CHILDREN WELCOME.

PORTHMADOG

Blossoms Restaurant

BORTH Y GEST, PORTHMADOG, GWYNEDD, LL49 9TP   TEL: (01766) 513500
Small informal restaurant specialsing in continental and vegetarian cuisine.
V STD. N/S UPSTAIRS DINING R. LICENSED. CHILDREN WELCOME. ACCESS, VISA.

TREFRIW

Chandler's Brasserie

TREFRIW, GWYNEDD, LL27 0JH   TEL: (01492) 640991
Small owner-run restaurant serving imaginative food prepared from fresh ingredients. Good vegetarian options.
V STD. NO SMOKING. LICENSED. CHILDREN WELCOME. ACCESS, VISA.

Powys

ACCOMMODATION

BRECON

BEACONS GUEST HOUSE, 16 BRIDGE ST, BRECON, POWYS, LD3 8AH
Beautiful Georgian family-run house close to the River Usk. The food is delicious - and very much prepared to suit guests' needs: there is a choice of a traditional or lighter continental breakfast, and light snacks, packed lunches and mid-day meals are served in the shop. The Beacons is "Taste of Wales Recommended" and as such offers wholesome home-cooked meals, prepared from fresh local produce (some home-grown);.
TEL: (01874) 623339 OPEN ALL YEAR. V, S.D. B/A. N/S DINING R. CHILDREN & PETS WELCOME. LICENSED. EN SUITE, BEVERAGES & TV IN ROOMS. CREDIT CARDS. B. & B. AROUND £20.

FORGE FARM HOUSE, HAY ROAD, BRECON, LD3 7SS
Beautiful 17th C. house with adjacent historical fulling mill in a quiet, secluded position in the valley of the River Honddu; good home-cooking including bread and jams.
TEL: (01874) 611793 OPEN ALL YEAR ex. Xmas. V, VE, S.D. B/A. WH WHEN AVAIL. NO SMOKING. CHILDREN WELCOME. BEVERAGES & TV IN SITTING ROOM. B. & B. AROUND £15.

BUILTH WELLS

THE COURT FARM, ABEREDW, NR BUILTH WELLS, LD2 3UP
Spacious stone-built house with working farm set in beauiful unspoilt valley; traditional home-cooking with home-produced meat, poultry, eggs, honey and organically home-grown vegetables and fruit. Farm, riverside and hill walking.
TEL: (01982) 560277 OPEN Easter - Nov. V B/A. NO SMOKING. CHILDREN: OVER 12S ONLY. 1 EN SUITE ROOM. BEVERAGES ON REQUEST. T.V. LOUNGE. B. & B. AROUND £15.

NANT-Y-DERW FARM, BUILTH WELLS, LD2 3RU   TEL: (01982) 553675
Working sheep farm 4 miles north of Builth Wells on a south-facing slope in the centre of
45 acres of farmland; home-produce used in cooking. Only four guests at any one time.
OPEN May - Dec. ex. Xmas.   V, VE, S.D. B/A.   ORG WHEN AVAIL. WH STD.   NO SMOKING.   DISABLED
ACCESS. OVER 7S ONLY. PETS B/A. PRIVATE BATHROOM. BEVERAGES IN ROOMS. T.V. IN LOUNGE.
B. & B. AROUND £18.

CHURCHSTOKE

The Old Barn
HYSSINGTON, NR CHURCHSTOKE, MONTGOMERYSHIRE, SY15 6AT TEL: (01588) 620660
The Old Barn is a delightful, stone-built, converted farm building with many exposed
beams, peacefully situated in the quiet conservation hamlet of Hyssington amidst the
pleasant hills and wooded valleys of the lovely countryside on the Shropshire Montgomeryshire border. There are three centrally heated and double-glazed guest rooms, and the
spacious guest lounge, with its TV and wide range of books, enjoys splendid country
views. Your hosts prepare delicious and nutritious vegetarian and vegan meals, mainly using
organic and wholefood ingredients, and guests dine in the large farmhouse kitchen.
OPEN ALL YEAR.   NO SMOKING.   V, VE, EXC.   OVER 6s WELCOME.   PETS B/A.
EN SUITE, TV & BEVERAGES IN ROOMS. B. & B. FROM £18.

CRICKHOWELL

THE DRAGON HOTEL, HIGH STREET, CRICKHOWELL, NP8 1BE
Early 18th C. building within original boundaries of Alisby Castle; a listed building full of
charm, open fires and oak beams; excellent food prepared from fresh, local produce.
TEL: (01873) 811868 OPEN ALL YEAR.   V STD. VE, S.D. B/A.   WH WHEN AVAIL.   N/S LOUNGE, PART OF
DINING R & SOME BEDRS. LICENSED. CHILDREN WELCOME. EN SUITE & TV IN MOST ROOMS. BEVER-
AGES IN BEDROOMS. ACCESS, VISA. B. & B. AROUND £18.

LLANBRYNMAIR

Barlings Barn
LLANBRYNMAIR, POWYS, SY19 7DY   TEL: (01650) 521479

When Terry and Felicity Margolis arrived at Barlings Barn some years ago they were prepared to
have to undertake a tremendous amount of reno-
vative work on their lovely 18th century stone
farm buildings. Their efforts were well rewarded,
however, and now, in addition to the main building, a cottage and self-catering wing now provide absolutely first-class accommodation to
guests; not only is there a microwave, automatic
washer and tumble dryer, but your hosts will
provide you with home-cooked frozen meals on
request, and will send you a grocery shopping list
when you book to ensure that your first few days'worth of provisions is there to greet you
when you arrive. A stay at Barlings Barn is healthy indeed; in addition to the excellent
cuisine which is prepared wherever possible from fresh and wholefood ingredients, there
is a first-class range of leisure and sports amenities including an outdoor heated pool,
squash court, sauna and solarium.
V STD. VE, S.D. B/A. ORG, WH ALMOST ALWAYS.   OPEN ALL YEAR.   CHILDREN WELCOME.   PETS B/A. N/S
MAIN LEISURE AREAS & DISCOURAGED THROUGHOUT. EN SUITE IN ALL ROOMS.   PRICES: VARIOUS.

CYFEILIOG GUEST HOUSE, BONT DOLADFAN, LLANBRYNMAIR, POWYS.
Licensed riverside guest house in delightful hamlet. Vegetarian Bonanza!
TEL: (01650) 521231 OPEN ALL YEAR.   V, VE STD. S.D. B/A. ORG, WH STD. CHILDREN WELCOME. LICENSED.
TV & BEVERAGES. B. & B. AROUND £15.

LLANDRINDOD WELLS

CORVEN HALL, HOWEY, LLANDRINDOD WELLS, LD1 5RE
Large Victorian house with spacious rooms and peaceful gardens. Traditional English and
Welsh cooking is a house speciality, and a variety of home-made dishes are freshly prepared
from local produce.
TEL: (01597) 823368 OPEN Feb. - Nov.   V, S.D. B/A.   N/S DINING R & LOUNGE.   LICENSED. DISABLED
ACCESS. CHILDREN WELCOME. PETS B/A.   EN SUITE. BEVERAGES.   T.V.   B. & B. AROUND £17.

THE METROPOLE HOTEL, TEMPLE STREET, LLANDRINDOD WELLS
TEL: (01597) 823700 OPEN ALL YEAR. V, VE, DIAB ST. LOW-CAL., LOW-FAT OR WHEAT-FREE B/A. ORG
ON REQUEST. WH WHEN AVAIL. LICENSED. CHILDREN WELCOME. PETS B/A. EN SUITE, TV &
BEVERAGES IN ROOMS. CREDIT CARDS. B. & B. AROUND £37.

V Stredders Vegetarian Guest House

PARK CRESCENT, LLANDRINDOD WELLS, POWYS, LD1 6AB   TEL: (01597) 822186
Spacious Victorian town house with period furniture. Comfortable lounge with open fire,
lots of books, huge video collection. Excellent food (accompanied by some first-class
organic wines).
OPEN ALL YEAR. V, VE, WH STD. DIAB., S.D. B/A. ORG. WHEN AVAIL. N/S DINING R., BEDR & B/A. LICENSED.
CHILDREN WELCOME. PETS B/A. BEVERAGES & TV IN ROOMS. B. & B. £15, D. £7

MACHYNLLETH

V Gwalia

CEMMAES, MACHYNLLETH, SY20 9PU TEL: (01650) 511377
Exclusively vegetarian, family-run 10 acre smallholding; lovely house with beautiful views
just outside Snowdonia National Park; virtually all food home-grown or home-produced
spring water. Therapeutic massage available.
OPEN ALL YEAR. V, VE STD. NO SMOKING. CHILDREN WELCOME. PETS B/A. BEVERAGES ON
REQUEST. B. & B. AROUND £15, D £8.

MONTGOMERY

THE DRAGON HOTEL, MONTGOMERY, POWYS, SY15 6AA

Black & white timbered 17th C.coaching inn. Panoramic views. Meals prepared from fresh,
local produce. The hotel has an indoor heated swimming pool.
TEL: (01686) 668359 OPEN ALL YEAR. V STD. VE, S.D.B/A. N/S SOME BEDRS & PART OF DINING R.
LICENSED. R EASONABLE DISABLED ACCESS. CHILDREN WELCOME. PETS B/A. EN SUITE, BEVERAGES
& TV IN ROOMS. CREDIT CARDS. B. & B. AROUND £30.

RHAYADER

TRE GARREG, ST HARMON, NR RHAYADER, LD6 5LU

Converted stone barn offering comfortable accommodation; log fires, wholesome food.
TEL: (01597) 88604 OPEN Easter - Oct. V, S.D. B/A. ORG WHEN AVAIL. NO SMOKING. ALL ROOMS EN
SUITE. BEVERAGES & T.V. IN LOUNGE. B. & B. AROUND £18.

RESTAURANTS

MACHYNLLETH

Old Mill Tea Shop, Felin Crewi

PENEGOES, MACHYNLLETH, POWYS, SY20 8NH TEL: (01654) 703113
V, VE & LOW-FAT STD. NO SMOKING. DISABLED ACCESS. CHILDREN WELCOME.

THE OLD STATION COFFEE SHOP, DINAS MAWDDWY, MACHYNLLETH, SY20 9LS
TEL: (016504) 338 V STD. NO SMOKING. LICENSED. DISABLED ACCESS. WELL-BEHAVED CHILDREN.

THE QUARRY SHOP, WHOLEFOOD CAFÉ & STORE, 13 MAENGWYN ST, MA-CHYNLLETH
Part of the Centre for Alternative Technology at Machynlleth.
V, VE, WH STD. NO SMOKING.

MIDDLETON, WELSHPOOL

Border Restaurant

MIDDLETOWN, WELSHPOOL, POWYS, SY21 8EN TEL: (01938) 570201
Coffee Shop and a Cellar Bistro. Excellent food. Home-made tea and cakes.
OPEN ALL YEAR. NO SMOKING. V STD (extensive menu). WHEELCHAIR ACCESS. CHILDREN. LICENSED.
RHAYADER

CAROLE'S CAKE SHOP AND TEA ROOM, SOUTH ST, RHAYADER, POWYS, LD6 5BH
TEL; (01597) 811060 V STD. NO SMOKING. CHILDREN WELCOME.